WASHINGTON D.C. MUSEUMS

A ROSS GUIDE

FORMERLY

A MUSEUM GUIDE TO WASHINGTON, D.C.

WASHINGTON D.C. MUSEUMS

A ROSS GUIDE

MUSEUMS • HISTORIC HOUSES •
ART GALLERIES • LIBRARIES •
AND OTHER SPECIAL PLACES OPEN TO
THE PUBLIC IN THE WASHINGTON
METROPOLITAN AREA

BY BETTY ROSS

AMERICANA PRESS • *Washington, D.C.*

To Richard
_____

Copyright © 1992 by Betty Ross
First edition published 1986.

All rights reserved.
No part of this publication may be reproduced, stored in a retrieval system, or transmitted, in any form or by any means, electronic, mechanical, photocopying, recording or otherwise, without the prior permission of the copyright owner or the publisher, Americana Press, Post Office Box 71004, Chevy Chase, Maryland 20813.

Quotation from John Walker's *Self-Portrait With Donors* reprinted by permission of the publisher, Little, Brown and Company.

All information in this book was accurate at the time of publication but admission fees and hours are subject to change without notice.

Library of Congress Cataloging-in-Publication Data

Ross, Betty
    Washington, D.C. museums : a Ross guide : museums, historic houses, art galleries, libraries, and other special places open to the public in the Washington metropolitan area / by Betty Ross.
      p.   cm.
Rev. ed. of: A museum guide to Washington, D.C. 2nd ed. 1988.
Includes bibliographical references and index.
ISBN 0-9616144-3-9
1. Museums—Washington (D.C.)—Guide-books.
2. Historic buildings—Washington (D.C.)—Guide-books.
3. Art museums—Washington (D.C.)—Guide-books.
4. Washington (D.C.)—Description—1981—Guide-books.
I. Ross, Betty. Museum guide to Washington, D.C.
II. Title.
AM13.W3R67   1992   91-39333
069'.09753—dc20   CIP

Printed in the United States of America

Cover: The Great Hall of the National Building Museum; National Building Museum, F. Harlan Hambright photo.

ACKNOWLEDGEMENTS

I am grateful to many friends and colleagues, without whose help this book could not have been produced.

Special thanks are due to Susan Bliss of the Arthur M. Sackler Gallery; Linda Goldstein of Woodlawn Plantation; Thomas Harney of the National Museum of Natural History; Sidney Lawrence of the Joseph M. Hirshhorn Museum and Sculpture Garden; Laura Lester of the Phillips Collection; Linda Mattingly of Dumbarton House; Betty C. Monkman at the White House; Naomi Paiss and Sam Eskenazi of the U.S. Holocaust Memorial Museum; Eleanor Preston of Tudor Place; Christopher With of the National Gallery of Art; Barbara Wolanin at the Capitol, and the many other public information officers and curators who double-checked facts and provided information.

Particular thanks are due to Betty and Brock Adams, June and John Hechinger, Olie and Joe Rauh, and Lillian Owen, who helped to launch the first edition of the book in June 1986. And I wish especially to thank Harriet Ripinsky and Linda Ripinsky for supervising the production of this book; Vicki Venker Johnson, for her superb editing, and my family—especially my husband, Richard Mullens—for their support and encouragement.

CONTENTS

PREFACE		1
INTRODUCTION		2
MAPS		5
THE MALL	Smithsonian Institution Building The "Castle"	12
	Arts and Industries Building	14
	Freer Gallery of Art	16
	Hirshhorn Museum and Sculpture Garden	22
	Holocaust Memorial Museum	26
	National Air and Space Museum	29
	National Gallery of Art	35
	National Museum of African Art	47
	National Museum of American History	51
	National Museum of Natural History	60
	Arthur M. Sackler Gallery	68
	S. Dillon Ripley Center	74
	Enid A. Haupt Garden	74
CAPITOL HILL	Capital Children's Museum	80
	Capitol	82
	Folger Shakespeare Library	90
	Library of Congress	94
	Marine Corps Museum	98
	Navy Museum	102
	Sewall-Belmont House	108
DOWNTOWN	National Archives	112
	Ford's Theatre	114
	National Building Museum	117
	National Museum of American Art	120
	National Museum of Women in the Arts	128
	National Portrait Gallery	132
	Petersen House The House Where Lincoln Died	138
	Lillian and Albert Small Jewish Museum Jewish Historical Society of Greater Washington	140
MIDTOWN	Art Museum of the Americas	144
	Bethune Museum-Archives	148
	B'nai B'rith Klutznick Museum	149
	Corcoran Gallery of Art	152
	Daughters of the American Revolution Museum	156
	Decatur House	158
	Diplomatic Reception Rooms	162
	Interior Department Museum	166
	National Geographic Society Explorers Hall	167
	Octagon	170
	Old Executive Office Building	174
	Organization of American States	180
	Renwick Gallery	181
	White House	186
DUPONT-KALORAMA	Anderson House	196
	Barney Studio House	199

	Fondo del Sol Visual Art and Media Center	203
	Historical Society of Washington, D.C.	205
	Heurich Mansion	
	Phillips Collection	208
	Textile Museum	214
	Woodrow Wilson House	218
GEORGETOWN AND UPPER NORTHWEST	Dumbarton House	224
	Dumbarton Oaks	228
	Old Stone House	234
	Tudor Place	236
	Hillwood	240
	Washington Dolls' House and Toy Museum	248
MARYLAND AND VIRGINIA	Clara Barton House	252
	National Capital Trolley Museum	256
	Stabler-Leadbeater Apothecary Shop	258
	Arlington House	260
	Carlyle House	264
	Gadsby's Tavern Museum	270
	Robert E. Lee Boyhood Home	274
	Lee-Fendall House	278
	Lyceum	282
	Mount Vernon	284
	Pope-Leighey House	289
	Woodlawn Plantation	293
ART GALLERIES		299
SPECIAL PLACES FOR PRIVATE FUNCTIONS		308
CHECKLIST OF SPECIAL COLLECTIONS		311
BIBLIOGRAPHY		314
PHOTO CREDITS		317
INDEX		318

PREFACE

This is a book for those who feel uncomfortable and overwhelmed by museums, as well as those who are dedicated museumgoers. Designed to make museum visits entertaining, as well as educational, it describes what lies behind the doors of sixty-five museums, historic houses, and other special places open to the public in the Washington metropolitan area.

The book was first published in 1986 as *A Museum Guide to Washington, D.C.* Since that time, it has gone through two editions and several printings. Now, with a new title and new, updated information, it joins a companion volume, *New York City Museums: A Ross Guide.*

The book includes biographies and historical backgrounds, in-depth reports on museum collections, anecdotes, and information on hours, admission fees, museum shops, restaurants, libraries, handicapped facilities, and public transportation. A list of 105 area art galleries and forty-nine museums, clubs, and historic houses available for private functions is also included.

Five museums are new to this edition of the guide. The U.S. Holocaust Memorial Museum, scheduled to open in 1993, is previewed. Also included are the U.S. Marine Corps Museum; Tudor Place, a magnificent Georgetown mansion built by Martha Washington's granddaughter; Woodlawn Plantation, the former home of another Washington descendant, and the Pope-Leighey House, designed by Frank Lloyd Wright.

For those with limited time, the book points out highlights that should not be missed. For others, it describes what can be seen when browsing at a leisurely pace. It is for those who live in Washington, as well as visitors to the nation's capital.

Hundreds of years of history, art, and science are encapsulated in Washington's museums. They contain everything from historic airplanes to moon rocks, from ancient glass to modern ceramics, from pre-Columbian figures to abstract sculpture, from icons to pop art. The museums are cross-referenced, and, as the Checklist of Special Collections indicates, there is something here for everyone.

Each entry was carefully researched, and the manuscript was read by museum officials to ensure its accuracy. Bear in mind, however, that museum exhibits are constantly changing. Works of art are often loaned to other museums, placed in storage temporarily, or removed for study or conservation.

Museums are dynamic institutions, interesting to read about and to visit. I hope that this guide will open the door for you to many hours of enjoyment inside the great museums in the Washington area. And I hope that you will share my fascination not only with what to see but also who created or donated it and why.

Betty Ross
Washington, D.C.
March, 1992

INTRODUCTION

Oddly enough, Washington was a late starter in the museum world. Charleston, South Carolina, had a public museum as early as 1773. Twelve years later, artist-naturalist Charles Willson Peale opened a museum in his Philadelphia home. His sons, Rembrandt and Rubens followed their father's example and opened Peale's Baltimore Museum in 1814. In New York, the museum established by the Society of St. Tammany at City Hall in 1790 flourished until the group's focus shifted from culture to politics.

While older, more established cities were opening museums, the citizens of Washington were busily transforming a rural village into the capital of a new nation. The nineteenth century was nearly half over before a national museum was established here. In 1846, after ten years of debate, Congress finally accepted James Smithson's bequest and the Smithsonian Institution was established.

Now, as the twentieth century draws to a close, few cities in this country are as rich in museums as Washington. And more are scheduled to open soon. The U.S. Holocaust Memorial Museum is previewed in these pages. Two other museums, honoring American Indians and African-Americans, are still on the drawing board as this book goes to press.

In addition to such world-class institutions as the Smithsonian, the National Gallery of Art, the Phillips Collection, and the Corcoran Gallery of Art, Washington has a host of specialized museums, such as Dumbarton Oaks, the Textile Museum, the Folger Shakespeare Library, and the Art Museum of the Americas—to name just a few.

The current cultural abundance is a post-World War II phenomenon. I can recall visiting Ford's Theatre in the 1950s, before it was restored. The Lincoln museum occupied a large, barnlike room filled with hundreds of objects in glass display cases. Footprints painted on the floor marked John Wilkes Booth's route across the stage the night of President Lincoln's assassination. There was no attempt to interpret the collection, no effort to separate the wheat from the chaff. What a difference today—not only at Ford's Theatre but at museums throughout the country.

When I visit a museum, I am curious not only about what to see but also about how a work of art fits into its period, who donated it, and why. To me, museums often reflect the personalities of their founders and benefactors. The art that appealed to Joseph Hirshhorn, for example, would probably have been of little interest to Duncan Phillips, Charles Lang Freer or Andrew Mellon.

In writing about museums, I try to imagine what sort of person would collect old masters, say, rather than modern sculpture. What was there about James McNeill Whistler that appealed so much to Charles Lang Freer that he built one of the largest Whistler collections in the world? And was it Pierre Bonnard's use of color or his subject matter that most interested Duncan Phillips? The story of museums is the story of people. Knowing about the founders—their personal and professional backgrounds and their tastes—adds another dimension to visiting museums.

The men who built our great museums on the Mall—Andrew W. Mellon, Charles Lang Freer, Joseph Hirshhorn, and Arthur M. Sackler—were dedicated collectors who shared a passion for art. We can appreciate Freer's singlemindedness, Mellon's insistence on quality, George Hewitt Myers's scholarly approach, and Hirshhorn's enthusiasm for art. Every collector shares those characteristics, in varying degrees.

In his *Self-Portrait With Donors,* John Walker quotes Armand Hammer as saying that "pictures are something more than just collecting. You are connecting yourself with something that really is immortal, something that has survived all these centuries. You are preserving something for posterity." Curators and collectors alike sense this connection with the past, and many museum visitors are aware of its importance, too.

In researching this book, I found the relationships between certain historical figures, their contemporaries, and their descendants intriguing. Even though he never lived in the White House, George Washington's footprints are all over this city. His spirit can be felt at Arlington House, Dumbarton House, Tudor Place, and Woodlawn Plantation, as well as at Mount Vernon. And the stern hero becomes considerably more human when you learn, for example, that he advised Martha's granddaughter, Eliza Parke Custis, to obtain a prenuptial agreement. As it turned out, Washington's advice saved Eliza's inheritance when she became one of the city's first divorcées in 1804.

A sense of history pervades the nation's capital. In visiting the historic houses described in this book, I could often sense the spirit of a former occupant. I could picture Dolley Madison entertaining at the Octagon; Susan Decatur grieving at Decatur House; Mrs. Robert E. Lee fleeing Arlington House before its occupation by Union troops; Britannia Peter storing some of her Lee cousins' possessions at Tudor Place during the Civil War; Woodrow Wilson reading in his library, and Clara Barton wearing her medals while she worked for the fledgling American Red Cross.

Perhaps the strongest personality among my historic friends was Alice Pike Barney, whose efforts to revitalize Washington's cultural life in the early years of this century led to the establishment of the Sylvan Theater at the Washington Monument. She lobbied for legislation permitting works of art to be imported tax free. Without such a law, many of the great collections we now enjoy in public museums might never have existed.

Through the years, a combination of acquisitiveness, national pride, and patriotism has given birth to many of the museums chronicled in this book. From Smithson, Freer, Folger, and Mellon to Phillips, Larz Anderson, Hirshhorn, and Sackler, the men whose fortunes were made elsewhere donated their collections to the nation's capital. And we are all the richer for their generosity.

If the 1980s were the Golden Age of Museums, what can one say about the 1990s? In a time of retrenchment, of budget cuts and congressional restraints, they must continue to play an important role in providing food for the spirit, in expanding horizons, and enriching lives.

If art is a mirror of the cultural and social, as well as aesthetic values of its time, then museums are truly the repositories of our civilization.

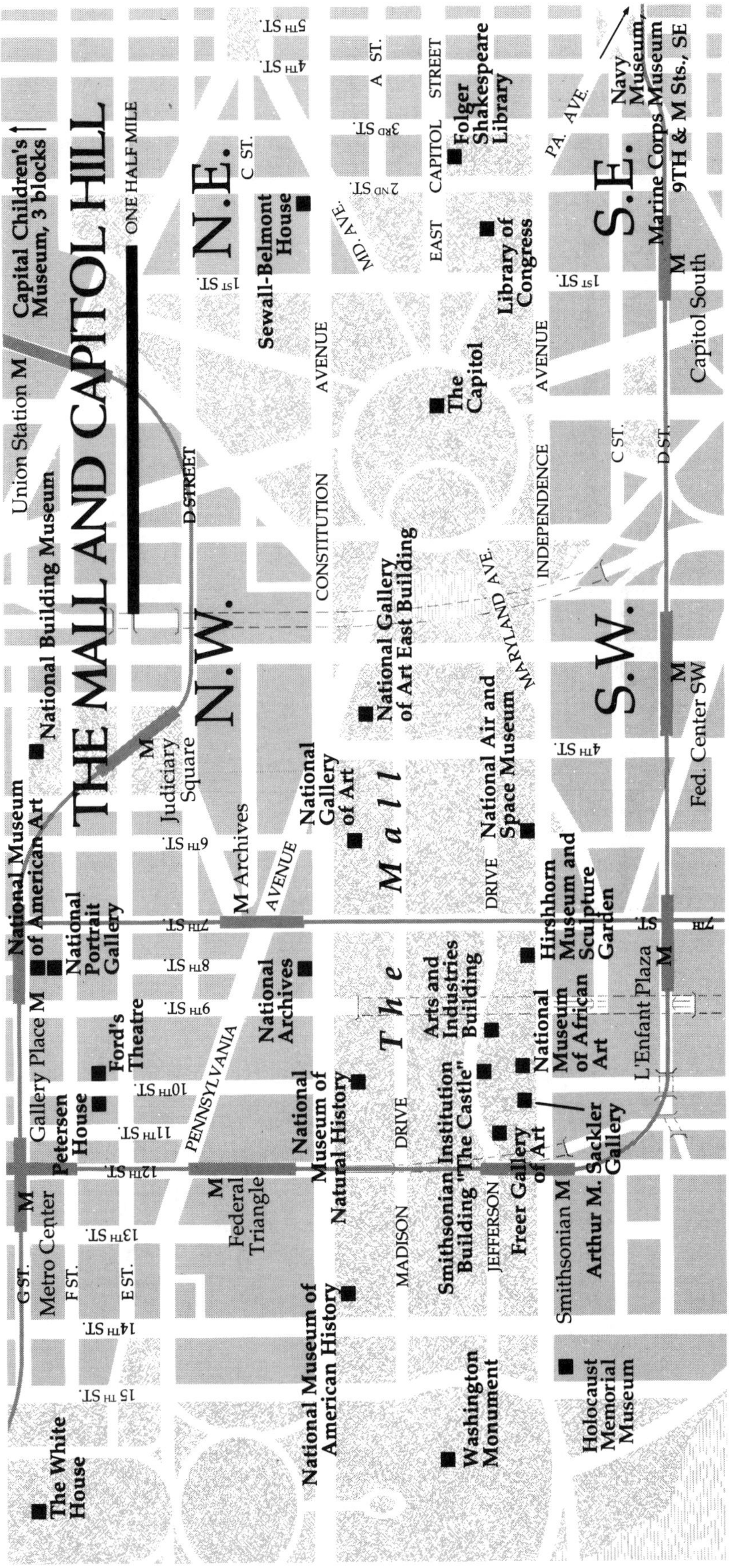
THE MALL AND CAPITOL HILL
ONE HALF MILE
N.W.
N.E.
S.W.
S.E.
The White House
Metro Center M
G ST.
F ST.
E ST.
15TH ST.
14TH ST.
13TH ST.
12TH ST.
11TH ST.
10TH ST.
9TH ST.
8TH ST.
7TH ST.
6TH ST.
4TH ST.
5TH ST.
3RD ST.
2ND ST.
1ST ST.
Gallery Place M
Petersen House
Ford's Theatre
National Portrait Gallery
National Museum of American Art
National Building Museum
Union Station M
Capital Children's Museum, 3 blocks
M Judiciary Square
D STREET
C ST.
Sewall-Belmont House
A ST.
MD. AVE.
EAST CAPITOL STREET
Folger Shakespeare Library
Library of Congress
The Capitol
CONSTITUTION AVENUE
INDEPENDENCE AVENUE
MARYLAND AVE.
PA. AVE.
PENNSYLVANIA AVENUE
M Federal Triangle
M Archives
National Archives
National Gallery of Art
National Gallery of Art East Building
The Mall
National Museum of Natural History
National Museum of American History
MADISON DRIVE
JEFFERSON DRIVE
Washington Monument
Smithsonian Institution Building "The Castle"
Arts and Industries Building
Freer Gallery of Art
Arthur M. Sackler Gallery
National Museum of African Art
Hirshhorn Museum and Sculpture Garden
National Air and Space Museum
Smithsonian M
L'Enfant Plaza M
M Fed. Center SW
M Capitol South
D ST.
C ST.
Holocaust Memorial Museum
Navy Museum, Marine Corps Museum, 9TH & M Sts., SE

MIDTOWN AND DOWNTOWN

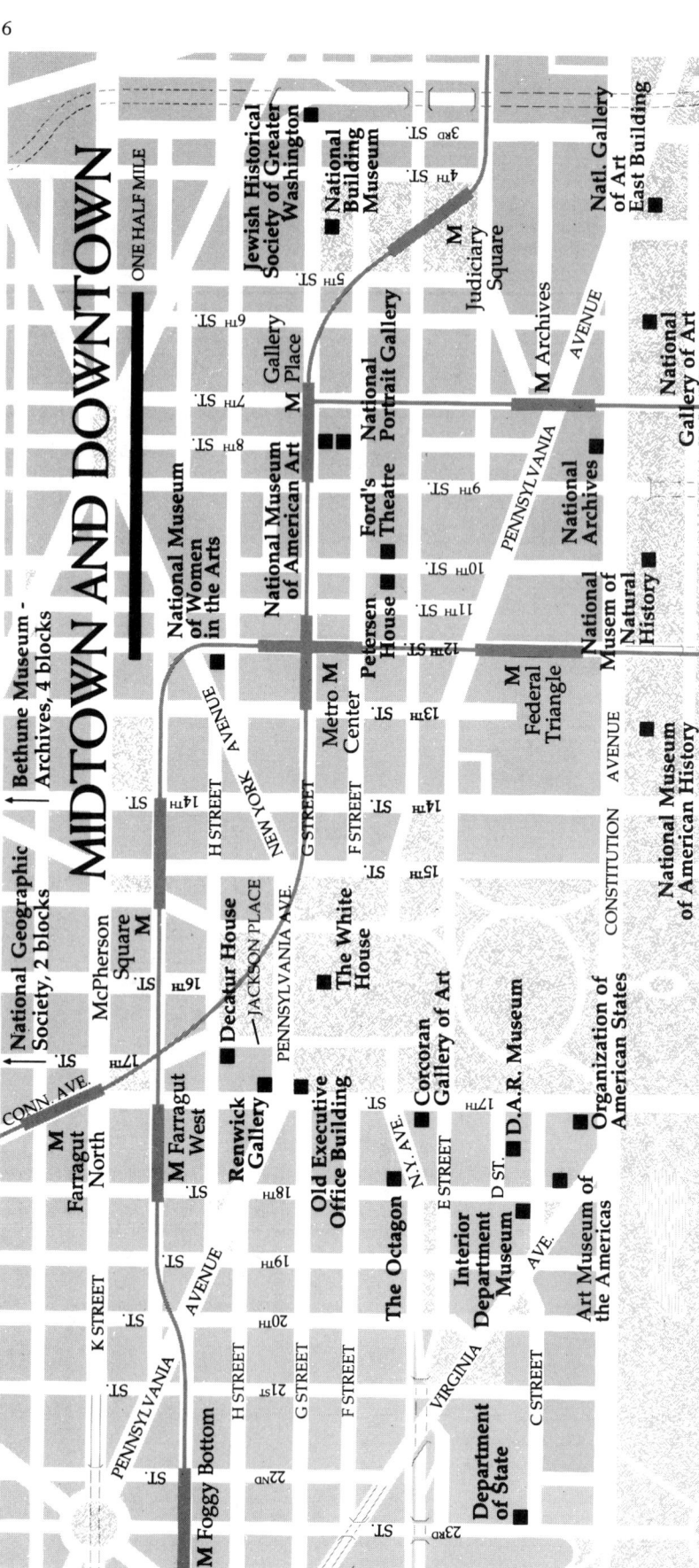

GEORGETOWN AND DUPONT-KALORAMA

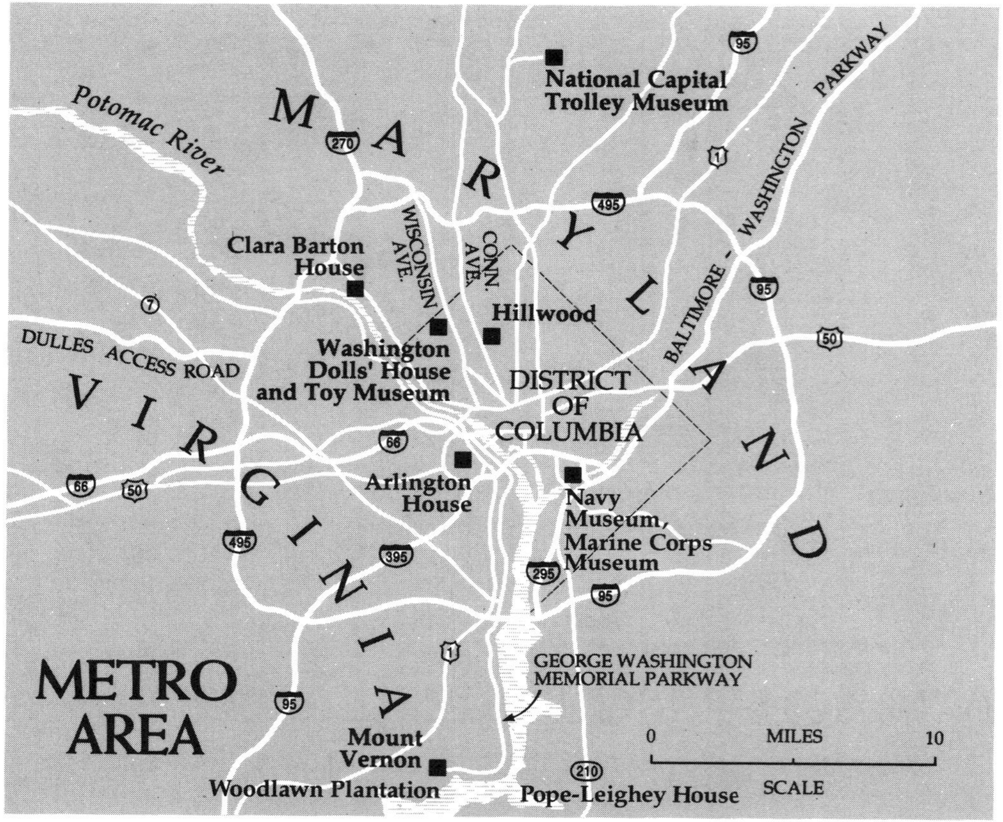
METRO AREA
MARYLAND
VIRGINIA
DISTRICT OF COLUMBIA
Potomac River
National Capital Trolley Museum
Clara Barton House
Hillwood
Washington Dolls' House and Toy Museum
Arlington House
Navy Museum, Marine Corps Museum
Mount Vernon
Woodlawn Plantation
Pope-Leighey House
GEORGE WASHINGTON MEMORIAL PARKWAY
BALTIMORE - WASHINGTON PARKWAY
DULLES ACCESS ROAD
WISCONSIN AVE.
CONN. AVE.
270
495
95
1
50
7
66
395
295
210
0
MILES
10
SCALE

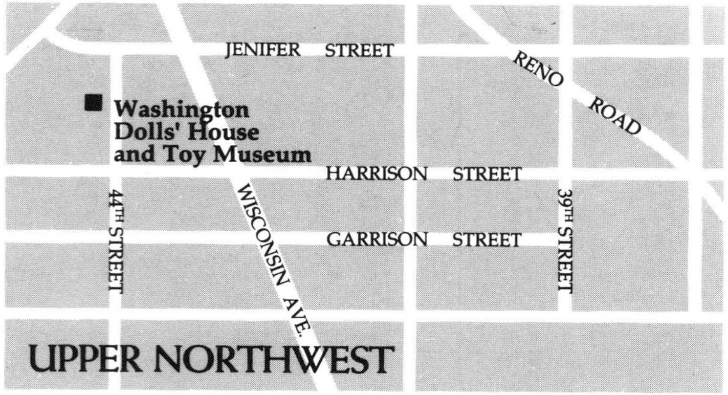
UPPER NORTHWEST
Washington Dolls' House and Toy Museum
JENIFER STREET
RENO ROAD
HARRISON STREET
GARRISON STREET
44TH STREET
39TH STREET
WISCONSIN AVE.

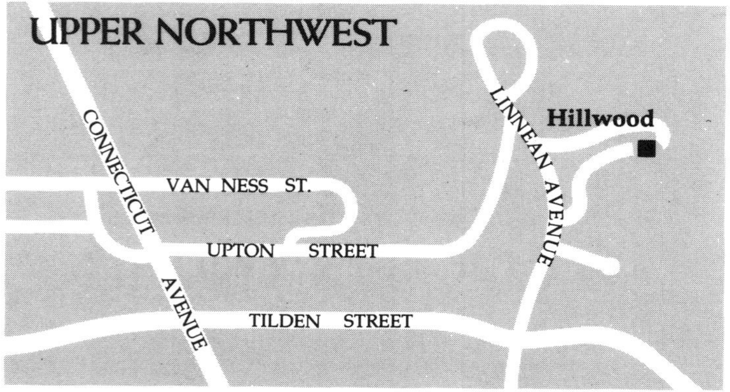
UPPER NORTHWEST
Hillwood
LINNEAN AVENUE
CONNECTICUT AVENUE
VAN NESS ST.
UPTON STREET
TILDEN STREET

OLD TOWN ALEXANDRIA

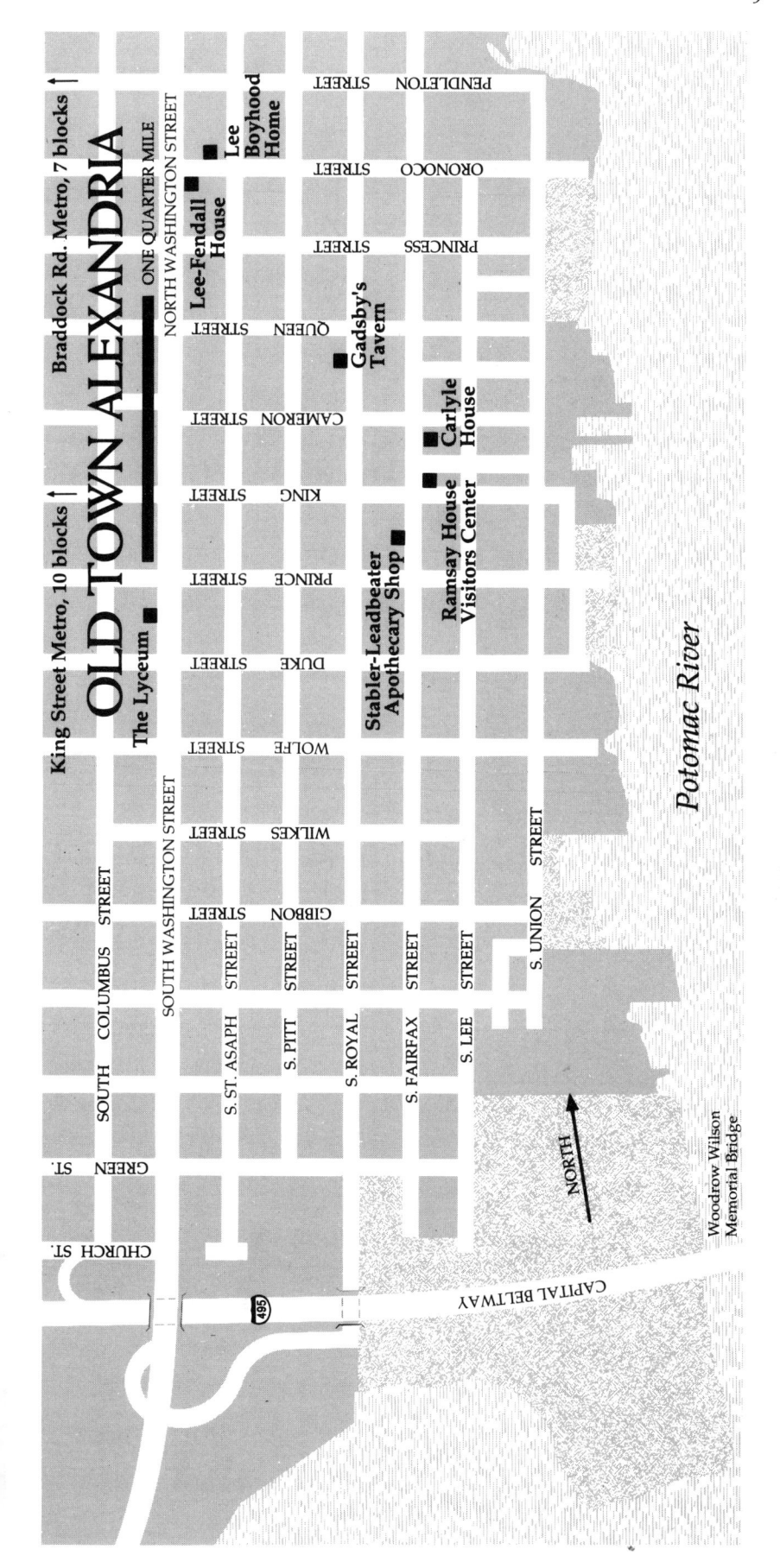

*The Arts and Industries
Building*

THE MALL

THE SMITHSONIAN INSTITUTION BUILDING

The Castle

1000 Jefferson Drive, S.W.
Washington, D.C. 20560
202/357-2700; 202/357-1300
202/357-1729 TDD for hearing-impaired visitors
202/357-2020 recorded Dial-a-Museum information

METRO	Smithsonian.
HOURS	9 A.M. to 5:30 P.M. daily. Closed Christmas Day. Spring and summer hours determined annually.
TOURS	Inquire at the information desk or call 202/357-2700 for specific times.
ADMISSION	Free.
HANDICAPPED FACILITIES	Accessible to the disabled. Wheelchair accessible via ramp west of porte cochere, main entrance on Jefferson Drive.
MEMBERSHIP	Smithsonian Associates.
AUTHOR'S CHOICE	James Smithson's tomb The building's Norman-style architecture

Designed by James Renwick, Jr., in 1847 and completed in 1855, this red sandstone building looks like a twelfth-century castle on the Mall, with its crenellated Norman-style towers.

Originally, the building housed a science museum, art gallery, lecture hall, research laboratories, offices, and living quarters for the secretary of the Smithsonian and his family. In short, everything needed by the institution in its early days was under this roof. Today, the Castle houses the Smithsonian Information Center, administrative offices, and the Woodrow Wilson International Center for Scholars.

To the left of the Mall entrance, a small chapel-like room contains James Smithson's tomb, as well as a few exhibits relating to his life.

Directly opposite the entrance, through the double doors, is the Smithsonian Information Center in the Great Hall. Twin theaters feature an award-winning, twenty-minute video orientation to the institution, and interactive touch-screen stations provide information on the Smithsonian in English and six other languages. Two electronic maps and four other interactive video stations provide information on citywide attractions.

You can obtain a previsit information package by writing to Smithsonian Information, Smithsonian Institution, Washington, D.C., 20560, or by calling 202/357-2700; 202/357-1729 TDD.

Joseph Henry, *first secretary of the Smithsonian Institution, at the mall entrance to the Smithsonian "Castle"*

SMITHSONIAN INSTITUTION

As the custodian of 137 million specimens and artifacts of historic and scientific interest, the Smithsonian Institution—

sometimes called "the nation's attic"—is a showcase for science, history, technology—past, present, and future—and cultures of the world.

The Smithsonian is the world's largest museum complex, with millions of visitors each year. It includes nine museums on the Mall between the Washington Monument and the Capitol, and four other museums and the National Zoo elsewhere in Washington. The Cooper-Hewitt Museum and the National Museum of the American Indian are in New York City. Although administered separately by their own boards of trustees, the National Gallery of Art, the Woodrow Wilson International Center for Scholars, and the John F. Kennedy Center for the Performing Arts all operate under the aegis of the Smithsonian.

What are the most popular exhibits? The original Star-Spangled Banner—the flag that flew over Fort McHenry and inspired Francis Scott Key to write the National Anthem—attracts some of the largest crowds. And so does the National Air and Space Museum. Only one percent of the Smithsonian's holdings are on public display. The rest are in study and reference collections, available to qualified researchers and scientists.

The Smithsonian Institution was founded by an Englishman who never visited America. Its founder, James Smithson, was born in France in 1765 and lived the early part of his life in Europe as James Lewis Macie. He was the illegitimate son of Hugh Smithson, who became Hugh Percy, the first Duke of Northumberland.

Smithson, a wealthy bachelor and prominent scientist, was presumably frustrated by his lack of family standing and recognition. He was nearly fifty before he applied to the Crown for permission to take his father's name.

Smithson's will provided that if a nephew, Henry James Hungerford, died without an heir, all of Smithson's property would be bequeathed "to the United States of America, to found at Washington, under the name of the Smithsonian Institution, an establishment for the increase and diffusion of knowledge." He added, "My name shall live in the memory of man when the titles of the Northumberlands and Percys are extinct and forgotten."

Smithson died in Genoa in 1829, and his nephew died childless in 1835. Smithson's body was brought to Washington in 1904.

The Smithson estate amounted to around $550,000, an enormous sum at that time. By law, the money is lent to the U.S. Treasury, which pays six percent interest on it in perpetuity. Congress accepted the Smithson bequest in 1835 but debated its purpose for the next decade. In 1846, the Smithsonian Institution was established to conduct scientific research and publish original findings. Through the years, the Smithsonian has evolved into an organization which now incorporates many branches of study—art history, air and space, Oriental art, American history, science, and even zoology.

The Smithsonian Institution is governed by a board of regents whose chancellor is the chief justice of the United States. The regents include the vice-president of the United States, three senators, three members of the House of Representatives, and nine private citizens.

ARTS AND INDUSTRIES BUILDING

900 Jefferson Drive, S.W.
Washington, D.C. 20560
202/357-1300
202/357-2700

METRO	Smithsonian.
HOURS	10 A.M. to 5:30 P.M. daily. Closed Christmas Day. Summer hours determined annually.
TOURS	Inquire at the information desk or call 202/357-2700 for specific times.
ADMISSION	Free.
HANDICAPPED FACILITIES	Ramp at north entrance (Mall side). Accessible to the disabled.
MUSEUM SHOPS	Cards, books, jewelry, and items of Victoriana. Experimental Gallery Support Center, merchandise reflecting changing exhibits.
SPECIAL EVENTS	Discovery Theater, live performances for young audiences. Presentations by puppeteers, dancers, actors, mimes, and singers Tuesday through Saturday. Call 202/357-1500 for show times, tickets, and reservations.
MEMBERSHIP	Smithsonian Associates.
AUTHOR'S CHOICE	Samuel F. B. Morse's original telegraph Turn-of-the-century machinery

Entrance to the Arts and Industries Building

A visit to the Smithsonian's Arts and Industries Building is like returning to the Victorian era.

The year is 1876, the year of the great Centennial Exposition in Philadelphia—the World's Fair that celebrated the achievements of the Industrial Revolution. When the exposition closed, forty carloads of memorabilia were brought to Washington and presented to the Smithsonian. Originally called the National Museum, this red brick and Ohio sandstone structure is the second oldest building on the Mall. Designed by Washington architect Adolph Cluss, it opened March 1881, in time for President James Garfield's inaugural ball.

The building was restored over a ten-year period, beginning in 1976, in honor of the nation's Bicentennial, and "1876: A Centennial Exhibition" was installed in the style of the original Philadelphia exposition.

A huge skylit rotunda with a fountain and fresh flowers is at the center of the building. Four high-ceilinged halls radiating from this hub are crammed with the products of the Industrial Revolution—manufactured items ranging from silks and porcelains to sewing machines, printing presses, and steam locomotives. Everything here was either shown at the Centennial Exposition or was made during that period.

NORTH HALL

The first gallery you enter through the Mall entrance on Jefferson Drive is filled with a variety of objects that once graced Victorian homes. Here are desks, clocks, keyboard instruments, lamps, and chandeliers, as well as silver teapots and porcelain dishes from the original Philadelphia exposition. Other exhibits show the types of medicines that were used, the books that were read (*Uncle Tom's Cabin, Little Women,* and popular cookbooks), and the clothes that were worn in the late nineteenth century.

On the wall to the right of the entrance is "L'Eau et Le Feu," a large Haviland tile mural by French artist Felix Bracquemond created for the Centennial Exposition. Nearby is a display of Minton tiles, made by the porcelain manufacturing company in England. Minton tile floors, which were the height of fashion in the late nineteenth century, can be seen in the Capitol and the Old Executive Office Building.

WEST HALL

Here are many of the industrial objects taken for granted today—a telegraph cable, a steam boiler, even an ice cream machine—that were considered revolutionary a hundred years ago. In the far left-hand corner of the room is the telegraph invented by Samuel F. B. Morse. Also in this hall are a hoist machine (precursor of the elevator), a printing press, rock drills, steam engines and pumps, and woodworking machinery.

SOUTH HALL

The Experimental Gallery, a changing exhibition space, opened in the South Hall in February 1991. It features innovative and creative exhibitions from Smithsonian museums and other institutions throughout the world.

The Experimental Gallery encourages risk-taking in exhibit techniques and styles, to take exhibitions into the twenty-first century. Featured are multicultural exhibitions in the humanities and sciences, and interactive exhibitions in the physical sciences.

EAST HALL

Jupiter, a beautifully restored locomotive engine built for the Santa Cruz Railroad of California in 1876, dominates this hall.

Glass cases display pottery from Spain and Turkey, stained glass from Germany, Thonet bentwood rockers from Austria, silks and brassware from Thailand, porcelain vases from Japan and Russia, and furniture from China—representing the best and most typical products of the countries participating in the Centennial Exposition.

Individual states also had exhibits at the exposition. The Virginia exhibit includes Patrick Henry's wallet and snuff box, one of President Madison's shoe buckles, and a small, worn leather purse once owned by Pocahontas. There are Hitchcock chairs from Connecticut, pieces of the Plymouth Rock from Massachusetts, and Lincoln memorabilia from Illinois. The Liberty Bell was a popular motif in 1876. Pennsylvania's exhibit included a bell made of sugar, while North Carolina's bell was crafted entirely of tobacco leaves.

FREER GALLERY OF ART

Jefferson Drive at Twelfth Street, S.W.
Washington, D.C. 20560
202/357-4880

Please note: The Freer Gallery of Art is closed for renovation and is scheduled to reopen in late 1992.

METRO	Smithsonian, Mall exit.
HOURS	10 A.M. to 5:30 P.M. daily. Closed Christmas Day.
TOURS	Daily tours; call 202/357-2700 for information.
ADMISSION	Free.
HANDICAPPED FACILITIES	Accessible to the disabled through the Independence Avenue entrance.
MUSEUM SHOP	Postcards, notecards, desk sets, slides, prints, books, ceramics, jewelry, and needlepoint kits.
SPECIAL EVENTS	Lectures, concerts, and other public programs.
SPECIAL FACILITIES	Reference library located in the Arthur M. Sackler Gallery open to the public.
MEMBERSHIP	Smithsonian Asociates. Friends of Asian Arts at the Freer and Sackler Galleries from $1,000.
AUTHOR'S CHOICE	James McNeill Whistler's Peacock Room Japanese screens Chinese bronzes

Charles Lang Freer

The elegant Renaissance façade of the Freer Gallery of Art and its superb collections reflect the refined, highly cultivated artistic taste of Detroit industrialist Charles Lang Freer.

Freer's life was a rags-to-riches story. Born in Kingston, New York, in 1854, he left school at fourteen, soon after his mother died. After working briefly in a cement factory, a general store, and for a railroad, he moved to Logansport, Indiana, for a job with the Eel River Railroad. A few years later, Freer and a colleague, Col. Frank J. Hecker, moved to Detroit and founded the Peninsular Car Works, the first factory to manufacture railroad cars in the Midwest.

It was the Golden Age of Railroads and the firm prospered. A year after organizing the American Car and Foundry Company (now ACF Industries, Inc.) by merging thirteen railroad car manufacturers, Freer sold his interest in the company for several million dollars and retired to concentrate on his art collection. The forty-six-year-old bachelor spent the next two decades, until his death in 1919, traveling, studying, and collecting Oriental art and the works of late nineteenth- and early twentieth-century American artists.

Freer's interest in art became all-encompassing. Fellow industrialists in Detroit complained that he would rather discuss the tariffs on early Italian art than the price of pig iron.

The Freer Gallery of Art

Sensing Freer's affinity for elegance and refinement, architect Stanford White introduced him to the works of contemporary artists Dwight William Tryon, Abbott Handerson Thayer, and Thomas Wilmer Dewing. White, who encouraged circus showman John Ringling to collect Baroque art, must have realized that the sinuous lines and vibrant colors of a Rubens or a Caravaggio would not appeal to Freer.

Freer had begun collecting etchings in the 1880s. In 1887, on a visit to New York City, he saw a friend's collection of more than three hundred Whistler etchings. The following day, Freer bought his first Whistler prints, *Venice, Second Series*. Anxious to meet the artist he admired so much, Freer knocked on Whistler's door in London one day in 1890. Despite twenty years' difference in their ages, the two men became close friends.

Born in Lowell, Massachusetts, in 1834, James Abbott McNeill Whistler attended the U.S. Military Academy at West Point but was discharged after three years. Although at the head of his class in drawing, he was near the bottom in chemistry and philosophy. A brief stint as a draftsman at the Coast and Geodetic Survey in Washington in 1854 provided him with an opportunity to learn etching. In 1855, at the age of twenty-one, he decided to become an artist and moved to Europe.

When Freer and Whistler met, the industrialist owned eighty Whistler etchings and one watercolor. By that time, Whistler had weathered a variety of critical storms and controversies and his works were selling well. Two museums had purchased his paintings. Whistler's portrait of his mother, *Arrangement in Grey and Black*, now in the Musée d'Orsay, had been bought by the Musée du Luxembourg in Paris and the University of Glasgow had purchased his portrait of author Thomas Carlyle.

Whistler was fascinated with Oriental art, especially blue-and-white porcelains and the Japanese woodblock prints that had recently been "discovered" in Paris wrapped around porcelains shipped from the Far East. A Japanese screen or kimono, Chinese porcelains, or an oriental rug often served as props in his paintings. Whistler introduced Freer to Japanese art and stressed the importance of further study. Freer's interest in Japanese paintings and ceramics led to an appreciation of Chinese art as well.

Freer admired Whistler because he believed that he embodied Western and Oriental art better than any other artist of his day. Following Whistler's advice, Freer consulted the foremost scholars of the period to add to his understanding and appreciation of Oriental art.

The two men saw each other frequently during Freer's trips abroad. In 1902, they traveled to Holland together to study Rembrandt paintings. And Freer was on his way to call for Whistler for their daily carriage ride when the artist died in London, July 17, 1903.

The following year, Freer wrote to President Theodore Roosevelt, offering to give his art collection to the nation. Although an art gallery had been part of the Smithsonian Institution since its founding in 1846, the federal art collection at that time consisted of a hodgepodge of Indian portraits, historical paintings, and miscellaneous works donated by public-spirited citizens. With a few notable exceptions, such as the Harriet Lane Johnston and William T. Evans collections, most of the art works were more important ethnographically or historically than aesthetically.

A committee headed by Alexander Graham Bell went to Detroit to inspect the Freer collection before accepting it on behalf of the government. Because there were more than two thousand objects to examine, and Freer insisted on showing each item individually, it took five days to complete the task. Finally, the regents of the Smithsonian agreed to accept the gift according to Freer's terms.

Freer proposed to keep the collection, adding to it periodically, during his lifetime. He offered to provide funds for acquisitions and for a new building on the Mall to house the collection after his death. The federal government would be responsible for maintaining the building and caring for the collections. Freer had often been disappointed to find that objects he wanted to see in museums had been loaned to other institutions, so he stipulated that nothing in the collection could be loaned. Nothing in the permanent collection could leave the museum and nothing could enter the museum except objects for the permanent collection. More than ten thousand Oriental objects have been added through gifts and purchases since the museum opened.

In May 1906, Freer promised $500,000 and 2,250 objects for the new museum. As the collection continued to grow with his full-time collecting, he realized that a larger building would be needed, and he increased the donation to a million dollars. In 1920, more than 9,400 objects, including the Peacock Room and the largest collection of works by James McNeill Whistler in North America (1,270 objects, including the Peacock Room) were transferred from Detroit to Washington. (The only other comprehensive Whistler collection is in the Hunterian Art Gallery of the University of Glasgow and, like Freer, its donor forbade loans.)

THE BUILDING

Charles Freer selected Charles A. Platt of New York as the architect and worked closely with him on all details of the museum's design. Built around a central courtyard faced with white Tennessee marble, the façade resembles a Florentine Renaissance palace. Stony Creek granite from Milford, Massachusetts, was chosen for the exterior and Indiana limestone for corridor walls. The building opened in the spring of 1923.

In addition to galleries, storage areas, offices, and a library, space was provided for a 320-seat auditorium for lectures, a technical laboratory, and an Oriental art restoration studio—all of which make the gallery an unparalleled resource for the study and exhibition of Oriental art.

THE COLLECTIONS

Freer travelled to the Near East and South Asia, as well as to China and Japan, adding to his collection. Approximately eight percent of the collection is on view at any time. Except for the Peacock Room, permanently installed in Gallery 12, the museum showcases temporary exhibitions drawn from the permanent collection, which now encompasses more than twenty-seven thousand objects.

It is virtually impossible to avoid superlatives when discussing the scope, depth, and quality of the collection. Consider the following:

• There are 128 paintings in oil and watercolor by Whistler, 163 of his works in pastel, pencil, and ink, and 944 Whistler prints.

• The Chinese bronze collection includes food containers, cooking vessels, wine goblets, servers, and water vessels dating back to the Shang dynasty (1523-1028 B.C.)

• Among the ceramics and porcelains are Chinese ceramics crafted in 2000 B.C., as well as outstanding examples of blue-and-white porcelain, stoneware, and polychrome ware.

• The collection of Islamic paintings is one of the most renowned in the world and certainly the finest in North America.

If your time is limited, be sure to see the Peacock Room. Enter from Jefferson Drive and turn left after mounting the steps to the main floor. Follow the corridor to the Peacock Room in the northeast corner of the building.

Chinese bronze ritual wine vessel, Western Zhou dynasty, 10th century B.C.

THE PEACOCK ROOM

In 1876, Frederick R. Leyland, a Liverpool shipowner and Whistler's first major patron, had the dining room of his London town house remodeled to display an extensive collection of blue-and-white Oriental porcelain.

Thomas Jeckyll, the architect in charge of the project, built a wooden shell behind the walls, ceiling, fireplace, and window shutters in the room. (This made it possible to dismantle the room years later and move it from London to Detroit and, finally, to Washington.) Jeckyll covered the walls with gilded leather. The porcelains were placed on specially designed walnut shelves, a red-bordered rug was laid on the floor, and a large Whistler painting, *Rose and Silver: The Princess From the Land of Porcelain*, was hung over the mantelpiece.

Whistler felt that the gilded leather, with its design of red flowers and pomegranates, and the red border on the rug detracted from the delicate colors of his painting, so Leyland gave him permission to tone down the room. Whistler began by cutting off the rug's red border and painting over the offensive red flowers. Then he experimented with blue paint on the gilded leather.

While Leyland was in Liverpool for several months, Whistler redecorated the entire room, gilding the walnut shelves and painting turquoise and gold peacocks and other decorative motifs on the walls, shutters, ceiling, and sideboard. Four places are marked with Whistler's characteristic butterfly signature: on the right shutter of the central window, in the southwest corner of the ceiling, on the upper left panel of the top of the sideboard, and near the lower left part of the large panel over the sideboard.

Whistler was proud of his work, which he called *Harmony in Blue and Gold*. He said, "Pictures have been painted often enough with consideration of the room in which they were to hang; in this case I have painted a room to harmonize with my picture."

According to legend, when Jeckyll saw what Whistler had done, his mind reportedly snapped and he was later found gilding the floor of his bedroom, babbling of peacocks and pomegranates. He died soon afterward in an insane asylum.

Leyland was equally shocked and asked Whistler how much he owed for the destruction of his dining room. When Whistler requested two thousand guineas, Leyland countered with one thousand pounds. Since pounds were used for tradesmen, not professionals, Whistler was incensed. According to some reports, he vented his ire by changing the large painting on the south wall of the room to show his patron as a rich peacock clutching a pile of silver coins in his claw. Others say that Whistler planned this version of the painting from the beginning. The artist himself is the poor but proud peacock who disdains the silver shillings.

After his initial displeasure with Whistler for ruining a valuable antique wallcovering, Leyland grew to admire the room and kept it intact until his death in 1892. The house and its contents were sold at auction, and the new owners occasionally allowed visitors to see the Peacock Room. When Freer saw it in 1902, he wanted to buy the large panel and the three sets of folding shutters—but not the entire room. He believed it would be impossible to move the room without damaging it severely.

In 1904, when a London dealer bought the Peacock Room and reinstalled it in his gallery, Freer agreed to purchase the entire room for $30,000. A wing was added to his Detroit home to accommodate the room, and *The Princess From the Land of Porcelain*, which he had acquired in 1903, was hung in its original location over the mantelpiece. After Freer's death in 1919, the room was dismantled again and installed in its permanent home at the Freer Gallery. The room has been

The Peacock Room

returned to its original splendor through a two-year program of conservation.

THE PRINCESS FROM THE LAND OF PORCELAIN

The Princess is a painting of Christine Spartali, daughter of the Greek Consul General in London, painted in 1863-64. Whistler, who was doing a series of so-called Japanese paintings at that time, asked her to pose with Oriental props. Mr. Spartali did not consider the painting a suitable portrait of his daughter and refused to buy it.

A collector who wanted the picture objected to Whistler's signature printed in large letters near the top of the canvas. When the artist refused to change the signature, the picture remained unsold for a while. Frederick Leyland bought the painting after its first owner had died. After Leyland's death in 1892, it was purchased by a Glasgow dealer, who loaned it to the World's Columbian Exposition in Chicago in 1893. The painting was later acquired by a Glasgow collector, from whom Freer bought it in 1903.

As a result of the controversy over his signature, Whistler began to change the way he signed his works, and his experiments led finally to the famous butterfly signature.

HIRSHHORN MUSEUM AND SCULPTURE GARDEN

Independence Avenue at Eighth Street, S.W.
Washington, D.C. 20560
202/357-2700

METRO	L'Enfant Plaza, Maryland Avenue Exit.
HOURS	10 A.M. to 5:30 P.M. daily. Summer hours determined annually. Closed Christmas Day.
TOURS	General tour of the collection at 10:30 A.M., Noon, and 1:30 P.M. Monday through Saturday; also at 2:30 P.M. Saturday; 12:30 P.M., 1:30 P.M., and 2:30 P.M. Sunday. Tour of special exhibitions 11 A.M. Wednesday. Group tours, including foreign language tours. Call 202/357-3235 for details.
ADMISSION	Free.
HANDICAPPED FACILITIES	Swinging doors at plaza entrance (Mall side). Accessible to the disabled. Ramps into the sculpture garden from the Mall. Sign language tours by appointment.
FOOD SERVICE	Outdoor café scheduled to reopen in 1993.
MUSEUM SHOP	Books, postcards, posters, and jewelry.
SPECIAL EVENTS	Free film series, October through June; concerts by the Twentieth Century Consort, lectures.
MEMBERSHIP	Smithsonian Associates
AUTHOR'S CHOICE	Sculpture garden *Woman With Baby Carriage* by Pablo Picasso, third floor *Sleeping Muse* by Constantin Brancusi, third floor Matisse sculptures, third floor Abram Lerner Room (third floor balcony room)

In 1966, Joseph Hirshhorn donated his entire art collection to the nation for the first federal museum of contemporary art. With funds appropriated by Congress for a building and an additional million dollars from Hirshhorn, the museum opened in October 1974. At that time, the Hirshhorn collection included four thousand paintings and drawings and two thousand pieces of sculpture. Since then, gifts from other donors and additional works from Hirshhorn have expanded the original holdings. Hirshhorn, a five-foot-four-inch bundle of energy, continued to collect until his death at eighty-two in 1981, when approximately six thousand more art works were bequeathed to the museum.

Hirshhorn, who came to the United States at the age of six from his native Latvia, never forgot his early impoverished years. His widowed mother supported her ten children by working at a purse factory in Brooklyn. As a child, Hirshhorn tacked pictures from insurance company calendars—scenes by such artists as Bouguereau and Landseer—on his bedroom wall.

He left school at fourteen to work on Wall Street, becoming a broker on the American Exchange at seventeen. With canny investments and the foresight to sell his stocks shortly before the stock market crash in 1929, he became a millionaire by the time he was thirty. Later, Hirshhorn's company mined a hundred million tons of uranium ore when he began investing in Canada's mineral-rich lands.

Hirshhorn, who evolved from looking at calendar art to buying etchings of Wall Street scenes in his teens, began buying modern art intensively—almost compulsively—in the 1930s. When he found an artist whose work he admired, he bought in quantity and was often among the first to recognize talent. Early on, he bought twenty works by Arshile Gorky. He acquired forty Milton Avery paintings in 1940, when few people cared for Avery's work. He bought three Kenneth Noland paintings from the artist's first New York show in 1959. Sculptor David Smith sold only eighty works during his lifetime; eleven were bought by Hirshhorn.

When a dealer once tried to discuss the investment value of one of his purchases, Hirshhorn said angrily,"Don't tell me how to make money. I don't collect art to make money. I do it because I love art."

With the collection growing, in the mid-1950s, Hirshhorn decided to hire Abram Lerner, an artist, gallery official, and friend, as curator. According to Lerner, who later served as founding director and guided the museum through its first ten years, Hirshhorn bought what he liked and would buy "a young painter he's never heard of as readily as a Rodin or an Eakins." By the 1960s, the Hirshhorn collection was eagerly being sought by museums in England, Israel, Italy, and Switzerland. New York Governor Nelson Rockefeller, himself a collector, wanted it to be located in New York State. However, having realized the immigrant's dream of success, Hirshhorn felt that his collection should go to the United States. The personal intervention of President and Mrs. Lyndon B. Johnson helped to ensure its place in Washington.

Today, donations from numerous other individuals, together with curatorial acumen in keeping up with the newest art, have added to the Hirshhorn legacy.

THE BUILDING
Architect Gordon Bunshaft of Skidmore, Owings, and Merrill, designed a cylindrical concrete structure encircling an open courtyard. This "doughnut" on the Mall measures 231 feet in diameter. Supported on four fourteen-foot-tall concrete piers, the building seems to float above a paved, three-acre plaza dotted with sculpture and filled with café tables in summer. (The restaurant and sculpture plaza will be closed for a redesign project until 1993.)

The permanent collection is displayed on the second and third floors, with temporary exhibitions and an auditorium located on the lower level. A glass-walled museum shop is in the lobby.

THE CORE COLLECTION
Originally, the paintings and sculpture were displayed in various Hirshhorn homes and offices, with many stored in

The Hirshhorn Museum and Sculpture Garden

warehouses. The large sculpture pieces were placed on the lawn of the Hirshhorns' Tudor-style mansion in Greenwich, Connecticut. When the museum opened in 1974, more than fifty truckloads of art were dispatched to Washington.

As developed by the donor, the collection touched on all major trends in late nineteenth- and twentieth-century art. Hirshhorn recognized the importance of Thomas Eakins and, with more than fifty paintings by that innovative artist—as well as drawings, sculpture, photographs, and memorabilia—the collection is second only to that of the Philadelphia Museum of Art.

So many artists are represented in depth that there are virtually collections-within-the-collection. There are dozens of works by Honoré Daumier, Henri Matisse, Auguste Rodin, Edgar Degas, Alexander Calder, Alberto Giacometti, Henry Moore, Willem de Kooning, David Smith, and Pablo Picasso.

TOURING THE MUSEUM

It is best to begin your tour on the third floor, proceeding clockwise through the galleries.

The development of American art unfolds, from late nineteenth- and early twentieth-century portraits by Eakins and John Singer Sargent, among others, to the vibrant paintings of Georgia O'Keeffe. After the American collection, there are galleries devoted to works by European Modernists, from Constantin Brancusi's *Sleeping Muse* to Fernand Léger's *Nude on a Red Background*, followed by Surrealists of the 1920s and 1930s, including works by Francis Bacon and Balthus, and a selection of German Expressionist paintings.

Don't miss the Joan Miró paintings and the spectacular view of the Mall from the balcony room, named in honor of founding director emeritus Abram Lerner. Alexander Calder's *Fish*, a four-foot-long mobile of glass, metal, wire, and cord on view here, formerly hung in the front hall of the Hirshhorns' Connecticut home.

The third floor sculpture galleries in the inner ring, adjacent to the painting galleries, are devoted to American and European artists from approximately 1910 to the present. *Woman With Baby Carriage*, a 1950 bronze by Picasso, stands near the inner ring entrance. Hirshhorn paid $300,000 for this sculpture, a price he said would have caused his mother to "turn over in her grave."

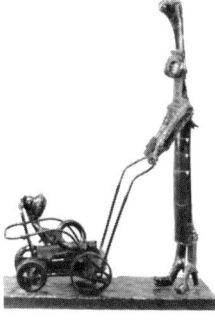

Woman With Baby Carriage by Pablo Picasso

Sculpture galleries on the second floor include the works of such nineteenth- and twentieth-century masters as Barye, Daumier, Degas, Gauguin, Maillol, Matisse, and Rodin.

Paintings on the second floor cover the period from approximately 1945 to 1986, and include the New York School, Postwar Abstract Expressionists, Pop Art, Color Field Painting, Funk, New Realists, Neo-Expressionism, Neo-Geo, and contemporary organic abstraction. Here the spirit of the post-Hirshhorn Hirshhorn comes through, as a publicly-funded contemporary art museum flexes its muscle in bringing visitors the finest, most up-to-date examples.

SCULPTURE

Hirshhorn's collection was particularly strong in sculpture of the late nineteenth and early twentieth centuries, and newly acquired works include today's sculptors.

Monumental abstract pieces are displayed on the plaza, including Henry Moore's bronze *Two Piece Reclining Figure: Points* near the Independence Avenue entrance, Alexander Calder's *Two Disks*, George Rickey's *Three Red Lines*, and the forty-two-foot high, thirty-ton *Isis* fashioned of scrap metal by Mark di Suvero. Newer works by William Tucker, Joan Van Alstine, and others also stand on the plaza, which is currently being redesigned.

The sculpture garden contains mostly figurative pieces, more intimate in scale than those on the plaza. The majority of the seventy-five works are cast in bronze, except for a few welded steel pieces by David Smith.

Particularly noteworthy is *The Burghers of Calais*, an 1886 bronze by Rodin, which commemoratoes the heroes of the city of Calais during the Hundred Years' War. Two rare bas-reliefs by Eakins depict scenes from the Battle of Trenton during the Revolutionary War, and a series of four bronze bas-reliefs, *Backs*, created by Matisse at intervals over a twenty-year period from 1909 to 1930, show his increasingly abstract style.

As you sit near the fish pond in the sculpture garden or stroll among the works arrayed here, think about the four men who have given the country a quartet of great art museums on the Mall. Despite the different circumstances that shaped their tastes and personalities, Andrew W. Mellon, Charles Lang Freer, Arthur M. Sackler, and Joseph Hirshhorn shared a passion for art and an acquisitiveness that has benefited succeeding generations.

The Burghers of Calais *by Auguste Rodin*

HOLOCAUST MEMORIAL MUSEUM

Raoul Wallenberg Place and Independence Avenue, S.W.
Washington, D.C. 20560
202/357-2700

Until Spring 1993:
2000 L Street, N.W., Suite 588
Washington, D.C. 20036
202/653-9220

Please note: The museum is scheduled to open in the Spring of 1993.

METRO	Smithsonian.
HOURS	10 A.M. to 5:30 P.M. daily. Closed Christmas Day.
TOURS	Call for information.
ADMISSION	Free.
HANDICAPPED FACILITIES	Accessible to the disabled. Ramp entrance.
SPECIAL EVENTS	Special exhibitions, lectures, symposia, films, concerts, and commemorative and educational programs.

Washington's newest landmark, the United States Holocaust Memorial Museum, is rising in the shadow of the Washington Monument as this book goes to press. Here is a preview of this unique museum, which is scheduled to open in April 1993.

HISTORY
The U.S. Holocaust Memorial Council was authorized by Congress in 1980 to educate the American people about the Holocaust and to create a living memorial to the millions of people who were murdered by the Nazis between 1933 and 1945. Although built on federal land, all funds for its construction have been raised through contributions from the private sector.

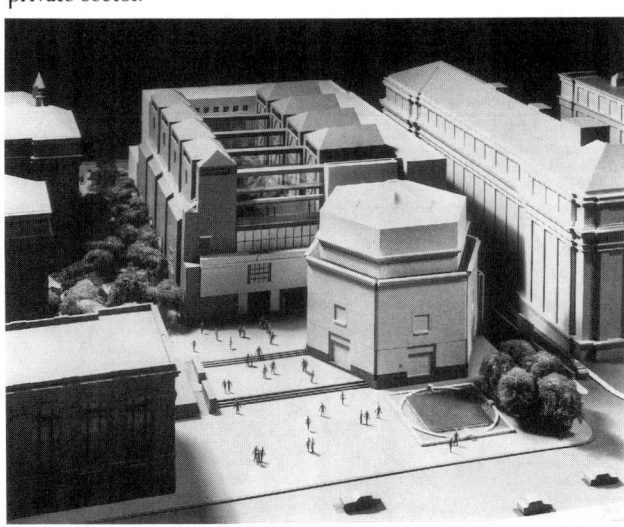

The Holocaust Memorial Museum

James I. Freed of Pei Cobb Freed and Partners of New York City developed the architectural design for the building, in association with Notter Finegold and Alexander, Inc. of Washington, D.C., and Boston. His mandate was to create a museum of "symbolic and artistic beauty that is visually and emotionally moving in accordance with the solemn nature of the Holocaust."

The five-story building adjoins the National Mall four hundred yards from the Washington Monument, on Raoul Wallenberg Place (formerly Fifteenth Street), near Independence Avenue, S.W.

Highlights include:

• *The Hall of Remembrance*, a hexagonal, sixty-foot-high, six-thousand-square-foot space that will be America's national memorial to the victims of the Holocaust.

• *The Hall of Witness*, a large, skylit space that will serve as a central gathering place for visitors. It will be connected to the Hall of Remembrance by a grand staircase at one end, and another staircase will lead down to the auditoriums and education center on the concourse level.

• *The permanent exhibition*, located on the second, third, and fourth floors, will depict the tragedy of the Holocaust through artifacts, audio-visual displays, documents, photographs, and eyewitness testimonies.

When you begin your tour of the permanent exhibition, you will be given an identification card resembling a passport. That card will tell the story of an actual victim or survivor whose age and sex are similar to yours and whose fate you will understand as you tour the exhibits.

The exhibition will be arranged chronologically, beginning on the fourth floor with the period from 1933 to 1939. During those years, various groups, including dissidents, Gypsies, Jehovah's Witnesses, the handicapped, and, especially, Jews were systematically excluded from society in Nazi Germany. The book burnings of 1933; the tragic impact of the Nuremburg Laws of 1935 isolating Jews from German society, and the state-sponsored terror of "Kristallnacht," November 9-11, 1938, when hundreds of synagogues and Jewish-owned businesses were burned, are vividly depicted.

The third floor will be devoted to the years from 1939 to 1945, a period that included the establishment of ghettos, the deportation of thousands of people, and mass murders in concentration camps. Beginning with state-authorized killings of handicapped German nationals, Nazi persecution reached its height in Auschwitz, Treblinka, and other death camps. The Nazis murdered six million Jews and millions of others, including Gypsies, Soviet prisoners of war, Polish dissidents, homosexuals, and Jehovah's Witnesses.

One artifact on this floor is boxcar #31599 G, the same type of railroad car that was used to transport thousands of Jews from the Warsaw Ghetto to their deaths in Treblinka.

Among the most interesting artifacts is a large, rusty milk can in which historian Emanual Ringelbaum placed scores of documents describing the life and destruction of the Warsaw Ghetto, the largest ghetto in Western Europe. Three such milk cans were secretly buried in separate locations in the ghetto, and only two have been discovered. The one which will be on display here, which is on long-term loan from the Jewish Historical Institute in Warsaw, was found by construction workers in 1950 under the ruins of a building. The other can was found in 1946 and is still in Poland at the Jewish Historical Institute. The Warsaw Ghetto was completely destroyed and nearly all of its inhabitants were killed in the Holocaust. Dr. Ringelbaum escaped from the ghetto in March 1943, but was discovered hiding on the "Aryan" side of Warsaw a year later and was murdered by the Nazis.

The exhibition emphasizes the heroism of the people of the ghetto, who resisted the Nazis and tried to maintain their educational and religious institutions and their community structure.

Exhibits on the second floor will show how survivors of the Holocaust have attempted to rebuild their lives from 1945 to the present in the United States, Israel, and elsewhere.

- *The Learning Center*, a computer-based learning facility on the second floor, will provide an opportunity to explore specific aspects of the Holocaust and the Nazi era by retrieving documentary films, photographs, eyewitness oral histories, maps, and music onscreen.

- *The Library and Archives*, located on the fifth floor, with additional stack space in the basement, will form the nucleus of the U.S. Holocaust Research Institute. It will include thousands of volumes and documents relating to the Holocaust, and will be available to general researchers, as well as scholars.

- *The Children's Wall of Remembrance*, on the concourse level, will serve as a memorial to the one-and-a-half million children killed by the Nazis. Six thousand tiles, handpainted by American schoolchildren, will depict their views of the Holocaust.

- Two *special exhibition galleries* on the first floor and concourse levels will house temporary exhibits, and two auditoriums on the concourse level will be used for lectures, films, concerts, and symposia.

NATIONAL AIR AND SPACE MUSEUM

Sixth and Independence Avenue, S.W.
Washington, D.C. 20560
202/357-2700

METRO	L'Enfant Plaza.
HOURS	10 A.M. to 5:30 P.M. daily. Summer hours determined annually. Closed Christmas Day.
TOURS	Ninety-minute tours at 10:15 A.M. and 1 P.M. daily. Group tours by appointment. Cassette recorded tours available in English, French, German, Spanish, Japanese, Italian, and Portuguese.
ADMISSION	Free.
HANDICAPPED FACILITIES	Ramp entrance on Jefferson Drive (Mall side). Accessible to the disabled.
FOOD SERVICE	Flight Lines cafeteria and Wright Place restaurant at east end of building.
MUSEUM SHOPS	Books, postcards, models, slides, posters, freeze-dried ice cream near the Mall entrance. Spacearium shop on the second floor, with books, posters, first-day stamp covers.
SPECIAL EVENTS	Films in Samuel P. Langley Theater: adults, $2.75; children, students, and senior citizens, $1.75. Shows in Albert Einstein Planetarium: adults, $2.25; children, students, and senior citizens, $1.25. Free lectures, film series, and concerts.
SPECIAL FACILITIES	Planetarium, library, IMAX film theater, Education Resource Center.
MEMBERSHIP	Smithsonian Associates and National Air and Space Museum Associates.
AUTHOR'S CHOICE	*Blue Planet*, Langley Theater Charles Lindbergh's *Spirit of St. Louis*, Milestones of Flight Hall Wright Brothers' 1903 Flyer, Milestones of Flight Hall Space shuttle exhibit, Space Hall

The Smithsonian's interest in flight dates back to 1857, when it began using balloons to collect weather data and the *Washington Evening Star* published daily Smithsonian weather reports. In 1861, the Smithsonian conducted studies on ballooning, and Joseph Henry, the institution's first secretary, persuaded President Lincoln to use balloons for military observations during the Civil War.

At the close of the Philadelphia Centennial Exposition in 1876, the Smithsonian acquired a group of kites from the Chinese Imperial Commission, which formed the nucleus of its aeronautical collection. The Smithsonian's third secretary, Samuel Pierpont Langley, began the institution's research in aerodynamics in 1887, and the Smithsonian Astrophysical Observatory was established three years later.

More recently, from 1916 to 1945, the Smithsonian

published major articles by Robert H. Goddard, father of the liquid-fuel rocket, and provided funding for his research.

Although the National Air and Space Museum contains some 200,000 square feet of exhibit space, there is not room to show all the major machines. For example, the fuselage of a Boeing 747 is longer than the building is wide, and a Saturn V rocket, which boosted men to the moon, is four times taller than the museum itself.

OUTDOOR SCULPTURES

The bronze, ribbon-like sculpture at the Independence Avenue entrance is *Continuum* by Charles O. Perry. The painted stainless steel sculpture on the Mall side is *Ad Astra* by Richard Lippold.

Delta Solar by sculptor Alejandro Otero, a Bicentennial gift from the Venezuelan government, stands above a reflecting pool at the Seventh Street side of the building. The 48-by-27 foot delta-shaped framework is filled with stainless steel rotary sails that move in the breeze.

TOURING THE MUSEUM

As soon as you enter this three-block-long glass and marble building, you are caught up in the wonder and excitement of flight. Groups of students swirl around you. Midwestern twangs and Southern accents mingle with the unfamiliar sounds of foreign languages. A dazzling array of airplanes, spacecraft, and flight-related artifacts are displayed overhead and all around. Films, puppet and slide shows, and dioramas add to the excitement. You can see objects as old as a seventeenth-century Chinese sundial and as modern as space food.

This is the world's most popular museum, visited by an average of ten million people each year. The building, designed by Gyo Obata of the St. Louis firm of Hellmuth, Obata, and Kassabaum, opened July 1, 1976, as part of the Bicentennial celebration. All objects displayed were either used on historic missions or are the backup craft for those flights.

Before you start your tour of the museum, buy a ticket for one of the film showings in the Samuel P. Langley Theater on the first floor. Then do your sightseeing and return at showtime. Films are shown on an IMAX motion picture projection system, with a giant screen five stories high and seven stories wide.

Take your choice of *Blue Planet*, a space film about the earth and its delicate environment; *The Dream Is Alive,* featuring spectacular inflight footage shot by fourteen astronauts on three 1984 missions; *To Fly*, a bird's eye view of America, or *On The Wing*, a comparison of the flight of birds with man's mechanical flight.

MILESTONES OF FLIGHT HALL (Gallery 100)

The best place to begin your tour is at the Milestones of Flight Hall, a two-level gallery at the Mall entrance. Several historic airplanes and spacecraft are here. Some of the earliest planes are delicate structures of fabric, wood, and wire. You can see the Wright brothers' 1903 Flyer, which made the first manned flight in 1903; Charles Lindbergh's *Spirit of St. Louis*, which made the first solo, nonstop, thirty-three-and-a-half-hour transatlantic flight in 1927, and John Glenn's Friendship 7, the

Charles Lindbergh's Spirit of St. Louis

first U.S. spacecraft to orbit the earth in 1962. Other *firsts* include: Gemini 4, the first U.S. space walk in 1965; Apollo 11 Command Module, *Columbia*, which returned the three astronauts from the moon in 1969, and Pioneer 10, the first spacecraft to explore Jupiter.

HALL OF AIR TRANSPORTATION (Gallery 102)
This two-story gallery to the west of Gallery 100 shows the history of air transportation of people, mail, and cargo. Suspended from the ceiling are the Ford Tri-Motor, which first offered safe and dependable service in 1926; the Pitcairn Mailwing, which carried mail in 1927; the Fairchild FC-2, which made the first nonstop flight from New York to Miami in 1928, and the first modern airliner, the Boeing 247D. The 17,500-pound Douglas DC-3 is the heaviest plane to hang from the museum's ceiling and is probably the most important aircraft in air transportation history.

Exhibits also show the history of air express and the development of air traffic control.

VERTICAL FLIGHT (Gallery 103)
Continuing to the left, this gallery displays helicopters, autogiros, and special vehicles. You can look inside the cockpit of the Marine helicopter UH-34D with its canvas seats for passengers. Also here are *The Spirit of Texas*, the Bell LongRanger helicopter, the first helicopter to fly around the world in 1982 in a little over twenty-nine days, and the Sikorsky XR-4, the first helicopter able to carry passengers and the first to travel across the United States in 1942.

WEST GALLERY (Gallery 104)
The changing exhibits in this gallery include recently restored aircraft. For example, you may see a Curtiss P-40, a World War II fighter plane; a Grumman *Gulfhawk II*, used for aerial acrobatics, and a Boeing P-26, a famous Army Air Corps fighter of the 1930s.

GOLDEN AGE OF FLIGHT (Gallery 105)
Across the hall from Gallery 103, this area pays tribute to the planes and people who made aviation history during the years between the two World Wars. An audiovisual show re-creates the era of the 1930s. Planes included are the Curtiss Robin *Ole Miss* that established a world record for sustained flight using air-to-air refueling in 1935, and the Northrop Gamma *Polar Star*, used in Antarctic exploration in 1935.

JET AVIATION (Gallery 106)
Here are landmarks of the first forty years of jet aviation, which began in 1939. Artifacts include a Messerschmitt Me

262, the world's first operational jet fighter, and a Lockheed XP-80, prototype of the first U.S. operational jet fighter. Keith Ferris's mural, *The Evolution of Jet Aviation* shows twenty-seven airplanes from a 1939 Heinkel He178 to a 1972 Airbus A300.

EARLY FLIGHT (Gallery 107)

Designed to look like an indoor aeronautical exhibition of 1913, this gallery shows the beginnings of modern aviation. You can see the Wright 1909 Military Flyer, the world's first military airplane; a 1911 Curtiss Headless Pusher, often used by U.S. exhibition pilots, and an 1894 hang glider with bat-like wings of cotton cloth designed by German pioneer Otto Lilienthal.

INDEPENDENCE AVENUE LOBBY (Gallery 108)

The museum's Information Desk and Recorded Tour Desk are here, beneath the Rutan *Voyager* aircraft which flew around the world, nonstop and unrefueled, in December 1986. Aeronautical and astronautical trophies are on display. The large mural on the east wall is Robert McCall's *The Space Mural, A Cosmic View*. Eric Sloane's *Earth Flight Environment* mural is on the west wall.

FLIGHT TESTING (Gallery 109)

You can see the evolution of flight testing, from the Wright brothers through World War II, as well as the importance of inflight and ground testing. Highlights include *Winnie Mae*, Wiley Post's Lockheed Model 5C Vega, used for stratospheric research in the 1930s and the Bell XP-59A Airacomet, the first U.S. turbojet aircraft. To keep jet engine research secret during World War II, officials disguised the XP-59A by adding a dummy propeller while the plane was being transported to the test site. The propeller was removed before the flight and replaced after landing.

LOOKING AT EARTH (Gallery 110)

This gallery traces the various ways in which man looks at the earth, from early balloon observations to aerial photography, spacecraft, and satellite photos. A DeHaviland DH-4 and a Lockheed U-2 are featured in the exhibit.

STARS: FROM STONEHENGE TO THE SPACE TELESCOPE (Gallery 111)

A small model of Stonehenge shows how this primitive astronomical observatory worked. Tracing the development of astronomy, the exhibit also includes Skylab's Apollo Telescope Mount and Uhuru, an X-ray telescope.

LUNAR EXPLORATION VEHICLES (Gallery 112)

In the area outside Gallery 111, you can see a backup of the Apollo Lunar Module, the spacecraft that carried astronauts to the surface of the moon. Suspended from the ceiling are Surveyor, which soft-landed on the moon to study its soil composition and physical properties; Lunar Orbiter, which circled the moon to map the entire lunar surface, and Ranger, which provided the first close-up photographs of the moon's surface.

ROCKETRY AND SPACE FLIGHT (Gallery 113)
Exhibits of rocket motors, engines, and various facets of space development show the fact and fantasy of space flight from the black powder rocket developed in thirteenth-century China to the present. A large exhibit is also devoted to the evolution of the space suit.

SPACE HALL (Gallery 114)
One of the most popular exhibits in the museum, this gallery featuring rockets, guided missiles, and manned spacecraft is dominated by a sixty-foot-tall Minuteman III ground-based Intercontinental Ballistic Missile. Here are the Apollo-Soyuz spacecraft, the first international manned space mission; the V-2, the first operational long-range ballistic missile; the Jupiter C and Vanguard boosters, the first two U.S. satellite launch vehicles, and an exhibit on the U.S. space shuttle.

Rockets in Space Hall

On the second floor, you can walk through the Skylab Orbital Workshop, the backup of Skylab, America's first space station. Skylab proved that astronauts can live and work in space for extended periods of time.

BEYOND THE LIMITS: FLIGHT ENTERS THE COMPUTER AGE (Gallery 213)
This gallery at the end of the hall, to the left of the escalator, explores the primary applications of the electronic digital computer in aerospace. You can see a CRAY-1 supercomputer and models of the Mariner 10 spacecraft and the Grumman X-29 research aircraft here.

WORLD WAR I AVIATION (Gallery 206)
Examples of popular World War I aircraft—a Fokker D. VII, General Billy Mitchell's Spad XVI, and an Albatros D. Va.—are included in this gallery.

PIONEERS OF FLIGHT (Gallery 208)
Some of the greatest aviators and their historic aircraft are honored here. Included are Amelia Earhart's bright red Vega, marking the first solo transatlantic flight by a woman, in 1932, and Calbraith Perry Rodgers's *Vin Fiz*, in which he made the first U.S. transcontinental flight in 1911. The Wright brothers taught Rodgers to fly earlier that year and he soloed after only ninety minutes of instruction. Rodgers crashed several times during his historic flight between Sheepshead Bay, Long Island, and Pasadena, California. Eighteen wing panels, twenty struts, and two engines had been replaced by the end of the trip.

You can also see the Douglas World Cruiser *Chicago*, which made the first around-the-world flight—a trip that took nearly six months—in 1924. The exhibit "Black Wings" recounts the history of African-Americans in aviation.

EXPLORING THE PLANETS (Gallery 207)
A full-scale replica of a Voyager spacecraft, which was designed to explore Jupiter, Saturn and Uranus, is the centerpiece of this gallery. You can test your knowledge of the planets, and listen to "The Family of the Sun," an audiovisual exhibit designed for children.

WORLD WAR II AVIATION (Gallery 205)
Fighter aircraft from five countries show the air history of World War II. Included are a North American P-51D

Mustang, considered the best fighter in terms of speed, range, maneuverability, and firepower; a Mitsubishi A6M5 Zero, used by the Japanese navy; the nose of a Martin B-26, flown in Europe by the U.S. Air Force; a British Supermarine Spitfire Mark VII; a Messerschmitt Bf.109G, used by the German Luftwaffe against Spitfires and American bombers, and a Macchi C.202 Folgore, an Italian fighter plane.

Fortresses Under Fire, a mural by Keith Ferris, shows the Eighth Air Force under attack over Germany. The B-17G *Flying Fortress* depicted here contributed significantly to the Allied victory in Europe.

SEA-AIR OPERATIONS (Gallery 203)
Across the hall from Gallery 205, you can step aboard a reproduction of an airplane carrier hangar deck. Aircraft include a Boeing F4B-4, a biplane fighter used from 1928 to 1939; a Douglas SBD Dauntless, the major carrier-based bomber used during World War II; a Grumman FM-1 Wildcat, the Navy fighter plane used at the beginning of World War II, and a McDonnell Douglas A-4C Skyhawk, known as Heinemann's "Hot Rod," named after its famous designer.

ALBERT EINSTEIN PLANETARIUM (Gallery 201)
A Zeiss Model VI planetarium device and other projectors simulate the heavens on a seventy-foot overhead dome. Regularly scheduled planetarium shows and special presentations are featured in this 220-seat auditorium.

APOLLO TO THE MOON (Gallery 210)
You can learn about manned space flights from 1957 to 1972, from Project Mercury through the Apollo moon landings. Highlights include the Mercury *Freedom 7* and Gemini 7 spacecraft, a Skylab 4 command module, a Lunar Rover, and a Saturn V rocket booster, as well as samples of lunar soil and rocks.

FLIGHT AND THE ARTS (Gallery 211)
Changing exhibitions of paintings, drawings, prints, sculpture, and photographs show the artist's unique perceptions of air and space. The whimsical sculpture, *S.S. Pussiewillow II*, by British sculptor Rowland Emett brings to life a space ship of the future.

THE PAUL E. GARBER PRESERVATION, RESTORATION, AND STORAGE FACILITY
If you would like to see more historic air and space craft and learn how they are restored, you can tour the Garber Facility, about half an hour from Washington in Suitland, Maryland.

Approximately ninety aircraft, as well as space vehicles, engines, and propellers are on display.

Free tours are given at 10 A.M. Monday through Friday and at 10 A.M. and 1 P.M. Saturdays, Sundays, and holidays. There is no heating or air-conditioning in the warehouse-type exhibit buildings, so dress accordingly.

Call 202/357-1400 between 9 A.M. and 5 P.M. Monday through Friday for reservations and further information.

NATIONAL GALLERY OF ART

West Building, Constitution Avenue at
  Sixth Street, N.W.
East Building, Fourth Street and
  Constitution Avenue, N.W.
Washington, D.C. 20565
202/737-4215

METRO Judiciary Square, Smithsonian, or Archives.

HOURS 10 A.M. to 5 P.M. Monday through Saturday; 11 A.M. to 6 P.M. Sunday. Closed Christmas and New Year's Day. Summer hours determined annually.

TOURS *Introduction to the West Building Collection* 1:30 P.M. and 3 P.M. Monday through Friday; 3 P.M. Saturday; 1 P.M. Sunday, West Building Rotunda. *Introduction to the East Building Collections* 11:30 A.M. Monday through Friday; 11 A.M. Saturday; 2 P.M. Sunday, East Building, Art Information Desk. *Foreign Language Tours* West Building, Noon Tuesday; East Building, 2 P.M. Tuesday.

ADMISSION Free.

HANDICAPPED FACILITIES Ramps in front of East Building and at Sixth Street and Constitution Avenue. Wheelchairs available at all entrances.

FOOD SERVICE Self-Service Buffet, concourse level, connecting link; Garden Café, West Building, ground floor; Terrace Café, East Building, upper level.

MUSEUM SHOPS West Building, ground floor; concourse level between the two buildings; East Building, concourse level. Art books, exhibition catalogs, slides, postcards, posters, and reproductions.

SPECIAL EVENTS Concerts by the National Gallery Orchestra or guest artists in the West Garden Court of the West Building 7 P.M. Sunday, except during the summer. Illustrated lectures by visiting experts in the East Building Auditorium 4 P.M. Sunday. Gallery talks by Education Department lecturers and Graduate Lecturing Fellows. Also, free films on art in East Building Auditorium.

SPECIAL FACILITIES Easels provided for artists who have obtained permission to copy paintings from the gallery's collections. Baby strollers available.

RESEARCH FACILITIES Center for Advanced Study in the Visual Arts, Index of American Design, extension services, photographic archive, research library available by permission.

AUTHOR'S CHOICE West Building
  Ginevra de Benci by Leonardo da Vinci
  Self-Portrait by Rembrandt van Ryn
  Alba Madonna by Raphael
  Rubens Peale With a Geranium by Rembrandt Peale
  A Girl With a Watering Can by Auguste Renoir
  The Rotunda

East Building
> Untitled mobile by Alexander Calder
> *National Gallery Ledge Piece* by Anthony Caro
> *Roses* by Vincent van Gogh
> Permanent twentieth-century collection
> Special exhibitions

Its permanent collections, special exhibitions, and contributions to conservation, art history, and related research make the National Gallery of Art the jewel in Washington's crown of museums. Even if you spent days there, you still could not see all of the treasures concealed within those marble walls. With this guide you can, at least, look for the highlights.

The National Gallery's collections encompass the entire history of Western art, from the twelfth century to the present. There are familiar masterpieces, including the only painting by Leonardo da Vinci in the Western hemisphere. The twentieth-century collection is particularly strong in French art before World War I and in American art of the 1950s and 1960s.

HISTORY

During the 1920s, Andrew W. Mellon, millionaire industrialist and secretary of the treasury, decided to begin an art collection that could form the nucleus of a national art gallery. As Mellon's plans became known, art dealers—especially Knoedler and Company and Duveen Brothers—vied to find works for his collection. Lord Duveen even rented an apartment directly below the Mellon apartment at 1785 Massachusetts Avenue (now the headquarters of the National Trust for Historic Preservation) and hung some of his most tempting treasures there. Mellon, who was given a key, could study the paintings at his leisure before deciding to buy.

After the Russian Revolution, when works of art from the Hermitage Museum in Leningrad were offered for sale, Mellon bought twenty-one paintings which he donated to the museum. The Hermitage group included Botticelli's *Adoration of the Magi*, Jan van Eyck's *Annunciation*, Raphael's *Alba Madonna* and *Saint George and the Dragon*, and Titian's *Venus with a Mirror*, as well as paintings by Rembrandt, Van Dyck, and Frans Hals.

In 1937, Congress made the new National Gallery of Art official by granting it a charter and giving it the name formerly used by a branch of the Smithsonian. The A.W. Mellon Educational and Charitable Trust donated funds for the construction of the building and salaries of the top executives. The museum, inaugurated by President Franklin D. Roosevelt, opened on March 17, 1941, with a nucleus of 121 paintings donated by Andrew Mellon. Although the federal government pays for the operation of the museum, all acquisition costs are contributed by private individuals and corporations.

Following the example set by Mellon, other great collections have been donated, including the Samuel H. Kress collection of Italian paintings and sculpture, Joseph E. Widener's paintings, sculpture, and decorative arts, Chester Dale's nineteenth- and twentieth-century French paintings, the Lessing J. Rosenwald collection of twenty-five thousand prints and drawings, and the Edgar William and Bernice Chrysler Garbisch collection of American folk art paintings.

Hundreds of gifts from other collectors have also enriched the gallery's holdings.

In honor of the gallery's fiftieth anniversary in 1991, more than two thousand works of art were presented by donors from the United States and abroad. The anniversary was also marked by special exhibitions, concerts, publications, a documentary film, and the ongoing re-installation of the permanent collection.

The anniversary gifts enriched virtually all of the gallery's collections. Highlights include the first drawings by Titian, Heinrich Aldegrever, Adrian van Ostade, Jean-Baptiste-Camille Corot, and Hans Bol to enter the collection; thirty-one of the surviving sixty-nine original wax sculptures modeled by Edgar Degas, and such masterpieces as Jusepe di Ribera's *The Martyrdom of Saint Bartholomew*, Vincent van Gogh's *Roses*, Paul Cézanne's *Boy in a Red Waistcoat,* Claude Monet's *Sainte-Adresse*, and the finest known impression of Pablo Picasso's etching *The Frugal Repast*. Artists Richard Diebenkorn, Robert Frank, Helen Frankenthaler, Jasper Johns, Ellsworth Kelly, and Roy Lichtenstein contributed works of art.

THE BUILDINGS

The West Building was designed by John Russell Pope, architect of the Archives Building and the Jefferson Memorial (whose dome bears more than a passing resemblance to the National Gallery). Inspired by the old Court House on Judiciary Square, which was built around 1820, the building contains paintings and sculpture from the twelfth to the twentieth centuries. Its 782-foot length makes this one of the world's largest marble structures, with more than 500,000 square feet of interior floor space.

When the National Gallery began to outgrow its quarters, Andrew Mellon's daughter, the late Ailsa Mellon Bruce, his son, Paul, and the Andrew W. Mellon Foundation carried on the family tradition by contributing funds for the construction of the East Building. Designed by I. M. Pei and Associates, the East Building opened on June 1, 1978.

Both East and West Buildings are works of art themselves. Each is built of Tennessee pink marble and is typical of its era. The West Building, with its rotunda lined with Italian green marble columns, is the last of the great neoclassical buildings by Pope, who—like Andrew Mellon—died without seeing it. I. M. Pei's East Building, with its sharp angles and crisply modern lines, is a metaphor for the last decades of the twentieth century.

In the West Building, galleries devoted to painting and sculpture are on the main floor; additional sculpture, decorative arts, prints, and drawings are on the ground floor.

THE WEST BUILDING

ITALIAN PAINTINGS

The first thirty-three galleries trace the development of Italian painting and sculpture.

You might begin your tour in the West Hall adjoining the Rotunda, visiting the galleries devoted to Italian painting from the Middle Ages to the eighteenth century. Among the earliest paintings is a thirteenth-century icon, *Madonna and Child on a Curved Throne* (Gallery 1), which is typical of the highly stylized, flat planes of the Byzantine School.

During the Middle Ages, paintings were generally of religious subjects because the church was the major art patron. In Siena, Byzantine elements combined with a more naturalistic approach (as typified by the sheep in the foreground) to produce Duccio di Buoninsegna's magnificent *Nativity With the Prophets Isaiah and Ezekiel* (Gallery 3). This was part of an altarpiece composed of nearly a hundred panels, commissioned for the high altar of the Cathedral in Siena in 1308. Duccio continued to influence Sienese artists for centuries after his death.

While Duccio drew his inspiration from Byzantine roots, Giotto, his contemporary, about forty miles away in Florence, was beginning to break with Byzantine traditions. As you can see in his *Madonna and Child* (Gallery 1), Giotto continued to place figures against a flat gold background, but their forms are much more solidly sculptural than the Byzantine-influenced paintings of Siena.

Florence was a major art center throughout the Renaissance. If anyone could be said to represent the Renaissance man, it was Leonardo da Vinci. An inventor as well as an artist, Leonardo anticipated many later discoveries in aeronautics and anatomy. He invented the first armored fighting vehicle and anticipated the submarine, as well as helicopters and several types of aircraft. Although his interests in science were varied, many of his ideas were never fully developed. In art, Leonardo was constantly experimenting—sketching drapery folds, horses, and hands, and developing new techniques of oil painting. When Leonardo died in 1519, he left thousands of notes and drawings but only a few paintings.

His haunting portrait of the young merchant's wife, *Ginevra de Benci* (Gallery 6), is the only painting by Leonardo in the Americas. Note the artist's pun on the name of his sitter—a juniper bush (*ginepro* in Italian) frames her head, and a drawing of a juniper sprig is on the reverse of the painting.

During World War II, *Ginevra*'s owner, the Prince of Liechtenstein, hid the painting in the wine cellar of his castle at Vaduz. The National Gallery purchased the portrait in 1967, after several years of negotiations. Using the same method that had previously been employed to bring the *Mona Lisa* from Paris for a special exhibition, the panel painting was placed in a Styrofoam-lined suitcase equipped with a gauge to record the temperature and humidity. The painting traveled to New York's Kennedy Airport in a first class seat, accompanied by two gallery officials. And, despite delays caused by a snowstorm, *Ginevra* reached her new home safely, completing the journey to Washington in a private jet.

Ginevra shares this gallery with several other superb Florentine Renaissance portraits that are fascinating personality studies. Virtually a collection-within-a-collection, the group includes Lorenzo de Credi's *Self-Portrait*, *Portrait of a Youth* by Filippino Lippi, and *Portrait of a Man* by Andrea del Castagno.

Gallery 7 contains several canvases by Sandro Botticelli, who was one of the most innovative painters in fifteenth-century Florence. As a young man, Botticelli's paintings were vigorously realistic, but by the time he reached maturity and painted *The Adoration of the Magi* Botticelli was more concerned with spiritual expression.

By the fifteenth century, portraiture was an important

Ginevra de Benci *by Leonardo; National Gallery of Art, Ailsa Mellon Bruce Fund.*

source of artists' commissions. You can see how two artists viewed the same subject, Guiliano de Medici, by comparing Botticelli's portrait of him (Gallery 7) with Andrea del Verrocchio's terracotta bust (Gallery 9). Both indicate the dandyish character of the popular Florentine hero.

Raphael, an Umbrian artist of the fifteenth and early sixteenth century, painted his *Alba Madonna* (Gallery 19) in Rome, at the same time that Michelangelo was painting the ceiling of the Vatican's Sistine Chapel. Michelangelo's experiments with circular compositions and monumental forms may have influenced this painting, which was acquired by Andrew Mellon from the Hermitage Museum.

Raphael's small painting, *Saint George and the Dragon* (Gallery 19) was probably created for an emissary of the English king, Henry VII. The panel depicts the legendary warrior Saint George, the embodiment of chivalry. The saint killed a dragon with his lance, thereby saving a pagan princess and prompting her father and his subjects to convert to Christianity.

Agnolo Bronzino's *A Young Woman and Her Little Boy* (Gallery 21) illustrates the Mannerist tradition which was important in Italy during the years from 1520 to 1600. Bronzino, court painter to Cosimo de Medici in Florence, specialized in this type of haughty, elegant court portrait.

Titian, the great sixteenth-century Venetian painter, admired classical Greek art, as is evident in the monumentality and dignity of his *Venus With a Mirror* (Gallery 23).

During the eighteenth century, when it was customary for wealthy gentlemen to embark on a Grand Tour of Europe, paintings of important landmarks were sought-after souvenirs of their travels. According to Gallery Director J. Carter Brown, the Canaletto and Guardi Venetian views they collected (Galleries 34 and 36) were the eighteenth-century equivalent of picture postcards.

In designing the National Gallery's Rotunda, John Russell Pope was inspired by the dome of the Pantheon in Rome. Giovanni Paolo Pannini's *Interior of the Pantheon* (Gallery 34) shows the source of Pope's inspiration.

SPANISH PAINTINGS

Although the National Gallery's Italian paintings outnumber those of other European schools, the quality—if not the quantity—of its other collections is superb. Consider, for example, the gallery (29) devoted to El Greco (Domenikos Theotocopoulos). Gathered together here are eight of El Greco's finest paintings, including his *Laocoon* and *Saint Jerome*.

El Greco was born in Crete, which then belonged to Venice, and he studied in Venice and Rome before going to Spain in 1576. He lived in Toledo until his death in 1614, painting Mannerist works remarkable for their intensity. With their vivid colors and sinuous lines, his paintings seem as modern as those of contemporary Expressionists.

FLEMISH AND GERMAN PAINTINGS

Flanders, now part of Belgium, was a prosperous country during the fifteenth and sixteenth centuries, with art patrons drawn from the ranks of wealthy merchants, the church, and the ruling ducal family.

Jan van Eyck, a master of detail, was court painter to Philip the Good, Duke of Burgundy, in the fifteenth century. Van

Eyck's *The Annunciation* (Gallery 39) shows the Virgin and the Angel of the Annunciation in a setting as richly ornamented and elegant as a cathedral, with vaulted Gothic arches, stained-glass windows, and handsome carpets.

Rogier van der Weyden's *Saint George and the Dragon* nearby is even smaller than Raphael's version of the same subject (Gallery 19) but of equally prime quality.

Perhaps the greatest Flemish artist was Peter Paul Rubens, whose *Daniel in the Lions' Den* (Gallery 45) is a fine example of the Baroque style that followed Mannerism. Rubens, born in Antwerp in 1577, was court painter to Vincenzo Gonzaga, Duke of Mantua, for several years. That position enabled him to study the works of Titian, Michelangelo, and Caravaggio. Called back to Antwerp by his mother's illness in 1608, he was planning to return to Mantua when he was appointed court painter to the Spanish Governors of the Netherlands—a post he held until his death in 1640. Although Rubens frequently permitted his assistants to work on his canvases, he described *Daniel in the Lions' Den* as "Original, entirely by my hand."

Portraits by Sir Anthony van Dyck are among the most beautiful paintings in Galleries 42 and 43. Note particularly his elegant *Marchesa Elena Grimaldi, Wife of Marchese Nicola Cattaneo*, painted in Genoa around 1623, and *Queen Henrietta Maria With Her Dwarf*. Van Dyck was lionized by wealthy Genoese merchants and nobles because of his ability to depict their personalities, as well as the details of their lavish clothing and palaces.

Albrecht Dürer is one of the stars of the German collection. Don't miss his *Lot and His Daughters*, tucked away in a secluded spot in Gallery 35.

DUTCH PAINTINGS

Works by Rembrandt van Ryn are among the glories of seventeenth-century Dutch painting, and the National Gallery has a number of Rembrandts (Galleries 48 and 49). Notice particularly his brooding *Self-Portrait* and *The Mill*, one of Rembrandt's few landscape paintings.

In the adjacent gallery (Gallery 51), Jan Vermeer's *Woman Holding a Balance* can be appreciated on various levels. At first glance, it appears to be simply a painting of a woman holding a balance scale. According to curator Arthur K. Wheelock, however, it is "an allegorical scene that urges us to conduct our lives with temperance and moderation." Clues to this moralistic interpretation include the large painting *The Last Judgment* in the background, as well as the scale and the woman's jewelry on the table, both materialistic symbols.

The realism of Dutch art was at its finest in architectural studies, such as Pieter Jansz Saenredam's *Cathedral of Saint John at 's-Hertogenbosch* (Gallery 51). Saenredam was a seventeenth-century Dutch painter whose specialty was precisely detailed church interiors.

Don't miss Willem Claesz Heda's *Banquet Piece With Mince Pie* (Gallery 47). Unknown to the art world until 1990, it was purchased by the gallery in 1991 for a reported $2.55 million. The detailed rendition of glass, pewter, and fruit make it, as Director J. Carter Brown has said, "a Dutch still life for people who don't think they like Dutch still lifes."

ROTUNDA

The bronze statue *Mercury*, messenger of the classical gods, atop the fountain in the center of the Rotunda is attributed to Francesco Righetti. It was part of Andrew Mellon's collection.

FRENCH PAINTINGS

In the East Hall adjoining the Rotunda are galleries devoted to seventeenth- and eighteenth-century paintings, including Jean-Honoré Fragonard's *Blindman's Buff* and *The Swing* (Gallery 55), and Jacques-Louis David's *Napoleon in His Study* (Gallery 56).

One of the most beautiful paintings is Fragonard's *A Young Girl Reading* (Gallery 55). This picture had been in a private collection in New York City for many years. John Walker, then director of the National Gallery, frequently visited the owner and discussed her collection over tea. After sixteen years and endless cups of tea, the gallery was finally able to buy the painting at auction with funds contributed by the late Ailsa Mellon Bruce in memory of her father, Andrew Mellon. According to Walker, *A Young Girl Reading* was one of Mrs. Bruce's favorite pictures. And, although she could have received the same tax benefit if she kept the picture during her lifetime instead of making an immediate gift to the gallery, Mrs. Bruce considered the painting too important to be privately owned. Years before, Andrew Mellon had made that same judgment about another painting, now in the National Gallery's collection, Reynolds's *Lady Caroline Howard*.

A Young Girl Reading *by Jean-Honoré Fragonard; National Gallery of Art, gift of Mrs. Mellon Bruce in memory of her father, Andrew W. Mellon.*

Painted nearly a century later than *A Young Girl Reading*, Edouard Manet's *Gare Saint-Lazare* (Gallery 80) combines elements of Realism with Impressionism. Its light colors and flat planes show the influence of Japanese woodcuts, which were being discovered in Paris at that time.

Paul Cézanne, whose ability to abstract nature into colored planes made him a forerunner of contemporary artists, is represented by several paintings in Gallery 83, including *The Artist's Father*, *Still Life With Apples and Peaches*, *Houses in Provence*, and *Still Life With Peppermint Bottle*.

The gallery's nineteenth-century French holdings are particularly strong, thanks to the Mellons, Chester Dale, Joseph E. Widener, and other donors. Among the paintings given to the National Gallery by Mr. and Mrs. Paul Mellon are Claude Monet's two light-filled views of *Waterloo Bridge, London*, at dusk and at sunset (Gallery 85); Mary Cassatt's *Child in a Straw Hat* (Gallery 72), Vincent Van Gogh's *Flower Beds in Holland*, and Georges Surat's *Lighthouse at Honfleur*.

One of the most appealing paintings in the gallery's collection is Auguste Renoir's *A Girl With a Watering Can* (Gallery 89), which supports the artist's belief that "A painting should be a lovable thing, gay and pretty . . . There are enough things to bore us in life without our making more of them."

A Girl With a Watering Can *by Auguste Renoir; National Gallery of Art, Chester Dale Collection.*

Other outstanding examples of nineteenth-century French art include Renoir's *The Dancer* (Gallery 89), Paul Gauguin's *Self-Portrait* (Gallery 84), Claude Monet's *Rouen Cathedral* (Gallery 85), Van Gogh's *Roses*, and Edouard Manet's *The Old Musician* (Gallery 80).

BRITISH PAINTINGS

Galleries devoted to British and American painters surround the East Garden Court. Among the highlights are Thomas Gainsborough's portrait *Mrs. Richard Brinsley Sheridan* (Gallery 59), wife of the eighteenth-century dramatist. The painting's loose brush strokes and naturalistic landscape background are contrary to the formal Grand Style of portraiture advocated by the influential British artist Sir Joshua Reynolds.

John Constable, a friend of the archdeacon of Salisbury Cathedral, painted many versions of his *A View of Salisbury Cathedral From Lower Marsh Close* (Gallery 57), showing the spire of the building and the surrounding countryside. Constable based his art on direct observation of nature—as did the Romantic poets of the period, Wordsworth and Keats. Constable said "Painting is with me but another word for feeling. I associate my 'careless boyhood' with all that lies on the banks of the Stour. Those scenes made me a painter, and I am grateful."

AMERICAN PAINTINGS

The gallery's American collection ranges from the eighteenth century to the present, and includes all major trends, from primitive to pop. Works of the eighteenth and nineteenth centuries are in the West Building; twentieth-century paintings are in the East Building.

Among the pictures to note are Thomas Cole's series of four canvases, *The Voyage of Life* (Gallery 60), in which this painter of the Hudson River School depicts characters representing Childhood, Youth, Manhood, and Old Age against romantic and symbolic landscape backgrounds.

Rembrandt Peale's 1801 portrait of his brother, *Rubens Peale With a Geranium* (Gallery 64) is half portrait and half still life. John Wilmerding, former deputy director of the National Gallery, called it "the first great American portrait," and pointed out that the picture "with its casualness and informality and its combination of art and science, suggests an American idiom." The twenty-three-year-old Rembrandt Peale and his brother were the sons of Charles Willson Peale, an artist-scientist who established the nation's first museum. The National Gallery purchased the painting at auction in 1985 for a record-breaking $4.07 million, with funds provided by its Patrons' Permanent Fund.

Rubens Peale With a Geranium *by Rembrandt Peale; National Gallery of Art, Patrons' Permanent Fund.*

The National Gallery owns forty-one Gilbert Stuart canvases, including portraits of the first five presidents, *George Washington*, *John Adams*, *Thomas Jefferson*, *James Madison*, and *James Monroe* (Gallery 60A), which are important historically as a set.

Thomas Sully's elegant style of portraiture, as seen in *Lady With a Harp: Eliza Ridgely* (Gallery 64), reflected his training in the fashionable British Grand Style. He believed that "Resemblance in a portrait is essential but no fault will be found with the artist—at least by the sitter—if he improve the appearance." The appearance of fifteen-year-old Eliza Ridgely hardly needed improvement.

John Singleton Copley painted the large group portrait *The Copley Family* (Gallery 62) soon after settling in London around 1776. The picture is noteworthy for its graceful composition and for Copley's skillful handling of such details as the folds of the drapery and the texture of the fabrics.

In a different vein, Copley's *Watson and the Shark* (Gallery 60B) depicts an actual incident in Havana harbor in which Brook Watson lost his leg to a shark. Copley's realistic portrayal of the scene caused a sensation when the painting was first exhibited in London in 1778.

The Luminists—Americans who shared the late nineteenth-century interest in the changing effects of light—are represented by, among others, Fitz Hugh Lane's *Lumber Schooners at Evening on Penobscot Bay* (Gallery 67).

Jasper Francis Cropsey's *Autumn on the Hudson River* (Gallery 67) is a fine example of the nineteenth-century Hudson River School of landscape painting that glorified the wonders of arcadian America.

In the next room (Gallery 68), the variety of subject matter sums up the diversity of American art in the last decades of the nineteenth century and the early years of the twentieth. Here are Thomas Eakins's *The Biglin Brothers Racing*, James McNeill Whistler's *Wapping on Thames*, William M. Harnett's *My Gems*, Winslow Homer's *Breezing Up*, Albert Pinkham Ryder's *Siegfried and the Rhine Maidens*, and *The Old Violin* by John Frederick Peto.

AMERICAN NAIVE PAINTINGS

Col. Edgar William and Bernice Chrysler Garbisch donated to the National Gallery more than three hundred folk art paintings of the early eighteenth to the late nineteenth century. Many of these naive paintings, including Edward Hicks's *Peaceable Kingdom*, are displayed in Gallery 65 on the Main Floor.

GROUND FLOOR GALLERIES

The ground floor is virtually three museums-within-a-museum, with special galleries devoted to decorative arts, graphic arts, and sculpture. With some two thousand objects to choose from, the depth and diversity of the exhibitions are dazzling—everything from Medieval tapestries and Renaissance bronzes to eighteenth-century French furniture, Old Master prints and drawings, and modern sculpture.

RENAISSANCE TAPESTRIES AND FURNITURE

To the left of the Seventh Street entrance are a lobby (GC 3) and a hall (GN 1) with fine examples of Renaissance tapestries, tables, and chairs from France and Italy. A massive fifteenth-century Italian chimneypiece is the focal point of the hall, whose walls are lined with rare antique tapestries. All of the furniture in these two galleries, originally owned by fifteenth- and sixteenth-century aristocratic families, was designed to be portable and to serve more than one function. For example, a table might be used as a desk, a banquet table, or a bed.

Don't miss *The Triumph of Christ*, a thirteen-foot-long tapestry, made in Brussels around 1500, which was once owned by Cardinal Mazarin, the seventeenth-century prime minister of France. The wool and silk fabric, interwoven with pure gold and silver threads, is considered the finest surviving Medieval tapestry, woven to twenty-two warps to the inch. The central panel depicts Christ presiding over the sacred and secular worlds, and the side panels show the triumph over paganism.

MEDIEVAL AND RENAISSANCE ECCLESIASTICAL ARTS

The pièce de résistance in this small gallery (GN2) devoted to liturgical objects is the chalice of the Abbot Suger of Saint-Denis. Designed to hold wine for Mass, it was first used in 1144 at the consecration of the altar chapels in the French royal abbey of Saint-Denis near Paris. The sardonyx cup was probably carved in Egypt during the Roman era, and the gold and precious stones were added by Medieval craftsmen.

EIGHTEENTH-CENTURY FRENCH FURNITURE AND DECORATIVE ARTS

Eighteenth-century French furniture and decorative arts, including the famed Joseph E. Widener collection, are displayed in four handsome white-and-gold rooms (Galleries GN14 A through D). Recent scholarship indicates that walls were often painted white in the eighteenth century—not left in original wood tones—with panels and moldings gilded and glazed. Every piece in the collection is either signed or attributed to known cabinetmakers, most of whom worked for the royal court.

One of the most historic pieces is a small writing table with gilded cupids by Jean-Henri Riesener. It was used by Marie Antoinette during her three-year imprisonment in the Tuileries. This piece and several other ladies' writing desks are displayed periodically in glassed-in cases where the desks can be opened to reveal their inner workings (Gallery GN14 D).

The Widener collection of polychrome vases, plates, and bowls—part of an outstanding assemblage of antique Chinese porcelains—fills many cases in Gallery GN 3.

SCULPTURE AND DECORATIVE ARTS

Honoré Daumier's *The Deputies*, thirty-six small bronze heads caricaturing members of the French Chamber of Deputies, are displayed in a glass case in Gallery GN 15.

In the adjoining gallery (GN 16) are sixteen of the sixty-nine surviving studies in wax or modeling clay done by Edgar Degas during his lifetime, as well as five bronze sculptures cast after his death.

Other highlights include Auguste Rodin's *Walking Man* and *Hand With Female Figure* (GN 17), Paul Gauguin's sculpture *Eve* (GN 18), and Wilhelm Lehmbruck's *Seated Youth* (GN 19).

PRINTS AND DRAWINGS

Fourteen galleries on the south side of the building show the history of graphic arts. Old Master and modern prints and drawings are exhibited continuously, with selections changed every few months. Artists represented range from Dürer, Rembrandt, Tiepolo, and Boucher to Homer, Whistler, and Picasso.

THE EAST BUILDING

The East Building is bounded by the two major avenues of Pierre L'Enfant's 1791 plan for the nation's capital. Here the Mall, bounded by Constitution Avenue (which L'Enfant envisioned lined with a row of "palaces"), meets Pennsylvania Avenue, the grand ceremonial route linking the Capitol and the White House.

In addition to designing a structure that would relate harmoniously to the neoclassical West Building and to the government buildings along Constitution and Pennsylvania Avenues, architect I. M. Pei had to cope with a trapezoidal site. His brilliant solution was to divide the trapezoid diagonally into two interlocking triangles. The larger isosceles triangle contains public exhibition galleries and auditoriums, while the smaller right triangle houses the gallery's

The interior of the East Building

administrative and curatorial offices and its Center for Advanced Study in the Visual Arts. Pei's geometrical solution to the design problem might also be considered a subtle bow to the classical symmetry of the West Building. Equally remarkable is the symmetrical façade Pei devised, despite the triangular geometry behind it.

Washington's artistic life has been enriched enormously since the East Building opened in 1978. The flexibility of the building's space, with galleries connected by bridges and balconies, has enabled the National Gallery to present special "blockbuster" exhibitions on various levels throughout the building, in addition to small, scholarly exhibitions.

At the Fourth Street entrance to the building stands a large bronze sculpture by Henry Moore, *Knife Edge Mirror Two Piece*. In creating it, Moore was concerned not only with the sculpture but also with its surrounding space. He adapted an earlier motif, enlarging the scale and reversing the composition. Moore said of this sculpture, "As you move around it, the two parts overlap or they open up and there's space between. Sculpture is like a journey. You have a different view when you return."

Entering the building, you come into the Central Court, a vast, glass-enclosed, skylit sculpture area whose greenery and spaciousness provide an easy transition from the Mall. You can see that the triangle is the leitmotiv of the building—a motif repeated in the interlocking blocks of marble in the floors and in the space-frame skylight, as well as in the overall design of the structure.

Several important works are visible here. Above, suspended from the skylight, is Alexander Calder's *Untitled* mobile, whose red, black, and blue petals move in response to air currents. The mobile, with honeycomb aluminum blades, is three stories high and seventy-six feet long, and weighs 920 pounds.

On the far wall, Anthony Caro's welded steel sculpture, *National Gallery Ledge Piece*, sits on a ledge directly over the entrance to the administrative offices. It was commissioned by the National Gallery's Collectors' Committee in 1978 in honor of the opening of the East Building.

A moving walkway on the concourse level links the East and West Buildings and leads to the Concourse Buffet, where a waterfall cascading behind a glassed-in wall creates both light and a sense of movement.

The galleries on the mezzanine, concourse, and ground levels are often used for special exhibitions. The National

Gallery's permanent collection of twentieth-century art is installed on the upper level and the concourse level, but it is sometimes moved to provide space for special exhibitions. So please bear in mind that some of the paintings and sculptures described here may not be in the galleries we have indicated.

Works by Pablo Picasso range from his early blue and rose periods—*Le Gourmet*, *The Tragedy*, and *Lady With a Fan*—through the *Family of Saltimbanques* to the cubist *Nude Woman* of 1910 (on the upper level).

Also in the collection are Henri Matisse's brilliantly colored *Large Composition With Masks*, the richly patterned *Pianist and Checker Players*, and a blue-and-white *Woman With Amphora and Pomegranates* (on the concourse level). Matisse executed these painted paper cutouts mounted on canvas in 1953, near the end of his life, when he was confined to a wheelchair.

Family of Saltimbanques *by Pablo Picasso; National Gallery of Art, Chester Dale Collection.*

Among a variety of modern styles represented are Yves Tanguy's surrealistic *The Look of Amber* (gallery 98 on upper level) and Piet Mondrian's characteristically grid-patterned *Diamond Painting, Red, Yellow and Blue* (gallery 97 on upper level). Abstract expressionist paintings include Jackson Pollock's black-and-white *Number 7, 1951* and *Lavender Mist* (on the concourse).

In several rooms, individual artists are represented in depth, providing mini-retrospectives of the work of Jasper Johns, Roy Lichtenstein, Robert Rauschenberg, and Mark Rothko.

David Smith's geometric stainless steel sculptures *Sentinel* and *Sentinel V* demonstrate another aspect of twentieth-century American art. They are part of a mini-retrospective of his work on view in the tower.

Washington Color Painters are represented by Kenneth Noland's *Another Time* (1973) and Morris Louis's *Beta Kappa* (1961).

"Pop" artist Roy Lichtenstein's *Look Mickey* (1961), a fiftieth anniversary gift of the artist, is his first mature adaptation of the subject, style, and source of comic illustration to his art.

The Mark Rothko Foundation has given over a thousand works of art, including paintings and drawings ranging from major oils to small sketches. Some of these works are usually on view. Rothko is only the second American artist to be represented in such depth at the National Gallery. The other is George Catlin, who painted the Indians' native customs.

NATIONAL MUSEUM OF AFRICAN ART

950 Independence Avenue, S.W.
Washington, D.C. 20560
202/357-4600 weekdays; 202/357-2700 weekends
202/357-2020 recorded Dial-a-Museum information
202/357-4814 TDD for hearing-impaired visitors

METRO	Smithsonian.
HOURS	10 A.M. to 5:30 P.M. daily. Closed Christmas Day.
TOURS	General tours and tours of special exhibitions offered weekly. Call museum for details.
ADMISSION	Free.
HANDICAPPED FACILITIES	Elevator to all levels. Accessible to the disabled.
MUSEUM SHOP	Books, postcards, jewelry, textiles, baskets, and carvings.
SPECIAL EVENTS	Lectures, demonstrations, workshops, courses, films, and gallery talks year-round.
SPECIAL FACILITIES	Eliot Elisofon Photographic Archives. Warren N. Robbins Library open to the public by appointment.
MEMBERSHIP	Smithsonian Associates.
AUTHOR'S CHOICE	Drum, Baga peoples, Guinea Mask, Western Pende peoples, Zaire *Female figure and children*, Yoruba peoples, Nigeria

The National Museum of African Art is the only museum in the United States devoted solely to the collection, study, and exhibition of the art of sub-Saharan Africa. It owes its existence to Warren Robbins, a dedicated collector, and S. Dillon Ripley, former secretary of the Smithsonian.

HISTORY

A former Foreign Service officer, Robbins became interested in African art through studying African influences on early twentieth-century artists. In 1964, he established the Museum of African Arts as a private educational institution. It was housed in a Victorian town house on Capitol Hill that was once the home of abolitionist Frederick Douglass. In 1979, the museum became a bureau of the Smithsonian Institution and the name was changed to the National Museum of African Art.

During the 1970s, Ripley decided to increase the Smithsonian's focus on non-Western art. Plans were developed for a Center for African, Near Eastern, and Asian Art on the 4.2-acre quadrangle of land south of the Smithsonian Castle. The National Museum of African Art, a major component of the quadrangle complex, opened September 1987.

THE BUILDING

The National Museum of African Art

Creating a design that would not block the view of the original Smithsonian Institution Building (the Castle) and that would also harmonize with the adjacent Arts and Industries Building and the Freer Gallery of Art was one of the most important issues faced by architect Jean Paul Carlhian of the Boston firm Shepley, Bulfinch, Richardson, and Abbott. He also had to devise a plan that would make the journey below ground inviting and attractive, since ninety-six percent of the museum complex—which includes the Arthur M. Sackler Gallery, the S. Dillon Ripley Center, and the Enid A. Haupt Garden, as well as the National Museum of African Art—is underground.

The circular motif Carlhian selected echoes the arches of the Freer Gallery. Similarly, the Arthur M. Sackler Gallery's diamond shapes are a subtle bow to the spires and pyramids of the Arts and Industries Building.

A sixty- by ninety-foot entrance pavilion with six copper-roofed domes is the only part of the museum above the ground. Its exterior is faced with light pink granite from Texas, which harmonizes with the red brick of the Arts and Industries Building and the Castle's red sandstone exterior. Floors are paved with pink New Hampshire granite and a limestone staircase leads to two levels of museum space.

The building covers 68,800 square feet and extends fifty-seven feet below grade. Since the water table is just below the second level, special waterproofing and concealed drainage were required. Four ten-foot-square skylights provide natural lighting to the concourse level.

Selections from the museum's permanent collection are displayed in four galleries on the first level. A second level gallery provides a showcase for temporary exhibitions. A striking architectural feature is the 285-foot-long concourse on the third level, linking the National Museum of African Art with the Arthur M. Sackler Gallery. Richard Haas's forty-by-forty-five-foot-high trompe l'oeil mural depicting the Smithsonian Castle and the Arts and Industries Building dominates the rear wall of the concourse.

THE COLLECTION
The collection includes approximately six thousand sculptures, textiles, jewelry, architectural elements, decorative arts, and items for everyday use from forty-eight independent African nations. It includes twenty-three objects from Benin, Nigeria, which were part of Joseph H. Hirshhorn's original gift to the Smithsonian Institution; the Venice and Alastair Lamb collection of 1,500 West African textiles assembled between 1968 and 1972; 2,500 field photographs taken by William Fagg in Nigeria and Zaire between 1949 and 1959; 2,000 pictures taken by Emile Gorlia, a Belgian colonial official, in southern Zaire, Angola, and Zimbabwe between 1905 and 1923, and a collection of historic photographs taken by Dr. Henry Reis, a missionary in French Cameroon, between 1909 and 1920.

The Benin art and approximately one hundred masterworks from the permanent collection are usually on view, in addition to temporary exhibitions. Objects from the permanent collection are grouped according to several major geographical and cultural regions, including:
 • *Western Sudan*, a vast area of West Africa including Ghana, Mali, and the Songhai empire with terrain ranging from wooded areas to desert-like grasslands.

Jewelry and other portable objects are an indication of

wealth and prestige among the nomadic Fulani women of Mali. The large earrings of hammered gold and red embroidery floss on view typify the Fulani workmanship.
- *Eastern Guinea Coast*, stretching along the Atlantic Ocean coast from Guinea Bissau to Cameroon.

Yoruba artists in the southwestern region of Nigeria create particularly impressive objects for ritual and ceremonial use. One outstanding work is a palace door by the artist Olowe of Ise. Lower Niger bronzes, such as the bells that represent royal or chiefly authority, also come from this area. The museum's vessel with chameleons, cast in one piece by the lost-wax process circa 1668-1773, is an important object in the collection.
- *Northeastern Zaire*, with the Ubangi and Hele Rivers and tropical forests, home of the Zande and Mangbetu peoples.

The Mangbetu established a major empire in the eighteenth century and influenced the artistic traditions of their neighbors, the Zande. The figurative harp in the exhibition, which was probably owned by a high-ranking member of the Zande group, is unusual, since most Zande art features geometric forms.
- *Ogowe River Basin Region* in Gabon, home of the Mbuti, or Pygmies, and the Kota.

The Kota frequently place reliquary guardian heads and figures, carved into abstract forms, on top of containers holding sacred ancestral relics. As you can see, copper or brass strips sometimes cover the strikingly modern wooden figures.
- *Cameroon Region*, comprising the dry mountainous area of the north, grasslands in the center, and southern and coastal rain forests bordering Gabon and Equatorial Guinea.

Cameroon art is noted for its brilliant colors, organic forms, and frequent use of beadwork. A rare, almost life-size wooden male figure from the grassfields area is embellished with fine red, white, and blue glass beads and cowrie shells. King Njoya, who ruled from 1886 to 1933, presented it as a grave figure commemorating the death of a German colonial officer in 1908.
- *Lower Congo Region*, characterized by rainforests along the riverbanks of the Zaire River and the Kwango River Basin in Zaire.

The Kongo peoples, including the Yombe, Vili, and Woyo, are noted for naturalistic, figurative art. Woman-and-child figures, representing fertility and continuity, and power figures with embedded medicines, used as protective devices, are characteristic. Particularly outstanding are a Yombe woman and child, an ivory power figure of a woman and child by a Vili carver, and a miniature wooden power figure carved by a Kongo artist.
- *Eastern Zaire River Basin*, a rain forest area in Zaire and Angola inhabited by the Luba, Songye, Chokwe, Tetela, Pende, and Lega peoples.

An ancestor mask of a beautiful Chokwe woman, crafted of wood with metal earrings and a raffia coiffure, was used in ceremonies associated with fertility. The delicately carved ivory pendants, which are miniature replicas of masks produced by the Pende people, were designed to heal their wearers or protect them from harm. The Songwe power figure of wood, metal, and shell with attached magical substances served a similar purpose.

A Cameroon grave figure

A carving of a Yombe woman and child from Zaire

Bronze head from Benin

- *Southern and Eastern Africa*, stretching along the eastern coast from Sudan to the south of Africa.

The area includes the Ndebele people of South Africa, noted for their beadwork, such as the museum's geometrically patterned blanket strip, and the Shilluk people of Sudan, who create elaborately carved figurative pipe bowls.

ROYAL BENIN ART

Twenty cast brass sculptures and a sixteenth-century ivory carving from the West African kingdom of Benin, Nigeria, are on view. Most of the plaques, figures, commemorative heads, and pendants, which were crafted between the fifteenth and nineteenth centuries, were given to the Smithsonian Institution by Joseph H. Hirshhorn.

During the fifteenth century, Benin was an important city-state with a wealthy and influential royal court. The Edo people of that area believed that brass objects, which resist corrosion, were associated with the permanence and continuity of royalty. Brass casting was considered to be so important that the king himself controlled the art. Anyone who cast brass without royal permission was executed.

The Edo also believed that they were protected by the spirits of their ancestors and placed cast commemorative heads of former kings on altars throughout the royal palace. (Technically, most of the objects on view are cast of copper alloy. Bronze is copper combined with tin. Zinc is combined with copper to form brass.)

The exhibition focuses on three different facets of Benin art. The first section contains commemorative heads and figures, ranging from the fifteenth through the nineteenth century, which relate directly to the *oba*, or king.

The second section, which shows some of the royal rituals and regalia, includes eight wall plaques with kings, courtiers, and warriors in bas-relief. The plaques, representing historical personages and events, served to illustrate the stories told by Benin's oral historians. The plaques were originally nailed on the walls and columns of royal palaces.

The stylistic influence of foreigners is emphasized in the third section of the exhibit. Trade with Portugal began in 1486 and continued until the mid-1500s. By the end of the sixteenth century, most of the trade with Benin was conducted by the Dutch, although the French and English also played a significant role.

THE ART OF THE PERSONAL OBJECT

More than a hundred objects, ranging from headrests, stools, and chairs to snuff containers, bowls, and baskets are showcased here. All of the items were made in the nineteenth or twentieth century, and indicate the creativity and versatility of African artists. The exhibition also proves that everyday objects can be beautiful as well as useful.

PURPOSE AND PERFECTION: POTTERY AS A WOMAN'S ART IN CENTRAL AFRICA

In this exhibition of pottery from Central Africa, drawn from the museum's collection, you can see that women potters are among the most talented and versatile of African artists. While men often created beautifully carved chairs, headrests, and other functional objects, women fashioned pottery bowls, jars, and other household objects.

NATIONAL MUSEUM OF AMERICAN HISTORY

Fourteenth Street and Constitution Avenue, N.W.
Washington, D.C. 20560
202/357-2700

METRO	Federal Triangle or Smithsonian.
HOURS	10 A.M. to 5:30 P.M. daily. Closed Christmas Day.
TOURS	Highlights of the collection 10 A.M., 11 A.M., 1 P.M., and 1:30 P.M. Monday through Friday; 10 A.M., 11 A.M., and 1 P.M. Saturday.
ADMISSION	Free.
HANDICAPPED FACILITIES	Sign language and oral interpreters, and tours for visually handicapped by appointment. Call 202/357-1481 (TDD 202/357-1563) Monday through Friday, 10 A.M. to 2 P.M. Auditorium equipped with a loop amplification system for hearing-impaired. Wheelchairs available.
FOOD SERVICE	Cafeteria on lower level; Palm Court ice cream parlor on first floor.
MUSEUM SHOP	Books, tape cassettes, posters, prints, toys, games, dolls, jewelry, and gift items.
SPECIAL EVENTS	Music and films.
MEMBERSHIP	Smithsonian Associates.
AUTHOR'S CHOICE	Great Historical Clock of America, first floor Original Star-Spangled Banner, second floor Foucault pendulum, second floor Ceremonial Court, second floor First Ladies exhibition, second floor

The collections of the National Museum of American History are so diverse that you might consider it to be several museums-within-a-museum. With more than sixteen million objects, it is a museum of transportation, communications,

The National Museum of American History

agriculture, military and physical sciences, medicine and pharmacology, stamps, coins, glass, ceramics, and textiles. The museum is much more than static collections of inanimate objects, however. It is a lively place with an ambitious program of exhibitions, audiovisual displays, and demonstration centers.

Currently in the midst of a ten-year reinstallation program, the museum is shifting its focus away from the traditional glorification of famous people to a presentation of American social history. The new focus is on the lives of real, ordinary citizens—an approach represented by the popular exhibitions, "After the Revolution: Everyday Life in America, 1780–1800" and "Engines of Change: The American Industrial Revolution, 1790–1860."

HISTORY

The Smithsonian Institution, founded in 1846, was housed in the "Castle" on the Mall until 1876, when most of the U.S. Centennial Exposition was transferred there from Philadelphia. To accommodate the expanded collection, the Arts and Industries Building was constructed in 1881.

The Smithsonian collections included both specimens from nature and objects representing history and technology. The naturalistic collections were moved into the Museum of Natural History Building in 1911. By the 1950s, more space was needed, so a new National Museum of History and Technology, designed by McKim, Mead and White (succeeded by Steinman, Cain, and White) opened in 1964. In 1980, the name was changed to the National Museum of American History.

TOURING THE MUSEUM

A nineteenth-century bandstand from Jacksonville, Illinois, is the focal point of an outdoor amphitheater near the west end of the museum. At the Mall entrance, *Infinity*, a 1967 stainless steel sculpture by José de Riviera, was the first piece of abstract art commissioned by the federal government. *The Gwenfritz*, a monumental black steel stabile by Alexander Calder, stands near Constitution Avenue and Fourteenth Street. The thirty-five-ton sculpture is approximately forty feet tall.

Exhibitions are installed on three floors. A large, well-stocked museum shop and bookstore, a cafeteria, and a special exhibition gallery are on the lower level.

The Mall entrance leads to the second floor; the Constitution Avenue entrance is on the first floor. Because several major exhibits are located on the second floor, this tour will begin at the Mall entrance.

SECOND FLOOR

STAR-SPANGLED BANNER

The flag that inspired Francis Scott Key to write a poem that later became our national anthem is one of the museum's most treasured possessions. Key, an American lawyer detained aboard a British truce ship in Chesapeake Bay during the War of 1812, watched the British bombardment of Fort McHenry throughout the night of September 13, 1814.

When he saw the American flag still flying over the fort the following morning, he wrote "The Defence of Fort McHenry," which was published in a Baltimore newspaper the following week. The verse, set to the tune of an English air, "To

Anacreon in Heaven," became a popular patriotic song and was declared our official national anthem in 1931.

The handsewn flag of English wool bunting with fifteen cotton stars and stripes, was made for the fort in 1813 by Mrs. Mary Pickersgill of Baltimore. It remained in the family of Major George Armistead, commander of Fort McHenry, until 1907, when it was presented to the Smithsonian.

In 1914, with a new backing of Irish linen attached, the thirty-by-thirty-four-foot flag was displayed in the Arts and Industries Building. It was installed in the Museum of History and Technology in 1963. After studies in 1982 revealed that dust composed of particles of grass, soil, tree leaves, and cotton fibers had settled on the flag, workers carefully cleaned its surface and backing, improved the museum's ventilation systems and lighting, and installed an opaque cover to protect the fabric from light and dust.

The original Star-Spangled Banner in Flag Hall

The historic flag is now kept behind a movable cloth panel decorated with a large painting of the stars and stripes, opposite the Mall entrance. Every hour on the half hour, from 10:30 A.M. to 4:30 P.M., the panel in front of the flag is slowly lowered to reveal the original star-spangled banner. A recording of the national anthem, played at tempos popular during the 1800s, accompanies the brief, moving presentation.

AMERICAN ENCOUNTERS

This Christopher Columbus quincentenary exhibit, scheduled for a ten-year run beginning in July 1992, focuses on the continuing encounters between Indian, Hispanic, African-American, and Anglo-American cultures in the Upper Rio Grande Valley of the Southwest. From the arrival of the Spaniards in 1539 to the present, members of those cultures have managed to preserve their cultural identities, despite pressures to become part of more powerful and complex cultures. One of the questions raised by the exhibit is how to create a balance between cultural diversity and cultural unity.

Through the use of film, sound, and images, an introductory area prepares visitors to understand encounters of unlike peoples. The exhibit is divided into five sections. The first section, Land, depicts the differing views held by the Pueblo Indians, Hispanics, Anglo-Americans, and African Americans about the land they inhabited.

The section devoted to Conflict shows some of the clashes between the various cultures, from the first encounter between Indians and non-Indians in New Mexico in 1539 to the present land grant controversies. The third exhibit section, Convergence, presents some of the institutional frameworks, such as churches and schools, that enable peaceful cultural encounters to take place.

In the Creativity section, you can see how various cultures share certain characteristics—such as speaking a particular language or preserving a craft tradition—that reinforce their cultural and individual identity.

The final section, Continuity, is designed to help you apply the past five hundred years to your own life, and to the future. In a culturally diverse society, everyone must develop creative ways to preserve his own culture while respecting that of his neighbors.

FOUCAULT PENDULUM

Invented by Jean Bernard Leon Foucault in 1851, the pendulum illustrates the earth's rotation. Although carefully suspended so that it swings in one plane, the pendulum appears to rotate in a circle, knocking down a series of small pegs. Nevertheless, it is the earth that rotates. By the end of the day, all of the pegs are down.

AFTER THE REVOLUTION: EVERYDAY LIFE IN AMERICA 1780–1800

This exhibition proves that "The past never changes; memory and perception do." In examining the post-revolutionary period, it focuses on three families of various backgrounds, showing how they lived and the objects they used in everyday life. A brief audiovisual program serves as a useful introduction to the diversity of America in the closing decades of the eighteenth century.

The homes of three actual families have been re-created: the 1793 log house of the Thomas and Elizabeth Springer family, farmers in New Castle County, Delaware; the parlor or hall from the plantation home (1797) of Henry and Anne Saunders in Isle of Wight County, Virginia, and a parlor similar to one in the home of Samuel and Lucy Colton, a wealthy merchant family in Longmeadow, Massachusetts.

A view of After the Revolution: Everyday Life in America, 1780–1800.

Other displays are devoted to Afro-Americans in the Chesapeake area, the Seneca Indians, and other Iroquois peoples. Objects ranging from delicate Oriental porcelains and ceramics to a fully equipped print shop reflect the activities of people living in Philadelphia, the largest city of the time.

There are also two small study galleries, and a Hands on History room where you can touch and work with reproductions of eighteenth-century artifacts.

CEREMONIAL COURT

This exhibition re-creates the front corridor of the White House as it appeared after its renovation in 1902 during Theodore Roosevelt's administration. Six gallery spaces showcase recent first ladies' gowns, presidential mementoes, and White House china, as well as period jewelry, porcelain, pottery, glassware, and silver.

A large trompe l'oeil painting of the Roosevelt children playing on the Grand Staircase in the White House, and a view of the State Dining Room in the early 1900s help to re-create the White House atmosphere.

Mannequins representing the wives of six recent presidents—Mrs. John F. Kennedy, Mrs. Lyndon B. Johnson, Mrs. Richard Nixon, Mrs. Gerald Ford, Mrs. Jimmy Carter, and Mrs. Ronald Reagan are on view.

Other objects included in the exhibition range from President Lincoln's top hat and Woodrow Wilson's golf clubs to eighteenth-century furniture and porcelains owned by George and Martha Washington.

FIRST LADIES: POLITICAL ROLE AND PUBLIC IMAGE

The museum's spectacular collection of gowns worn by former First Ladies is the focal point of this exhibition. In addition to the clothing, such items as jewelry, fans, calling cards, photographs, and political campaign memorabilia help to illustrate the increasingly important role of the First Lady.

The idea of exhibiting the gowns worn by First Ladies originated in the early 1900s with Mrs. Rose Gouverneur Hoes, a descendant of President Monroe, and Mrs. Julian James, who were particularly interested in the Smithsonian's costume collections. In 1912, when Mrs. William Howard Taft presented a dress she had worn at the White House, this collection—one of the Smithsonian's most popular—was launched.

The First Ladies Hall was closed for renovations for over four years, from 1987 until March 1992. During that period, many of the gowns received much-needed repairs ranging from cleaning to textile conservation.

FROM PARLOR TO POLITICS: WOMEN AND REFORM IN AMERICA, 1890-1925

The political role of women in championing social reform around the turn of the century is highlighted in more than 700 objects and 275 photographs. Among the issues covered are education, the women's temperance movement, woman suffrage, labor reforms, social work, and peace activism.

Part of the exhibit re-creates Chicago's Hull House, established in 1889 as a community center for social and political action.

Temperance banners, buttons, and badges; Susan B. Anthony's desk set and gavel, and Jane Addam's Nobel Peace Prize help to dramatize women's struggles for social justice.

GEORGE WASHINGTON STATUE

A bigger-than-life-size marble statue of George Washington by Horatio Greenough stands in a corridor of the west wing. Commissioned by Congress in 1832, the toga-clad figure was placed in the Capitol rotunda in 1841, where it shocked the public. Charles Bulfinch, architect of the Capitol, pointed out that people wanted "to see the great man as their imagination has painted him," and feared the statue would "give the idea of entering or leaving the bath." The twenty-ton statue was moved to the Capitol grounds in 1843, and given to the Smithsonian in 1908. The pose, with upraised arm, is based on a statue of the god Zeus by the Greek sculptor Phidias.

ENTERTAINMENT
In special cases devoted to entertainment, you can see the chairs used by Carroll O'Connor and Jean Stapleton as Archie and Edith Bunker on the seventies' television program, "All in the Family"; a pair of sequin-studded ruby slippers from the 1939 film, *The Wizard of Oz*, and the brown leather jacket worn by Henry Winkler as Fonzie in "Happy Days."

FIRST FLOOR

A MATERIAL WORLD
This exhibition near the Constitution Avenue entrance serves as an introduction to the museum. It shows that Americans, throughout their history, have transformed resources into materials and have used those materials to create artifacts for the household, the workplace, and recreation. As a result, such artifacts reflect changing American cultural values.

The exhibition is divided into five main sections. "A Material Panorama" shows how the materials used in making artifacts have changed from natural materials, such as wood and stone, to manufactured materials such as steel and rubber and, finally, to synthetics.

The second section shows the attributes that make one material different from another. In the third section, a Brush runabout—a rare 1912 automobile composed of steel, rubber, glass, ceramics, hardwood, and aluminum—helps to illustrate the variety of different materials used to create most objects.

In the next section, wicker, plywood, and fiberglass chairs; ash, aluminum, and carbon fiber tennis rackets; ivory, boxwood, platinum, and ebonite flutes, and coffee mugs ranging from earthenware to polystyrene proves that artifacts designed for the same purpose may be made from many diverse materials.

The first dragster to exceed 270 miles per hour in the quarter-mile is featured in the final section, which highlights the use of synthetic materials.

ENGINES OF CHANGE: THE AMERICAN INDUSTRIAL REVOLUTION, 1790–1860
This exhibition focuses not only on the machines of the Industrial Revolution but on the people who invented, built, operated, and owned them. The world's oldest operable locomotive, the first powered textile machines, the first iron railroad bridge, and a variety of early production machines are included in the exhibit's six sections.

The exhibit begins with a display of some of the products that were shown at the 1851 Crystal Palace World's Fair, including the Chickering piano and the Palmer artificial leg. That fair marked the first international recognition for American technology, with Americans winning more prizes than any other nation in proportion to the number of entries.

In the second section, set in 1790, a piece of a sawmill from Chester County, Pennsylvania; the tool chest of a New York cabinetmaker; a clock, and an air pump bear witness to the skills of those who paved the way for the Crystal Palace success.

Next, the exhibition shows how Americans used the technology of the British Industrial Revolution. The locomotive *John Bull*, the oldest operable self-propelled vehicle in the world, was shipped to this country from England in 1831. It is shown crossing the first iron railroad bridge in

America. A piece of a Newcomen steam engine, shipped to America in 1753, and a spinning machine from a spinning mill established in Pawtucket, Rhode Island, in 1790, are other examples of early technology transfer.

The next section shows how federal, state, and local governments have encouraged the development of industry through tariffs, taxes, and direct investment. The patent models of many important inventions are on display, including the Whitney cotton gin, the Howe sewing machine, the Morse telegraph, and the steam engine.

"Machines, Factories, and American Society," is devoted to a series of ten case studies of American industry. They include an automated grist mill, a clock shop, an iron foundry, and a machine shop. Other exhibits explain the importance of transportation, steam and water power, and production machinery.

In the final section of the exhibition, a variety of manufactured objects, ranging from clocks, candlesticks, candles, and pitchers to books, shoes, and clothing represent the Industrial Revolution in 1860. This section also depicts the nature of the American working class and indicates the human, social, and environmental costs of America's industrial development.

PALM COURT

Near the entrance to this Edwardian ice cream parlor is part of an original Horn and Hardart *Automat*, the first self-service restaurant, opened in Philadelphia in 1902. Opposite, are the counter and displays from Stohlman's confectionery store, formerly located on Wisconsin Avenue in Georgetown.

EAST WING

The collection includes exhibits on timekeeping, power machinery, electricity, transportation (including railroads, automobiles, ships, bridges, and tunnels), and agriculture.

You can trace the origins of clocks, from sixteenth-century timepieces to contemporary electronic watches, and see the Great Historical Clock of America, with its scenes from American history. It was built in 1880 in imitation of the clock in the cathedral of Strasbourg, France.

The displays of power machinery, trains, and tractors show the development of the country from an agricultural to an industrial nation. The railroad hall contains the museum's largest displays, including the *1401* locomotive that required eleven days to move from Alexandria, Virginia, to this hall. It dwarfs the passenger coach nearby, built in 1836, that features decorative wallpaper and fabric window shades.

Early automobiles have a special fascination for visitors. The museum collection includes an 1893 Duryea, one of the first gas-powered vehicles; a 1903 Winton touring car, which made the first cross-country trip in the United States, and a Ford Model A deluxe roadster that cost $495 in 1931.

WEST WING
INFORMATION AGE: PEOPLE, INFORMATION AND TECHNOLOGY

In this, one of the largest and most ambitious exhibitions ever mounted by the Smithsonian, sophisticated, state-of-the-art technology is both the message and the medium.

A complete computer network ties together interactive workstations, video, films, and radio recordings in the exhibition hall. If you use a special bar-coded brochure distributed at the Information Age entrance, you can receive a printout of information on what you did as you toured the displays.

Objects from the museum's collections, including the Morse telegraph, components of Alexander Graham Bell's first telephone, and early personal computers illustrate how people's lives have been changed by the dramatic technological advances of the past 150 years.

The section of the exhibition devoted to People, Information and Technology, 1835–1939, depicts both the processing of information and the development of the wireless, telephone, and radio.

In the World War II: The Information War, 1940–45 section, you can learn about radar and sonar in a re-created Combat Information Center. And when you enter the People, Information and Technology, 1946–Present area, you can see early television programs, transistor radios, high-fidelity records, color television sets, and personal computers.

Foundations, 1946–60 displays several early, room-size computers, while Into the Mainstream, 1961–75 looks at computers as part of American culture. Their use in airline reservations, retail sales, and banking is featured.

The gallery space devoted to Control Central shows how interactive computers are used in international currency trading and in producing television news programs. At the end of the exhibition, a ten-minute presentation, shown as a video wall with twelve high-resolution projection cubes, reveals how much our lives, work, travel, entertainment, and education are affected by information technology.

THIRD FLOOR   **EAST WING**

"A More Perfect Union: Japanese Americans and the U.S. Constitution" explores the constitutional process by considering the experiences of Americans of Japanese ancestry, many of whom were interned during World War II.

Other exhibits are devoted to money and medals, the armed forces, firearms, and underwater exploration. George Washington's Revolutionary War uniform, his camp chest, and his eighteen-by-twenty-two-foot headquarters tent are near the entrance to the armed forces section.

In addition to a large display of military uniforms and weapons, there is a historic flag, *Old Glory*, made for Navy Captain William Driver of Salem, Massachusetts, when he was given command of his ship in 1824. Driver later left the navy and moved to Nashville, Tennessee. In 1862, when the city was captured by Union army forces during the Civil War, he flew this flag over the State House, symbolizing Tennessee's restoration to the Union.

Don't miss the gunboat, *Philadelphia*, the oldest American man-of-war in existence. Built and sunk in 1776, the ship was raised in 1935 with its twelve-pound bow gun and nine-pound broadside guns intact. An exhibit of pewter spoons, nails, rigging hooks, and other objects found aboard the forty-four-man craft is nearby.

DOLLS' HOUSES

You can see a dolls' house made by the White House gardener for the children of President Grover Cleveland (1893–97). Nearby is a twenty-three-room dolls' house designed, collected, and donated to the Smithsonian by Faith Bradford, which is home to the Doll family.

The Bradford dolls' house

WEST WING

A large part of this exhibit area is devoted to communications—photography, printing, and the graphic arts. The remainder of the space is devoted to musical instruments.

The hall of musical instruments displays rare and beautiful instruments, such as the Hellier violin, a Stradivarius made in 1679 and formerly owned by Lord Samuel Hellier of England; an eighteenth-century Nuremberg trumpet, and a piano with delicate Sheraton legs, made in Philadelphia in 1798.

Also on display is a model of the U.S. Capitol by Mitsugi Ohno of Manhattan, Kansas, in honor of the Bicentennial. Crafted of fused and manipulated glass rods, even the flags and the tiny statue on top of the dome are made of glass.

NATIONAL MUSEUM OF NATURAL HISTORY

Tenth Street and Constitution Avenue, N.W.
Washington, D.C. 20560
202/357-2700

METRO	Smithsonian or Federal Triangle.
HOURS	10 A.M. to 5:30 P.M. daily. Closed Christmas Day. Summer hours determined annually. *Discovery Room* open Noon to 2:30 P.M. Monday through Thursday; 10:30 A.M. to 3:30 P.M. Friday, Saturday, and Sunday. *Naturalist Center* open 10:30 A.M. to 4 P.M. Monday through Saturday; Noon to 5 P.M. Sunday.
TOURS	One-hour highlight tour of exhibits daily at 11:30 A.M. and 1:30 P.M.
ADMISSION	Free.
HANDICAPPED FACILITIES	Main (Constitution Avenue) entrance equipped for the disabled. Wheelchairs available.
FOOD SERVICE	Cafeteria near the museum shop on the first floor. The Court, private dining room for Smithsonian Associates, near Baird Auditorium on the ground floor.
MUSEUM SHOPS	Natural history and anthropology books, postcards, posters, jewelry, and crafts. Also, two shops on second floor rotunda balcony; one specializing in gems and minerals, and the other a "Dino" store.
SPECIAL EVENTS	Free natural history film and lecture series Friday at Noon in Baird Auditorium.
SPECIAL FACILITIES	Discovery Room, Learning Center, and Naturalist Center.
MEMBERSHIP	Smithsonian Associates.
AUTHOR'S CHOICE	African bush elephant, rotunda Blue whale, first floor Dinosaur and Ice Age Halls, first floor Hope diamond, second floor Insect zoo, second floor

The building of the National Museum of Natural History, opened in 1910, was originally called the "new" National Museum. More than 120 million objects are stored for research and display, including many collected on scientific expeditions dating back to the nineteenth century. If you are curious about man and his natural environment, you will find dozens of exhibits to whet your intellectual appetite.

"Uncle Beazley," a life-size model of a *Triceratops* dinosaur, is outside the Mall entrance, across Madison Drive from the museum. Also see the two huge fossil logs and boulder of iron ore flanking the Mall steps. The logs from the petrified forests

The National Museum of Natural History

of the southwest have been cut and polished so visitors can see their colors and growth rings.

There are entrances on Constitution Avenue and the Mall, and the collection is exhibited on three floors.

GROUND FLOOR

Inside the building's ground floor Constitution Avenue entrance is a large lobby with comfortable chairs and an information desk for visitors. Three towering Northwest Coast totem poles stand in the east stairwell. Straight ahead is the special exhibition gallery, where large traveling exhibitions are shown, and the Baird Auditorium, where lectures, concerts, films, and other special events are presented.

An exhibit devoted to birds of the Washington, D.C., region is near the auditorium. Nearly three hundred species of mounted birds native to the eastern United States are shown here, from tiny chickadees to egrets, herons, and swans.

Ask at the information desk in the Constitution Avenue lobby or the rotunda for directions to the Naturalist Center, a resource and reference center with collections of plants, insects, rocks, and minerals, as well as specimens of vertebrates and invertebrates. A library, microscopes, and other scientific equipment are available to help you identify objects that you have found, do research for papers, or get answers to questions. A small audiovisual lab is also available with films, videotapes, and slide sets. (Note that children under twelve and groups larger than six are not admitted without special permission.)

ROTUNDA

FIRST FLOOR

The rotunda, which most people enter from the Mall, is the largest public space in the building. This four-story-high, marble-pillared, and domed room is dominated by a huge mounted African bush elephant. One of the largest animals in the world, this eight-ton, thirteen-foot-tall bull elephant was killed in Africa in 1955.

FOSSILS: THE HISTORY OF LIFE

Entering the museum's large complex of fossil exhibits from the rotunda, you can see an animated film about the formation

Mounted African bush elephant, the rotunda

of organic compounds, the basis of life. On view are the oldest fossils in the world, colonies of algae from western Australia that grew on tidal flats 3.5 billion years ago.

An adjoining section displays the fossil evidence of the rich variety and abundance of animals that appeared in the oceans 600 million years ago, including weird and enigmatic creatures discovered in 1910 by the Smithsonian's fourth secretary, geologist Charles D. Walcott. These creatures have defied all efforts to link them with any other known form of life.

Another exhibit illustrates how plants and animals made the transition from water to land. On view here are the dramatic, floor to ceiling, sixteen-foot-tall fossil of *Callixylon*, one of the earliest trees; the fossil remains of *Ichthyostega*, the earliest-known amphibian; an exhibit on the origin of the seed, and plant fossils of the coal age. When flowering plants emerged 120 million years ago, the nature of life on land changed dramatically. Fossils of some of these early plants are shown in a diorama of a Potomac River scene from the Early Cretaceous Period, about 105 million years ago.

Dinosaurs are the dramatic focal point of the central gallery of the fossil exhibit complex. The museum's largest skeleton is the eighty-foot-long *Diplodocus longus*, whose skeleton was found embedded in limestone in Utah in 1923. It took one year to move the fossil out of the rock and seven years to reconstruct the skeleton.

Suspended from the ceiling of the dinosaur gallery is a life-size model of a pterosaur. This spectacular long-necked flying reptile, twice as large as any bird that ever lived, is posed as if it were in a slow, diving turn, its gold-and-black eyes seemingly scanning the floor below in search of a meal.

With the opening of the Life in the Ancient Seas exhibit in 1990, the museum completed its paleontological complex (a series of exhibition halls, which includes the Dinosaur Hall), a thirteen-year project. Displays chronicle the evolution of life in the sea, from the beginning of the Paleozoic Era (570 milllion years ago) through the Mesozoic and Cenozoic Eras to the present day. Many of the creatures seen here became extinct as a result of the global changes that occurred at the end of the Paleozoic and Mesozoic Eras.

Models of fish, squid, and other creatures suspended overhead seem to move through imaginary waters. Two spectacular murals by noted artist Ely Kish depict life-size prehistoric animals swimming under water. More than thirty marine animals, including a twenty-foot-long mosasaur (marine lizard) and a forty-five-foot-long *Basilosaurus* (ancient whale) are included in one of the carefully researched paintings.

Other highlights include a diorama of a 250-million-year-old Paleozoic Era reef, with more than 100,000 models of marine animals.

An exhibit on sharks can be seen on the dinosaur gallery balcony. The reconstructed jaws of a forty-foot-long prehistoric shark—with fossil teeth up to six inches long—are on view.

Following the extinction of dinosaurs sixty-five million years ago, mammals began to diversify and flourish. The next section, Mammals in the Limelight, chronicles this development. Large murals depict the landscape and evolving species at four different periods, from fifty-five to three million years ago. One of the most dramatic and beguiling fossil reconstructions on view is an eighteen-inch ancestral horse. In a small, intimate, circular theater you can see a mural and a film that traces the evolution of horses as they developed the long legs needed to escape from predators and the complex teeth that enabled them to chew abrasive grasses.

The latest of earth's Ice Ages, which took place from about three million to ten thousand years ago, is the focus of the next section. An audiovisual program explains the processes of glaciation that have gone on many times throughout history. Among the Ice Age mammals on view are a woolly mammoth with curved tusks, a mastodon, giant ground sloths from Panama, dire wolves and a saber-toothed cat from the Rancho La Brea tar pits, and a 28,000-year-old big-horned bison, now extinct, that was found freeze-dried in a creek in Alaska.

The emergence of man in the last Ice Age is symbolized by a cast of a 24,000-year-old mammoth tusk, engraved by a prehistoric artist. A life-size tableau shows a 70,000-year-old Neanderthal burial site, reconstructed from a similar site in a French cave. The exhibit indicates that ancient people buried their dead and believed in an afterlife.

CULTURES OF THE PACIFIC, ASIA, AND AFRICA

These exhibits explain the religious and cultural rituals, as well as the hunting and farming activities, music, arts, and crafts of natives of Africa, Asia, the Middle East, and the Pacific.

African artifacts include Benin sculpture, Yoruba wood figures, and Amharic religious paintings, as well as examples of African metal working, including brass pieces excavated in Nigeria that were crafted nearly a thousand years ago.

From the Middle East come Moslem pottery and musical instruments, and Jewish ceremonial objects, including a Torah scroll and silver spice containers.

Asian cultures are represented by Japanese folk crafts, shadow puppets from Malaysia, Thai silver boxes and lacquer bowls, and a figure representing Bali, the Monkey King of Kish Kindhya, a Hindu mythological figure. Also on view is an armored suit of a Japanese Samurai warrior, crafted between 1850 and 1875. It was presented to President Theodore Roosevelt after the Portsmouth Peace Conference that ended the Russo-Japanese War in 1905.

A massive stone head from Easter Island stands guard near the rotunda entrance to the Pacific Islands section. Among the exhibits on view are magnificent feather capes from Hawaii; beautiful examples of *tapa*, a cloth made from bark in Polynesia, and superbly carved war clubs from the Fiji Islands. Many of these objects were collected in 1838-42 by the U.S. Exploring Expedition, which assembled one of the most important and earliest American collections of anthropological artifacts from the South Seas.

SPLENDORS OF NATURE

This small exhibit is a dazzling display of the beauties of nature. Included are rare shells, butterflies, fossils, insects, and crystal formations, in addition to beautifully crafted American Indian artifacts.

ESKIMO AND INDIAN CULTURES

At the entrance to this hall, off the rotunda, is a diorama showing a family of Greenland Polar Eskimos. The boy has just caught an undersized seal through the ice and the other members of the family are laughing because he has called for the dog team and sled to bring home such a little animal. Created at the turn of the century by Smithsonian anthropologist and artist William H. Holmes, this appealing scene, which illustrates details of Eskimo culture in the polar environment, is still popular with museum visitors and is considered one of the masterpieces of museum exhibition.

The exhibits of Indian cultures include a birchbark canoe, tomahawks, lacrosse sticks (lacrosse was invented by Indians), and a tepee made of buffalo hides, decorated with porcupine quills. The tepee, part of a diorama showing the home life of an Arapaho Indian family, was exhibited at the 1876 Centennial Exposition in Philadelphia, and is thought to be the oldest full-sized Plains Indian tepee in existence.

Other dioramas illustrate aspects of Indian cultures of the southwestern United States, Mexico, the West Indies, and parts of Central and South America. Note particularly the Zuni, Hopi, and Pima pottery and the Mexican papier-mâché figures.

DISCOVERY ROOM

Here is your chance to touch a crocodile head, a piece of petrified wood, a chunk of coral, or dozens of other objects that may have piqued your interest. You can experiment with minerals, compare your teeth with those of a bobcat, or try on jewelry and costumes from around the world. And there are objects to smell and taste, including herbs such as coriander, fennel, and anise. This room, staffed by volunteers, is open only a limited number of hours (see above), and children under twelve must be accompanied by an adult.

MAMMALS

Hundreds of mammals from all parts of the world are exhibited here, including some in their natural settings. You can see everything from antelope to zebras. The section devoted to North American mammals includes bears, bison, caribou, deer, and moose. Of particular interest are the families of animals, showing, for example, the connections between dogs, foxes, and wolves, as well as lions, leopards, and tigers. Many of the big game animals on display were shot by President Theodore Roosevelt on an African safari in 1909.

BIRDS OF THE WORLD

Models of feathered creatures from throughout the world are displayed here, some in their native habitats. Particularly appealing are the penguins from Antarctica, looking like a group of tuxedo-clad conventioneers. Also shown are birds that are now extinct, including the dodo bird, the great auk, and the heath hen.

LIFE IN THE SEA
The sea green walls provide a fitting background for models of sharks, sailfish, porpoises, and a walrus. You can watch a film about pinnipeds, a group of mammals that includes the seal, the sea lion, and the walrus.

The largest single exhibit in the museum dominates this hall. Suspended from the ceiling is a ninety-two-foot-long model of a blue whale, which is now an endangered species.

Near the entrance to this hall, off the rotunda, are two three-thousand-gallon aquariums, designed by a Smithsonian scientist to house two contrasting marine ecosystems—one transplanted from a tropical Caribbean reef and the other from the subarctic waters off the rocky coast of Maine.

Both systems are microcosms of the actual wild environment, preserving the natural ecological relationships of the plants and animals living in two representative marine communities. Electronic and mechanical devices, including wave generating machines, simulate actual conditions on the reef and on Maine's rocky coastline. In the warm water tank, you can see colorful tropical fish, spider crabs, corals, and the blue-green, brown and red algae "turf" that grows like a lawn on the reef.

In the cold water tank, live lobsters move among clams, scallops, mussels, kelp, rockweed, and marsh grass as mechanically induced waves splash against rocks in this six-foot-deep, twelve-foot-long aquarium. The tides rise and fall in the tank about a foot twice a day, with excess water pumped into a holding tank as the tide goes out.

Most aquariums present sea creatures in an artificial environment. This is one of the few places in the country where you can study the interaction of fish, plants, and other types of marine life in their natural environment.

A film shown continuously in a small theater nearby, provides a glimpse of Smithsonian research in the Caribbean and Maine that led to development of the two microcosm systems.

ROTUNDA BALCONY GALLERY
Temporary exhibits of photographs and paintings with a natural history or anthropological theme are displayed on the balcony and in an adjacent gallery.

SECOND FLOOR

MINERALS AND GEMS
The mineral gallery, entered from the balcony, features an encyclopedic display of minerals, drawn from the museum's collection, which is considered to be the best in the world. Look for the dazzling display of California gold rush nuggets and smithsonite, a zinc carbonate identified by English chemist and mineralogist James Smithson, founder of the Smithsonian. Another display shows how minerals are formed and identifies their characteristics.

Once you understand the origins and characteristics of gems and minerals, you will be ready for the Hall of Gems, adjoining the Mineral Hall. This spectacular display features more than a thousand precious and semiprecious stones.

The best-known gem here is the fabulous Hope diamond, a

The Hope diamond, Hall of Gems

45.5-carat deep blue diamond named for a former owner, Henry Philip Hope of England. In 1668, the "French Blue" diamond was brought to France from India to become part of the crown jewels of King Louis XIV. The stone was stolen in 1792 and never recovered. In 1830, Hope bought his rare diamond, which may have been cut from the missing jewel. Despite a curse that is said to accompany the jewel, its last private owner, Mrs. Evalyn Walsh McLean of Washington, wore the stone frequently as the centerpiece of a necklace. New York jeweler Harry Winston, who acquired the gem from the McLean estate in 1949, presented it to the Smithsonian Institution in 1959.

You may be dazzled by the Hope diamond, but don't overlook other gems: the 127-carat Portugese diamond, the largest cut diamond from Brazil in existence; the 138.7-carat Rosser Reeves ruby, the largest and finest ruby in the world; the 423-carat Logan sapphire from Ceylon; the deep green 37.8-carat Chalk emerald, once owned by the royal rulers of Baroda, India; the 31-carat heart-shaped Eugénie blue diamond, formerly owned by French Empress Eugénie, and the 330-carat Star of Asia, which is considered to be one of the world's greatest cabochon-cut star sapphires.

Historical treasures include a pair of diamond drop earrings that King Louis XVI gave to Marie Antoinette shortly before the French Revolution; a tiara containing 950 diamonds, once owned by French Empress Marie Louise, and a 275-carat diamond necklace Napoleon I gave to his wife, Marie Louise, to celebrate the birth of their son in 1811. The tiara and the necklace were bequeathed to the Smithsonian Institution by Mrs. Marjorie Merriweather Post.

Magnificent Chinese jade carvings of the sixteenth to the nineteenth centuries are displayed near the north elevators. Although some of the objects date from the late Ming Dynasty, most are from the Ching Dynasty (1644-1912), when the art of jade carving reached its peak. In one of the cases, note the exquisite chrysanthemum-shaped dish and bowl carved in translucent spinach jade; the pair of altar boxes in the shape of the "Divine Tortoise" carved in spinach green jade, and the large covered vessel shaped like a Tibetan teapot, crafted of dark green jade.

EARTH, MOON, AND METEORITES

A huge revolving globe, depicting a geologist's view of the earth, is the focal point of this hall, entered off the rotunda balcony. It illustrates the great movements that have changed—and will continue to change—our planet. Exhibits explain the formation of the basic types of rock found on earth, ore deposits, and dynamic geological phenomena, such as volcanoes and earthquakes. A working seismograph is here to record earthquakes as they occur. A number of striking geological specimens are exhibited, including a three-ton mass of copper from Michigan, known to prehistoric Indians and first seen by a white man in 1766.

In an adjoining area, you can see moon rocks brought back by the Apollo astronauts and learn what they have taught scientists about the first 1.5 billion years of planetary evolution.

The meteorite hall displays huge chunks of meteorites that have fallen to earth, including the sculpture-like, 1,371-pound "Ring" meteorite that was found in Tucson, Arizona. Between five and ten meteorites are recovered each year, and a map shows the sites of nearly eight hundred meteorites that were found in the United States before 1976.

SOUTH AMERICA: CONTINENT AND CULTURE

This hall, off the rotunda balcony, takes you through four South American regions—the Patagonian grasslands, the tropical forests, the Pacific coastlands, and the high Andean mountain valleys—explaining how people have adapted to the varying conditions in these distinctive environments. One of the highlights is a re-creation of the market place in a modern Andean town, where you can see clothing, architecture, ceramics, tapestries, and gold and silver ornaments that reflect a mixture of prehistoric, colonial and twentieth-century cultural influences.

WESTERN CIVILIZATION: ORIGINS AND TRADITIONS

The ancient civilizations of the Mesopotamians, Egyptians, Greeks, Etruscans, and Romans and the heritage they have left us are featured in this hall. Among the two thousand objects in this exhibit are richly painted Egyptian mummy coffins from the tombs of Thebes; royal drinking goblets from Homer's legendary city of Troy; a massive mosaic from a Roman temple in Carthage; a signet ring that probably belonged to Jotham, one of the kings of Judah, and cuneiform tablets from Mesopotamia that represent some of the earliest business records in existence.

Murals, films, and dioramas supplement this material and explain two of the exhibit's main themes: how human affairs became increasingly complex as civilized cultures developed in Europe and the Middle East, and how early cultural traditions have survived to the present day. The exhibit concludes with a fine film about the development of Winchester, an ancient English town, where archaeological excavations have revealed occupation from the Iron Age through Roman times, the Anglo-Saxon and Norman periods to the present.

BONES

Skeletons of various mammals, birds, reptiles, amphibians, and fishes are posed characteristically and grouped by orders to demonstrate their relationships in this hall, which is entered from the rotunda balcony.

On view here is the skeleton of *Lexington*, the famous nineteenth-century race horse.

REPTILES

An exhibit re-creates a scene in the Florida Everglades, with alligators and snakes. Realistic models of snakes from the Malayan jungles and the Amazon are also shown. Other displays illustrate the food habits of lizards, toads, turtles, snakes, and crocodiles.

INSECT ZOO

This area of the museum is especially popular with children. It is one of the few places in the world where you can observe ants, bees, spiders, grasshoppers, and other insects in plastic-walled cages that re-create their native habitats. A beehive and an ant colony are prime attractions. Keepers are on hand to care for the insects, answer questions, and provide tours of the insect zoo.

ARTHUR M. SACKLER GALLERY

1050 Independence Avenue, S.W.
Washington, D.C. 20560
202/357-2700

METRO	Smithsonian, Mall Exit.
HOURS	10 A.M. to 5:30 P.M. daily. Closed Christmas Day.
TOURS	11:30 A.M. and 2:30 P.M. Monday through Friday; 11:30 A.M. Saturday and Sunday.
ADMISSION	Free.
HANDICAPPED FACILITIES	Building entrance at ground level; all areas served by elevators. Wheelchairs available. Accessible to the disabled.
MUSEUM SHOP	Books, jewelry, textiles, cards, and reproductions.
RESEARCH FACILITIES	Art reference library open 10 A.M. to 5 P.M. Monday through Friday. Ernst Herzfeld Archive of Persian and Near Eastern architecture and archaeological sites; Myron Bement Smith Archive relating to the Islamic world, the Carl Whiting Bishop Collection of photographs of China, the Henri Vever papers, and the correspondence of Charles Lang Freer.
MEMBERSHIP	Smithsonian Associates. Friends of Asian Arts at the Freer and Sackler Galleries from $1,000.
AUTHOR'S CHOICE	Chinese jade carvings, first level Iranian silver-and-gilt rhytons, first level Ancient Chinese bronzes, first level Chinese paintings and furniture, first level

The Arthur M. Sackler Gallery's holdings and exhibition policies complement those of the adjacent Freer Gallery of Art. And its innovative architectural design lends new meaning to the term "buried treasure."

HISTORY
In the late 1960s, S. Dillon Ripley, then secretary of the Smithsonian, began to urge a greater emphasis on international exhibition and research programs, particularly in the field of Asian art. By the 1970s, it became apparent that the Smithsonian's facilities were inadequate to meet the needs of the times. Part of the problem stemmed from restrictions in Charles Lang Freer's 1906 donation of the Freer Gallery, the Smithsonian's great museum of Asian art. Freer specified that only objects from the permanent collection may be shown and nothing may be loaned to other institutions. As a result, the Freer Gallery is unable to exhibit loan collections or to take advantage of the wealth of archaeological material that has become available in recent years.

In 1975, planning began for a new international museum and research complex to be built on the quadrangle of land just south of the Smithsonian Castle on the National Mall. In

1979, the government of Japan donated $1 million toward construction of an Asian art museum. The Japan Foundation and the JEC Fund, another Japanese organization, also contributed significantly to the project. The government of Korea donated $1 million in 1981.

In 1982, the late Dr. Arthur M. Sackler, a New York City medical researcher, publisher, and art connoisseur, donated $4 million toward construction of the museum and pledged approximately a thousand masterworks from his collection of Asian art. Dr. Sackler began collecting art after graduating from medical school. During the 1940s, his interests centered on pre- and early Renaissance art, as well as the French Impressionists, post-Impressionists, and contemporary American painters. He began collecting Chinese ceramics in 1950, later adding Chinese bronzes, jades, and sculpture.

In June 1983, construction began on a $73.2 million museum, research, and education complex adjacent to the Castle and the Arts and Industries Building. In addition to the Sackler Gallery, the complex, which opened in September 1987, includes the National Museum of African Art, the Smithsonian's International Center and Gallery, and the Enid A. Haupt Garden.

Unfortunately, like Charles Lang Freer, Henry Clay Folger, and Andrew W. Mellon, Dr. Sackler did not live to see the museum that bears his name. He died in May 1987 at seventy-three years old.

THE BUILDING

The decision to build the three-level, 360,000-square-foot museum below ground presented a variety of structural and aesthetic problems. The architect had to create a design that harmonized with the historic buildings nearby, while also making the journey underground attractive and inviting. The entire structure had to be waterproofed, since it reaches fifty-seven feet beneath the garden and extends below the water table. The roof, which provides support for the four-acre garden above, had to be specially designed. And a hundred-year-old European linden tree had to be preserved.

Architect Jean Paul Carlhian of the Boston firm Shepley, Bulfinch, Richardson, and Abbott inherited a plan for a two-pavilion museum complex from Japanese architect Junzo Yoshimura. Carlhian's task was to integrate his design with the

The Arthur M. Sackler Gallery

Renaissance Revival façade of the Freer, the Romanesque Revival architecture of the Castle, and the exuberant Victorian architecture of the Arts and Industries Building. He selected Minnesota gray granite to blend with the Freer's cream-colored exterior and a diamond-shaped motif to echo the spires of the Arts and Industries Building. (The pink New Hampshire granite of the National Museum of African Art harmonizes with the red brick of the Arts and Industries Building and its domes, arches, and circles reflect the Freer's arched exterior.)

A sixty-by-ninety-foot pavilion at garden level serves as the entrance to the museum, while an adjacent copper-domed kiosk provides a separate entrance for Smithsonian offices in the complex. The walls in the pavilion and the grand stairway are faced with blocks of Indiana limestone. The stairway angles right and left, repeating the diamond motif, down to a diamond-shaped reflecting pool at the bottom. Two large skylights bring daylight into the museum.

The first and second levels are devoted to exhibitions; a sculpture court is on the third level.

THE COLLECTIONS

Selections from the permanent collections—as well as works loaned by collectors and other museums—are shown in rotating exhibitions.

Dr. Sackler's $75 million gift—the nucleus of the museum's growing, permanent collections—included 153 Chinese bronzes from the Shang through the Han dynasties; 475 Chinese jades from the Neolithic period to the twentieth century; sixty-eight Chinese paintings from the tenth to the twentieth centuries, and forty-six examples of Chinese lacquerware. In addition, he donated 247 ancient Near Eastern works in silver, gold, bronze, ceramic, and minerals, and twenty stone and bronze sculptures from South and Southeast Asia.

The Sackler Gallery also houses the spectacular Vever collection, one of the world's most distinguished collections of ancient Persian art. Henri Vever, a Paris jeweler who died at eighty-nine during World War II, began collecting Asian and Islamic art at the turn of the century. He acquired more than five hundred rare Persian and Indian miniatures, texts, illustrations, books, and textiles, dating from the eleventh to the mid-nineteenth century. The collection comprises some of the most important Persian works, including the *Shahnama* or *Book of Kings*, an illuminated manuscript completed in 1010 A.D.

Secretly shipped from France during the German occupation, the collection was stored in a New York warehouse for more than forty years before the Smithsonian purchased it for $7 million in January 1986. Selections from the Vever collection are on view in a series of rotating exhibitions.

The permanent collection has also grown in the areas of Japanese art, especially twentieth-century prints and ceramics, as well as in Chinese and South Asian art. The museum maintains a lively schedule of international loan exhibitions.

ENTRANCE PAVILION

GROUND LEVEL

Indian terracotta sculpture is the focal point of the entrance lobby.

MONSTERS, MYTHS, AND MINERALS

FIRST LEVEL

A pair of Tang dynasty ceramic tomb guardians on either side of the exhibition entrance establishes the theme of these galleries—animals in Chinese folklore. The exhibition includes 123 jade, bronze, ceramic, stone, and marble objects, ranging from the eleventh century B.C. into the eighteenth century.

In Chinese legends, animals and fantastic creatures have special symbolic connotations. Such creatures were often represented in jade, bronze, stone, and lacquer.

In the first gallery, a variety of animals—a dragon, a tiger, and a tortoise, among others—decorate bronze mirrors from the early Western Han dynasty. Notice the magnificently carved dragon finial of pale green jade from the Yuan dynasty, which was probably intended to be mounted at the top of a staff. In Chinese folklore, the dragon (*long*) symbolizes imperial power and represents male vigor and vitality.

Several display cases are filled with intricately carved jade birds and animals. Variations in the color of the jade indicate the birds' plumage. Birds (*niao*) are believed to watch over the graves of pious men, to protect people, and to help them become rich. The reclining elephants seen here symbolize strength, sagacity, and prudence.

Jade horses and dogs are also on view. Horses (*ma*) are traditionally associated with magical travel. According to the sixteenth-century *Chinese Book of Medicine*, horses have eyes on their knees, enabling them to travel at night. Dogs (*gou*) have been companions of the Chinese for thousands of years. As long ago as the Shang dynasty, dogs were buried in tombs with their masters. And tenth-century paintings show hunting dogs sitting behind their owners on horseback, presumably ready to jump down and follow the prey.

Fantastical creatures, such as the chimera (*bixie*) are thought to bring good luck, if treated properly. With the body of a lion, the head of a dragon, and the wings of a phoenix, they often appear in Chinese legends, assuming the characteristics of other animals, as well as their own individual traits.

The twelve-year cycle of the Chinese zodiac is featured in a special display, with each year represented by a different animal. The exhibit describes the similarity in personality characteristics between people born during particular years and the animals for whom the year is named. The zodiacal cycle was first used in the Shang dynasty.

ART OF CAMBODIA

The five sandstone sculptures from tenth to thirteenth century Cambodia portray Buddhist and Hindu deities and themes.

THE ARTS OF CHINA

A spectacular assemblage of over two hundred masterworks from China, including ancient jades and bronzes, Buddhist sculpture and wall paintings, lacquer, scroll paintings, and furniture drawn largely from Dr. Sackler's gift, which forms the core of the permanent collection, is displayed in seven galleries.

The exhibit opens with jades and bronzes from the late

Neolithic period, dating from the fourth millennium B.C. to the third century A.D. During that period, most jade implements and bronze vessels were status symbols, used in religious, court, or burial ceremonies. Bronzes were decorated with masklike images, angular spirals, and other stylized designs. Note, for example, the Shang dynasty ritual wine container (*hu*) crafted in the thirteenth century, B.C. Dragons and birds were also favorite decorative motifs. Be sure to see the Shang dynasty bronze tripod with six dragons, dating from the thirteenth to the twelfth century, B.C.

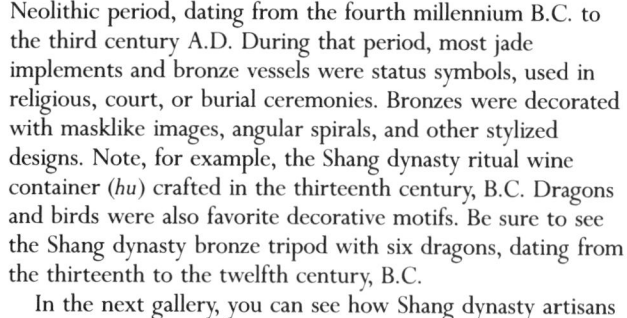

In the next gallery, you can see how Shang dynasty artisans used jade to create miniature birds and animals. And an owl formed the base of certain bronze ritual wine containers.

During the Western Zhou dynasty (ca. 1050-771 B.C.), the forms of bronze vessels showed a transformation from those of the preceding Shang dynasty. Western Zhou jade carvings included stags with antlers and birds with long tail feathers.

When the capital was moved from what is now Xi'an to Luoyang in Henan Province during the Eastern Zhou dynasty, ritual bronze vessels began to symbolize political power and courtly grandeur among feudal lords. They were used for secular, as well as religious functions. Bronzemaking flourished, and new decorative techniques were developed.

Chinese bronze ritual wine vessel, Shang dynasty, 13th century B.C.

During this period, artisans learned to create relief designs in jade. Several dragon pendants dating from the late sixth to fifth century, B.C. and a fourth century, B.C. fish-dragon pendant are fine examples of this technique.

In recent years, improved communication with scholars in China has broadened our knowledge of that country's ancient culture. Archaeological excavations in 1956-61 near Houma in Shanxi Province, 150 miles north of Luoyang, unearthed the site of a major sixth-century bronze foundry. More than a thousand decorated clay fragments of molds and models for bronze castings were found in what were apparently separate workshops for creating bells, vessels, coins, and other objects.

During the Late Eastern Zhou and Han Dynasties, luxury items were in great demand. Bronze objects, such as the garment hooks seen here, were inlaid with gold and semi-precious stones. Don't miss the cleverly designed gilt bronze lamp, which is really three separate lamps that fit together into a cylindrical shape. An intense interest in man and nature was expressed in naturalistic carvings of animals. A Han dynasty bear (symbolic of strength and endurance) scratching his ear is one of the most appealing jade animals on view.

A selection of Buddhas and *bodhisattvas* (enlightened beings) in gilt bronze, jade, and other media illustrates Buddhist art in China. Objects span the fifth to the eighteenth century.

The gallery devoted to later Chinese art contains paintings, furniture, jade, and lacquered objects. You can see an exquisite seventeenth- to eighteenth-century jade lotus-leaf bowl embellished with dragons; an early fifteenth-century cup stand with floral designs in carved lacquer on wood; *Feng River Landscape*, a series of black-and-white sketches by the seventeenth-century artist Hongren, and *Landscape and Portrait of Hong Zhengzhi*, a scroll painting by two early eighteenth-century artists, Shitao, a Buddhist monk, and a man known simply as Mr. Jiang.

Lotus, Chinese hanging scroll, Republic period, 1939

Included here are hanging scrolls by Qi Baishi (1863-1957) and Huang Binhong (ca. 1864-1955) which are among the first works of contemporary Asian art to be collected by the Smithsonian.

NOMADS AND NOBILITY: ART FROM THE ANCIENT NEAR EAST

Two basic techniques—casting and hammering—were used to produce metal objects that were used both in daily life and in special ceremonies.

Among the most outstanding items in the collection are three silver and gilt *rhytons* dating from the Parthian period in Iran (ca. 100 B.C.-100 A.D.). (A *rhyton* is a ritual drinking vessel incorporating the head or forepart of an animal, such as a bull, a lion, a gazelle, or an antelope.) As you can see from the fourth-century Iranian *rhyton* nearby, the animal's head became a more prominent feature of the design in later years.

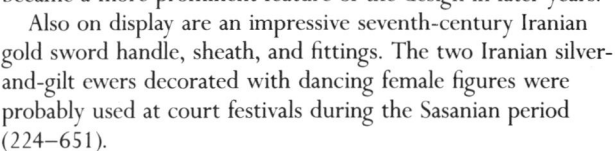

Iranian silver and gilt rhyton, 4th century

Also on display are an impressive seventh-century Iranian gold sword handle, sheath, and fittings. The two Iranian silver-and-gilt ewers decorated with dancing female figures were probably used at court festivals during the Sasanian period (224–651).

An important collection of silver figurines, bowls, jars, and jewelry dating from the second millennium in Iran is also on view. The various sizes of silver animals seen here may have been used as weights.

SOUTH INDIAN HINDU TEMPLE SCULPTURE

The seven sculptures exhibited here date from the tenth to the fourteenth century. Crafted of bronze, schist, and granite, the works include a sculpture of the omnipotent Shiva and a Hindu goddess, one of the Seven Mothers, or *Sapta-Matrka*, who is said to have risen from the blood of Shiva and other gods.

There is also a particularly fine image of Ganesh, the elephant god, who brings good fortune to his worshippers. Ganesh is the god who blesses new endeavors—an appropriate connotation for this relatively new museum.

In addition to this sculpture exhibition on the first level, a small selection of South Asian sculptures can also be seen on the third level, near the reflecting pool.

CHINA: CHRONOLOGY OF DYNASTIES

Neolithic period	ca. 5000–ca. 1700 B.C.
Shang dynasty	ca. 1700–ca. 1050 B.C.
Anyang period	ca. 1300–ca. 1050 B.C.
Zhou dynasty	ca. 1050–221 B.C.
Western Zhou	ca. 1050–771 B.C.
Eastern Zhou	770–221 B.C.
Qin dynasty	221–206 B.C.
Han dynasty	206 B.C.–220 A.D.
Six dynasties period	
Three Kingdoms	220–265 A.D.
Jin dynasty	265–420 A.D.
Northern and Southern	
dynasties	420–589 A.D.
Sui dynasty	581–618 A.D.
Tang dynasty	618–907 A.D.
Five dynasties	907–960 A.D.

Song dynasty	960–1279 A.D.
Northern Song	960–1127 A.D.
Southern Song	1127–1279 A.D.
Yuan dynasty	1271–1368
Ming dynasty	1368–1644
Qing dynasty	1644–1911
Republic period	1911–
People's Republic	1949–

THIRD LEVEL **S. DILLON RIPLEY CENTER**

A copper-domed kiosk serves as the entrance to the S. Dillon Ripley Center, which is named for the eighth secretary of the Smithsonian.

Located on the third level underground, it includes the International Center, a two-hundred-seat lecture hall, an education center, and offices for the Smithsonian Institution Traveling Exhibition Service (SITES) and the Smithsonian's resident and national associate programs. Exhibitions are presented in the International Center Gallery.

A three-story trompe l'oeil mural of the Castle and the Arts and Industries Building by New York artist Richard Haas is the focal point of a 285-foot-long, plant-filled concourse linking the Arthur M. Sackler Gallery and the National Museum of African Art.

ENID A. HAUPT GARDEN

HISTORY

James Renwick's 1847 design for the Smithsonian Castle called for a main entrance on the Mall side, with open space to the south. In 1853, a Magnetic Observatory, where scientists could conduct experiments, was built in the south yard. The observatory was torn down when the Smithsonian's second building, the Arts and Industries Building, was erected in 1881.

Approximately a hundred animals, including two buffalo who grazed in the yard, lived here until the National Zoological Park opened in 1890.

Through the years, a series of "temporary" buildings—some lasting as long as forty years—sprouted on this four-acre plot of ground. There was a greenhouse where scientists studied the effects of sunlight on plants. Secretary Samuel P. Langley had a workshop here, in which he built his "aerodrome," an unmanned vehicle that made the first successful flight of a heavier-than-air, powered machine. And Secretary Charles Abbot turned a carriage house into a laboratory, which later became the Smithsonian's "bug house."

During World War I, the engines of fighter airplanes were repaired in a metal hut in the south yard. After the war, the building housed the aeronautical collection that formed the nucleus of the National Air and Space Museum. Some of the artifacts, including the Wright brothers' airplane and Charles Lindbergh's *Spirit of St. Louis*, overflowed into the Arts and Industries Building. During the 1960s, huge rockets that were too large to fit indoors stood on the grounds. Also during this period, part of the south yard became a parking lot.

When the National Air and Space Museum opened in 1976, all of the outbuildings were torn down. In their place, the Smithsonian created a three-acre Victorian garden that stretched from the south door of the Castle to the sidewalk on

Independence Avenue. The garden lasted until 1983, when construction began on the quadrangle museum complex.

THE GARDEN

Enid A. Haupt, a magazine publisher and philanthropist, donated $3 million for construction of the garden, which opened in May 1987. Architect Jean Paul Carlhian and landscape architect Lester Collins collaborated with the Smithsonian's Office of Horticulture to create a four-acre garden with special areas: an oriental-style garden, a fountain garden, and an English Victorian garden in the center, in keeping with the Castle's architecture.

The diamond-shaped and circular motifs that characterize the Arthur M. Sackler Gallery and the National Museum of African Art are repeated in the gardens. To tie the composition together, however, Carlhian and his design team switched motifs, using the Sackler's diamonds in the African garden and the African's circles in the oriental garden.

The oriental garden, to the west of the central parterre, is entered through a moongate—a characteristic feature of Chinese design—that leads to a square reflecting pool with a circular stone island in the center. Weeping Japanese cherry trees stand on opposite sides of the pool.

The eastern garden features an Indian *chadar*, or small waterfall, that splashes down a stone incline, with cockspur hawthorn trees surrounding a circular pool.

Directly in front of the Castle, the Victorian-style parterre, curved walkways, and elaborate hanging baskets are designed to conjure up images of an English Victorian garden. Nineteenth-century-style lampposts, Victorian benches, and plant-filled urns add to the nostalgic mood.

View of the Enid A. Haupt Garden

Plantings in the Haupt Garden include Japanese threadleaf maples, Katsura trees, willow oaks, sour gums, and magnolias, as well as wisteria and climbing hydrangea.

Since this is a "rooftop" garden, many of the plants and trees are designed to conceal the skylights, emergency stairways, and operating equipment of the below-ground museums and offices.

RENWICK GATE

When James Renwick designed the Castle, he also planned a carriage gate for the Independence Avenue entrance. According to historian James Goode, former curator of the Castle, either the gate was never built or it was built, rejected by the Smithsonian, and sold to the Oakhill Cemetery in Georgetown. A woodcut illustration in *Hints on Public Architecture*, an 1849 book by Robert Dale Owen, showed Renwick's design—an elaborate black iron central gate for carriages and two smaller side gates for pedestrians, framed by four large stone pillars or piers.

In 1977, then-Secretary S. Dillon Ripley decided to re-create Renwick's gate after his special assistant, Richard Howland, showed him an illustration of it. In the interests of historical accuracy, it was decided to try to match the Castle's red sandstone. Although the original quarry in Poolesville, Maryland, was closed, Goode, who supervised the project, found that the same sandstone had been used in two local buildings. He obtained the needed stone from the old District of Columbia Jail, which was being torn down, and the Sumner School, which was being renovated.

It took nearly a year to complete the three massive gates, which are crafted of black wrought and cast iron. Four steel columns, or I-beams, support the gates and the hand-carved sandstone pillars. The Renwick gate was installed in time for the dedication of the Enid A. Haupt Garden in May 1987.

Sketch of the Renwick gate after the original 1849 design by James Renwick

Freedom *by Thomas Crawford, on the Capitol dome*

CAPITOL HILL

CAPITAL CHILDREN'S MUSEUM

800 Third Street, N.E.
Washington, D.C. 20002
202/543-8600

METRO	Union Station.
HOURS	10 A.M. to 5 P.M. daily.
TOURS	Group tours 10 A.M., 11:30 A.M., and 2 P.M. by appointment only. Groups of ten or more receive a 25% discount on admission.
ADMISSION	$5, per person; $2, senior citizens aged 60 and over; children under 2 years and members, free.
HANDICAPPED FACILITIES	Ramps, elevators, parking, and special tours.
SPECIAL EVENTS	Puppet shows, live performances, and arts and crafts activities.
MEMBERSHIP	From $40.
AUTHOR'S CHOICE	Hall of Changing Environments Communication

> "I see and I forget,
> I hear and I remember,
> I do and I understand."
> Chinese proverb

This ancient Chinese proverb provides the inspiration for the Capital Children's Museum, a "hands-on" center of learning and discovery for children of all ages. A child can drive a mock-up of a bus, slide down a fireman's pole, print a poster, make a cartoon, talk on the telephone, make tortillas, or pat a live goat. It all adds up to a learning experience that is fun for children from preschool age to the teens. (Don't be surprised, however, if staff members, hired to demonstrate exhibits to youngsters, sometimes appear a bit disinterested.)

HISTORY
Educator Ann White Lewin conceived the idea for the museum in the 1970s. The museum opened in 1979 after receiving a $1.7 million grant from the Department of Housing and Urban Development. It is located half a dozen blocks from Union Station in a group of red brick buildings that formerly housed a convent and nursing home of the Little Sisters of the Poor.

In 1981, the International Telephone and Telegraph Corporation (ITT) underwrote the cost of Communication, the museum's largest and most ambitious exhibition area. Mexican government officials provided some of the furnishings for the Mexican plaza, and the fireman's hats, boots, and brass pole were contributed by the Washington, D.C., Fire Department.

The museum is part of the National Learning Center, an

organization dedicated to innovative education. The Learning Center also operates Options, a School for New Skills, and LAB IV, a research and development center for creating new educational methods and materials.

NEK CHAND SCULPTURE GARDEN
Life-size sculptured figures, crafted by Indian folk artist Nek Chand, line a skylit entryway. Chand's miniature Indian village includes sari-clad women, children, birds, and animals created from bits of broken glass, ceramics, and other found objects. Like James Hampton, whose *Throne of the Third Heaven of the Nation's Millennium General Assembly* can be seen at the National Museum of American Art, Chand turns cast-offs into art.

A former municipal public works inspector, Chand created a twelve-acre rock garden at Chandigarh near Delhi, using found materials. After seeing Chand's Chandigarh garden, Ann Lewin, president of the National Learning Center, asked him to create a similar sculpture garden here.

THE EXHIBITS
Temporary art exhibitions and an auditorium are on the first floor. The museum's three main exhibition halls are located on the second and third floors.

COMMUNICATION
In a series of exhibits, children can observe the development of communications, from primitive cave drawings to television and the computer. They can type on a Braille typewriter, learn Morse code, write with a quill pen, and print a poster on a Ben Franklin printing press. The film and photography section includes equipment that enables children to make their own film slides and cartoons.

The Future Center, equipped with twenty Atari 800 computers, explores the world of computers, while a radio studio, television theater, news wire machine, and telephone hall reveal other aspects of modern communications.

HALL OF CHANGING ENVIRONMENTS
Young visitors enjoy the Metricville Room, where a make-believe shoemaker's shop, grocery store (complete with working cash register), and metric scales convey information in a play environment. Putting puzzles together and sorting cards by their shapes helps children learn about patterns. A pint-size maze, the MetamorphoMaze, and a room where children can play with a pulley, a lever, and a wheel and axle are nearby.

The most popular section of this hall is the City Room, which includes a mock-up of a bus that can be "driven," and a fire station with a brass pole to slide down.

INTERNATIONAL HALL
A re-creation of a Mexican marketplace features a tiled fountain, the façade of a church, and an assortment of serapes and sombreros that can be tried on. In an adjoining area, Rosie the goat lies on her straw bed waiting to be petted.

Children can learn how to make tortillas and how to grind chocolate into a fine powder for Mexican cocoa. Staff members are on hand to show visitors how to make paper flowers, as well as yarn and wax necklaces.

THE CAPITOL

Washington, D.C. 20515
202/224-3121

METRO	Capitol South or Union Station.
HOURS	9 A.M. to 4:30 P.M. daily. Rotunda and Statuary Hall open until 8 P.M. in summer. Closed Thanksgiving, Christmas, and New Year's Day. House and Senate wings remain open during night sessions.
TOURS	From the rotunda every fifteen minutes, beginning at 9 A.M. Last tour at 3:45 P.M.
ADMISSION	Free.
HANDICAPPED FACILITIES	Ramp entrances at North and South Wings, and at Document Door, East Front. Call Office of Special Services, 202/224-4048, for details. Accessible to the disabled.
FOOD FACILITIES	Public Dining Room, first floor, open 8 A.M. to 11 A.M., 11:30 A.M. to adjournment; until 3:30 P.M. when there is no session. (Cafeterias in the House and Senate Office Buildings are open to the public from 7:30 A.M. to approximately 3 P.M. but are reserved for congressional staff members from 11:30 A.M. to 1:30 P.M.)
GIFT SHOP	Books, postcards, souvenirs at desk, East Front entrance.
SPECIAL EVENTS	Free concerts by Army, Navy, Marine, and Air Force bands on West Terrace during the summer, except Thursday. Also, special concerts on Memorial Day, July 4, and Labor Day.
AUTHOR'S CHOICE	The Rotunda Statuary Hall The House and Senate Chambers The Old Supreme Court Chamber The Old Senate Chamber

Here is the picture postcard view of Washington—the sparkling white dome that symbolizes the nation's capital. Within these walls, historic debates have taken place and landmark legal decisions have been handed down. Here, too, are hundreds of paintings and statues commemorating nearly two centuries of American history.

In planning the new federal city, Pierre Charles L'Enfant placed the Congress House and the President's Palace at opposite ends of Pennsylvania Avenue, as physical symbols of the separation of the legislative and executive branches of government. He considered Jenkins Hill to be "a pedestal waiting for a monument"—the ideal spot for the Capitol.

HISTORY

In 1792, approximately fifteen drawings were submitted in the competition to design the Capitol. Although Stephen Hallett's design was considered the best, the judges were not enthusiastic about his entry. They allowed Dr. William Thornton, a physician, painter, and amateur architect, to submit his design three months after the competition closed.

According to Secretary of State Thomas Jefferson,

Thornton's design, with its columned portico and low dome, "captivated the eyes and judgment of all." George Washington was impressed with its "grandeur, simplicity and convenience." Thornton received $500 and a lot in the new city as his prize. Runner-up Hallett was appointed supervisor of construction.

Washington, wearing a Masonic apron embroidered by the wife of French General Lafayette, laid the cornerstone in a Masonic ceremony September 18, 1793. The building was constructed in several stages and has gone through a series of additions and renovations up to the present day.

The north wing, built 1793–1800, contained the Senate Chamber, which was first occupied November 17, 1800, during the second session of the Sixth Congress. (The capital had just been moved to Washington at that time.)

As architect of the Capitol and one of three District commissioners, Thornton clashed with Hallett (who was fired in 1794 for not adhering to Thornton's design) and with professional architects who wanted to alter his plans. In 1802, Thornton was appointed head of the Patent Office, which was then located near the site of the present National Museum of American Art/National Portrait Gallery.

The following year, President Thomas Jefferson appointed Benjamin Henry Latrobe as surveyor of public buildings, a position that included responsibility for construction of the Capitol.

Members of Congress, the Supreme Court, the Circuit Court, and the Library of Congress were all housed in the rectangular north wing of the Capitol.

In 1807, the south wing containing the House Chamber (now Statuary Hall) was completed. It opened in time for the first session of the 106-member Tenth Congress, October 26, 1807.

On August 24, 1814, during the War of 1812, Rear Admiral Sir George Cockburn and his British troops took control of the Capitol building. Standing on the speaker's chair, Cockburn asked, "Shall this harbor of Yankee democracy be burned?" He was answered by a chorus of "ayes" as his men set fire to books, draperies, and furniture in both the House and Senate wings. Elsewhere in the city, British troops set fire to the White House and other federal buildings. A torrential downpour put out the flames that night, and the following day, a violent wind storm sent the British forces back to their ships.

That fall, Congress met in the Patent Office Building, originally Blodget's Hotel, which was the only undamaged federal structure in the city. William Thornton, head of the Patent Office, is credited with urging a British officer to spare that building. While some members of Congress talked of moving to another city, a group of Washingtonians hastily constructed a new building, known as the Brick Capitol, on the site of the present Supreme Court Building. Congress met there from 1815 to 1819, while the Capitol was being rebuilt. It was at the Brick Capitol that President James Monroe became the first president to have an outdoor inaugural ceremony.

Under Latrobe's direction, both wings of the Capitol were strengthened and restored. Sandstone columns capped with corn and tobacco leaf carvings were a major decorative feature in the Senate wing, and the House Chamber was redesigned into the semicircular shape of today's Statuary Hall. Although the magnificence of the House Chamber was undeniable, its acoustics left much to be desired. Later, scarlet draperies were hung behind the columns to muffle the troublesome echoes. (Samuel F. B. Morse's 1822 painting, *The Old House of Representatives*, at the Corcoran Gallery of Art depicts the chamber during this period.)

Disagreements with the commissioner of public buildings led to Latrobe's resignation in 1817 and his replacement by Boston architect Charles Bulfinch.

The House and Senate moved back into their chambers December 6, 1819, and Bulfinch completed the Capitol in 1829. He supervised construction of the central portion of the building, including the east and west fronts, and a central rotunda with a low copper-covered dome. The cornerstone of the center section was laid August 24, 1818—exactly four years after the building had been gutted by the British.

In October 1824, a gala reception in the rotunda honored the visiting Marquis de Lafayette. Two months later, in December, the aging general became the first foreign visitor to address a joint session of Congress.

NEW HOUSE AND SENATE WINGS

The nineteenth century was a time of expansion, as states were added to the Union and its population mushroomed. By 1850, the country stretched across three thousand miles, from the Atlantic to the Pacific. The sixty-two senators and 232 representatives were beginning to clamor for more space. Led by Senator Jefferson Davis, later president of the Confederacy, Congress appropriated $100,000 in September 1850 to create "ample accommodations for the two houses of Congress."

Thomas U. Walter, a Philadelphia architect appointed by President Millard Fillmore, was in charge of building the Capitol extension. The cornerstone was laid by Fillmore July 4, 1851, in a civil and Masonic ceremony. The event is remembered now chiefly for the two-hour dedication speech of silver-tongued Secretary of State Daniel Webster.

The large new House and Senate wings reduced the original portions to mere links between the central rotunda and the new structures. Despite bureaucratic struggles over authority, difficulty in obtaining materials, and an 1851 fire in the Library of Congress, both wings were completed by 1865. The House held its first session in the partially completed new south building December 16, 1857, and the Senate moved into its new quarters January 4, 1859.

The new halls were handsomely decorated with painted walls, glass skylights, and new gas lighting fixtures. Minton tile floors, manufactured by the same company that produced Minton porcelain in Stoke-on-Trent, England, embellished other parts of the building. But tensions were rising in the bitter North-South debates over slavery, and early in 1861, southern members left the Congress.

When Confederate forces fired on Fort Sumter and the Civil War began, the Capitol played a new role. It became a barracks for as many as three thousand northern soldiers, who referred to the building as the "Big Tent." Basement committee rooms were transformed into a bakery producing hundreds of loaves of bread for the army each day. For six weeks, the Capitol served as a temporary hospital for soldiers wounded at the battles of Second Manassas and Antietam, with fifteen hundred cots set up in the rotunda, halls, and meeting rooms. Red Cross founder Clara Barton and poet Walt Whitman were among those who tended the sick and wounded.

In spite of the war, work continued on the Capitol dome, which President Abraham Lincoln viewed as "a sign we intend the Union shall go on." Walter, assisted by army engineer Montgomery C. Meigs (later architect of the Pension Building), replaced Bulfinch's dome with one of cast iron, weighing nine million pounds. The massive dome was needed to balance the size of the two new wings.

President Lincoln's second inauguration, 1865; Frank Leslie's Illustrated Weekly

American sculptor Thomas Crawford was commissioned to design a statue for the top of the dome. (Art collector William Wilson Corcoran considered Crawford the greatest sculptor of his day and installed his statue, along with those of ten other artists, including Raphael, Michelangelo, and Rembrandt, in niches in the façade of what is now the Renwick Gallery.) Crawford first called the sketch of the nineteen-and-a-half-foot-tall bronze figure "Armed Liberty," and planned to place on her head a liberty cap similar to those worn by freed Roman slaves. When Jefferson Davis, then secretary of war, objected to the connotation, Crawford substituted a helmet with eagle head and feathers, in tribute to the American Indian.

The plaster cast, modeled in Crawford's Rome studio, was placed aboard a ship bound for the United States in 1858. The ship ran into heavy gales and, leaking badly, managed to reach Bermuda, where it was condemned and sold. The statue was placed in storage and finally reached Washington in March 1859, eight months after starting the transatlantic journey. Cast at a foundry on Bladensburg Road in Washington, D.C., "Freedom" was hoisted into place December 2, 1863, to the accompaniment of a thirty-five-gun salute—one for each state in the Union.

Although the east portico of the new Senate wing was completed in the fall of 1864, several more years elapsed before its north and west porticoes were finished. On the House side, the tympanum was completed by 1867, but the carvings in the east pediment were not commissioned and installed until 1916, almost fifty years later.

In 1959, President Dwight D. Eisenhower laid the cornerstone—again in a Masonic ceremony—for the thirty-

two-and-a-half-foot extension of the east central front of the Capitol. Nearly a century earlier, Walter had called for this addition to give an adequate base for the dome. It caused a controversy among critics who opposed any changes to the historic façade. Most observers now agree, however, that extending the central portico of the building has provided more balanced proportions for the 751-foot-long façade.
In the 1959 renovation, the original sandstone façade was replicated in marble and the dome was refurbished for the first time. Thirty-two layers of paint were removed in the process. Congress gained more than a hundred additional rooms, elevators, and corridors as a result of the east front extension, but the primary benefit was the preservation of the east front.

In recent years, there has been talk of a similar extension of the west front. Despite Congress's perennial need for additional space, the members voted to restore the west front, rather than to enlarge it. The recent renovation, which was completed in November 1987, reinforced the stone walls with stainless steel rods and replaced approximately thirty percent of the façade's sandstone that was chipped and crumbling.

TOURING THE BUILDING

THE ROTUNDA

The rotunda—more than 180 feet high and approximately ninety-six feet in diameter—is the center of the building. Because all streets radiate from the Capitol, this is the symbolic center of the city as well. Here, distinguished citizens, including presidents from Lincoln to Johnson, have lain in state.

Eight monumental paintings encircle the walls of the rotunda. Important events of the revolutionary period, as depicted by John Trumbull, include *The Declaration of Independence*, *The Surrender of General Burgoyne* and *The Surrender of Lord Cornwallis*, and *Washington Resigning His Commission as General of the Army*. Trumbull served with Washington in the Continental army and painted the portraits of many early patriots. He received $8,000 for each of the paintings here.

The other four paintings deal with the discovery and colonization of America.

A marble statue of *President Abraham Lincoln* by sculptor Vinnie Ream, the first woman to receive a government commission, stands near the Trumbull paintings. Through a congressional friend, Ream, a seventeen-year-old aspiring artist, obtained permission to sculpt a bust of Lincoln in the White House during the last five months of his life. The busy president agreed when he learned that she was young and poor. She was also talented, and created the full length statue from her earlier work.

Constantino Brumidi painted the fresco in the eye of the dome, *The Apotheosis of Washington*, in 1865 when he was sixty years old. Brumidi, an Italian artist, introduced fresco painting in the United States when he came here in search of political freedom. In fresco, paint is applied to fresh plaster. The artist must work quickly, before the plaster dries. Brumidi's aim was "to make beautiful the Capitol of the one country on earth in which there is liberty," and he devoted the last twenty-five years of his life to the task.

On a scaffold high above the ground, he finished the *Apotheosis*, or glorification of Washington, in eleven months. The figures near the outer edge of the dome represent Armed

The eye of the dome, painted by Constantino Brumidi

Freedom (modeled after Brumidi's young wife), Arts and Sciences, Marine, Commerce, Mechanics, and Agriculture. Near the eye of the dome, Washington is seated between Liberty and Victory. Thirteen figures crowned with stars represent the thirteen original colonies.

Brumidi is also responsible for the scenes from American history in the remarkable frieze that encircles the rotunda. Although the frieze appears to be three dimensional, it is actually fresco. In 1879, while working on the scene of William Penn's treaty with the Indians, the seventy-four-year-old artist slipped from a scaffold fifty-eight feet above the floor but managed to hold on until help came. He died a few months later, and Filippo Costaggini, using Brumidi's sketches, finished all but the final thirty-foot panel. In 1953, New York artist Allyn Cox completed the scenes showing the Civil War, the Spanish-American War, and the Wright brothers.

Brumidi's inspired artistry—his portrait medallions, landscapes, birds, flowers, and patriotic motifs—can also be seen in the Senate reception room, the President's Room, committee rooms, and corridors. Don't miss the Brumidi corridor on the first floor of the Senate side of the building.

The changing exhibits in the crypt beneath the rotunda, which provide information about the artists and architects responsible for building the Capitol, generally include a display about Brumidi's life and work.

STATUARY HALL

The House of Representatives met in this grandiose marble hall for half a century, from 1807 to 1857. For several years after that, the hall resounded to the cries of hucksters selling oranges and root beer. In 1864, Congress evicted the vendors and created Statuary Hall, permitting each state to send statues of two of its most distinguished deceased citizens. By the 1930s, the bronze and marble figures were too heavy for the floor. The collection now occupies the Hall of Columns on the House side and other locations throughout the building.

A small bronze marker in the floor indicates the spot where John Quincy Adams collapsed on February 21, 1848. He died soon afterward in the adjoining Speaker's Office, ending a seventeen-year congressional career. According to legend, Adams reportedly discovered that—among other acoustical quirks in the hall—he could hear his adversaries whispering across the room while sitting at his desk. Sound waves are carried across the hall in a phenomenon known as parabolic reflection.

THE HOUSE AND SENATE CHAMBERS

The guided tour of the Capitol includes a brief visit to the House chamber. If you would like to see the chambers on your own, you must obtain a pass to the Visitors' Gallery from your senator or congressman. Foreign visitors may obtain passes from the sergeant-at-arms. Sessions usually begin at noon, and committees meet during the morning. You can find daily congressional schedules in the *Washington Post*.

In both houses, the Democrats are seated to the right of the presiding officer, with Republicans on the left. The 435 members of the House of Representatives do not have assigned seats. Their 100 counterparts in the Senate, however, have desks that are assigned in order of seniority, with the most senior members seated near the front of the chamber.

A system of bells signals members who are not present what is happening on the floor. Each number of bells has its own special meaning. For example, in the House three bells indicates a quorum call, and more than half of the members must be present for business to continue. In the Senate, however, three bells is a call of absentees.

In the House chamber, two important paintings flank the rostrum. To the right of the speaker is *George Washington* by John Vanderlyn. *General Lafayette* by Ary Scheffer, a gift from the artist which has hung in the House since 1825, is on the speaker's left.

OLD SUPREME COURT CHAMBER

The first joint session of Congress took place in this ground floor area November 22, 1800. Thomas Jefferson was sworn in as president here in 1801 and again in 1805. In 1807, after the House of Representatives had moved to its own wing, Benjamin Henry Latrobe proposed certain changes to improve the facilities of the Senate and the Supreme Court. Structural problems were corrected, including a leaky roof, flaking plaster, and rotting timbers. Latrobe created this low-vaulted, Doric-columned room for the Supreme Court and a two-story Senate chamber directly above.

The Supreme Court was housed here for fifty years, from 1810 to 1860, with Chief Justices John Marshall and Roger B. Taney presiding. Before then, the court had met in various rooms, including members' boardinghouses and even at a tavern across the street.

The Old Supreme Court Chamber

In 1844, Samuel F. B. Morse, surrounded by justices and congressional supporters, sent the first telegraph message, "What hath God wrought," from this room to Baltimore.

When the new Senate wing was completed, the Supreme Court moved upstairs into the Old Senate Chamber, and this room became a law library. The justices remained upstairs until the Supreme Court Building opened in 1935. In 1976, a remodeling, which cost $478,000, restored the room to its appearance of the 1860s, with many of the original furnishings.

The Old Senate Chamber

OLD SENATE CHAMBER

The Senate occupied this room from 1810 until 1859, when the present Senate chamber was completed. The decor of the room, with its handsome gray marble Ionic columns and red-canopied dais surmounted by a gilt eagle, was much admired. More than the decorations, however, it was the senators' oratorical ability and the issues they debated on the eve of the Civil War that attracted overflow crowds to the chamber.

In *Democracy in America,* Alexis de Tocqueville reported that the Senate chamber "contains within a small space a large proportion of the celebrated men of America . . . eloquent advocates, distinguished generals, wise magistrates, and statesmen of note, whose arguments would do honor to the most remarkable parliamentary debates of Europe."

Senators Henry Clay, John C. Calhoun, Daniel Webster, and their colleagues provided an unparalleled source of entertainment and enlightenment, especially for society women. The galleries were so crowded that chivalrous senators sometimes gave their seats on the floor to the ladies. Senator Sam Houston distributed hearts he had whittled from pieces of pine, while others passed fruit tied to long sticks to the ladies in the galleries. Because of their frequent attendance, a third of the gallery was reserved for ladies, beginning in 1835.

In honor of the Bicentennial, the chamber was restored in 1976. The presiding officer's desk, the shield and eagle over the dais, and Rembrandt Peale's "porthole" *George Washington* directly above it (one of the finest works of art in the Capitol) are all original. The red carpet with gold stars, the mahogany desks with inkwells, sand shakers (to blot the ink), and ivory nameplates re-create the golden age of oratory represented in this small, historic room.

FOLGER SHAKESPEARE LIBRARY

201 East Capitol Street, S.E.
Washington, D.C. 20003
202/544-7077

METRO	Union Station or Capitol South.
HOURS	10 A.M. to 4 P.M. Monday through Saturday. Closed federal holidays.
TOURS	Walk-in tours 11 A.M. to 1 P.M. Monday through Friday. Group tours by appointment.
ADMISSION	Free.
HANDICAPPED FACILITIES	Parking and entrance at rear of building. Call security staff at 202/544-4600 for assistance.
MUSEUM SHOP	Folger Shakespeare Library publications, books, notecards, gift items with a Shakespearean theme.
SPECIAL EVENTS	Concerts by Folger Consort, resident early music ensemble; Evening Poetry Series, PEN/Faulkner fiction readings, Shakespeare's Birthday Open House, educational programs for schools, Folger Institute lectures.
SPECIAL FACILITIES	Reading rooms and research facilities open to persons with professional equivalent of a doctoral degree or a special need to refer to rare material.
MEMBERSHIP	Friends of the Folger Library membership from $100.
AUTHOR'S CHOICE	Great Hall exhibition gallery Elizabethan Theatre

The title page from the First Folio of 1623 with Martin Droeshaut's engraving of William Shakespeare

Perhaps it should be called the "Folger Renaissance Library." Although it contains the world's largest collection of the plays and poetry of William Shakespeare, the library also includes works by Shakespeare's contemporaries and volumes of social and political history, law and economics, science and geography. With approximately 280,000 books and manuscripts, nearly a third of which are considered rare, the Folger is an unparalleled source of information on life in England and western Europe in the sixteenth and seventeenth centuries. In addition, the library is a showcase of theater history, as revealed in theatrical prints, drawings, and paintings, and the promptbooks, costumes, and playbills of eighteenth- and nineteenth-century Shakespearean productions.

The Folger is much more than a collection of books and memorabilia, however. The library brings Shakespeare's world to life through a variety of seminars, symposia, lectures, and concerts that help to recapture some of the excitement of the period in which Shakespeare lived. Highlights of the collection are shown in special exhibitions year-round; the

Folger Consort, the library's resident early music ensemble, presents concerts each season; free lectures by visiting scholars are sponsored by the Folger Institute, and every April there is a Shakespeare's Birthday Open House, a free celebration featuring demonstrations and performances. Noted for its critical essays, the *Shakespeare Quarterly* has been published for over forty years. Educational programs range from Shakespeare performance festivals for students to a summer institute for high school teachers on innovative ways to teach Shakespeare.

HISTORY

In 1879, after hearing a lecture by Ralph Waldo Emerson during his senior year at Amherst College, and reading Emerson's essay on the tercentenary of Shakespeare's birth, Henry Clay Folger purchased a small edition of Shakespeare's works. Emerson's comment that "Shakespeare taught us that the little world of the heart is vaster, deeper, and richer than the spaces of astronomy" stuck a responsive chord with Folger, who spent many hours reading Shakespeare's plays and sonnets.

Folger was a tenth-generation descendant of Peter Folger, a schoolmaster and surveyor on Martha's Vineyard, who had emigrated from England to Massachusetts about 1635. (Peter Folger's daughter, Abiah, was Benjamin Franklin's mother.) After graduating from Amherst and Columbia University Law School, Folger—in true Horatio Alger style—progressed from clerk to president and, finally, to chairman of the board of directors of the Standard Oil Company of New York.

In 1885, he married Emily Jordan, a schoolteacher with a deep and abiding interest in literature. Soon after their marriage, he gave his bride a reduced facsimile of the 1623 First Folio edition of Shakespeare's works, which cost $1.25. She considered this "the cornerstone of the Shakespeare Library."

In 1889, Folger made his first major purchase, buying a Fourth Folio edition of 1685 for $107.50. Later, he acquired an outstanding Shakespeare collection when he purchased the library of the Earl of Warwick from a Rhode Island collector. Intrigued with the textual variations in different copies of the same play, as a result of alterations or errors made by printers, copyists, and actors, the Folgers began collecting different copies of the same edition for comparison. By 1930, they had acquired one-third of the approximately 240 First Folios known to exist. When Mrs. Folger obrtained a Master of Arts degree from Vassar College in 1896, her thesis, "The True Text of Shakespeare," was based on her study of various editions of Shakespeare's plays from the sixteenth to the nineteenth century.

The Folgers had no children and lived rather quietly in Brooklyn Heights, New York. They traveled to England eleven times to visit libraries and booksellers. As word of their scholarly interest spread, agents throughout the world kept them informed when sought-after volumes became available.

In 1904, they paid $10,000 for the library's rarest book, the only surviving quarto of *Titus Andronicus*, which had been found in a cottage in Sweden. (A quarto is a book made by twice folding a sheet of paper, or quartering it.) They also acquired a copy of the First Folio that the printer William Jaggard gave to his friend Augustine Vincent of the College of Heralds. In

1599, Vincent had helped Shakespeare's father, the mayor of Stratford-upon-Avon, acquire the family coat-of-arms. (It showed a silver falcon on a gold shield shaking a golden spear.)

As these treasures arrived, they were cataloged, packed, and stored in fireproof warehouses. With the collection growing, the Folgers decided to build a research library and considered various locations in both England and America. Mrs. Folger's fondness for Washington, where she had lived as a child during the Civil War (her father had been solicitor of the Treasury under President Lincoln), coupled with patriotic feelings about the nation's capital and its cultural development, led them to select a site on Capitol Hill.

In 1930, two years after Folger retired from Standard Oil, the cornerstone for the library was laid. He died two weeks later after a serious operation. President Herbert Hoover participated in the dedication of the building on the anniversary of Shakespeare's birthday, April 23, 1932.

Over two thousand boxes of books were taken out of storage, shipped to Washington, and unpacked, in a process that took six months. The library opened with seventy-five thousand books and thousands of prints, engravings, and manuscripts. Mrs. Folger supplemented the library's budget during the Depression and was actively involved in its operation until her death in 1936.

A private, nonprofit institution, the Folger Shakespeare Library is administered by the trustees of Amherst College.

The Folger Shakespeare Library

THE BUILDING

The building was designed by Paul P. Cret, architect of the OAS Building, and consulting architect Alexander Trowbridge. The neoclassical exterior of white Georgia marble is designed to blend with the surrounding federal buildings. Decorating the façade just below the windows are nine bas-reliefs by sculptor John Gregory depicting scenes from Shakespeare's plays.

In the garden, carved on the base of a statue of Puck, is a line from *A Midsummer Night's Dream*—"Lord, what fools these mortals be." The sculptor Brenda Putnam was the daughter of the librarian of Congress at the time.

If the exterior appears to be a bow to the architectural spirit of the 1930s, the interior of the building is vastly different. The great hall exhibition gallery, with its oak paneled walls, molded plaster ceiling, and carved Elizabethan doorways, is a re-creation of a Tudor long gallery.

At the west end of the great hall, toward the Capitol, is the shield and eagle of the United States. At the opposite end is the coat-of-arms of Shakespeare's queen, Elizabeth I. The tiled border on the floor connecting the two entrances is inscribed with the titles of Shakespeare's plays. In many ways, the library represents a link between this country and Shakespeare's.

Dominating one end of the Folger Reading Room is a bust of Shakespeare that is a copy of the one by Geraert Janssen in Trinity Church, Stratford-upon-Avon, where the Bard is buried. Frank O. Salisbury's portraits of the Folgers in their Amherst College honorary academic robes flank Shakespeare's bust. The Folgers' ashes are behind a memorial plaque here.

At the opposite end of the room, a stained glass window by Nicola D'Ascenzo pictures the seven ages of man, from infancy to old age, that Shakespeare described in *As You Like It*.

The Sedgwick-Bond Reading Room, which opened in 1982, adjoins the original reading room. While modern in design, it borrows from the Renaissance style.

One of the Folger's most unique features is its fully equipped theater. This little jewel is an adaptation of an outdoor Elizabethan theater, with comfortable seats instead of the pit where spectators stood in Shakespeare's day. The Shakespeare Theatre at the Folger and the Folger Consort perform here regularly. The theater is open to visitors during the same hours as the library, except during performances or rehearsals.

THE COLLECTIONS

Although the Folgers were interested primarily in the literary works of Shakespeare, the scope of the collection has far exceeded its original bounds. Six years after the library opened, the director, Joseph Quincy Adams, acquired nine thousand volumes from the collection of Sir Leicester Harmsworth. His rare books, printed in England between 1475 and 1640, focus on such subjects as history, economics, politics, science, law, and music. In 1937, on a visit to Harmsworth's widow, Adams found four hundred more early English books in a barn. The collector had purchased them just before his death, and his widow was unaware of their existence. The library acquired this collection, too.

Puck *by Brenda Putnam*

The Folger's next director, Louis B. Wright, added background materials published in England and Europe before 1800, as well as modern critical commentaries.

Director O. B. Hardison, Jr., continued in the same tradition, adding a special collection for the Reformation period. One priority of the library's present director, Werner Gundersheimer, is building the book acquisition endowment. The collection increasees by approximately fifteen hundred titles each year. Present holdings include about half of all of the known titles published in England or in English before 1640.

In addition, the collections include editions owned by Shakespearean actors Edmund Kean and David Garrick, and Walt Whitman's copy of the poems. Many other copies owned by authors, statesmen, and monarchs, including William Thackeray, Percy Bysshe Shelley, George Bernard Shaw, Presidents James Buchanan, Theodore Roosevelt, and Franklin D. Roosevelt, George III, Louis XIV, and Napoleon III, testify to the universal appeal of the man many people consider to be the world's greatest dramatist and poet.

LIBRARY OF CONGRESS

10 First Street, S.E.
Washington, D.C. 20540
202/707-5000
202/707-8000 recorded information

Please note: The Thomas Jefferson Building, the Main Reading Room, and the Coolidge Auditorium are closed for renovation and are scheduled to reopen in 1993.

METRO	Capitol South.
HOURS	*Exhibition halls* open 8:30 A.M. to 9:30 P.M. Monday through Friday, 8:30 A.M. to 6 P.M. Saturday, and 1 P.M. to 5 P.M. Sunday. *Reading rooms* open 8:30 A.M. to 9:30 P.M. Monday through Friday, 8:30 A.M. to 5 P.M. Saturday, and 1 P.M. to 5 P.M. Sunday. Closed legal holidays.
TOURS	10 A.M., 1 P.M., and 3 P.M. Monday through Friday from the lobby of the Madison Building. A 22-minute film, "Tour of the Library of Congress" runs continuously from 8:30 A.M. to 9:30 P.M. Monday through Friday, and from 8:30 A.M. to 6 P.M. Saturday and Sunday in Room 139, Madison Building. Group tours by appointment; call 202/707-5458.
ADMISSION	Free.
HANDICAPPED FACILITIES	Ramp at main entrance of each of the three buildings. Accessible to the disabled.
FOOD SERVICE	Cafeteria, Madison Building, sixth floor; snack bar on ground level.
GIFT SHOP	Library of Congress publications, postcards, recordings, slides, posters, and gift items.
SPECIAL EVENTS	Free chamber music concerts and literary programs. Free folk music performances on Neptune Plaza during spring and summer. Symposia, lectures, and exhibits year-round. Call 202/707-8000 for schedule of events and exhibitions.
SPECIAL FACILITIES	National Library Service for the Blind and Physically Handicapped provides reading material in large print, tape, and braille formats through selected libraries throughout the U.S.
AUTHOR'S CHOICE	The *Gutenberg Bible* The *Giant Bible of Mainz* Special exhibitions

Scholars, students, and visitors know the Library of Congress as the greatest storehouse of knowledge in the United States and one of the finest worldwide. Less well known, perhaps, is its role as the repository of fine prints and photographs, the owner of rare musical instruments, and the site of free chamber music concerts.

Each year since its founding in 1800, the library's holdings have grown through gifts, purchases, and copyright deposits.

Today, more than eighty-three million books, pamphlets, documents, newspapers, maps, motion pictures, microfilms, prints, and photographs are stored in its three-building complex. In addition to a legislative reference service for members of Congress, there is a law library and a music division that both commissions and presents live and recorded music.

When you visit the library, think of it as a multimedia encyclopedia divided into halls of knowledge.

HISTORY

As early as 1783, James Madison headed a Continental Congress committee to select a reference library for members of Congress. When some congressmen balked at spending money for books, Madison argued that it was "indispensable that Congress have at all times at command such authors on the law of nations, treaties and so forth. . . . It was regretted that the want of this information was manifested in several important acts of Congress."

The bill that provided for the capital to be moved to Washington in 1800 also called for the establishment of a congressional library. An appropriation of five thousand dollars was approved "for the purchase of such books as may be necessary for the use of Congress—and for putting up a suitable apartment for containing them therein." A case of maps and 740 books were purchased from Messrs. Cadell and Davies, London booksellers, and installed in the office of the clerk of the Senate in the Capitol. These volumes were burned, along with other House and Senate property, when the British set fire to the Capitol August 24, 1814.

Within a month, Thomas Jefferson, who was living in retirement at Monticello, offered to sell his personal library to the nation. Acquired during a period of fifty years, it was considered to be the finest library in the United States. While serving as American envoy to France, Jefferson had spent many hours browsing in Parisian bookstalls, "turning over every book with my own hands, putting by everythng which related to America, and indeed whatever was rare and valuable in every science." When he offered his library to Congress, Jefferson wrote, "I do not know that it contains any branch of science which Congress would wish to exclude from their collection; there is, in fact, no subject to which a Member of Congress may not have occasion to refer." After several months of debate, Jefferson's offer was accepted, and, in January 1815, Congress purchased his 6,487 books for $23,950.

THOMAS JEFFERSON BUILDING

The library remained in the rebuilt Capitol until 1897, when the Thomas Jefferson Building was opened across the Capitol Plaza. Built 1886-97, it was designed in Italian Renaissance style by two Washington architects, John L. Smithmeyer and Paul J. Pelz. (They also designed Georgetown University's Healy Building in 1879.) The aim was to create a showplace, not merely a functional library. New Hampshire granite was used for the exterior and fifteen kinds of marble grace the interior. Fifty American artists and twenty sculptors, ranging from Elihu Vedder to Daniel Chester French, embellished the building with works of art devoted to the twin themes of

The Gutenberg Bible

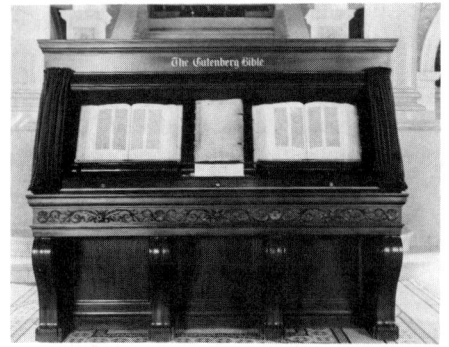

knowledge and learning. Sculptors turned unfinished rooms into studios where they carved bas-reliefs and other decorations.

The great hall is dominated by a series of broad marble columns, set off by mosaics, murals, stained glass, and sculpture. While the building is undergoing an $81.5 million renovation, two bibles that are usually displayed near the entrance to the main reading room, are now on view in the Madison Building. Among the library's rarest treasures, they are the *Gutenberg Bible* (1455), the first important book printed from movable metal type in the western world and the only perfect copy on vellum (a fine parchment made of animal skin) in the United States, and the *Giant Bible of Mainz*, an illuminated manuscript of 1452-53 also on vellum.

Unlike most national libraries, three-fourths of the collections are in foreign languages. Included, for example, are the world's largest printed encyclopedia, in 5,040 Chinese volumes, completed in 1726, and a fifteenth-century copy of the Book of Psalms in Hebrew, believed to be the first appearance in print of any part of the Hebrew bible.

Carefully preserved here are a draft of the Declaration of Independence bearing the hand written changes made by Thomas Jefferson; Abraham Lincoln's first drafts of his Gettysburg Address; the papers of twenty-three presidents, from George Washington to Calvin Coolidge, and the manuscripts of musical compositions by Ludwig van Beethoven, Johannes Brahms, Joseph Haydn, and Wolfgang Amadeus Mozart.

From the visitor's gallery, you can see the 160-foot-high main reading room, the heart of the library. Eight statues placed around the room symbolize "civilized life and thought." Daniel Chester French carved *History* holding a backward-looking mirror (as well as a bronze *Herodotus* on the upper balustrade). French is noted for his statue of *Abraham Lincoln* at the Lincoln Memorial. Augustus Saint-Gaudens created *Art*, a nude figure holding a model of the Parthenon, with an artist's palette and brushes beside her feet.

Forty-five thousand reference books are housed here, with desks that can accommodate 250 readers. A computer catalog center provides access to the automated catalog files. The library ceased to be the sole province of members of Congress in 1898, and now the resources of the library are available to all scholars and students over high school age. It is a research and reference library, however, not a lending library.

Special collections available in twenty reading rooms range from the archive of folk culture, children's literature, and

The Thomas Jefferson Building, Library of Congress

science to rare books, local history and genealogy, and foreign languages. On the ground floor, special exhibitions showcase items from the library's permanent collections.

When the renovation is completed in 1993, chamber music concerts will resume in the five-hundred-seat Coolidge Auditorium of the Thomas Jefferson Building. Rare Stradivarius and Guarnieri violins from the library's collections are frequently used by the artists who perform here.

JOHN ADAMS BUILDING

The simple lines of the John Adams Building at Second Street and Independence Avenue, S.E., contrast with the ornate style of the Thomas Jefferson Building. Completed in 1939, the façade is of white Georgia marble. Twelve historic figures credited with giving their people the tools for writing are depicted in bas-relief on the heavy bronze doors. They include Ts'ang Chieh, Chinese patron saint of pictographic letters; Cadmus, credited by ancient Greeks with inventing the alphabet, and Sequoyah, who invented the Cherokee alphabet and taught his people to read.

Special reading rooms devoted to science and social science, African, Asian, Hebraic, and Near Eastern studies are on the first and fifth floors. Murals of Chaucer's *The Canterbury Tales* enliven the fifth-floor reading room.

JAMES MADISON MEMORIAL BUILDING

The James Madison Memorial Building at First Street and Independence Avenue, S.E., more than doubled the library's space on Capitol Hill when it opened in 1980. It is the largest library building in the world. As the official memorial to the fourth president, it contains the James Madison Memorial Hall, exhibition space, eight reading rooms, offices, and storage for more than fifty million items in the library's special-format collections. Included here are the U.S. Office of Copyright, the Congressional Research Service, the law library, and the recorded sound reference center, as well as reading rooms for geography and maps; manuscripts; motion pictures and television; newspapers and current periodicals; performing arts, and prints and photographs.

All three buildings are connected by a series of underground pedestrian tunnels for the protection of the materials moved by staff from one building to another. The tunnels also contain conveyor belts for transferring books from one building to another. Electric book carriers in each building transport materials between floors. It usually takes less than an hour to serve a reader with a particular book.

James Madison, James Madison Building, Library of Congress

MARINE CORPS MUSEUM

**Washington Navy Yard
Building 58
Ninth and M Streets, S.E.
Washington, D.C. 20374
202/433-3267; 202/433-3534**

METRO	Eastern Market (fifteen-minute walk).
BUS	52, 54, 92, and 94.
HOURS	10 A.M. to 4 P.M. Monday through Saturday; Noon to 5 P.M. Sunday and holidays.
TOURS	Museum is self-guiding but group tours may be arranged.
ADMISSION	Free.
HANDICAPPED FACILITIES	Accessible to the disabled.
MUSEUM SHOP	Articles relating to the U.S. Marine Corps.
SPECIAL FACILITIES	Library, reference collection, archives, manuscripts, and oral history collections in U.S. Marine Corps Historical Center open to qualified researchers.
MEMBERSHIP	Marine Corps Historical Foundation from $25.
AUTHOR'S CHOICE	Flag raised on Iwo Jima Special exhibitions

The entire panorama of Marine Corps history, from the eighteenth century to the present, is revealed here in exhibits of uniforms, weapons, art, and documents. They convey a sense of the important role played by Marines throughout the world.

HISTORY
The Marine Corps Museum occupies the first floor of the Marine Corps Historical Center adjacent to Leutze Park. The building was constructed in the 1840s for use as a naval storehouse and a sail loft. From 1941 to 1975, it was a Marine barracks. The museum was established in 1960 at Quantico, Virginia, and moved to the Navy Yard in 1977. The exterior has been restored to its appearance at the turn of the century, while the interior has been renovated and converted into research and exhibit facilities and offices.

THE COLLECTIONS
Original art works by or about Marines, over six hundred personal papers relating to Marines, and an outstanding collection of military music are included in the collection. Of particular interest are music and memorabilia relating to John Philip Sousa, as well as research materials on the U.S. Marine Band and composers of martial music. These collections can be studied by interested researchers during normal working hours.

In addition, there are various study collections at the museum's ordnance and technology storage and exhibit facility at Quantico. Among the most interesting are the aircraft, tanks, artillery, and other equipment on display in the Air-Ground Museum. To view these exhibits, you must write or call the Officer-in-Charge, Marine Corps Museums Activities, Marine Corps Development and Education Command, Quantico, Virginia 22135, 202/640-2606, for an appointment.

TOURING THE MUSEUM
Turn to the right when you enter. Several historic flags and the guns used in support of landing forces are displayed in the entrance area. Exhibits proceed chronologically along one wall. On the opposite wall are documents, photographs, and artifacts devoted to the accomplishments of individual Marines.

MARINES IN THE REVOLUTION 1775–83
In 1775, the Second Continental Congress authorized two battalions of Marines for an amphibious landing force against the British at Halifax, Nova Scotia. Marines served on Continental ships throughout the Revolutionary War. On display are the commission of Captain Samuel Nicholas, a powder horn, uniform button, and cartridge pouch.

On the opposite wall, notice a 1779 recruitment ad for "a few good men," a phrase that has become synonymous with the Marine Corps.

MARINES AND THE FRIGATE NAVY
A separate Marine Corps was authorized by Congress July 11, 1798. By 1812, the corps numbered thirty-seven officers and 1,294 enlisted men. A private's pay was six silver dollars each month.

SECOND WAR OF INDEPENDENCE 1812–15
Muskets of the period, a uniform coat, and the muster roll of the Marine detachment at the Battle of Bladensburg are on view.

THE AGE OF ARCHIBALD HENDERSON 1816–59
Archibald Henderson, commandant of the Marine Corps from 1820 to 1859, established the place of the corps within the military system. A sword, similar to one seen here, was authorized in 1826, and is still worn by officers.

MEXICAN WAR 1846-48
The Marines, who fought in California and Mexico, raised the U.S. flag atop the former Mexican National Palace September 14, 1847. The exhibit includes a diagram showing the formation of landing boats on the Mexican coast. By May 1848, the corps was almost double its pre-war strength, with seventy-one officers and 2,170 enlisted men.

CIVIL WAR 1859–65
Marines captured abolitionist John Brown at Harper's Ferry October 16, 1859. Almost one-third of the Union Marines resigned and joined the Confederates, including nearly half of the captains and lieutenants. By 1865, there were seventy-eight officers and 3,177 men, with 460 known Marines killed.

FROM SAIL TO STEAM 1865–99
In addition to other duties, Marines took part in landings and interventions in Panama, Argentina, Chile, Formosa, the Bering Sea, China, Samoa, Egypt, and Hawaii during this period.

MARINES IN THE SPANISH-AMERICAN WAR 1898–99
The United States fought a war against Spain in 1898 over Spanish efforts to crush a Cuban war for independence. Americans were incensed by the blowing up of the battleship *Maine* in Havana harbor February 15, 1898. Weapons on display include a machete; the first automatic machine gun used by Marines, the six-millimeter M1895; the Colt-Browning M1895, and the first modern rifle, the six-millimeter Lee M1895.

MARINES IN THE FAR EAST
Marines served in the Far East from the Boxer Rebellion in 1900 until America's entry into World War II.

MARINES IN THE CARIBBEAN 1899–1934
Marines landed and sometimes stayed in Nicaragua, Panama, Honduras, the Dominican Republic, Cuba, Mexico, and Haiti. This experience helped to form the basis for the corps' knowledge of jungle and counter-guerilla tactics.

WORLD WAR I 1917–18
Marines served in France, both on the ground and in the sky, with the U.S. Navy bombing group. The exhibit includes uniforms and other items of Marine aviation, captured German weapons and equipment, and a woman Marine's hat. For the first time, women served at headquarters during World War I.

PREPARATION FOR AMPHIBIOUS WAR 1898–1941
Amphibious warfare was planned during the 1920s and 30s. In 1940, there were 1,556 officers and 26,369 enlisted men.

WORLD WAR II DEFENSE AND COUNTERATTACK 1941–44
Marines participated in some of the bloodiest fighting of the war in the Pacific, from the landing at Guadalcanal through the battles of the Solomon Islands and New Britain. Notice the bugle that was used to sound the call to arms at the Marine Barracks during the attack on Pearl Harbor December 7, 1941.

WORLD WAR II . . . VICTORY 1943–45
A Japanese Samurai sword and flag help to recall the fighting on Tarawa, Guam, Saipan, and Tinian. Also here is the U.S. flag that was raised after Marine victories at New Britain, Palau Island, and Okinawa.

EVOLUTION OF VERTICAL ENVELOPMENT 1946–65
Marine helicopters were first used in the Korean War.

KOREAN WAR 1950–53
You can see some of the modern body armor that was used in Korea, and the U.S. flag that was raised at Wolmi-Do Island, the key to the Inchon landing.

FORCE IN READINESS 1954–65
Cuba, Vietnam, the Dominican Republic, Guatemala, Taiwan, and Mexico are among the places Marines went in humanitarian or contingency roles. An M14 rifle and an M60 machine gun, the first new weapons since World War II, are on view, together with items from the 1962 Cuban missile crisis.

VIETNAM WAR 1965–71
Marines were the first to arrive in Vietnam in the winter of 1964–65. Captured enemy weapons, Marine uniforms, and equipment used in Vietnam are on display. By 1971, the corps numbered 24,994 officers and 289,423 enlisted men.

CONTINGENCY OPERATIONS 1972–76
At various times, Marines were deployed in Vietnam, the Mediterranean Sea, Cyprus, and Cambodia. On the wall opposite this exhibit you can see the brass bell from the *S.S. Mayaguez*, which was recaptured from the Cambodians in May 1975. Since the Vietnam War, the Marine Corps has numbered approximately 19,000 officers and 177,000 enlisted men.

THE MARINE CORPS TODAY
This exhibit describes the organization of the corps today, with three combat divisions, three aircraft wings, and the U.S. Marine Corps Reserve.

SPECIAL EXHIBITIONS
Special exhibitions are devoted to such topics as the current "Marines in Operation Desert Storm." The story of the war in Iraq is told graphically through the use of maps, photographs, artifacts, paintings, and drawings. A statement of General Alfred M. Gray, commandant of the U.S. Marine Corps, sums up the spirit of the corps: "There are four kinds of Marines: those in Saudi Arabia, those going to Saudi Arabia, those who want to go to Saudi Arabia, and those who don't want to go but are going anyway." Look for the U.S. and Marine Corps flags that were flown at Kuwait International Airport February 27, 1991.

MARINES IN MINIATURE 1800–1918
Meticulously detailed miniature dioramas depict some of the most decisive events in Marine Corps history. Included are the capture of the privateer, *Sandwich,* May 11, 1800; action off Tripoli harbor, August 3, 1804; the attack on Derna April 27, 1805; Marines at Bladensburg August 24, 1814; the first into Mexico City September 13, 1847; the capture of John Brown October 18, 1859; Sergeant Quick at Cuzco Well June 14, 1898, and Sergeant Dan Daly at Belleau Wood June 10, 1918.

HISTORIC FLAGS
As you leave the museum, notice two U.S. flags that marked significant moments in World War II—the first flag raised at Suribachi and the famous flag that flew over Iwo Jima. There is also a small scale model of Felix de Weldon's *Iwo Jima* statue, which was based on Joe Rosenthal's Pulitzer Prize-winning photograph.

NAVY MUSEUM

**Washington Navy Yard
Building 76
Washington, D.C. 20374
202/433-2651**

METRO	Eastern Market (fifteen-minute walk).
HOURS	September through May: 9 A.M. to 4 P.M. Monday through Friday; June through August: 9 A.M. to 5 P.M. Monday through Friday; 10 A.M. to 5 P.M. weekends and holidays. Closed New Year's Day, Thanksgiving, Christmas Eve, and Christmas Day.
TOURS	Free tours available Monday through Friday; walk-in and pre-arranged school programs available.
ADMISSION	Free.
HANDICAPPED FACILITIES	Accessible to the disabled.
FOOD SERVICE	Officers club open to the public.
MUSEUM SHOP	Books, models, prints, naval memorabilia. Open 9:30 A.M. to 3:30 P.M. Monday through Friday; 10:30 A.M. to 4:30 P.M. Saturday and Sunday.
SPECIAL EVENTS	Annual fall festival (October).
AUTHOR'S CHOICE	Fighting top from the frigate *Constitution* Gunmounts from World War II fighting ships Submarine room

Located in the historic Washington Navy Yard, this is the only museum in the country that focuses exclusively on the two-hundred-year history of the U.S. Navy from the Revolutionary War era to the present. In addition to depicting the navy's role in wartime, exhibits present such peacetime pursuits as exploration, diplomacy, navigation, space flight, and humanitarian service.

HISTORY
The history of the Navy Museum is intertwined with that of the Washington Navy Yard.
  Approved by Congress in 1799, the Navy Yard was the first land acquired by the U.S. Navy and its oldest establishment onshore. It was created originally to construct forty-four-gun frigates to protect American ships from post-Revolutionary War attacks by Barbary pirates and other threats to merchantmen.
  Benjamin Henry Latrobe, architect of the White House and the Capitol, was the architect for the Navy Yard. The one-story entrance gate and the flanking gatehouses he designed in 1804 at Ninth and M Streets, S.E., are among the earliest examples of Greek Revival architecture in the United States. Larger, Victorian-style guardhouses were added in the 1880s. The Latrobe Gate is the country's oldest continuously manned U.S. Marine sentry post.

Captain Thomas Tingey, the first commandant of the shipyard, was in charge when British troops occupied Washington in 1814. Tingey was ordered to burn the yard to keep it from falling into enemy hands. The sawmill, rigging loft, paint shops, and timber sheds, as well as the new frigate *Columbia* and the sloop of war *Argus*, were put to the torch. Only Tingey's own house—a handsome Federal structure built in 1804—was saved from the flames. Strong winds spread the fire to nearby homes, whose residents looted Tingey's house in revenge. Tingey House, originally the home of Washington Navy Yard commandants, is now the official residence of the Chief of Naval Operations.

Before the War of 1812, the Navy Yard was the largest shipbuilding facility in the nation, but its importance as a shipbuilding center declined after the war. Manufacturing weapons replaced shipbuilding as the primary function of the yard, with the first ordnance facility established in 1820. John Dahlgren began to design and manufacture new naval guns in 1847, and he continued his weapons research as commandant of the yard during the Civil War.

During World War I, the navy's first sixteen-inch guns and the fourteen-inch naval railway batteries that were used in France were manufactured here. During World War II, the yard became the largest naval armament plant in the world.

The yard has also played an important role in developing new technology. Its "firsts" include the first marine railway, built here in 1822; the first shipboard catapult, constructed in 1912, and the first navy wind tunnel, built in 1916. In 1898, David W. Taylor built a model basin here to study the effect of water on ships' hulls.

The yard also serves as a ceremonial gateway to the nation's capital.

In 1961, Admiral Arleigh Burke, the Chief of Naval Operations, recommended the establishment of a navy museum. The location selected was Building 76, the six-hundred-foot-long Breech Mechanism Shop of the old Naval Gun Factory. The northern section of the building, constructed in 1887, and the southern portion, which dates from 1899, provided forty thousand square feet of display space. The museum opened in 1963 and is now part of the Naval Historical Center, which includes a library, archives, and other research facilities.

Embroidered seabag, circa 1842-62

THE COLLECTION

The collection includes more than five thousand artifacts, ranging from Revolutionary War swords to space-age mementoes. It includes ship models, weapons, uniforms, tools, and documents that commemorate the navy's role in aeronautics, ordnance, electronics, exploration, marine engineering, navigation, oceanography, and space flight.

Twenty-six eighteenth- and nineteenth-century bronze guns that were captured in various battles, as well as a collection of iron guns that date from the Civil War era, are displayed outdoors near the museum. Also outdoors are a six-inch gun from the battleship *Maine*, sunk in Havana Harbor at the beginning of the Spanish-American War; the antenna from the navy's first shipboard radar; a 1950s Navy Regulus missile, and more than sixty other weapons and naval hardware that are too large to be accommodated in the museum.

The destroyer *Barry* (DD-933) is moored at the dock in front of the museum. Commissioned in 1956, the ship saw service in the Cuban quarantine and the Vietnam War before being decommissioned in 1982. The ship, which is open to the public, is permanently berthed here.

TOURING THE MUSEUM

Exhibits to the right of the entrance are arranged chronologically; those on the left are thematic. All exhibits are on ground level.

Destroyer U.S.S. Barry (DD-933)

A replica of the fully rigged fighting top from the frigate *Constitution* dominates the center of the museum, and scale models of such ships as the navy's first post-Civil War steel monitor, *Miantonomoh*; the two-masted schooner *Shark*, and the aircraft carrier U.S.S. *Forrestal* are placed at intervals throughout the hall. A complete collection of U.S. Navy decorations and awards is displayed in glass cases near the center of the building.

The museum shop, near the entrance, is housed in the former pilot house of the Naval Militia Drill Hall in Brooklyn.

THE AMERICAN REVOLUTION

In a series of exhibits dealing with the Revolutionary War, a model of the twenty-six-gun frigate *La Flore* recalls the support provided by France after the 1778 Treaty of Alliance.

The achievements of John Paul Jones, commander of the *Bonhomme Richard*, are commemorated here. When the commander of the larger, better armed British ship *Serapis* demanded his surrender after a fierce battle, Jones replied with the often-quoted words, "I have not yet begun to fight."

A weathered timber with rusty, hand-hewn nails from one of the galleys that served General Benedict Arnold on Lake Champlain, is on display. The ship was sunk in battle in October 1776.

THE FORGOTTEN WARS OF THE NINETEENTH CENTURY

The Quasi War with France, an undeclared naval war, was fought primarily in the West Indies from 1798 to 1801. Captain Thomas Truxtun commanded the thirty-eight-gun frigate *Constitution*, which won the name of "Old Ironsides" when cannon balls bounced off its hull. The ship, now berthed in Boston harbor, also saw service in the Barbary Wars and the War of 1812 and is the oldest commissioned navy ship afloat. A scale model is on display here.

After 1775, the American colonies were no longer protected by Great Britain. The attacks by Barbary pirates that had led to the establishment of the U.S. Navy in 1798 escalated when the pasha of Tripoli declared war in 1801. American Navy vessels were sent to the Mediterranean, and the *Constitution*, under the command of Commodore Edward Preble, established a blockade of the Barbary coast that helped to end the war in 1805. On view here is Stephen Decatur's certificate of membership in the Society of the Cincinnati, signed by George Washington. Decatur built his home on Lafayette Square with prize money won by fighting the Barbary pirates.

One of the most interesting documents in the museum is a letter from John Paul Jones to John Jay, the minister of foreign affairs, written in August 1785. Jones reports that the Algerians have declared war on the United States. Copies of the letter were sent on several different ships in order to be sure that the message would arrive safely.

In the early nineteenth century, when flogging with a cat-o-nine-tails was a customary naval punishment, American seamen were frequently taken from their ships and pressed into service in the British Navy. By June 1812, when the United States declared war on Great Britain, ten thousand Americans had been taken against their will to serve in the Royal Navy. The burning of Washington on August 24, 1814, climaxed a two-year campaign in the Chesapeake Bay during the War of 1812.

THE MEXICAN WAR, THE CIVIL WAR, AND THE SPANISH-AMERICAN WAR

An exhibit on the Mexican War, 1846 to 1848, points out that the war served as a training ground for Civil War leaders. Bowie knives, shells, rifle bullets, engravings, and other artifacts recall the naval blockade of the South during the Civil War. Also featured is a model of the U.S.S. *Hartford*, the flagship of Admiral Farragut, who said, "Damn the torpedoes, full speed ahead."

Various commemorative items recall the Spanish-American War in 1898, including Admiral Dewey's gold presentation sword and a fruit bowl and silver tray from the battleship *Maine*, whose sinking in Havana harbor ignited the war.

WORLD WAR I

Exhibits depict the anti-submarine warfare, mine warfare, and naval aviation of the first World War.

A mine that is typical of those used in the North Sea mine barrage, when approximately fifty-seven thousand mines were laid, is displayed here.

WORLD WAR II

By pushing a button on a vintage radio, you can hear President Franklin D. Roosevelt's speech to Congress on December 8, 1941, the day after the bombing of Pearl Harbor. More than sixty million Americans—the largest audience in the history of radio—heard Roosevelt call for a declaration of war against Japan.

Among the most popular artifacts in the museum are the bridge from the U.S.S. *Fletcher* and the forty-millimeter quadruple gunmount, an anti-aircraft weapon from the U.S.S. *South Dakota*, which visitors are permitted to climb on and touch.

The largest exhibition of its kind, "In Harm's Way" is a comprehensive look at the role of the U.S. Navy in World War II. Divided in two sections, "In Harm's Way" allows the visitor to follow both the war in the Atlantic and the war in the Pacific. A highlight of the Atlantic story is a German Enigma machine and a uniform of a beachmaster worn during the invasion of Normandy.

UNDERSEA EXPLORATION

This section presents an overview of the history of diving and exploration. It is dedicated to the memory of Robert D. Stethem, a member of the U.S. Navy's underwater construction team who was killed by a terrorist on a TWA plane in Beirut in 1985.

Dioramas show that men tried to invent a diving apparatus as early as the sixteenth century.

SPACE
The exhibit devoted to navy astronauts includes the space suit worn by Captain John W. Young on the Apollo 16 flight in April 1972.

VIETNAM
Artifacts of the Vietnam War include medals, a field medicine kit, a mine, and submachine guns captured from the Viet Cong. Two metal sensors, each resembling a tree with four branches, were dropped by U.S. aircraft to detect the movement of enemy supplies and equipment. Also of interest are artifacts from prisoner of war camps, including a chess set whose pieces are made of stale bread, ink, and painted toothpaste.

BRITISH-AMERICAN COOPERATION
This exhibit, focusing on the special relationship between Great Britain and the United States, shows how Americans have adopted many of the practices, customs, and traditions of the British Navy.

A portrait of British Admiral Edward Vernon recalls that he obtained a midshipman's warrant for fourteen-year-old George Washington. Only his mother's objections kept Washington from entering the Royal Navy. His older brother, Lawrence, served under Vernon in the Caribbean and named his estate Mount Vernon in honor of his former commander.

Don't miss the cutaway model of a 120-gun ship of 1750. It is complete, down to the miniature maps, chairs, tables, crates, and ballast. The builder spent two thousand hours during a three-year period making the ship model.

Also worth noting are a collection of watercolors of Lord Nelson's ships, painted by a retired navy commander, and a 1781 hand-colored print of the battle of the *Bonhomme Richard* and the *Serapis*, which can be seen through the lens of a perspective glass, an early three-dimensional device.

UNIQUE SHIP MODELS
The models include a *Chan Chuan*, a fifteenth-century Chinese ship; a late sixteenth-century Korean "tortoise" boat whose upper deck is covered with spiked iron plates to prevent boarding; a Greek trireme of the fifth century B.C., and a mid-nineteenth-century fantasy galleon crafted of German silver.

NAVAL ELECTRONICS
This exhibit covers the history of shipboard radio communications, from its inception in 1899 to 1963, when messages were first transmitted by satellite. You can see how sonar is used for underwater ranging, depth sounding, and detection. You can also learn how radar indicates an object's range and direction through pulses of radio energy beamed from its antenna.

NAVIGATION
Some of the earliest devices for celestial navigation are on display. They include a mariner's astrolabe, an octant, and a sextant that date from the sixteenth and seventeenth centuries. A collection of nineteenth-century ship chronometers is also on view.

POLAR EXPLORATION
The North and South Poles have long held a special fascination for explorers. Polar exploration and discovery are chronicled here, from the first American exploring expedition of 1838-42 led by Lieutenant Charles Wilkes, through the Greely expedition of 1881-84, the Scott expeditions of 1901-04 and 1910-13 and Commander Robert E. Peary's trek to the North Pole in 1909.

Among the historic artifacts and photographs that document the navy's role in exploring the vast, frozen Arctic and Antarctic are a model of the *Bear*, one of the ships that sailed in the Greely expedition, and the special paper and wood prefabricated hut in which Rear Admiral Richard E. Byrd lived for seven months during his second expedition to Antarctica, 1933-35.

COMMODORE PERRY AND JAPAN
A collection of nineteenth-century Japanese woodblock prints shows such scenes as a procession of foreigners at Yokohama, an American steamboat, and foreign ships anchored in Yokohama harbor.

One of the most interesting objects is a large broadside that features a picture of Commodore Perry and a poem in Japanese. Also on view is a model of a sidewheel steamer, *Powhatan*, Perry's flagship when he negotiated the treaty opening Japan to U.S. trade in 1854. *Powhatan* carried the treaty back to the United States in 1856 after a two-year voyage from Japan.

THE *CONSTITUTION*: "OLD IRONSIDES"
In addition to seeing the fighting top of the historic *Constitution*, you can walk through a replica of the gun deck of "Old Ironsides" and visualize the excitement as cannons were loaded in this cramped, low-ceilinged space.

A unique object on display is a 650-pound careening block that was used before drydocks were invented. Blocks such as this one enabled sailors to pull a ship down on its side in order to clean the bottom of the hull.

TEMPORARY EXHIBITIONS
Temporary exhibitions are presented in this space to the left of the entrance. Various themes are depicted, such as a recent show devoted to the Battle of Midway in June 1942, the turning point for the Japanese in World War II.

SUBMARINES
A submarine room has been re-created, with working periscopes, steering wheels, torpedo data computers, and submarine memorabilia. You can peer into the periscopes and imagine that you are deep below the surface of the ocean in a U.S. Navy submarine.

SEWALL-BELMONT HOUSE

**144 Constitution Avenue, N.E.
Washington, D.C. 20002
202/546-3989**

METRO	Union Station or Capitol South.
HOURS	10 A.M. to 3 P.M. Tuesday through Friday; Noon to 4 P.M. Saturday and Sunday.
TOURS	Upon arrival. Group tours by appointment.
ADMISSION	Free.
MUSEUM SHOP	Books, publications, and items related to women's suffrage.
MEMBERSHIP	National Woman's Party membership from $15.
AUTHOR'S CHOICE	Women's suffrage memorabilia

Inside this red brick, Federal building, headquarters of the National Woman's Party, issues have been debated ranging from the Louisiana Purchase and the Treaty of Ghent to women's suffrage and the Equal Rights Amendment.

HISTORY

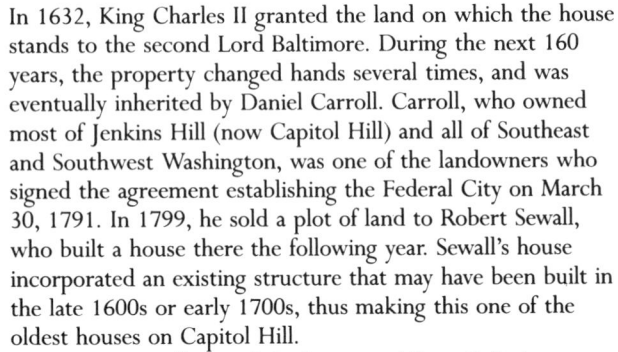

In 1632, King Charles II granted the land on which the house stands to the second Lord Baltimore. During the next 160 years, the property changed hands several times, and was eventually inherited by Daniel Carroll. Carroll, who owned most of Jenkins Hill (now Capitol Hill) and all of Southeast and Southwest Washington, was one of the landowners who signed the agreement establishing the Federal City on March 30, 1791. In 1799, he sold a plot of land to Robert Sewall, who built a house there the following year. Sewall's house incorporated an existing structure that may have been built in the late 1600s or early 1700s, thus making this one of the oldest houses on Capitol Hill.

In 1801, Sewall rented the house to Albert Gallatin, secretary of the treasury under Presidents Thomas Jefferson and James Madison. Gallatin, who remained as a tenant until 1813, was one of the few cabinet officers who chose to live near the Capitol, rather than the White House. And, instead of taking a lengthy carriage ride to his office every day, Gallatin conducted much of his business at home. Reportedly, financial details of the Louisiana Purchase, which nearly doubled the size of the United States, were negotiated here. Gallatin also may have conducted some of the preliminary negotiations for the Treaty of Ghent in this house. (The treaty was signed by President Madison at the Octagon in 1815.)

In 1814, American patriots in or near the house reportedly fired on British troops during the War of 1812, and the house was damaged by fire when the British retaliated.

The Sewall family owned the house for 123 years. Sewall's granddaughter married Senator John Strode Barbour of Virginia, and the house became a lively social center late in the

Alice Paul, founder of the National Woman's Party

nineteenth century. Vermont Senator Porter Dale purchased it in 1921 and restored the house and gardens.

In 1929, the National Woman's Party bought the property and renamed it the Alva Belmont House in honor of Mrs. Oliver H. P. Belmont, its major benefactor. From 1922 to 1929, the organization had been headquartered in the Old Brick Capitol, where Congress met for four years after the British burned the Capitol (on the site of the present Supreme Court Building).

Alice Paul, who founded the National Woman's Party and wrote the Equal Rights Amendment in 1923, lived and worked here. The house memorializes her efforts—and those of her colleagues—to gain the vote for women.

In the 1950s, there was talk of replacing the building with a parking lot. The building was saved by President Dwight D. Eisenhower and others who recognized its significance as the only remaining house in the United States with historic ties to the women's suffrage movement. In 1974, the Sewall-Belmont House, renamed to reflect its origins, was declared a National Historic Site. It is jointly maintained by the National Woman's Party and the National Park Service.

TOURING THE MUSEUM

The house combines a variety of architectural styles, reflecting the changes wrought by nearly two hundred years of occupancy. F. Morris Leisening of the American Institute of Architects has called it an "interesting example of the development of architecture in the District of Columbia ... from the primitive type of colonial farm house through the Georgian, the Early American, the Federal, Classic Revival, Victorian, and French Mansard periods."

The Sewall-Belmont House

One detail worth noting is the "peacock fan" stained glass window above the front door, installed by the Sewall family. The two silver-hinged doors leading to the living room and the drawing room reportedly came from Daniel Webster's home and were purchased by Senator Dale before the Webster house was razed.

The house is filled with portraits, statuary, memorabilia relating to feminism, and furnishings contributed by members. Portraits of prominent women hang in every room. Marble busts of Susan B. Anthony, Lucretia Mott, Elizabeth Cady Stanton, and Alice Paul line the entrance hall. Alva Belmont's furniture is in the living room and her china is in the dining room. The Victorian furniture in the parlor where Gallatin hammered out the Louisiana Purchase was contributed by publisher William Randolph Hearst in memory of his mother.

On the first floor, Paul's former office contains a rolltop desk formerly owned by Susan B. Anthony, Paul's table-desk, and Henry Clay's desk, which had been in the Old Brick Capitol. Also on the first floor, you can see the kitchen, which is in the oldest part of the house. Now modernized with a refrigerator and microwave oven, it still includes an enormous brick fireplace with a space above it where gunpowder was reportedly stored to keep it dry.

Paul's bedroom and two guest bedrooms can be seen on the second floor. Paul, who was approximately four feet, eight inches tall, needed a stool to reach her high, four-poster bed.

*The Great Hall of the
National Building
Museum*

DOWNTOWN

NATIONAL ARCHIVES

Eighth Street and Constitution Avenue, N.W.
Washington, D.C. 20408
202/501-5000 schedule information
202/501-5400 research information

METRO — Gallery Place, Federal Triangle, or Archives.

HOURS — April 1 through Labor Day: 10 A.M. to 9 P.M. daily; After Labor Day through March 31: 10 A.M. to 5:30 P.M. daily for exhibitions. Closed Christmas Day. *Central Research and Microfilm Research Rooms* open 8:45 A.M. to 10 P.M. Monday through Friday; 8:45 A.M. to 5:15 P.M. Saturday. Closed federal holidays.

TOURS — 10:15 A.M. and 1:15 P.M. Monday through Friday by appointment only. Call 202/501-5205.

ADMISSION — Free.

HANDICAPPED FACILITIES — Accessible to the disabled. Ramp entrance at Eighth Street and Pennsylvania Avenue.

GIFT SHOP — Books, prints, posters, games, facsimiles of documents, and souvenirs.

SPECIAL EVENTS — Free noontime and evening films and lecture series.

AUTHOR'S CHOICE — Declaration of Independence, Constitution, and Bill of Rights, rotunda

The nation's most precious documents are preserved in this neoclassical granite-and-limestone building, along with millions of letters, reports, maps, architectural drawings, films, photographs, and other official government records.

HISTORY
The need for preservation of the nation's records was recognized more than two hundred years ago. Thomas Jefferson warned that "Time and accident are committing daily havoc on the originals deposited in our public offices." After a series of disastrous fires, the National Archives was finally established in 1934.

The entire history of the United States unfolds here, with some documents written as early as 1774. Best known are the great charters—the Declaration of Independence, the Constitution, and the Bill of Rights—which are on permanent display. But this is also the repository for such papers as the Louisiana Purchase Treaty signed by Napoleon Bonaparte; the Japanese surrender document that ended World War II, and the manifests of ships that brought immigrants to America.

Although only those federal records judged to have historical value—approximately one to two percent—are kept each year, the total is now enormous. In addition to billions of pages of documents, there are over six million still photos, including Mathew Brady's Civil War pictures; nearly 112,000 reels of motion picture film, comprising documentaries, newsreels, and combat films; over 187,000 sound and video recordings of congressional hearings, Supreme Court arguments, and the Nuremberg trials; census records from 1790 to 1910, and nearly twelve million maps, charts, and aerial photographs.

The National Archives also publishes the Federal Register, a daily record of government regulations; operates nine presidential libraries, and maintains twelve field branches and fourteen records centers throughout the country.

THE BUILDING

John Russell Pope, architect of the National Gallery of Art and the Jefferson Memorial, designed the building. President Herbert Hoover laid the cornerstone in 1933, and the building was completed four years later. Because the Archives Building was erected on marshy Tiber Creek, it was necessary to drive more than eighty-five hundred concrete piles twenty-one feet into the ground to support the structure.

The focal point of the ground floor is a vast rotunda that soars seventy-five feet above the ground. The Declaration of Independence, the Constitution, and the Bill of Rights are enshrined here, surrounded by exhibits that document the struggle for independence and a democratic government.

On your left is a mural, *The Declaration of Independence*, by Barry Faulkner, showing twenty-eight delegates to the Continental Congress of 1776. A companion piece on the right wall, Faulkner's version of *The Constitution*, depicts George Washington and twenty-four other delegates to the Constitutional Convention.

Temporary exhibits are located in the circular gallery to the left of the Constitution Avenue lobby. The Pennsylvania Avenue entrance on the opposite side of the building leads to the research areas where visitors may conduct historical or genealogical research.

The National Archives Building

EXHIBITS

Throughout much of the nineteenth century, the Declaration of Independence was displayed in the Old Executive Office Building, formerly the State, War, and Navy Building. Beginning in 1924, both the Declaration and the Constitution were exhibited at the Library of Congress. Since 1952, they have been on view here in special helium-filled glass and bronze cases that keep out dust, excess moisture, and pollutants. Filters over the documents protect them from harmful light rays. Each evening the documents are lowered electrically about twenty feet into a fifty-five-ton vault made of steel and reinforced concrete.

FORD'S THEATRE

511 Tenth Street, N.W.
Washington, D.C. 20004
202/426-6924
202/426-1749 TDD for hearing-impaired visitors

METRO	Metro Center, Eleventh Street Exit.
HOURS	9 A.M. to 5 P.M. daily, except during rehearsals and performances. Closed Christmas Day.
TALKS	On the history of the theater and the assassination twice an hour, unless stage work, matinee performances, or rehearsals prevent use of the theater.
ADMISSION	Free.
HANDICAPPED FACILITIES	Ramp to lobby of theater but no access to museum without using staircase. Video of museum exhibits available in lobby. Sign language tours available upon request. Visually impaired visitors may be escorted into the presidential box if a National Park Service ranger is available.
MUSEUM SHOP	Books relating to Abraham Lincoln and the Civil War; copies of Lincoln speeches.
SPECIAL EVENTS	Lectures and special walking tours presented throughout the year.
AUTHOR'S CHOICE	The clothing President Lincoln wore when he was killed John Wilkes Booth's pistol Booth's diary

Ford's Theatre

Five days after General Robert E. Lee's surrender at Appomattox, when the Civil War was finally winding down, President and Mrs. Lincoln planned an evening at the theater.

The play was *Our American Cousin*, starring Laura Keene. The date was April 14, 1865. The place was Ford's Theatre. And the rest, as they say, is history.

John Wilkes Booth, an actor and Confederate sympathizer, had originally planned to kidnap the president and exchange him for Confederate prisoners of war. The kidnap plan failed, and Booth decided on assassination instead.

Booth slipped into the theater during the performance and watched the president through a peephole in the door of Box 7. At a predetermined moment during the third act, he shot the president and jumped to the stage, catching the spur of his boot in the flag that was draped across the box and breaking his leg. Limping across the stage, Booth shouted, "Sic Semper Tyrannis" ("Thus always to tyrants").

The president was carried to William Petersen's house across the street and died the following morning. Meanwhile, Booth, who had dashed through the stage door and escaped on horseback, made his way into the southern Maryland countryside. He was found twelve days later hiding in a barn, and was captured and shot. Eight of Booth's accomplices were tried by a military tribunal and found guilty.

THE BUILDING

Ford's Theatre was built in 1863 to replace Ford's Atheneum, which had been destroyed by fire the previous year. The War Department closed it immediately after the assassination. Although impresario John T. Ford wanted to reopen two months later, the public outcry made it impossible, and the theater remained closed. The government leased and then bought the building to use as a center for processing Union Army records and as the site of the Army Medical Museum after its conversion into a three-story office building and warehouse. In 1893, all three floors collapsed, killing twenty-two government workers and injuring sixty-eight. In 1932, the Oldroyd Collection of Lincolniana was installed in a small museum on the ground floor.

As early as 1947, there was talk of restoring the theater to its original condition. Not until the 1960s, however, did Congress appropriate funds for an architectural study of the building, and in 1964, approved full restoration at a cost of more than $2 million. By researching period newspapers, photographs, sketches, and drawings, the furnishings were faithfully reproduced, down to the wallpaper and the furniture in the presidential box.

Original sofa in the box occupied by President Abraham Lincoln April 14, 1865

The flag-draped, upper righthand stage box was occupied by President and Mrs. Lincoln and their guests, Major Henry Rathbone and his fiancée, Clara Harris, on the night of the assassination. You can see the original red damask sofa on which Major Rathbone was seated. A reproduction of the rocker used by President Lincoln, which John Ford brought from his own home for the president, is near the front of the box. Next to it are copies of Mrs. Lincoln's straight-backed chair and the upholstered one used by Harris.

The building reopened as a theater February 13, 1968. The National Park Servcice administers Ford's Theatre, the Lincoln Museum, and the House Where Lincoln Died. The Ford's Theatre Society is responsible for theatrical performances.

THE LINCOLN MUSEUM

The museum reopened in June 1990 after a two-year renovation. The history of Ford's Theatre and the Lincoln assassination are revealed in nearly four hundred artifacts and graphics.

The exhibits are divided into seven sections, beginning with the assassination and its aftermath, which focuses on the events of April 14-15, 1865, at Ford's Theatre and the Petersen House.

Display cases devoted to the accused show the conspirators,

their trial and punishment, with items used as evidence in their trial included.

Lincoln's funerals in Washington and other cities, and the funeral train which carried his body to Springfield, Illinois, for burial are depicted in another exhibit. This is followed by a display that reveals the tension and chaos of Lincoln's presidency and attempts to show why Booth shot Lincoln.

Mourning badges, photographs, paintings, prints, and statuary depict the Lincoln legacy. And Lincoln's life in Washington is interpreted through objects from the White House.

In the final section of the exhibit, you can see original playbills, graphics, tickets, and posters that depict the history of the building, its restoration, and current use as a theater. Here are the single-shot Deringer pistol Booth used to kill the president, the diary he kept while he was in hiding, and knives owned by his fellow conspirators. In addition, you can see Dr. Samuel Mudd's medical kit and Booth's boot, which Dr. Mudd slit in order to set Booth's broken leg.

The tailcoat, overcoat, and boots the president wore the night he was shot are in a glass case nearby.

Some of the items in the museum were originally in the Osborn H. Oldroyd Collection. In 1860, Oldroyd, a resident of Mount Vernon, Ohio, read a booklet about President-elect Lincoln. He was so impressed with Lincoln that he decided to collect everything he could relating to the president.

After serving in the Union Army during the Civil War, Oldroyd moved to Springfield, Illinois, where he leased the former Lincoln home and, in 1883, displayed his collection there. Four years later, Robert Lincoln, son of the slain president, presented the Springfield home to Illinois for a museum. The collection remained in the house until 1893, when Oldroyd moved to Washington.

Finding the Petersen House vacant, Oldroyd rented the building and installed his museum there on October 17, 1893. The federal government purchased the Petersen House in 1896 and acquired the Oldroyd Collection in 1926. The collection, numbering more than three thousand items, was moved to Ford's Theatre. It opened to the public on Lincoln's birthday, February 12, 1932, as the forerunner of the present Lincoln Museum.

After visiting the museum, cross the street to see the Petersen House where Lincoln died.

NATIONAL BUILDING MUSEUM

401 F Street, N.W.
Washington, D.C. 20001
202/272-2440

METRO	Judiciary Square, F Street Exit (across the street).
HOURS	10 A.M. to 4 P.M. Monday through Saturday; Noon to 4 P.M. Sunday. Closed Thanksgiving, Christmas, and New Year's Day.
TOURS	12:30 P.M. Monday through Friday; 12:30 P.M. and 1:30 P.M. Saturday and Sunday. Group tours by appointment. Write or call 202/272-2448.
ADMISSION	Free.
HANDICAPPED FACILITIES	Ramp entrance on Fifth Street.
MUSEUM SHOP	Books, posters, games, souvenirs, and objects of good design related to building.
SPECIAL EVENTS	Lectures, films, and lunchtime concert series.
MEMBERSHIP	From $25.
AUTHOR'S CHOICE	The Great Hall "An Architectural Wonder: The U.S. Pension Building"

The National Building Museum, dedicated to the glorification of the building arts in America, is housed, appropriately, in a structure that is itself a monument to the building arts. Adapted from an Italian Renaissance palace plan, it is one of the most astonishing—and historic—buildings in Washington.

HISTORY

So many veterans were entitled to pensions after the Civil War that the Pension Bureau soon grew to a work force of fifteen hundred. General Montgomery C. Meigs, the retired quartermaster general of the Union army, was commissioned to design a building to house the agency. Designed in 1881, it was built during a five-year period from 1882 to 1887. The budget-conscious Meigs accounted for every penny of the building's $886,614.04 cost.

The 1885 inaugural ball of President Grover Cleveland took place in the partially completed building. Since then, twelve other balls have been held here, celebrating the inaugurations of Presidents Harrison, McKinley, Theodore Roosevelt, Taft, Nixon, Carter, Reagan, and Bush.

The Pension Bureau occupied the building until 1926. Various other government tenants followed, including the General Accounting Office and the Civil Service Commission.

In 1980, Congress approved a National Building Museum to commemorate and encourage the building arts. It appropriated $2.56 million to clean and restore the Pension Building's exterior and Great Hall, and to create an auditorium and several exhibition galleries. The museum opened in 1985. Although the federal government provides space for the museum free of charge, a private nonprofit group is responsible for operating it.

THE BUILDING

A cream-colored terracotta frieze of Union army veterans in seemingly endless procession encircles the exterior. Designed by the sculptor Caspar Buberl, it is three feet high and twelve hundred feet long. Meigs, who lost a son in the war, considered the frieze a tribute to all those who have given their lives for an ideal.

Detail of the 1,200-foot frieze encircling the Pension Building

Bricklayers, paid four dollars an hour, were hired from as far away as Philadelphia to ensure the finest workmanship. More than fifteen million bricks were used to construct the building and the mortar, colored to match the bricks, is almost invisible.

The visual impact of the Great Hall is intensified by entering through a dimly lit vestibule that gives no hint of the splendors to come. It is a bit like the first surprising glimpse of the Taj Mahal after you pass through its dark tunnel-like entrance area.

The colors of the Great Hall—lime-green and rose-beige—are historically correct. Meigs believed that "bright colors can set off good architecture when they adorn and emphasize it instead of concealing it." He envisioned a park-like setting here but lacked the funds to fulfill his plans. The twenty-eight-foot fountain basin in the center was restored in 1980.

Meigs was impressed by the architecture of the sixteenth-century Farnese palace and the ruins of the baths of Diocletian in Rome, which he had visited during a European trip. He adapted the Farnese's central courtyard and arcaded loggia with interconnecting rooms, and added Corinthian columns based on—although considerably larger than—Diocletian's. The result is a Great Hall of staggering proportions—316 feet long and 116 feet wide. Its 159-foot height is the equivalent of a fifteen-story building. No wonder architect Philip Johnson has called this "the most astonishing interior space in America."

Meigs, an engineer who designed Washington's water system and collaborated with Thomas U. Walter on the Capitol's iron dome, broke all records for size with the eight Corinthian columns in the center of the hall. They are eight feet in diameter and seventy-five feet high—larger than the columns in the Roman temple of Baalbek, built in the first century A.D. and, until the Pension Building, the biggest columns in the world. Each one is constructed of seventy thousand bricks. In 1895, the columns were painted to resemble Siena marble, and their bases and capitals were given the appearance of bronze. The columns were painted over in 1951 but restored in 1984.

Seventy-two Doric columns of terracotta covered with cement, each thirteen feet high, grace the first floor arcade. The next arcade is lined with seventy-two cast iron Ionic columns, eleven feet high. On the third floor, seventy-six gilded terracotta urns with eagle-head handles, copies of the original urns, surround the parapet.

High above, Meigs placed 244 portrait busts in niches below the cornice. Meigs's original plan—to use life-size busts of prominent Americans—was scrapped because he could not find enough of them. Instead, he used the Smithsonian collection of life casts of American Indians. The plaster casts were removed in 1911.

Replacing the portrait busts was a major goal of the 1985 restoration. To reflect the new role of the Pension Building, Washington sculptor Gretta Bader modeled eight heads of men and women, representing those who have devoted their lives to creating the built environment of America.

Concerned about workers' health and a proponent of fresh air, Meigs conceived a novel plan to increase the flow of air throughout the building. He created air vents under each window sill. This allowed the air—hot in summer, cold in winter—to waft through the office cubicles, into the Great Hall and out the windows in the upper stories.

The historic Pension Building, home of the National Building Museum

THE EXHIBITIONS

"An Architectural Wonder: The U.S. Pension Building," on permanent display, explains the history, architecture, and construction of this historic building. An audiovisual program narrated by television host David Brinkley, "Meet the Architect: General Montgomery C. Meigs," provides a helpful introduction to the exhibition and to the building itself.

"Washington: Symbol and City," describes how Washington has evolved as a symbol to the nation and the world and as home to more than 650,000 people. The exhibition, featuring hands-on activities, large-scale models, drawings, and artifacts, serves as an orientation to visitors to the nation's capital, illustrating the history of the monuments and the city during the past two hundred years. It includes two historic models created by the Senate Park Commission in 1901 showing the Mall and downtown at the turn of the century and the commission's plans for the Mall's development.

NATIONAL MUSEUM OF AMERICAN ART

Eighth and G Streets, N.W.
Washington, D.C. 20560
202/357-2700

METRO	Gallery Place, Ninth Street Exit; Metro Center, Eleventh Street Exit.
HOURS	10 A.M. to 5:30 P.M. daily. Closed Christmas Day.
TOURS	Walk-in tours Noon Monday through Friday; 2 P.M. Saturday and Sunday; group tours by appointment. Call 202/357-3111.
ADMISSION	Free.
HANDICAPPED FACILITIES	Ramp entrance at Ninth and G Streets. Accessible to the disabled.
FOOD SERVICE	Patent Pending restaurant, first floor, open 11 A.M. to 3 P.M. daily.
MUSEUM SHOP	Art books, exhibition catalogs, slides, postcards, posters and reproductions.
SPECIAL EVENTS	Lectures, symposia, concerts, and other public programs in conjunction with exhibitions. Call 202/357-2700 or 202/357-3095 for information.
RESEARCH RESOURCES	*Inventory of American Paintings Executed Before 1914*; *Pre-1877 Art Exhibition Catalogue Index*; *Peter A. Juley and Son Collection* of 127,000 photographic negatives from 1896 to 1975; *Smithsonian Art Index*; *Inventory of American Sculpture, Slide, and Photographic Archives*; *Joseph Cornell Study Center*; and 80,000-volume library shared with the National Portrait Gallery. Graphic arts study room open by appointment; call 202/357-2593.
MEMBERSHIP	Smithsonian Associates
AUTHOR'S CHOICE	Thomas Hart Benton mural, first floor *Throne of the Third Heaven* by James Hampton, first floor American landscapes and impressionism, second floor

The National Museum of American Art, the oldest federal art collection in the United States, has had several different names but only one purpose—to collect and exhibit American art from the eighteenth century to the present.

HISTORY

As early as 1829, an enterprising Washingtonian named John Varden had begun collecting specimens of natural history, historical relics, coins, pictures, and miscellaneous works of art that he planned to exhibit in the nation's capital. An 1836 advertisement for the "Washington Museum, John Varden Proprietor" announced that his collection of between four hundred and five hundred specimens was now open to the public in specially built rooms at the corner of John Marshall Place and D Street, near City Hall.

In 1841, the Varden Collection was incorporated into a similar collection of the National Institute, which had been organized the previous year. These collections were displayed in the Patent Office Building.

The art and artifacts of the first national museum were displayed in galleries on the third floor (now the Lincoln Gallery) alongside glass cases containing thousands of patent models. Visitors could see paintings and sculptures, as well as the original Declaration of Independence (now at the National Archives), George Washington's commission as commander-in-chief of the Continental Army (now at the Library of Congress), and Benjamin Franklin's printing press (now at the National Museum of American History).

In 1858, the historic and scientific objects in the government's collection were transferred to the Smithsonian Institution. And in 1862, the National Institute's art collection, including the Varden Collection, also became part of the Smithsonian. The museum was known as the National Gallery of Art from 1906 until 1937, when the name was given to the Andrew W. Mellon collection. Its next incarnation was as the National Collection of Fine Arts. This lasted until October 1980, when Congress and the president approved the current, more accurate name, the National Museum of American Art (NMAA).

The Renwick Gallery, on Pennsylvania Avenue at Seventeenth Street, N.W., is a curatorial department of the National Museum of American Art, and the Smithsonian acquired Barney Studio House on Sheridan Circle for the NMAA in 1960.

THE BUILDING

The Old Patent Office Building, housing both the National Museum of American Art and the National Portrait Gallery, is the fourth oldest public building in Washington. Only the White House, the Capitol, and the Treasury building are older. In 1796, when Pierre Charles L'Enfant designed the city of Washington, he envisioned a pantheon, a building that would honor the nation's heroes, at this location, midway between the White House and the Capitol.

When the Patent Office was created in 1790, Secretary of State Thomas Jefferson personally examined every patent application. His standards were so rigid that only three patents were granted during the first year. In 1836, nearly fifty years and seven thousand patents later, the Patent Office Building was destroyed by fire. William Parker Elliot's Greek Revival design for a new building—whose porticoes are said to be exact reproductions of the Parthenon in Athens—was quickly approved by Congress. President Andrew Jackson appointed Robert Mills, architect of the Washington Monument, to supervise the construction, and the Patent Office was installed in the South Wing on F Street upon its completion in 1840. Nearly thirty years elapsed before the other three wings were completed, in 1867. At the time, it was the largest building in the country.

Only American materials were used in the building's construction. The sandstone came from the Aquia Creek quarries in Virginia, originally owned by George Washington. The marble was quarried in Baltimore County, and the granite came from Maine, Massachusetts, Connecticut, and Maryland.

The building had all the latest amenities, including marble-topped washstands and a cuspidor-sterilizing plant. And a guidebook of the period called the Patent Office Building "one of the greatest ornaments of the city."

The building's functions have gone far beyond the original intention of granting patents, collecting patent models, and displaying museum collections. During the Civil War, it was a makeshift barracks, hospital, and morgue. The First Rhode Island Militia was quartered in the north wing, "with a laundress and three ladies who utterly refused to be left at home." After the battles of Second Bull Run, Antietam, and Fredericksburg, two thousand beds were placed between the glass display cases and in the gallery above the exhibition hall. Clara Barton, founder of the Red Cross and a Patent Office copyist, nursed wounded soldiers here. And poet Walt Whitman came to "soothe and relieve" the wounded by reading his poetry to them.

Near the end of the Civil War, on March 6, 1865, the Patent Office Building, complete except for the north portico, was the site of President Lincoln's second inaugural ball. The event was a benefit for families of Union Army soldiers. A $10 entrance fee entitled any gentleman to bring one or more ladies, and over four thousand guests attended the gala event. Guests walked through the south portico and up the curving double staircase to the great exhibition hall with its vaulted ceiling. After admiring the frescoes and Pompeiian-style tiles, the guests proceeded to the eastern hall. Now called the Lincoln Gallery, this hall runs the entire length of the block between F and G Streets.

In later years, as the government's need for office space grew, the Department of the Interior and the Civil Service Commission were housed here. In the 1950s, after those agencies had moved into their own buildings and the Patent Office had been installed in a wing of the Department of Commerce building, the building was slated to be razed and replaced with a parking garage. President Dwight D. Eisenhower was among those who opposed the plan and helped to save the historic building, which was eventually given to the Smithsonian Institution. After extensive renovation and restoration, the Old Patent Office Building reopened in 1968 as a showcase of America's cultural heritage.

THE COLLECTION

The museum presents a panoramic view of the history of American art, from the colonial era to today. Since 1968, the collections have more than quintupled and now include more than thirty-five thousand paintings, sculptures, folk art, prints, drawings, photographs, and crafts.

The works begin with such colonial-era masters as Charles Willson Peale, Benjamin West, and John Singleton Copley. Among the nineteenth-century holdings are eighteen oils by Albert Pinkham Ryder, the largest collection in the country; Impressionist works by Mary Cassatt, Childe Hassam, and John Twachtman; the contents of Hiram Powers's sculpture studio in Florence; a large Thomas Wilmer Dewing collection, and a comprehensive selection of works by American artists who worked abroad. Major paintings by portrait painter John Singer Sargent and landscape artists Albert Bierstadt, Thomas Cole, George Inness, Frederic Church, and Thomas Moran are also included, as are figure subjects by Winslow Homer and Eastman Johnson.

Twentieth-century artists Romaine Brooks, William H. Johnson, Morris Kantor, Man Ray, and Paul Manship are represented in depth. The museum has the largest collection in the United States of the art of the 1930s, especially works produced under various federal art programs during the Depression. Works by artists William Baziotes, Adolph Gottlieb, Franz Kline, and Clyfford Still represent the New York School. And representatives of the Washington Color School include Gene Davis, Morris Louis, Leon Berkowitz, and Kenneth Noland.

The NMAA's graphics department began in 1966 with noted artist Jacob Kainen as curator. Its holdings include more than twenty-two thousand prints, drawings, and photographs. Among these are major collections of prints by Howard Norton Cook, Werner Drewes, Louis Lozowick, and J. Alden Weir; and works by contemporary artists, such as Jim Dine, Helen Frankenthaler, and Robert Rauschenberg. In 1983, with the transfer of photographs from the National Endowment for the Arts, the museum began a collection of contemporary photography.

In recent years, significant gifts—the Martha Jackson Memorial Collection, the S.C. Johnson Collection, the Sara Roby Foundation Collection, the Container Corporation of America Collection, the Patricia and Phillip Frost Collection, and the Herbert Waide Hemphill, Jr., Collection of American Folk Art, as well as gifts from individual artists and collectors—have added major works to the museum's collection of twentieth-century art.

Una, Lady Troubridge by Romaine Brooks

The collection shows the evolution of American art through the past two-and-a-half centuries. The historical sequence is flexible, however, so that in certain cases groupings are based on subject matter or other considerations.

LOBBY AND COURTYARD

FIRST FLOOR

An information desk is near the main (G Street) entrance. Nearby is *Achelous and Hercules*, a 1947 mural by Thomas Hart Benton, originally commissioned by Harzfeld's department store in Kansas City. To the right are print study rooms, a corridor where graphic arts are displayed, and the Granite Gallery for special exhibitions.

Sculpture is installed in the tree-shaded courtyard, with Alexander Calder's *Nenuphar* and Bryan Hunt's *Stillscape I* and *Stillscape II* featured.

HAMPTON THRONE

To the left of the lobby is James Hampton's *The Throne of the Third Heaven of the Nations' Millennium General Assembly*, a remarkable room-size work with 177 glittering objects sheathed in aluminum and gold foil. Robert Hughes of *Time* Magazine called this possibly "the finest work of visionary religious art produced by an American." Hampton, the son of a black gospel singer and an itinerant preacher, was a janitor for the General Services Administration for nearly twenty years until his death in 1964. He worked on the *Throne* every night in an unheated, poorly lit garage, believing that God visited him there to guide his hand. Using discarded materials—old furniture, cardboard, bottles, burnt-out light bulbs, aluminum and gold foil—he fashioned intricately designed objects, including some which suggest a throne, pulpits, and offertory tables. Objects on the left refer to the New Testament, Jesus, and Grace; those on the right, to the Old Testament, Moses, and Law.

FOLK ART
A selection of nineteenth- and twentieth-century folk art is displayed in first-floor corridors and galleries, reflecting the inventiveness of people from diverse geographic, ethnic, religious, political, and economic backgrounds. Particularly featured are works from the recently acquired Herbert Waide Hemphill, Jr., Collection. Among the objects on view are bottlecap animals, carvings, memory and genre paintings, trade signs, decorative arts, visionary and political paintings, and sculpture.

ART OF THE WEST
In the gallery on the right at the end of the corridor, America's fascination with the West is evident in a compelling work by Charles Bird King, *Young Omahaw, War Eagle, Little Missouri, and Pawnees* and a 1907 oil painting, *Fired On*, by Frederic Remington. Although best-known today as a sculptor of cowboys and Indians, Remington was also an illustrator and painter. He prophetically wrote his friend, novelist Owen Wister, "My water colors will fade but I am to endure in bronze."

Paintings of Indians by John Mix Stanley and George Ctalin hang in the corridor leading to the cafeteria. (The museum owns 459 paintings by Catlin.)

Ju-ah-kis-gaw, Woman With Her Child in a Cradle *by George Catlin*

After seeing a delegation of Indians on their way to discuss a treaty in Washington, Catlin was so impressed by their dignity that he decided to devote his life to recording the Indian way of life. Catlin gave up his law practice to become a portrait painter in Philadelphia. He gained the Indians' confidence and, with the help of General William Clark, governor of the Missouri Territory, and other friends in Washington, traveled throughout the Great Plains for six years. Catlin captured the mood and character of Indian chiefs on canvas, in addition to faithfully reproducing the costumes, homes, and tribal rituals of forty-eight Indian tribes. His books, lectures, and paintings preserved information about Indian customs that might otherwise have been lost.

SECOND FLOOR

LOUNGE
To the right of the elevator, three monumental works by Thomas Moran—*The Chasm of the Colorado* and two views of *The Grand Canyon of the Yellowstone*—epitomize the flowering of

American landscape painting. Moran was a member of the nineteenth-century Hudson River School of landscape painters who followed William Cullen Bryant's advice to "Go forth, under the open sky, and list to Nature's teachings."

Included among a large group of paintings by other Hudson River School artists is Thomas Cole's *The Subsiding of the Waters of the Deluge*.

In the corridor to the left of the elevator, works of nineteenth-century artists are on view. These include two elegant portraits by John Singer Sargent—*Elizabeth Winthrop Chanler* in a black dress and *Betty Wertheimer* in red.

ALBERT PINKHAM RYDER

Albert Pinkham Ryder was both America's last great romantic painter and its first modern expressionist, inspiring generations of artists with the power of his nocturnal marines and idyllic landscapes. With his eccentric and experimental techniques, he was the most revolutionary American artist of his time. His paintings include the brooding and mysterious *With Sloping Mast and Dipping Prow*, *Flying Dutchman*, and *Jonah*. Other major works in these galleries include Eastman Johnson's *The Girl I Left Behind Me*, Albert Bierstadt's *Among the Sierra Nevada Mountains, California*, and Frederic Church's *Aurora Borealis*.

NINETEENTH-CENTURY AFRICAN-AMERICAN ART

With more than fifteen hundred African-American works by over a hundred black artists, ranging from early portraiture to contemporary art, the collection is the largest in any general museum. This second floor gallery includes sculpture by Edmonia Lewis and paintings by Edward Mitchell Bannister, Robert Scott Duncanson, and Henry Ossawa Tanner. In a third floor gallery are works by such twentieth-century artists as William H. Johnson, Jacob Lawrence, Palmer Hayden, and Lois Mailou Jones.

LATE NINETEENTH CENTURY

A monumental plaster, *The Falling Gladiator* by William Rimmer, stands next to Abbott Handerson Thayer's *Stevenson Memorial*. Be sure to see Thomas Eakins's masterful *William Rush's Model*.

Among Hiram Powers's classically inspired works displayed here are *Eve Tempted* and *The Greek Slave*. When *The Greek Slave*, a statue of a nude, was exhibited at the Corcoran Gallery of

The Stevenson Memorial *by Abbott Handerson Thayer*

Art around 1880, there were separate visiting hours for men and women, and no one under sixteen was admitted.

Mrs. James Smith and Grandson *by Charles Willson Peale*

TURN-OF-THE-CENTURY
Paintings by turn-of-the-century artists, such as Thomas Wilmer Dewing's *The Spinet*, *Summer*, and *Lady in White* and Maria Oakey Dewing's *Garden in May* are here.

Don't miss James McNeill Whistler's *Valparaiso Harbor* in the corridor. Whistler painted this gray and turquoise scene during a visit to Chile in 1866. Whistler's *Head of a Young Woman* (2L) was executed nearly twenty-five years later, around 1890. Also in these galleries is a charming, small sculpture of *Narcissa* by Daniel Chester French, which contrasts sharply with his brooding *Abraham Lincoln* in the Lincoln Memorial. Abbott Henderson Thayer is represented by a surprisingly contemporary *Flower Studies*.

AMERICAN IMPRESSIONISTS
Turn right at the end of the corridor to see Mary Cassatt's *The Caress*, a 1902 painting of a mother and two children. Also here are John Henry Twachtman's snowy, impressionistic landscape *Round Hill Road* (1890–1900), Childe Hassam's sun-dappled *South Ledges, Appledore* (1913), and William Merritt Chase's evocative *Shinnecock Hills* (1895).

EARLY AMERICAN ART
To the right of the lounge area, selections from the permanent collection include the classically inspired *Helen Brought to Paris*, painted in 1776 by Benjamin West, as well as West's *Self-Portrait* and his portrait of *Mary Hopkinson*. Nearby, a meticulously detailed *Still Life With Fruit* by Severin Roesen is reminiscent of a seventeenth-century Dutch painting.

The galleries also contain fine examples of colonial portraiture—particularly *Mrs. Lucy Parry* by John Wollaston, one of the earliest American portrait artists, and *Mrs. James Smith and Grandson* by Charles Willson Peale.

Among the early American portraits in the next room are Gilbert Stuart's *Portrait of a Lady*; *Edward Shippen Burd of Philadelphia*, painted by Rembrandt Peale, son of Charles Willson Peale, and two 1835 portraits of *Georgianna Frances Adams* and *Mary Louisa Adams* by Asher Brown Durand.

THIRD FLOOR

The third floor is devoted to the permanent collection of twentieth-century American art and to special exhibitions. Special exhibitions are mounted in galleries to the right of the elevator; the permanent collection is displayed to the left.

S.C. JOHNSON AND FROST GALLERIES

Pre-war abstraction, surrealism, and paintings from the Federal Art Projects are the focus of these galleries. Among the works are Ralston Crawford's *Buffalo Grain Elevators*, Yasuo Kuniyoshi's *Strong Woman and Child*, Theodore Roszak's *Construction in White*, and Reginald Marsh's *George Tilyou's Steeplechase*. From the museum's rich holdings of the Federal Art Projects are Douglass Crockwell's *Paper Workers*, Pedro Cervantez's *Los Privados*, and Edward Hopper's *Ryder's House*. Jackson Pollock's *Going West*—a gift to the museum from Pollock's teacher, Thomas Hart Benton—also hangs in these galleries.

Paper Workers *by Douglass Crockwell*

THE LINCOLN GALLERY

Architect Philip Johnson has called this gallery, which measures 264 feet by 63 feet, "the greatest room in America." Designed by Robert Mills as an exhibition gallery for the Patent Office, it was completed in 1852. The Lincoln Gallery (so-called because it was the site of President Lincoln's second inaugural reception) is the only area on the third floor that retains its original architectural features, with thirty-two marble pillars and a twenty-eight-foot-high vaulted ceiling.

Highlights of modern American art on display include:
- Hans Hofmann's *Fermented Soil*
- Isamu Noguchi's *Grey Sun*
- Robert Rauschenberg's mixed media *Reservoir*
- Gene Davis's *Raspberry Icicle*
- Franz Kline's *Merce C.*
- Andrew Wyeth's *Dodges Ridge*
- Larry Rivers's *The Athlete's Dream*
- Frederick Brown's *Stagger Lee*
- Helen Frankenthaler's *Small's Paradise*

Ryder's House *by Edward Hopper*

NATIONAL MUSEUM OF WOMEN IN THE ARTS

1250 New York Avenue, N.W.
Washington, D.C. 20005
202/783-5000

METRO	Metro Center, 13th Street Exit.
HOURS	10 A.M. to 5 P.M. Monday through Saturday; Noon to 5 P.M. Sunday.
TOURS	Walk-in tours Noon and 2 P.M. Monday through Saturday. Group tours available.
ADMISSION	Free; voluntary contributions suggested.
HANDICAPPED FACILITIES	Ramp at entrance. Elevator to all floors. Wheelchairs available.
FOOD SERVICE	Palette Café on the mezzanine level open 11:30 A.M. to 3 P.M. Monday through Friday.
MUSEUM SHOP	Books relating to women artists, posters, reproductions, gift items.
SPECIAL EVENTS	Concerts, lectures, seminars, and films.
SPECIAL FACILITIES	Library and research center with monographs, reference books, exhibition catalogs and information on women artists open 9 A.M. to 5 P.M. Monday through Friday.
MEMBERSHIP	From $25.
AUTHOR'S CHOICE	*Lady With a Bowl of Violets* by Lilla Cabot Perry, ground floor *Portrait of a Noblewoman* by Lavinia Fontana, third floor *Portrait of a Young Boy* by Elisabeth Vigée-Lebrun, third floor Botanical prints by Maria Sibylla Merian, third floor

The National Museum of Women in the Arts

The National Museum of Women in the Arts, located several blocks from the White House, is the only institution in the country whose primary purpose is to celebrate the achievements of women artists. Ironically, it is housed in a landmark building that was formerly an all-male bastion.

HISTORY
In 1965, Washington collector Wilhelmina "Billie" Holladay and her husband were touring Europe. At the State Museum in Vienna, they admired a still life composed of a pair of goblets, some gold coins, and a spray of tulips, painted in 1594 by Clara Peeters. The following week at the Prado in Madrid, they found other Peeters paintings. Back in Washington and eager to learn more about this artist whose work they admired, Mrs. Holladay consulted various reference works and found that Peeters was not included. And neither was Mary Cassatt or any other well-known woman artist. H. W. Janson's *History of Art*, a standard art history book, failed to mention

any woman artist. (Not until the third edition, in 1986, were women included in the Janson text.)

At that point, the Holladays decided to focus on women artists in building their collection. As the collection grew, the idea of establishing a museum was suggested to them by the late Nancy Hanks, former chairman of the National Endowment for the Arts, and other arts administrators. The museum was incorporated in 1981 and fundraising began. A building was purchased in 1983. By the time the museum opened in April 1987, there were over seventy-two thousand members and more than fifteen million dollars had been raised from individuals and corporations.

The idea of a museum devoted exclusively to women artists has aroused a certain amount of controversy in art circles. Some people believe that segregating art according to sex, race, or any other nonartistic factor detracts from the work itself. Museums should simply show the best works.

On the other hand, supporters of the National Museum of Women in the Arts, recognizing that women are under represented in museum collections, see this museum as a means of encouraging greater awareness of the role of women in the arts and of the contributions women have made to the history of art. According to Mrs. Holladay, "As people are exposed to great art by women, they will develop a richer understanding and appreciation of the contributions women have made throughout the course of history."

Traditionally, women painters have been the relatives of male artists, working alongside their better known fathers, husbands, and brothers. Women artists flourished during the Renaissance, serving popes and princes. Later, however, they were not admitted to art schools and were forced to study at home. In the sixteenth and seventeenth centuries, Lavinia Fontana, Elisabetta Sirani, and Charlotte Mercier were among those trained by their fathers. Fontana, a sixteenth-century artist who executed many church commissions, supported her husband and eleven children with her painting. Sirani carried on her father's work from the time he was crippled by arthritis until her death, presumably by poisoning, at age twenty-seven.

Virgin and Child *by Elisabetta Sirani*

Since women were not admitted to art schools, they were forced to study art at home, often concentrating on such subjects as portraiture and still life. Filial duty led many women to copy their father's styles, sometimes signing his name to their work. They also made engravings or miniature copies of their relatives' works. Frequently, a daughter even married her father's most promising student and continued to assist her father in his studio.

Not until 1897 were women admitted to the École des Beaux-Arts in Paris, although their work had been accepted in the annual Salons des Beaux-Arts beginning in the 1790s. Certain women artists, such as Mary Cassatt and Berthe Morisot, did not have a financial need to sell their paintings, so art works created by women were often kept in the family and not seen publicly.

Ironies abound. Although Angelica Kauffmann was a founder of England's Royal Academy of Art, she was not permitted to exhibit her paintings there because she was a woman. But the Academy permitted her portrait—painted by a male artist—to be shown.

THE BUILDING

Completed in 1911, the building at the intersection of New York Avenue, Thirteenth, and H Streets, was designed as a Masonic temple by Waddy B. Wood, architect of the Textile Museum and the Woodrow Wilson House. The aim of the Renaissance Revival design was to create a structure "of great dignity and simplicity and entirely in keeping with the classic public buildings for which Washington is well known." With seventy thousand square feet of space and sixteen-foot-high ceilings, it originally housed meeting rooms, archives, and offices of the Masonic order.

In the early 1980s, a movie theater operated on the ground floor of the building. In 1983, the Masons sold the property to the National Museum of Women in the Arts for $4.8 million. In an $8 million renovation, the Washington architectural firm of Keyes Condon Florance converted the interior into galleries, offices, a library and research center, and a two-hundred-seat auditorium for lectures and concerts.

THE COLLECTION

The collection spans five centuries, from the sixteenth to the twentieth, and includes over twelve hundred paintings, prints, drawings, sculptures, and pottery by nearly four hundred artists from twenty-eight countries. Included are approximately three hundred works donated by the Holladays, which form the nucleus of the permanent collection.

In addition to loan exhibitions and shows drawn from the museum's permanent collection, the work of regional artists is exhibited periodically.

There are no galleries on the ground floor. Selections from the permanent collection can be seen on the third floor. Temporary exhibitions and part of the permanent collection are on the second floor. The library is on the fourth floor and the auditorium is on the fifth floor.

GROUND FLOOR

On entering the building, visitors sometimes feel that they have entered a palace instead of a museum—an impression created by the three sparkling crystal chandeliers, plush fabric walls, marble floors, and staircase in the Martin Marietta Hall. Hanging on the far wall, near the entrance to the museum shop, is Lilla Cabot Perry's *Lady With a Bowl of Violets*.

THIRD FLOOR

The gallery to the right of the elevator usually displays works on paper, including *Alligator Pears in a Basket*, a charcoal drawing by Georgia O'Keeffe; Sonia Terk Delaunay's colorful gouache, *Study for Portugal*, and Helen Frankenthaler's *Ponti*. Also in this gallery are a bronze sculpture, *The Farewell*, and a bronze relief, *Rest in His Hands*, by Kathe Kollwitz.

A remarkable collection of hand-colored engravings by Maria Sibylla Merian is generally on view in an adjoining gallery. The prints illustrated a 1719 book, *Dissertation in Insect Generations and Metamorphosis in Surinam*, by Merian, an artist and naturalist. Born in Germany in 1647, Merian spent two years in Surinam, a Dutch colony in South America, studying insect life. As a result of her observations, Merian disproved the then-common theory that insects emerged spontaneously from dirt and mud. Her pioneering engravings, which show the life cycle of plants and insects in graphic detail, became the model for later zoological and botanical illustration.

The next gallery to the right contains some of the earliest paintings in the collection, including Lavinia Fontana's *Portrait of a Noblewoman*, painted in 1580, Clara Peeters's *Still Life of Fish and Cat*, and *Flowers in a Vase* by Rachel Ruysch.

A few of the works of Hester Bateman and other notable women silversmiths are also on view here. Objects include a delicately crafted cake basket, teapot, and saltcellars.

As you move on to the next gallery, notice Marie Laurencin's *Portrait of a Girl in a Hat*, a self-portrait that was once owned by writer Gertrude Stein.

Nineteenth-century art is featured in the gallery across the hall. Included here are *The Cage* by Berthe Morisot, Mary Cassatt's pastel *Study of Reine*, Rosa Bonheur's *Sheep by the Sea*, Cecilia Beaux's portrait of Ethel Page, and Lilla Cabot Perry's *Lady in Evening Dress*. Perry helped to introduce Impressionism into the United States when she brought to Boston a painting by Claude Monet, whom she had met while studying art in Paris in 1889. For the next ten years, Perry spent her summers with her family in Giverny, where Monet, a close friend, regularly critiqued her work.

Contemporary art is displayed in the next gallery. Included are Joan Mitchell's *Dirty Snow*, Anne Truitt's sculpture, *Summer Day*, *Bacchus #3* by Elaine Fried de Kooning, *Rheo* by Nancy Graves and two radiant paintings by Alma Thomas, the colorful *Iris, Tulips, Jonquils, and Crocuses* and *Orion*, a study in red, painted in 1973, five years before her death. Thomas taught art at Shaw Junior High School in Washington for thirty-five years before retiring in 1960 to paint full time.

Portrait of a Girl in a Hat (Self-Portrait) *by Marie Laurencin*

W orks here range from Suzanne Valadon's *Nude Doing Her Hair* and *Bouquet of Flowers in an Empire Vase* to Helen Frankenthaler's *Spiritualist*, Bridget Riley's *Cerise, Olive, Turquoise Disks*, Frida Kahlo's *Self-Portrait Between the Curtains (Dedication to Trotsky)*, and Lolo Sarnoff's plexiglass sculpture, *Gateway to Eden*.

SECOND FLOOR

Alligator Pears in a Basket *by Georgia O'Keeffe*

NATIONAL PORTRAIT GALLERY

F Street at Eighth, N.W.
Washington, D.C. 20560
202/357-2700

METRO	Gallery Place.
HOURS	10 A.M. to 5:30 P.M. daily. Closed Christmas Day.
TOURS	10 A.M. to 3 P.M. Monday through Friday; 11 A.M. to 2 P.M. Saturday, Sunday, and holidays. Group tours available upon request. Call 202/357-2920.
ADMISSION	Free.
HANDICAPPED FACILITIES	Ramp entrance at Ninth and G Streets. Accessible to the disabled.
FOOD SERVICE	Patent Pending café, first floor, open 11 A.M. to 3 P.M. daily.
MUSEUM SHOP	History and art books, exhibition catalogs, slides, postcards, posters, reproductions, jewelry, scarves, china, and silver.
SPECIAL EVENTS	Portraits in Motion, a dramatic and musical series; lunchtime lectures.
MEMBERSHIP	Smithsonian Associates.
AUTHOR'S CHOICE	*Mary Cassatt* by Edgar Degas, second floor Presidential portraits, Hall of Presidents, second floor Great Hall, third floor

"It is for the artist . . . in portrait painting to put on canvas something more than the face the model wears for that one day; to paint the man, in short, as well as his features."
James McNeill Whistler

The National Portrait Gallery is one of Washington's youngest museums with some of the oldest—as well as newest—paintings in town.

HISTORY
Not until 1857 did the federal government express an interest in collecting portraits of noted Americans. In that year, Congress commissioned George Peter Alexander Healy to paint a series of presidential portraits for the White House. As the Smithsonian began to develop an art collection, the idea of a separate gallery for portraits gained support. And in 1962, Congress established the National Portrait Gallery. Nearly two-thirds of the art works in the permanent collection are gifts; the remainder have been purchased with funds appropriated by Congress.

THE BUILDING
The National Portrait Gallery shares space with the National Museum of American Art in one of Washington's most historic structures, the Old Patent Office Building. The fourth oldest public building in Washington—only the White House,

the Capitol, and the Treasury building are older—it formerly housed the Department of Interior and the Civil Service Commission. During the 1950s, plans were underway to raze the building and replace it with a parking garage, but President Dwight D. Eisenhower and other influential citizens intervened. Instead, the building was restored and reopened in 1968. The courtyard linking the two buildings is a pleasant place to bring your lunch or to sit and rest.

(See the National Museum of American Art section for more information about the history of the Old Patent Office Building.)

FIRST FLOOR

Guided tours start at the information desk immediately to the right, inside the main (F Street) entrance. Major temporary exhibitions are installed in the first floor galleries. Recent acquisitions are exhibited immediately to the right of the entrance and in the first floor lobby.

THE PERFORMING ARTS IN THE TWENTIETH CENTURY (East Corridor)
Nearly every facet of the performing arts is represented in paintings, prints, photographs, and sculpture. Among those included are playwrights Eugene O'Neill, Tennessee Williams, and Thornton Wilder; actors John Barrymore, Alfred Lunt, and Lynn Fontanne, and singer-dancer Josephine Baker.

At the far end of the corridor hangs Augustus John's 1930 painting of actress Tallulah Bankhead. She described it as her most precious possession and said, "I'll live in a hall bedroom and cook over a sterno before I give it up."

CHAMPIONS (South Corridor)
Photographs, paintings, and sculpture line the corridor nearby that leads to the Patent Pending Café. Particularly noteworthy are James Montgomery Flagg's large oil painting of the 1919 Dempsey-Willard fight, five *Time* magazine covers from August 1957 to September 1980, and a full-length marble sculpture of boxer John L. Sullivan, carved in 1888.

Tallulah Bankhead *by Augustus John*

STAIRWAY
Jo Davidson's stone head of President Franklin D. Roosevelt is at the foot of the staircase leading to the second floor.

On the wall above, *Grant and His Generals*, an 1865 oil painting by Ole Peter Hansen Balling, shows the Civil War hero with twenty-six of his generals. Balling, a Norwegian artist who served briefly in the Union Army, sketched President Lincoln at the White House and then spent five weeks in the field drawing army officers. His portrait of General Custer in this painting is said to be the only image of Custer done from life. Mrs. Grant thought Balling's portrait of Grant at Vicksburg (also in the National Portrait Gallery collection) accurately portrayed her "careworn and weary" husband as he looked during the siege.

SECOND FLOOR

Turn right as you leave the elevator. Directly ahead are the Hall of Presidents and the rotunda.

George Washington *and* Martha Washington *by Gilbert Stuart*

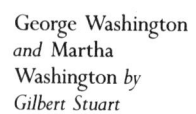

ROTUNDA

Presidential portraits by Gilbert Stuart hang in this impressive high-vaulted area. The "Lansdowne" portrait of George Washington, painted in 1796, is one of more than a dozen life portraits of the first president in the Portrait Gallery's collection. The "Athenaeum" portraits of George and Martha Washington are jointly owned with the Boston Museum of Fine Arts, and are exhibited at the Portrait Gallery every alternate three years. When the Washington portraits are in Boston, Stuart's portrait of Thomas Jefferson, which is jointly owned with Monticello, the Thomas Jefferson Memorial Foundation, Inc., is on view.

HALL OF PRESIDENTS

At the west end of the second floor, this gallery is a panorama of presidential portraits, from George Washington to George Bush. The styles vary from the aristocratic portraits of the Founding Fathers through the pensive Abraham Lincoln and the victorious Ulysses Grant to a denim-clad Ronald Reagan.

LINCOLN AND HIS CONTEMPORARIES (Gallery 203)

This selection of photographs by Mathew Brady, drawn from the Frederick Hill Meserve collection, shows the leading personalities of mid-nineteenth-century America. Soon after arriving in Washington in February 1861, President-elect Lincoln posed for Brady in his gallery on Pennsylvania Avenue between Sixth and Seventh Streets. Brady photographed the leading politicians, military heroes, religious leaders, writers, artists, and entertainers—as well as ordinary citizens—in his New York and Washington galleries. These are modern prints, made from Brady's original glass-plate negatives.

GEORGE WASHINGTON (Gallery 202)

Portraits of the popular first president include a marble bust by Jean-Antoine Houdon and Rembrandt Peale's "porthole" portraits of George and Martha Washington. Peale, the son of artist Charles Willson Peale, was only seventeen years old when he painted Washington in 1795.

AUGUSTE EDOUART SILHOUETTES (South Lounge)

One of the most prolific silhouette artists, Auguste Edouart executed four thousand profile likenesses in six years, beginning in 1839. He pasted the paper cutouts on a lithograph whose subject matter was appropriate to the sitter. For example, Joel Roberts Poinsett, U.S. minister to Mexico, is shown in a garden setting, because he introduced the poinsettia plant into this country. Artist Thomas Sully is pictured in front of an easel. And a portrait of author-editor Sarah Josepha Hale shows her reading a manuscript.

GALLERY OF NOTABLE AMERICANS, 1600 TO THE PRESENT DAY

The galleries are devoted to outstanding Americans from the Colonial era to the twentieth century. Artists and writers are shown in the main corridor. The adjacent rooms are arranged thematically and chronologically.

In the main corridor are:
- A portrait of Rubens Peale by Rembrandt Peale
- A self-portrait by Samuel F. B. Morse painted in England in 1812, many years before he abandoned art in favor of electrical experiments. Morse invented the telegraph in 1838.
- A self-portrait of Thomas Hart Benton with his wife Rita
- A full-length portrait of Samuel Clemens (Mark Twain) by John White Alexander
- A terracotta bust of artist James Abbott McNeill Whistler by Joseph Edgar Boehm (1872). Whistler reportedly was so fond of this bust that he kept it on view in his home for many years—the only work of art by another artist that he displayed.
- A portrait of Mary Cassatt by her good friend and fellow artist Edgar Degas (1880-84) is at the far end of the hall. Alan Fern, director of the National Portrait Gallery, considers this to be one of the most important works in the collection and has called it "portraiture at its finest."

Mary Cassatt by Edgar Degas

COLONIAL AMERICA (Gallery 204)

Don't miss John Singleton Copley's self-portrait in a roundel near the entrance to Gallery 204. One of the gems of the Portrait Gallery's collection, it was painted in a loose, freely brushed style around 1780–84, early in the artist's career. Portraits of Pocahontas, Robert "King" Carter, William Shirley by Thomas Hudson, and Dr. John Morgan by Angelica Kauffmann are among those included here.

THE ROAD TO INDEPENDENCE (Gallery 206)

A terracotta bust of Benjamin Franklin, after Jean-Antoine Houdon; a Copley oil miniature of Andrew Oliver, and his oil portrait of Henry Laurens, and Edward Savage's engraving of *Congress Voting Independence* are highlights of Gallery 206. Other signers of the Declaration of Independence, including Thomas Stone, Robert Morris, Charles Henry Lee, and Thomas McKean, are also portrayed here.

THE AMERICAN REVOLUTION (Gallery 208)

In the room next door, the marble bust of the Marquis de Lafayette is also modeled after one by Houdon. A charming miniature portrait of naval officer John Paul Jones was painted by Constance de Lowendal in 1780.

THE EARLY REPUBLIC (Gallery 210)

A striking self-portrait by George P. A. Healy hangs near the entrance to this room. Early leaders are shown, including Alexander Hamilton by sculptor Giuseppe Ceracchi, Chief Justice John Marshall by William James Hubard, Winfield

Scott by William Rush, Associate Justice Bushrod Washington by Chester Harding, and John Randolph by John Wesley Jarvis.

PRE-CIVIL WAR SCIENCE AND INVENTION (Gallery 209)

Important scientists and inventors, including Joseph Henry, first secretary of the Smithsonian, by LeClear, and Elias Howe, primary inventor of the sewing machine, after Charles Loring Elliott, are portrayed across the hall. Christian Schussele's mural-size, 1862 canvas, *Men of Progress*, shows an imaginary scene of nineteen inventors engaged in conversation.

THE EXPANDING FRONTIER (Gallery 207)

Images of John Jacob Astor, Sam Houston, John C. Fremont, and Davy Crockett are shown here. Also on view are an 1859 ambrotype of General George Armstrong Custer, and an 1850 daguerreotype of Mormon leader Brigham Young.

THE GILDED AGE (Gallery 211)

Go to the end of the corridor and turn right to see portraits of some of the men who left their mark on the twentieth century, such as Alexander Graham Bell, Cornelius Vanderbilt, August Belmont, Andrew Carnegie, Isaac Merrit Singer, and J. P. Morgan.

PERFORMING ARTS IN THE NINETEENTH CENTURY (Gallery 212)

The gallery across the hall is dominated by Orlando Rowland's full-length portrait of Richard Mansfield as Beau Brummel. Other portraits include those of Edwin Booth, Julia Marlowe, Minnie Maddern Fiske, Charlotte Cushman, John Phillip Sousa, and Ira Aldridge.

THE IMPULSE FOR REFORM (Gallery 213)

This gallery chronicles the men and women who championed often unpopular political causes, including suffragists Susan B. Anthony, Elizabeth Cady Stanton, and Belva Ann Lockwood, as well as Eugene V. Debs, a founder of the American Socialist Party and three-time presidential candidate, labor leader Samuel Gompers, and Booker T. Washington, a turn-of-the-century spokesman for black Americans.

PROGRESSIVISM AND WORLD INFLUENCE (Gallery 214)

Philosopher John Dewey, suffragist Carrie Chapman Catt, labor organizer Mary Harris "Mother Jones", and William Jennings Bryan are among those portrayed. Also note Jo Davidson's head of Robert LaFollette, founder of the National Progressive League.

WORLD WAR I AND THE TWENTIES (Gallery 216)

The room next door features notable Americans of the World War I era and the 1920s, ranging from General John J. Pershing and pioneer aviator Charles A. Lindbergh to Chief Justice Charles Evans Hughes and Andrew W. Mellon, donor of the National Gallery of Art. A large painting depicts the signing of the Treaty of Versailles, June 28, 1919, by John C. Johansen.

Gertrude Stein *by Jo Davidson*

JO DAVIDSON PORTRAIT SCULPTURE (Gallery 219)
A massive terracotta sculpture of writer Gertrude Stein and portrait heads of Albert Einstein, Clare Boothe Luce, and W. Averell Harriman are among the outstanding works of art in this gallery devoted to sculptor Jo Davidson (1883–1952).

SOCIAL CHANGE (Gallery 217)
Paintings of Robert F. Kennedy and Chief Justice Earl Warren by Gardner Cox, and a handsome head of Rachel Carson by sculptor Una Hanbury are shown here, as well as portraits of Sam Rayburn, Hubert Humphrey, George Washington Carver, and Martin Luther King.

THE NEW DEAL AND WORLD WAR II (Gallery 215)
Paintings of Winston Churchill by Douglas Chandor and General Douglas MacArthur by Howard Chandler Christy; a Ben Shahn ink drawing of physicist Julius Robert Oppenheimer, and Reuben Nakian's striking bronze head of White House aide Harry Hopkins are displayed here.

THE CIVIL WAR   **MEZZANINE**
Portraits of major Civil War figures line the mezzanine. The exhibit traces the history of the conflict from its inception through the battles on land and sea to the final Union victory. William Cogswell's full-length painting of a melancholy Abraham Lincoln dominates the exhibition.

The centerpiece is the Great Hall, once the largest room in America. When the Patent Office occupied this building, glass cases displayed thousands of miniature patent models, as well as the art and artifacts of the first national museum.   **THIRD FLOOR**

After a disastrous fire in 1877, the room was redecorated in American Victorian Renaissance style, with stained glass windows and colorful tile floors. Bas-relief portraits of Fulton, Franklin, Jefferson, and Whitney, and classically inspired carved friezes decorate the walls.

PETERSEN HOUSE

The House Where Lincoln Died
516 Tenth Street, N.W.
Washington, D.C. 20004
202/426-6830

METRO	Metro Center, Eleventh Street Exit.
HOURS	9 A.M. to 5 P.M. daily. Closed Christmas Day.
ADMISSION	Free.
AUTHOR'S CHOICE	The room in which President Lincoln died.

President Lincoln was too seriously wounded in Ford's Theatre to risk being carried over mud streets to the White House or even to a hospital. A man standing on the steps of a house across the street from the theater urged that he be brought there.

William Petersen, a tailor, had built the house in 1850. Like many other residents of the nation's capital, he rented rooms to lodgers, because there was a severe housing shortage in wartime Washington. The man who beckoned to the doctors attending Lincoln was a resident of the boardinghouse. He knew that William T. Clark, a Union Army soldier who rented a ground floor bedroom, was out for the evening.

The unconscious president was carried up the steps of the three-story red brick house and through a narrow hall to Clark's room. He was placed diagonally across the bed, as it was too short for his six-foot, four-inch frame. Mrs. Lincoln, her son Robert, and other visitors spent the long night in the front parlor.

Secretary of War Edwin M. Stanton set up a miniature command post in the back parlor bedroom, interviewing witnesses and trying to piece together clues to the killer's identity. Secretary of the Navy Gideon Welles sat in a rocking chair at the foot of the president's bed.

Dr. Charles A. Leale, who had been in the audience when the president was shot, gently probed the president's skull, removed a blood clot, and knew there was no hope of recovery. Because of the nature of the wound, Leale realized that if the president ever regained consciousness, he would be blind. Leale held the president's hand so that he would know he was not alone. At 7:22 A.M. the following morning, Lincoln died.

The three ground floor rooms open to visitors are furnished in Victorian style, as they might have appeared the night Lincoln died. Note that the clock on the mantelpiece in the front parlor is stopped at 7:22—the time of Lincoln's death. In the back parlor, which was a bedroom for the lodgers, Corporal James Tanner took dictation as a steady stream of witnesses filed in to give accounts of the slaying.

You can visualize the scene in the back bedroom, where chairs were pulled up to the bed for family, friends, and cabinet members to watch during the president's final hours.

The room is sparsely furnished, with a bed, a dresser, and a few chairs. The original pillow, stained with Lincoln's blood, is on the bed. Currier and Ives prints and a Rosa Bonheur engraving hang on the walls. Perhaps because of its simplicity, the room makes a strong impression on visitors.

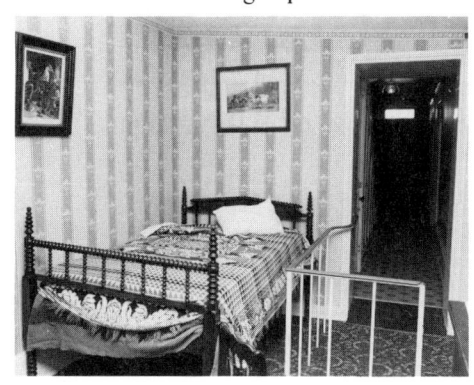

The room where Lincoln died

The Petersen House remained in the family until 1878 when William and Anna Petersen's heirs sold it to Mr. and Mrs. Louis Schade for $4,500. Schade, editor of *The Washington Sentinel*, published his newspaper in the basement. The room in which Lincoln died became a playroom for the Schade children.

In 1893, Osborn H. Oldroyd rented the house to display his collection of Lincoln relics. And three years later, the federal government purchased the house from the Schades for $30,000. The Oldroyd collection was displayed here until 1932, when it was installed in glass cases on the ground floor of Ford's Theatre, across the street from the Petersen House.

LILLIAN AND ALBERT SMALL JEWISH MUSEUM

Jewish Historical Society of Greater Washington
701 Third Street, N.W.
Washington, D.C. 20001
202/789-0900

METRO	Judiciary Square, F Street Exit.
HOURS	11 A.M. to 3 P.M. Sunday through Thursday and by appointment.
TOURS	By appointment.
ADMISSION	Free.
HANDICAPPED FACILITIES	First floor accessible to the disabled.
MEMBERSHIP	Jewish Historical Society of Greater Washington membership from $25.
AUTHOR'S CHOICE	Restored sanctuary of 1876 Adas Israel Synagogue Special exhibits on Washington Jewish community

Perched at the edge of a superhighway in the middle of a rather bleak landscape, this red brick, Federal-style building was once a synagogue, twice a church and, most recently, a grocery store and carryout.

HISTORY
In 1869, thirty-five members of the Washington Hebrew Congregation, dissatisfied with certain liturgical reforms, decided to organize their own synagogue, Adas Israel. After meeting in members' homes or rented rooms for several years, they built this synagogue, which then stood at the corner of Sixth and G Streets, N.W. President Ulysses S. Grant was among the dignitaries attending the dedication of the building in 1876. In those days, Seventh Street was the heart of the business district, and a large Jewish community lived nearby.

The Adas Israel congregation soon outgrew the building and, in 1908, moved to larger quarters at Sixth and Eye Streets, N.W. The original building was rented to St. Sophia's Greek Orthodox Church and later housed the Evangelical Church of God. In later years, various small businesses used the first floor, while the second floor, the original sanctuary, became a storage area. The last occupants were a grocery store and carryout.

Lillian and Albert Small Jewish Museum in the original Adas Israel Synagogue

THE BUILDING
The Federal-style architecture seems surprising, since Byzantine and Romanesque styles were much more fashionable when the synagogue was built in the late nineteenth century.

The first floor originally contained two classrooms and a chapel for daily services. A *mikvah*, or ritual bath, was located in a corner of the present office.

In 1968, the old Adas Israel Synagogue was scheduled for

demolition because of subway construction. To save the building, it was placed on the National Register of Historic Places, as the first synagogue built in the nation's capital. (It is the second synagogue in the country—after Newport's Touro Synagogue—to be included in the National Register.) The District of Columbia government agreed to acquire the building and lease it to the Jewish Historical Society of Greater Washington.

The rescue operation was complicated by the need to move the building. Because some of the brick walls on the ground floor had been replaced with storefront windows, it was not considered to be sturdy enough to move. Therefore, in December 1969, the top two floors of the building—270 tons of brick and lumber—were placed on a 28-wheeled dolly, moved three blocks to the present location, and placed on a new foundation. Surprisingly, all of this took only three hours.

The building reopened in 1975 as a museum and historical society headquarters. Longtime Washington residents Lillian Small and the late Albert Small, for whom the museum is named, donated a major portion of the restoration funds in honor of Mr. Small's seventieth birthday.

Despite nearly a hundred years of ups and downs, parts of the interior, as well as the exterior, have survived in their original condition. These include portions of the *bimah*, or raised platform, the railing around it, the ark for the Torah, part of the women's gallery, the cupola, the wood sunburst design over the main entrance, and many of the windows.

The wrought iron fence, with its Star of David and menorah motifs, was inspired by the design in a four-hundred-year-old synagogue on the island of Rhodes. A member of the Adas Israel congregation who saw the Rhodes synagogue contributed the fence as a memorial to his father.

THE SANCTUARY

The sanctuary on the second floor is as much of a surprise as the exterior of the building. Its plain white, unadorned walls are reminiscent of a Quaker meetinghouse or an eighteenth-century synagogue.

Hard, narrow pews of red-painted pine are placed in four rows on either side of the aisle. The first pew on the left was in the original synagogue and had been given to the Charlotte Hall A.M.E. Church in St. Mary's County, Maryland. It was returned to the old Adas Israel Synagogue in 1970. The Turner Memorial A.M.E. Church, which now occupies the second Adas Israel building at Sixth and Eye Streets, N. W., returned two other pews from the original building in 1984.

EXHIBITS

On the ground floor, a slide show and a small permanent exhibit tell the history of the restored synagogue building. The museum serves as the central archive and display center of Washington Jewish history. Two or three changing exhibits each year focus on various facets of Jewish communal life in the nation's capital. The exhibits frequently contain photographs and documents borrowed from public sources, such as the National Archives and the Library of Congress, as well as the museum's own growing collection. Also included are treasured family memorabilia, loaned by or copied from local area residents, which help to personalize and dramatize the displays.

The Octagon

MIDTOWN

1799

ART MUSEUM OF THE AMERICAS

201 Eighteenth Street, N.W.
Washington, D.C. 20006
202/458-6022

Mailing address
1889 F Street, N.W.
Washington, D.C. 20006

METRO	Farragut West.
HOURS	10 A.M. to 5 P.M. Tuesday through Saturday. Closed Sunday, Monday, and holidays.
TOURS	Guided tours in English or Spanish by appointment.
ADMISSION	Free.
MUSEUM SHOP	Catalogs and films about Latin American art and artists.
SPECIAL EVENTS	Films, lectures, and rotating exhibits.
SPECIAL FACILITIES	Extensive archives, available by appointment, contain monographs, catalogs, and photographs related to Latin American art.
MEMBERSHIP	Friends of the Art Museum of the Americas membership from $25.
AUTHOR'S CHOICE	Works by Japanese-Brazilian artists

In 1957, the representative of Mexico to the Organization of American States (OAS), Ambassador Luis Quintanilla, proposed that one painting from each OAS art show be purchased to build a permanent collection representing the best contemporary art of the hemisphere. Corporate and individual donations added to the collection, which soon began to outgrow its exhibition space. Many paintings were hung in OAS offices; others were loaned periodically to museums in Europe and the Americas.

In 1976, the representative of Venezuela to the OAS, Ambassador José Maria Machin Acosta, proposed that a Museum of Modern Art of Latin America be established in Washington, in honor of the U. S. Bicentennial. The resolution was adopted unanimously, and funds were appropriated to convert the former residence of OAS Secretaries General into the Museum of Modern Art of the Americas, the first museum in the world devoted exclusively to contemporary Latin American and Caribbean art. Its name was changed to the Art Museum of the Americas in 1990.

THE BUILDING

The museum building's white walls, iron grillwork, and red tile roof are typical of Spanish colonial architecture. Designed by architects Albert Kelsey and Paul Cret, the building was completed in 1912 with funds provided by philanthropist Andrew Carnegie. OAS secretaries general lived here until 1968, when the building was converted into office space.

The museum's audiovisual department is housed in a small,

stucco building next door to the museum, and has an interesting history. Originally a carriage house, it is the only remaining structure of the Van Ness estate, which was one of the first parcels of land allocated when the City of Washington was laid out in the late eighteenth century. The Van Ness house was torn down around the turn of the century to make room for the Pan American Union building, later the Organization of American States.

THE PERMANENT COLLECTION

All important art trends in the hemisphere during the past forty years are represented in the collection, which includes approximately eight hundred works of art. Selections from the permanent collection are rotated periodically, and loan exhibitions are presented two or three times a year. Roughly one-third of the collection is usually on display in five galleries on the second and third floors of this elegant Spanish colonial house, with its high ceilings, curved stairways, and sculpture gardens.

Approximately fifty percent of the holdings are prints and drawings, thirty-five percent are paintings, and fifteen percent sculptures. The sculpture is displayed in niches along the staircase—as well as in the galleries—and on the loggia behind the museum, which opens on to the Aztec Garden and reflecting pool.

As the only institution in North America devoted exclusively to Latin American artists, the museum provides a unique opportunity to compare and contrast the work of artists of widely varying cultures. The collection gained special attention during the early 1960s with the Kennedy Administration's Alliance for Progress and its emphasis on Latin America. But today even some longtime Washingtonians are unaware of its existence.

Caribbean Enchantment *by Cuban artist Mario Carreño*

STAIRWAY AND HALL

SECOND FLOOR

A Fernando Botero bronze of a seated woman and an Everald Brown ironwood *Totem* are in niches along the staircase. *Hermala II*, a large painting by Chilean surrealist painter Roberto Matta, hangs at the top of the stairs.

PIONEERS AND TEACHERS

The first gallery on the right showcases major Latin American artists, including Rufino Tamayo of Mexico, Joaquin Torres-Garcia and Pedro Figari of Uruguay, and Cuban painter

Wilfredo Lam. Many experts consider Tamayo, who was born in 1899, the most important influence on modern art in Latin America. His *Man Contemplating the Moon* lithograph shows Tamayo's love of vibrant colors.

Joaquin Torres-Garcia (1874–1949) studied in Paris and returned to Montevideo in 1932 to become a proponent of constructivism, rediscovering the pre-Hispanic roots of his country. Works such as his *Constructivism*, painted in 1943, influenced many Uruguayan artists, who continue to follow his theories. Figari (1861–1938) did not devote himself completely to art until he was sixty, after a successful career as a lawyer, writer, professor, parliamentarian, and philosopher. Primarily a colorist, he often painted scenes of nineteenth-century life, such as *The Market Place*.

Lam, the son of a Chinese father and an Afro-Cuban mother, studied in Madrid and Paris before returning to his native Cuba and to the United States. His *Lisamona* shows the influence of Picasso and African masks.

GEOMETRIC ART

Latin American artists began to explore geometric forms in the 1940s, particularly in Argentina and Venezuela. In the latter country, artists frequently experimented with kinetic effects.

Included in the museum collection of Argentine abstract paintings are Rogelio Polesello's *Orange on Magenta*, Miguel Angel Vidal's *Equilibrium*, and Ary Brizzi's *Interaction No. 10*.

Examples of kinetic art include Carlos Cruz-Diez's *Physiochrome No. 965* and Jesus Rafael Soto's *Hurtado Scripture*, a mixed media work of wire, wood, and nylon cord.

THIRD FLOOR

LYRIC ABSTRACTION

Departing from the rigidity of geometric abstraction in the 1950s, many Latin American artists developed a more subjective approach that has been labeled Lyric Abstraction. Their works may remind you of the Abstract Expressionists working in this country at that time.

Representative works include Peruvian artists Fernando de Szyszlo's *Cajamarca* and Estuardo Maldonado's *Pictography*, which features a patterned sequence of symbols based on pre-Colombian textiles. *Composition* by Bolivian artist Maria Luisa Pacheco, known for her skillful handling of white paint, is also noteworthy.

In Brazil, a number of artists who had been born in Japan or were of Japanese ancestry exhibited at the São Paolo Biennials in

Man Contemplating the Moon, lithograph by Rufino Tamayo of Mexico

Andean Family by Venezuelan artist Hector Poleo

the 1950s and 1960s. These artists combined Japanese traditions of abstraction and symbolism with elements derived from their Hispanic environment. In paintings such as *Number 9* by Tomie Ohtake—a leader of the Japanese-Brazilian artists—broad irregular areas of color fill vast spaces on the canvas to create an effect of calm and serenity.

Also note Tikashi Fukushima's *Green*, Kazuo Wakabayashi's *Blue and Black* and Manabu Mabe's powerful *Agony*. Yutaka Toyota's *In the Time Before Nothing* expresses Toyota's view that "an artist's work should be simple—something precise and elementary that transmits information to the viewer without thematic distortion."

LATIN AMERICAN FOLK VISIONS

The folk art of Haiti is internationally known and admired. Less well-known, perhaps, is the primitive art of other Latin American countries. The subject matter varies from village street scenes to religious works, from portraits to mountain landscapes, from themes of national history to social protest. Yet, these primitive works share a common theme—an unsophisticated point of view that is at once appealing and direct.

Consider, for example, *Walking With Her Blue Umbrella* by Panamanian Victor Lewis, *San Antonio* by José Antonio Velasquez of Honduras, Joseph Jean-Gilles's *Haitian Landscape*, Jamaican Sidney McLaren's *Creative Imagination*, and Haitian sculptor Georges Liautaud's *Crucifixion*. And don't miss the charming paintings by Nicaraguan artist Asilia Guillen, *Rafaela Herrera Defending the Castle Against the Pirates* and *Heroes and Artists Come to the Pan-American Union to Be Consecrated*.

San Antonio de Oriente *by José Antonio Velasquez*

THE AZTEC GARDEN

A statue of Xochipili, the Aztec god of flowers, watches over a reflecting pool in the center of the Aztec Garden. Azaleas, boxwood, and seasonal plantings border the pool. The garden, linking the Art Museum of the Americas with the Organization of American States building, is a popular background for fashion photographs.

Several sculptures by Latin American artists can be seen here, including *Setember* by Argentinian artist Marta Minujin; *Gran Diagonal* by Rolando Peña, and *The Integration* by Beatriz Blanco, both from Venezuela; *Big Shoal* by José Sancho of Costa Rica, and *Carnival in the Caribbean* by Puerto Rican Pablo Rubio.

BETHUNE MUSEUM-ARCHIVES

1318 Vermont Avenue, N.W.
Washington, D.C. 20005
202/332-1233

METRO	McPherson Square.
HOURS	10 A.M. to 4:30 P.M. Monday through Friday; weekends by appointment for tours.
TOURS	By appointment.
ADMISSION	Free for walk throughs; $1 per person for tours.
SPECIAL EVENTS	Films, concerts, lectures, and children's programs.
MEMBERSHIP	Bethune Museum-Archives, Inc., membership from $25.
AUTHOR'S CHOICE	Current historical exhibitions

Mary McLeod Bethune, *founder of the National Council of Negro Women*

This three-story brick Victorian row house, built in 1876, memorializes a noted black activist and educator.

Mary McLeod Bethune, one of seventeen children born to ex-slaves in South Carolina in 1885, founded Bethune-Cookman College in Daytona, Florida. In addition, she founded and was the first president of the National Council of Negro Women (NCNW) and served as an advisor to President Franklin D. Roosevelt on black affairs and youth.

The building, known as Council House, was the Bethune home from 1943 to 1950. As early as 1939, Bethune dreamed of a museum-archive, a goal that was finally achieved when the institution opened in 1979.

The museum mounts two special exhibitions each year focusing on various aspects of black women's history. Five rooms on the first and second floors are used for exhibitions.

The nineteenth-century carriage house behind the museum is home to the National Archives for Black Women's History. Several collections are here: Bethune's papers from her Washington years; the papers of other black women leaders; the records of the National Committee on Household Employees, and the files of the National Council of Negro Women from 1935 through the 1970s. The archive is available by appointment only.

Except for a large painting of Bethune and photographs of her with the Roosevelts and other world leaders, the house itself—a handsome building with high ceilings and a bay window—bears few reminders of its former owner, who died in 1955. Her furniture and personal effects are not here—not even in the second-floor study. Her spirit remains, however. And the museum makes its point: that a remarkable black woman achieved gains for her people and for all women by being in the right place at the right time. Mary McLeod Bethune's work continues in the museum-archive she dreamed of creating.

B'NAI B'RITH KLUTZNICK MUSEUM

1640 Rhode Island Avenue, N.W.
Washington, D.C. 20036
202/857-6583

METRO	Farragut North, L Street Exit.
HOURS	10 A.M. to 5 P.M. Sunday through Friday. Closed Saturdays, legal and Jewish holidays.
TOURS	Group tours by appointment
ADMISSION	Free; suggested contribution $2, adults; $1, children.
HANDICAPPED FACILITIES	Wheelchair available. Museum is barrier-free.
MUSEUM SHOP	Jewish books, ceremonial objects, original art, crafts.
SPECIAL EVENTS	Lectures, films, and holiday workshops.
MEMBERSHIP	Friends of the B'nai B'rith Klutznick Museum membership from $25.
AUTHOR'S CHOICE	Silver spice boxes Parchment marriage contracts Torah crowns and pointers Seventeenth-century candlesticks from Danzig

A colorful mural, *The Hearts and Minds of B'nai B'rith* by Yankel Ginzburg, brightens the entrance to what appears to be just another office building. In addition to serving as the headquarters of B'nai B'rith International, this building houses a comprehensive collection of ceremonial and folk art, spanning more than twenty centuries of Jewish history.

Founded in 1843, B'nai B'rith International is the world's largest and oldest Jewish service organization. The museum, founded in 1957, is named for the Honorable Philip M. and Ethel Klutznick of Chicago, Illinois. Klutznick, a former U. S. secretary of commerce, was formerly international president of the organization.

THE COLLECTION
To the left of the main entrance are the museum shop and a gallery for temporary exhibitions. On the right are a large hall, also for temporary exhibitions, and several galleries which house the permanent collection.

Jewish artistic tradition dates back to biblical times. After the Exodus from Egypt, God called upon Bezalel to fashion the Tent of Meeting, filling him with "the Spirit to devise artistic designs."

The exhibits illustrate how Jewish art has enhanced the religious experience, touching every aspect of Jewish daily life. More than five hundred objects on permanent display illustrate the Jewish life cycle and Jewish festivals.

Silver spice containers from Poland and Germany

THEATER GALLERY—JEWISH HISTORY

The first gallery of the permanent collection, which features a slide show on the history of B'nai B'rith, chronicles Jewish history in works of art. Objects range from ancient Babylonian coins and pottery incantation bowls to a yellow Jewish star and currency used in the Theresienstadt concentration camp near Prague during the 1930s, and a growing collection of contemporary Israeli and Soviet Jewish art.

One of the most historic documents is a copy of a letter from George Washington to the president of the Touro Synagogue in Newport, Rhode Island, following Washington's visit there in August 1790. Washington wrote, ". . . the government of the United States, which gives to bigotry no sanction, to persecution no assistance, requires only that they who live under its protection, should demean themselves as good citizens, in giving it on all occasions their effectual support."

THE LIFE CYCLE

Here are objects related to the Jewish life cycle, from birth to bar and bat mitzvah, marriage and death.

Parchment *ketubot* or marriage contracts dating from the seventeenth, eighteenth, and nineteenth centuries are particularly interesting. Especially rare is an eighteenth-century Italian *ketubah* decorated along the border with signs of the zodiac. Other cases are filled with bridal jewelry, hairpieces, prayer books, amulets, and good luck charms. Memorial candleholders and ornate clocks mark the end of the life cycle.

THE FESTIVAL CYCLE

The next three galleries demonstrate a wide variety of artistic inspiration in such functional items as Passover plates, kiddush cups, Hanukkah lamps, and other objects used to celebrate Jewish holidays. The exquisite antique silver spice containers were used in a special ceremony marking the end of the Sabbath, as a reminder of the sweetness of the day. The most unusual ones in the collection are crafted like miniature Gothic turrets with banners flying.

Don't miss the pair of silver candlesticks, made in Danzig, Poland, around 1680 with biblical scenes fashioned on the base.

You will also find a group of elaborately embroidered Torah covers, crowns, breastplates and finials, as well as the pointers that readers use to follow the text when reading the Torah before a congregation.

The collection of Torah binders is among the finest in the world. Note particularly the eighteenth-century examples, including two in German linen and a delicately embroidered blue silk binder from Italy.

A Sabbath candlestick from Danzig, Poland, circa 1680

HERMAN AND SARA PERLMAN COLLECTION

This small but choice collection of religious and historical subjects etched in glass was a gift to the museum from its creator, Herman Perlman, a local artist.

PHILIP LAX GALLERY OF B'NAI B'RITH HISTORY AND ARCHIVES

Books, files, photographs, and memorabilia relating to B'nai B'rith are available here. Documents on display are changed periodically. They range from the 1872 charter of a B'nai B'rith lodge in Davenport, Iowa, to artifacts from the Gold Medal USA softball team supported by B'nai B'rith in the 1984 Maccabiah Games in Israel.

HAROLD AND SYLVIA GREENBERG SCULPTURE GARDEN

A sculpture garden behind the museum contains bronze works on biblical themes by Washington sculptor Phillip Ratner.

JEWISH AMERICAN SPORTS HALL OF FAME

The Hall of Fame highlights the careers and honors the accomplishments of athletes, including Hank Greenberg, Al Rosen, Sandy Koufax, Sid Luckman, Dolph Schayes, Dick Savitz, Mark Spitz, Benny Leonard, coach "Red" Auerbach; sportswriter Shirley Povich; broadcaster Mel Allen, and entrepreneurs Eddie Gottlieb and Abe Pollin.

CORCORAN GALLERY OF ART

**Seventeenth Street and New York Avenue, N.W.
Washington, D.C. 20006
202/638-3211**

METRO	Farragut North or West.
HOURS	10 A.M. to 5 P.M. Tuesday through Sunday; until 9 P.M. Thursday. Closed Monday, Christmas Day, and New Year's Day.
TOURS	12:30 P.M. Tuesday through Sunday. Group tours by appointment.
ADMISSION	Donation, $3, adults; $1, students and senior citizens; $5, families/groups; free, members and children under 12.
HANDICAPPED FACILITIES	Ramp entrance on E Street. Elevator to first and second floors; some areas not accessible to the disabled.
FOOD SERVICE	Café at the Corcoran, 10 A.M. to 4:30 P.M. Tuesday through Sunday; until 8 P.M. Thursday. Afternoon tea 2:30 P.M. to 4:30 P.M.
MUSEUM SHOP	Books, prints, posters, notecards, jewelry, art glass, and gift items.
SPECIAL EVENTS	Films, concert series, lectures, and gallery talks.
SPECIAL FACILITIES	Workshops for children, fine arts courses for teens and adults at the Corcoran School of Art.
MEMBERSHIP	From $35.
AUTHOR'S CHOICE	*The Old House of Representatives* by Samuel F. B. Morse *Mount Corcoran* by Albert Bierstadt *Niagara Falls* by Frederic Edwin Church *The Greek Slave* by Hiram Powers The grand salon of the Hotel d'Orsay

The Corcoran Gallery of Art, founded in 1859, is Washington's first art museum and one of the three oldest in the country. It was chartered in 1870, when New York's Metropolitan Museum of Art and the Museum of Fine Arts in Boston were also chartered. Its collection of American art—particularly landscapes and genre paintings—is one of the finest in the country.

In addition, the museum contains the Edward and Mary Walker collection of French Impressionists and the William A. Clark collection, which includes fine seventeenth-century Dutch and Flemish paintings, a thirteenth-century French stained glass window, and an eighteenth-century French salon. Founder William Wilson Corcoran was photographed by Mathew Brady in the 1850s, and the museum has been collecting photographs for more than a hundred years. The collection now numbers nearly two thousand nineteenth- and twentieth-century images.

The Corcoran averages fifteen to twenty special exhibitions

William Wilson Corcoran by Charles Loring Elliott

each year, including major international shows, photography, artists' retrospectives, and Washington regional art. Since 1907, the museum's biennial exhibitions have been an important and sometimes controversial showcase for contemporary art.

The Corcoran School of Art, a fully accredited four-year art college, is the only professional art school in the metropolitan area, with a full-time enrollment of 250 fine arts, photography, and visual communications students.

HISTORY

In 1854, after making a fortune in business and serving as co-founder of Riggs Bank, William Wilson Corcoran retired to devote his time to philanthropy and art collecting.

A trip abroad in 1849 introduced him to European painting and architecture. Corcoran took to one but not to the other. He commissioned architect James Renwick, Jr., to design a building "dedicated to art" at Seventeenth Street and Pennsylvania Avenue in the fashionable Second French Empire style (now the Smithsonian's Renwick Gallery). Although Corcoran bought European art on that trip and later purchased more than a hundred bronzes by French *animalier* Antoine-Louis Barye, he preferred to concentrate on "the American genius." Hoping that his museum might become a national portrait gallery, Corcoran acquired the portraits of every president, along with other American heroes.

In 1897, when the collection of nearly seven hundred works of art outgrew its original building, the Corcoran opened at its present site a few blocks away. In 1925, Montana Senator William A. Clark donated his European paintings, antiquities, and decorative art to the museum, stipulating that the collection be exhibited intact. Mr. and Mrs. Edward Walker also donated their collection of forty-nine late nineteenth- and twentieth-century paintings and two matched sets of priceless string instruments. The Stradivarius violins once owned by Nicolo Paganini are on loan to the Cleveland Quartet, and instruments crafted by Niccolo Amati (teacher of Stradivarius), have been loaned to the Tokyo String Quartet. Both groups perform regularly at the Corcoran.

A privately funded institution governed by a self-perpetuating board of trustees, the Corcoran in former years tended toward conservatism in its acquisition and exhibition policies. In 1962, a few of its trustees, concerned by the museum's lack of interest in contemporary art, joined other sponsors in founding the Washington Gallery of Modern Art (WGMA). Six years later, the Corcoran acquired the collection and assets of the financially troubled WGMA, which included a building at Twenty-first and P Streets that became the Corcoran Gallery-Dupont Center and, later, the Corcoran Workshop. Washington's first regularly scheduled photography exhibitions were shown in the Corcoran Gallery-Dupont Center. During the mid-1970s, the Corcoran discontinued its outreach programs and sold the building on Twenty-first Street.

In 1966, an exhibition spanning 250 years of American art included more than seven hundred works from the permanent collection. It marked a milestone—the first major survey of American art ever presented in the nation's capital.

THE BUILDING

Designed by architect Ernest Flagg, this building of white Georgia marble with its green copper roof and ornate grillwork is considered to be the finest Beaux Arts structure in Washington. It was reportedly Frank Lloyd Wright's favorite; he called it "the best designed building in Washington." Charles Platt designed the wing in 1927 to house the Clark collection.

Like I. M. Pei's East Building of the National Gallery of Art, the Corcoran stands on a trapezoidal site. Flagg placed a semicircular amphitheater facing New York Avenue, at the acute angle of the triangle, that is balanced by a wing at the opposite end of the building.

A frieze under the cornice bears the names of eleven artists—Phidias, Giotto, Dürer, Michelangelo, Raphael, Velásquez, Rembrandt, Rubens, Reynolds, Allston, and Ingres. The inclusion of landscape painter Washington Allston (1779–1843) in such stellar company seems a curious choice. If Corcoran had been alive at that time, he might have included Thomas Crawford, the man he considered to be the greatest contemporary sculptor, whose statue *Freedom* stands atop the Capitol dome. In *Washington Itself*, E. J. Applewhite suggests that architect Flagg compiled the list and included Allston, who happened to be his mother's uncle.

The major interior architectural details are a double atrium on the first floor and a grand marble staircase leading to a rotunda and the second floor. Barye bronzes are displayed in niches on either side of the staircase and portraits—notably John Singer Sargent's *Mrs. Henry White*, *William Wilson Corcoran* by Charles Loring Elliott, and *Andrew Jackson* by Thomas Sully—line the stair walls.

THE COLLECTION

Paintings from the permanent collection are shown in galleries on the first floor, as well as in the atrium and the upper atrium. Selections may range from nineteenth-century landscape and history paintings to the hard-edge works of the Washington Color School. Temporary exhibitions are usually installed in galleries adjoining the south side of the atrium, in the rotunda, and in galleries on the second floor.

With a permanent collection that is rotated frequently and an active schedule of temporary exhibitions, paintings are often rehung in various galleries. Here are a few of the major works to see when you visit the museum.

- *The Old House of Representatives* by Samuel F. B. Morse shows a congressional session at the Capitol in 1822. Morse painted eighty-six identifiable people, including sixty-seven congressmen, six Supreme Court justices, reporters, a visiting Indian chief, and the artist's father (in the upper right galleries). Although Morse had hoped for both artistic and financial success when the painting was exhibited, critics complained that there were too many small figures and that the scene lacked historical significance. Morse's disappointment with the public response led him to abandon painting during the next decade. However, subsequent experiments with electricity resulted in his invention of the telegraph and the Morse code.

- Frederic Edwin Church's monumental *Niagara Falls*, one of the most important paintings in the Corcoran collection, is considered to be the finest representation of the subject ever

Niagara Falls by Frederic Edwin Church, 1857

painted. When Church exhibited it soon after its completion in 1857, the painting drew unprecedented crowds both in England and in America. The grandeur of nature, as represented by Niagara Falls, was a favorite subject of both amateur and professional artists throughout the nineteenth century.

• *Mount Corcoran* was painted by Albert Bierstadt after he had traveled through Yosemite Valley and the Sierra Nevada in 1858, 1863, and 1871. Originally called *Mountain Lake* when it was exhibited at the National Academy of Design in 1877, Bierstadt changed the title and presented maps supporting the *Mount Corcoran* designation when he decided to sell the painting to William Wilson Corcoran. (Bierstadt's *Mount Whitney* in the Rockwell Museum, Corning, New York, bears a striking similarity to this painting.)

• John Singer Sargent's elegant portrait of *Mrs. Henry White*, wife of an American diplomat in Europe, helped to establish his reputation as a leading portrait artist. Mrs. White hung it in her London dining room where it was seen by socialites who flocked to Sargent's studio to have their portraits painted. The Corcoran also owns Sargent's *Madame Edouard Pailleron*, his first important commission, in addition to his *Simplon Pass* and *The Oyster Gatherers*.

• *The Greek Slave* by Hiram Powers was considered so scandalous when it was first exhibited at the old Corcoran Gallery (now the Renwick) that separate viewing hours were set aside for men and women. No one under sixteen was admitted. The marble statue no longer causes raised eyebrows. Powers was a classically inspired nineteenth-century American sculptor who worked in Italy. The plaster cast of *The Greek Slave*, along with the contents of Powers's sculpture studio in Florence, can be seen at the National Museum of American Art.

• Thomas Eakins's *The Pathetic Song* is a portrait of three of his musician friends, as well as a re-creation of a popular form of Victorian entertainment, the home musicale. The singer, Margaret Alexina Harrison, was an Eakins pupil at the Pennsylvania Academy of the Fine Arts; the cellist was a seventy-one-year-old performer with the Philadelphia Symphonic Society, and Eakins's future wife, Susan McDowell, was at the piano.

• The grand salon of the Hotel d'Orsay is an elaborate gold-and-white drawing room from a late eighteenth-century Parisian town house built for the Duc de la Trémouille. Despite the cherubs, garlands, and other rococo touches, the room's fluted pilasters give it a neoclassical air. Senator William A. Clark bought the room in 1904 and installed it in his New York town house. Bequeathed to the Corcoran in 1925, it was re-created in the Clark wing in 1928. Notice the needlepoint-covered gilt armchairs and settees, the marble-topped marquetry commodes, and the painted panels on the doors.

The Greek Slave by Hiram Powers

DAUGHTERS OF THE AMERICAN REVOLUTION MUSEUM

1776 D Street, N.W.
Washington, D.C. 20006
202/879-3240

METRO	Farragut West and Farragut North (seven blocks down 17th Street).
HOURS	8:30 A.M. to 4 P.M. Monday through Friday; 1 to 5 P.M. Sunday. Closed to the public three weeks each April.
TOURS	10 A.M. to 3 P.M. Monday through Friday; 1 to 5 P.M. Sunday.
ADMISSION	Free.
HANDICAPPED FACILITIES	Special ramped entrance at 1775 C Street and elevators in building. Accessible to the disabled. Advance notice suggested.
MUSEUM SHOP	Books, notecards, needlepoint, ceramics, and other gift items.
SPECIAL EVENTS	Student tours and quilt workshops by advance arrangement. *Touch of Independence* discovery area for children.
SPECIAL FACILITIES	Genealogical library open to the public for a fee.
AUTHOR'S CHOICE	Museum Gallery with pre-1830 decorative arts Early American period rooms Quilt displays

The Daughters of the American Revolution (DAR) Museum has assembled an outstanding collection of antique furniture, ceramics, silver, glass, and paintings in an exhibition gallery and thirty-three period rooms in the Beaux-Arts-styled Memorial Continental Hall.

Founded in 1890, the year the DAR was formed by descendants of men who fought in the Revolutionary War, the museum contains more than thirty thousand objects that trace the development of life in America during the eighteenth and nineteenth centuries.

The period rooms—each reflecting the style of a particular period or region—are furnished and maintained by individual DAR state chapters.

Highlights of the period rooms include:

New Jersey Room One of the earliest period installations in any American museum, this room's paneling and Jacobean furniture were carved from the oak timbers of the Revolutionary frigate, *Augusta*.

Rhode Island Room A music room, with a selection of eighteenth- and nineteenth-century American and European instruments.

Georgia Room Based on the "long room" in Peter Tondee's tavern in Savannah, a meeting place of the "Sons of Liberty."

California Room A re-creation of an 1860s whaling station with whitewashed walls and exposed ceiling beams.

Massachusetts Room Modeled after a bedroom in the Hancock-Clarke house in Lexington, Massachusetts.

New York Room A formal drawing room whose furnishings reflect the Chinese influence that was important after trade with China began near the end of the eighteenth century.

Oklahoma Room A composite view of eighteenth- and nineteenth-century American kitchens.

New Hampshire Room Eighteenth- and nineteenth-century games, toys, and dolls in an attic setting.

South Carolina Room An early nineteenth-century bedroom.

AMERICANA ROOM

Located on the second floor, the Americana Room houses approximately five thousand letters, diaries, wills, deeds, engravings, newspapers, and rare books concerning Colonial America, the American Revolution, and the early Republic, as well as the signatures of presidents, First Ladies, and the signers of both the Constitution and the Declaration of Independence.

A 1953 painting of the *Battle of Bennington, August 16, 1777*, by Anna Mary Robertson ("Grandma") Moses, a DAR member, usually hangs in this room, and was a gift from the artist.

NATIONAL SOCIETY OF CHILDREN OF THE AMERICAN REVOLUTION MUSEUM

Also on the second floor, at the end of the corridor, wall cases display Americana exhibits especially designed for children. Objects range from seventeenth-century maps of the New World and an eighteenth-century spinning wheel to silver spoons, tea sets, and children's clothes. The collection of miniature furniture and dolls' house accoutrements is particularly interesting. Don't miss the tiny turn-of-the-century crystal punch bowl with matching cups.

DAR LIBRARY

Established in 1896, this is an extraordinary historical and genealogical resource, with more than 110,000 books and tens of thousands of files of genealogical material from all periods of American history. Thousands of Americans have conducted their family research here.

A French doll, circa 1880

Now housed in the former auditorium of Memorial Continental Hall, the library is open weekdays from 9 A.M. to 4 P.M. and Sunday afternoons from 1 to 5 P.M. (except on holiday weekends). Non-DAR members pay $5 per day. The library is closed to nonmembers part of April each year during the annual DAR Continental Congress.

QUILT WORKSHOPS

More than 230 examples of pieced, appliquéd, and whole cloth quilts are included in the museum collection. The quilts date from approximately 1780 to 1870.

A ninety-minute quilt workshop is generally held on the first Thursday of the month. There is a modest fee and reservations are required. Approximately twenty-five quilts are shown and discussed during each workshop.

DECATUR HOUSE

748 Jackson Place, N.W.
Washington, D.C. 20006
202/842-0920

METRO	Farragut North or West.
HOURS	10 A.M. to 2 P.M. Tuesday through Friday; Noon to 4 P.M. Saturday and Sunday.
TOURS	On the hour and half-hour. Adult and school group tours by reservation.
ADMISSION	$3, adults; $1.50, students and senior citizens; free, members of the National Trust for Historic Preservation.
HANDICAPPED FACILITIES	Advance notice suggested. Elevator to second floor.
MUSEUM SHOP	Books, notecards, jewelry, specialty foods, and gift items.
SPECIAL EVENTS	Preservation Week in May, open house in May and October, marketplace for nineteenth-century crafts in November, nineteenth-century Christmas decorations, and "Tactile Architecture" quilt exhibit in late January and early February. Also, walking tours of Lafayette Square by reservation.
SPECIAL FACILITIES	Reconstructed carriage house for museum programs and party rentals.
AUTHOR'S CHOICE	Latrobe's classical architectural details Decatur bedroom, first floor Drawing room, second floor

The first house built on what is now Lafayette Square, Decatur House was also the last to be privately owned. At various times, it served as the French, Russian, and British embassies, and was home to a naval hero, three secretaries of state, members of Congress, and a man who tried to popularize the use of camels in the desert of the Southwest.

HISTORY
Stephen Decatur's exploits in hand-to-hand combat against the Barbary pirates and against the British during the War of 1812 made him one of the most popular heroes of the early nineteenth century. Decatur's likeness was reproduced on souvenir mugs and pitchers; grateful citizens gave balls in his honor, and he received valuable gifts and prizes. He is still remembered for a toast he gave at a dinner in Norfolk that ended, "Our country . . . right or wrong."

Appointed to the board of navy commissioners, Decatur and his beautiful young wife, Susan, moved to Washington from New York in 1816. Decatur decided to invest some of his prize money in Washington real estate and selected a site on the northwest corner of the President's Square, the large lawn in front of the Executive Mansion. Land was available there when President Jefferson, believing that Pierre L'Enfant's plan for a President's Square was too pretentious, reduced its size. Saint John's Church, designed by Benjamin H. Latrobe, was

Commodore Stephen Decatur

the only other building on the square, which was then an open field that had been used by the local militia in the War of 1812. (The President's Square was renamed in honor of Lafayette in 1825.)

Decatur selected Latrobe, the country's first professional architect, to design his three-story brick town house. Latrobe, who was rebuilding the Capitol and the President's House after the British burning of 1814, created a symmetrical, classically inspired design.

The Decaturs moved into their new house in 1819, and it soon became a center of social life in the capital. In March 1820, they gave a ball in honor of President Monroe's daughter, Maria, who was the first presidential daughter to be married in the White House. Soon afterward—fourteen months after moving into his elegant new home—the forty-one-year-old naval hero was killed in a duel with his longtime foe, Commodore James Barron. (In 1807, Barron had surrendered his ship, *Chesapeake*, to the British and in the ensuing trial—in which Decatur was one of the judges—was sentenced to five years without pay. Barron blamed Decatur for ruining his career.)

The grief-stricken Susan Decatur moved to Georgetown and rented her house to a succession of tenants. The first occupant, the French minister, Baron Hyde de Neuville, was followed in 1822 by the Russian minister, Baron de Tuyll.

Henry Clay moved in when President John Quincy Adams appointed him secretary of state; he entertained lavishly until Andrew Jackson's election sent him back to Kentucky. Martin Van Buren followed Clay as secretary of state and resident of Decatur House. Van Buren and his close friend, President Jackson, reportedly sent secret signals to each other from their windows across the square. The next secretary of state, Edward Livingston, was also a tenant, from 1832 to 1833.

After a brief rental by the British minister, the house was purchased for $12,000 by John Gadsby, owner of hotels in Baltimore, Alexandria, and Washington. After Gadsby's death in 1844, the house was leased to a number of federal officials and was appropriated by the government during the Civil War.

In 1871, Decatur House was acquired by the colorful and adventurous Edward Fitzgerald Beale. In 1848, Beale had brought to Washington—in a record-breaking, forty-seven-day, cross-country trip—news of the discovery of gold in California. Later, Beale, who served as general superintendent of Indian affairs for California and Nevada, persuaded

Secretary of War Jefferson Davis to import camels from the Near East for transportation in the southwestern desert instead of pack mules. Two paintings in Decatur House, *The Search for Water* and *The Horses Eagerly Quenching Thirst, Camels Disdaining*, are souvenirs of this 1856 experiment.

During the 1870s, fashionable Victorian-style homes were being built on the square by William Wilson Corcoran, John Hay, and Henry Adams. To keep up with his neighbors, Beale lengthened the first floor windows, added sandstone trim, and removed the fanlight over the front door.

Beale's son, Truxtun Beale, inherited Decatur House in 1902, and once again it became a center of social life. The Beales were particularly noted for the parties they gave each year following the White House reception for the diplomatic corps. In 1944, Mrs. Beale retained architect Thomas T. Waterman to restore the house to its original Federal appearance.

The Truxtun-Decatur Naval Museum, established in the carriage house in 1950, was moved to its present location at the Navy Yard in 1982.

In 1956, Mrs. Beale bequeathed Decatur House to the National Trust for Historic Preservation.

TOURING THE MUSEUM

Six rooms are open to the public on the first and second floors. On the first floor, the rooms are furnished in Federal style, similar to the furnishings of the Decaturs. The second floor reflects the Beales' occupancy, with Victorian styles and souvenirs of their travels. Ceilings on the second floor are fifteen feet high, while those on the first floor are twelve feet—an indication of the relative importance of the rooms on the two stories.

The museum shop is located in an adjoining wing added by John Gadsby.

FIRST FLOOR

ENTRANCE HALL
Latrobe's classical inspiration is evident the moment you step inside the beautifully proportioned entrance hall, with its domed ceiling and symmetrically placed doors. Curved double doors leading to a winding staircase are reminiscent of those in the Octagon House. Like the Octagon, an ivory "amity button" in the newel post indicates that all work has been completed and all bills have been paid.

PARLOR
As owners of a high-style urban home, the Decaturs would have used fashionable Argand whale oil lamps, such as those

The parlor

on the mantelpiece—named for Swiss inventor Aimé Argand—rather than candles. In the breakfront are Decatur commemorative pitchers and green-and-white Fitzhugh Chinese export porcelain. Stephen Decatur's ivory-handled presentation sword and other memorabilia are in a glass display case nearby. An unusual nineteenth-century armchair that converts to library steps stands near the fireplace.

FAMILY DINING ROOM

Portraits of Stephen Decatur's mother and father, a handsome mahogany sideboard, and a set of rush-seated Sheraton fancy chairs are notable features of the room. After Decatur's death, his widow, in need of money, sold the silver tea urn on the sideboard. Sympathetic friends bought it back for her *twice* before she finally decided to keep it. The Chinese export porcelain punch bowl is a commemorative piece honoring Decatur's father, a naval officer who fought in the Revolutionary War.

DECATUR BEDROOM

Originally, the room to the right of the entrance hall had a false door (for symmetry), instead of the door that now opens on to the hall. The room is furnished with original Decatur pieces—his parents' four-poster bed with 1816 French toile fabric, a dressing table with a simulated marble top, Hepplewhite chairs, a Delaware Valley Chippendale high chest and table, and Decatur's Louis XVI-style writing desk. The black lacquer Chinoiserie sewing table is reputed to have been a gift from Decatur to a former fiancée.

SMALL SITTING ROOM

SECOND FLOOR

The random-width pine floor in this room to the right of the stairs is the only original floor exposed in the house. Used as a morning room by Mrs. Beale, it is furnished with comfortable sofas and family photographs. The camels Edward Fitzgerald Beale introduced to California, seen in paintings here, were kept on his 200,000-acre ranch near Bakersfield, California.

The silver Truxtun Urn, presented to Captain Thomas Truxtun in 1800, stands on a table beneath a portrait of Truxtun, who was a Beale ancestor.

SOUTH DRAWING ROOM

Victorian sofas and chairs of laminated rosewood, two paintings, *The French Legation Visiting the Turkish Empire*, (school of Tiepolo), an eighteenth-century French painting of *Diana and Her Handmaidens*, and nineteenth-century Dutch marquetry chairs reflect the eclectic tastes of Marie Beale, the last private owner of Decatur House. The ceiling decoration of grape leaves and ivy dates from around 1950, and includes elements of painted decoration first installed in the 1870s. The crystal chandelier, made in Philadelphia around 1876, was originally lit by gas.

NORTH DRAWING ROOM

The furnishings are similar to those in the adjoining drawing room. The most unusual feature is the state seal of California, inlaid with almost two dozen woods from North, Central, and South America, in the center of the floor. The seal symbolizes California's importance in the lives of Edward Fitzgerald Beale and his son, Truxtun.

DIPLOMATIC RECEPTION ROOMS

Department of State
Twenty-third and C Streets, N.W.
Washington, D.C. 20520
202/647-3241

METRO	Foggy Bottom.
TOURS	9:30 A.M., 10:30 A.M., and 3 P.M. Monday through Friday by appointment only.
ADMISSION	Free.
HANDICAPPED FACILITIES	Entrance accessible to the disabled. Elevators available.
AUTHOR'S CHOICE	John Quincy Adams State Drawing Room Thomas Jefferson State Reception Room Benjamin Franklin State Dining Room

Stepping into the elevator to the eighth floor of the State Department Building is like entering a time machine that transports you to eighteenth-century America. What you are about to see is a $50 million collection of museum-quality American furniture and decorative arts from approximately 1740 to 1825.

These—together with the White House—are the most beautiful rooms of period furniture in Washington and clearly among the finest in the United States.

Since 1961, the fine arts committee of the State Department has been assembling this collection under the chairmanship of curator Clement E. Conger, who has been called "The Grand Acquisitor." Funds from individuals, corporations, and foundations—not the federal government—have helped to transform an entire floor of a government office building into a showcase of the finest late eighteenth- and early nineteenth-century American design and decorative arts.

Virtually the only thing that has not changed in the remodeling is the spectacular view of the Lincoln Memorial and the Potomac River visible from the terrace. Oriental rugs now cover mahogany floors, where once wall-to-wall carpeting was laid over concrete. Reproductions have given way to antiques, and acoustic ceiling tiles have been replaced with plaster. Sparkling crystal chandeliers have replaced more mundane light fixtures. And eighteenth-century architectural details, such as pilasters and pediments, now grace formerly plain walls.

Approximately twenty percent of the furnishings are on loan to the State Department. The renovation continues, with the fine arts committee still seeking donors for furniture, paintings, and accessories for these rooms, as well as for offices of the secretary of state and his deputy. The committee also hopes to find donors for architectural improvements to the rooms.

EDWARD VASON JONES MEMORIAL HALL

This elevator hall, along with the entrance hall and the passageway to the gallery, set the tone for the splendors to come. Edward Vason Jones was an Albany, Georgia, architect who—without compensation—spent the last fifteen years of his life, from 1965 to 1980, designing and remodeling the Diplomatic Reception Rooms.

The *faux marbre* pilasters and entablature are adaptations of those at Marmion, a Virginia house whose parlor is now in the Metropolitan Museum of Art. The marble for the floor came from King of Prussia, Pennsylvania, out of a quarry that closed more than a hundred years ago.

ENTRANCE HALL

Completed in 1979, the paneling in this room was inspired by the great James River plantations in Virginia. Highlights include a Massachusetts secretary whose corkscrew finials and bombé base signal its Boston origin. Signed by Benjamin Frothingham in 1753, this is the earliest dated bombé piece in the country. A Chippendale highboy on another wall has a peanut carved on the apron, which was characteristic of eighteenth-century Philadelphia craftsmen.

In the adjacent passageway, *The Landing of the Pilgrims* by Michele Felice Cornè takes a few amusing liberties with history, since passengers in the boat include British Redcoats as well as Pilgrims.

The breakfront filled with early American silver is one of two American Chippendale breakfronts in the collection (the three others on view are English). Since glass was heavily taxed in the colonies, few Americans could afford a piece such as this.

The tall case clock in the corner, made in the workshop of Thomas Harland of Connecticut in 1776, chimes an eighteenth-century tune every third hour. Another great Philadelphia 1775 Chippendale tall case clock has the most ambitious features and dials ever attempted in North America.

GALLERY

In 1969, Edward Vason Jones solved the difficult architectural challenge of this long narrow room by installing Palladian windows in each of the two end walls. Much of the Queen Anne and Chippendale furniture was made in the Townsend and Goddard workshops in Newport, Rhode Island. They were particularly noted for their skill in creating blockfront designs.

A small bombé chest with a serpentine front is one of only six such pieces in the country.

Portraits include *George Washington* by Gilbert Stuart, and *Mrs. John Montresor* and *Alice Hooper* both by John Singleton Copley. The Honduran mahogany secretary near the painting of Alice Hooper originally belonged to her father, Robert "King" Hooper, a late eighteenth-century Marblehead, Massachusetts, shipping magnate.

A sixty-five-piece dinner service of Chinese export porcelain, in the green-and-white Fitzhugh pattern, can be seen in the breakfront. The china, which had been ordered for a Philadelphia family, was never used. It was still in its original cartons when loaned to the State Department in 1965.

JOHN QUINCY ADAMS STATE DRAWING ROOM

Used by the secretary of state, the vice-president, and cabinet members to receive guests at official luncheons and dinners, this is one of the largest reception rooms in the United States. It is furnished in the style of an elegant American drawing room of the late eighteenth century, with Chippendale pieces that could have been found in a large Philadelphia home.

Portraits of *George* and *Martha Washington* by Rembrandt Peale, *James Monroe* by Thomas Sully, and *Thomas Jefferson* by Dr. William Thornton are among the most important portraits in the room. Thornton, architect of the Octagon and the Capitol building, copied a classically inspired Gilbert Stuart profile portrait of Jefferson.

In January 1986, the State Department acquired *John Jay* by Gilbert Stuart, which is considered to be one of Stuart's greatest portraits. The painting, which was owned by a descendant of John Jay, secretary of foreign affairs during the second Continental Congress, had been loaned to the State Department for the previous twelve years. Its $990,000 auction price was contributed by two members of the fine arts committee.

Be sure to see the English Sheraton desk on which the Treaty of Paris was signed in 1783. American diplomat John Jay's chair in front of the desk contains a secret compartment under the seat.

Over the mantel, *The American Commissioners*, from the studio of Benjamin West, depicts American commissioners Jay, John Adams, Benjamin Franklin, Henry Laurens, and Temple Franklin signing the preliminary Treaty of Paris in 1782, ending the Revolutionary War.

Other historic furniture includes the architect's table-desk that Thomas Jefferson used in his Philadelphia apartment while attending the Continental Congress. Portions of the Declaration of Independence were drafted on it.

On the backs of six Chippendale chairs along the long north wall you can see carved peanuts, which mark them as Philadelphia pieces.

English Sheraton writing desk used for the final signing of the 1783 Treaty of Peace between England and the United States.

Rare Philadelphia Chippendale mahogany highboy attributed to Joseph Deleveau, circa 1775.

The large breakfront contains part of George Washington's Order of the Cincinnati Chinese export porcelain dinner service. Also in the breakfront are a Chinese porcelain punch bowl commemorating the surrender of British General John Burgoyne (whose officers are shown with oriental features), and one of Martha Washington's saucers. This extremely rare saucer was part of a "States" series that had the names of all the states inscribed around the border and an "M.W." monogram in the center.

THOMAS JEFFERSON STATE RECEPTION ROOM

In creating this room, Edward Vason Jones used the same design books that Thomas Jefferson used to create an elegantly simple, neoclassical effect. Completed in 1974, the doric entablature is based on designs by Andrea Palladio and Jefferson. An eighteenth-century white Carrara marble mantelpiece, supported by two classically draped figures, is the focal point of one wall.

A full-length statue of Jefferson is a modern copy of the 1833 bronze by David d'Angers in the U.S. Capitol. On a table near the entrance is the world's only known sterling silver knife box, made in England in 1797-98, which holds seventy-two knives.

Two portraits are worth noting. *Thomas Jefferson* by Thomas Sully was painted in 1822, four years before Jefferson's death. *Benjamin Franklin*, in a handsome fur-trimmed coat, was done from life by Jean Baptiste Greuze in Paris in 1777.

The Thomas Jefferson State Reception Room

BENJAMIN FRANKLIN STATE DINING ROOM

Redesigned by Philadelphia architect John Blatteau in 1985, this room features fluted *scagliola* Corinthian columns which resemble marble, and eight Adam-style chandeliers that were copied from the original London 1790 chandelier in the Thomas Jefferson State Reception Room.

One hundred feet long and forty-five feet wide, the room accommodates two hundred and fifty people for seated dinners and three hundred and fifty for receptions.

A floral still life by Severin Roesen hangs above a mahogany sideboard formerly owned by descendants of President Martin Van Buren.

The portrait of *Benjamin Franklin* by David Martin over the mantel—reportedly Franklin's favorite—is a contemporary replica of the one that hangs in the Green Room of the White House. The original was painted from life in London in 1767.

INTERIOR DEPARTMENT MUSEUM

Eighteenth and C Streets, N.W.
Washington, D.C. 20240
202/343-2743

METRO	Farragut West.
HOURS	8 A.M. to 5 P.M. Monday through Friday. Closed weekends and holidays.
TOURS	Group tours by appointment.
ADMISSION	Free.
HANDICAPPED FACILITIES	Accessible to the disabled. Handicapped entrance on E Street.
FOOD SERVICE	Cafeteria open 7:30 A.M. to 2:30 P.M. Monday through Friday.
AUTHOR'S CHOICE	Indian arts and crafts Early land patents Mineral specimens Mapmaking exhibits

This rather old-fashioned museum on the first floor of the Interior Department building—near the C Street entrance—is popular with school groups. They sometimes overflow the rows of benches that fill the first two galleries.

The museum, said to be the brainchild of former Secretary of the Interior Harold Ickes, has been part of the building ever since it opened in 1937. Exhibits tell the story of the Department of the Interior, with displays devoted to the National Park Service, the Geological Survey, the Fish and Wildlife Service, and the Bureaus of Land Management, Reclamation, Mines, and Indian Affairs.

Dioramas show the meeting of George Washington and the Marquis de Lafayette in 1780 and an Indian trading post as it looked in 1835. Cases filled with mineral specimens illustrate the geology of the United States; old surveys and land patents help to shed light on the country's growth, and other exhibits show the topographical mapping of Antarctica. Moose, buffalo, and bear heads on the walls and an Indian bark canoe suspended from the ceiling add to the atmosphere.

American Indian kachina, basket, and pottery bowl

A new exhibit, installed in the summer of 1991, uses hundreds of photographs and contemporary artifacts to present an overview of the department's changing responsibilities and current activities.

The display of Indian crafts in the first gallery to the left of the entrance appeals to many visitors. The artifacts include an Indian chief's headdress, Navajo rugs, Hopi kachinas, beadwork of the Plains, and a variety of woven baskets, including some made by the Tlinget, Pima, Hopi, and Mohawk tribes. The pottery ranges from rough-hewn Pueblo pieces to the elegant black Santa Clara ware. Note especially a Zuni polychrome jar decorated with butterflies and carved frogs.

The Indian Craft Shop across the hall, in Room 1023, sells fine quality Indian jewelry, baskets, pottery, and other crafts from 8:30 A.M. to 4:30 P.M., Monday through Friday.

NATIONAL GEOGRAPHIC SOCIETY EXPLORERS HALL

Seventeenth and M Streets, N.W.
Washington, D.C. 20036
202/857-7000
202/857-7588 recorded information

METRO	Farragut North, L Street Exit.
HOURS	9 A.M. to 5 P.M. Monday through Saturday and holidays; 10 A.M. to 5 P.M. Sunday. Closed Christmas Day.
ADMISSION	Free.
HANDICAPPED FACILITIES	Ramp at M Street entrance. Accessible to the disabled.
GIFT SHOP	The only place to buy National Geographic Society books, other than by mail order. Also postcards, maps, atlases, and globes.
SPECIAL EVENTS	Films and lectures.
MEMBERSHIP	National Geographic Society membership $18 per calendar year.
AUTHOR'S CHOICE	Earth Station One National Geographic Globe Henry, a live macaw

Explorers Hall is a lively, participatory place filled with objects, photographs, displays, and videotapes of society-sponsored and other scientific explorations. The current exhibit, Geographica, uses state-of-the-art technology to explain the earth and its geography through interactive displays.

THE BUILDING
Designed by Edward Durrell Stone, architect of the John F. Kennedy Center for the Performing Arts, this marble and glass building at the corner of Seventeenth and M Streets has been home since 1964 to the far-flung scientific and publishing operations of the National Geographic Society. The National Geographic complex also includes two other buildings—its original home on Sixteenth Street, which now houses the society's library, and a new pyramidal building slightly reminiscent of the Hanging Gardens of Babylon, which is entered through the M Street courtyard.

TOURING THE HALL
Start your tour by turning left inside the main (Seventeenth Street) entrance, on the first floor. You can make a complete

The National Geographic Society complex

circle of Explorers Hall and end at the publications desk, which is to the right of the main entrance.

In an hour or so, you can learn fascinating facts about the earth's surface—its mountains, rivers, oceans, and deserts—through dioramas, maps, and audiovisual displays. An introductory film sets the scene.

EARTH SCIENCE

In an exhibit devoted to earthquakes and volcanoes around the world, you can learn about the eruption of Mount St. Helen's in Washington, as well as volcanoes in Hawaii, and earthquakes in California and Japan.

EARLY HUMANS

This exhibit traces the evolution of man from tree-dwelling apes to ground-dwelling hominoids.

METEOROLOGY

You can see the current weather patterns in the United States. A highlight of the display about weather conditions is a simulated tornado that can be touched.

GLOBAL ACCESS

You can play an electronic game about the countries of the world, testing your knowledge of geography.

EARTH STATION ONE

Earth Station One, a seventy-two-seat amphitheater, simulates an orbital flight twenty-three thousand miles above the earth. In an interactive program, the "Captain" poses questions about geography which the audience answers electronically. Programs last approximately fifteen minutes, and run several times an hour. (Groups of fifteen or more should call 202/857-7689 for reservations.)

The society's eleven-foot, hand-painted, fiberglass globe is the focal point of Earth Station One. It is the world's largest unmounted sphere, and weighs nearly 1,100 pounds. The globe can revolve in any direction to show different parts of its surface. And, to give you an idea of its scale—a sixty-mile hike would take you just one inch on this huge model.

SEA EXPLORERS
Four prominent oceanographers are introduced and followed on their respective adventures to unlock the secrets of the oceans.

BIOLOGY
You can use a cyberscope to see an ant colony, a grasshopper, a spider, and other creatures.

HENRY, THE MACAW
Henry, a blue-and-gold macaw native to Central and South America, has been a resident of the National Geographic Society since 1964.

Nearby is the preserved specimen of the world's largest frog. This goliath frog weighed seven pounds when found in Cameroon, West Africa, in 1967.

EXPLORATION
In the center of the gallery stands a huge basalt head, a copy of an Olmec head found by a National Geographic Society-Smithsonian archaeological expedition in the jungles of Tabasco, Mexico. The lost Olmec civilization, a predecessor of the Mayas and Aztecs, flourished in Mexico from 1200 to 400 B.C. A nearby display case contains pottery and a thousand-year-old turquoise necklace crafted by the Anasazi Indians.

The exhibit salutes the achievements of various explorers, including Admiral Richard E. Byrd, the first man to fly over both the North and the South Pole. His bronze bust by sculptor Felix de Weldon can be seen here.

Another exhibit is devoted to Admiral Robert E. Peary, the first man to reach the North Pole in 1909. Peary adopted the diet, dress, and travel of the Eskimos. Accompanied by Matthew Henson, he learned to drive the hand-made sled, drawn by a team of huskies, that is shown here.

During Peary's trip to the Pole in 1909, he carried an American flag made by his wife, and marked his route by depositing small pieces of the flag at various places. On April 6, 1909, he finally raised the flag over the North Pole, after cutting a long diagonal strip down the middle to mark the end of his journey. Later explorers found the two fragments in this exhibit at Cape Columbia and Cape Thomas Hubbard.

SPACE SCIENCE
The current night sky over Washington, D.C., is visible in a small planetarium here. There is also information about space and the solar system.

EXPLORER THEATER
You can see a dazzling, multi-image collage of some of the most memorable footage from National Geographic Television Specials and Explorer TV.

IN THE PICTURE
You can wind up your visit to Geographica by taking a photograph of yourself which is then superimposed on the cover of *National Geographic*.

THE OCTAGON

1799 New York Avenue, N.W.
Washington, D.C. 20006
202/638-3105

METRO	Farragut West.
HOURS	10 A.M. to 4 P.M. Tuesday through Friday; 1 to 4 P.M. Saturday and Sunday. Closed Monday and major holidays.
TOURS	Walk-in tours available whenever the house is open.
ADMISSION	$2 tax-deductible contribution suggested.
HANDICAPPED FACILITIES	Ramp entrance at the back of the house. First floor accessible to the disabled.
MUSEUM SHOP	Exhibition catalogs and books on history and architecture.
SPECIAL EVENTS	Lectures; architecture, history, and design-related exhibitions; special re-creations of historical events, including Twelfth Night Celebration in December and Madison Ice Cream Festival in September.
AUTHOR'S CHOICE	Federal period rooms, first floor Treaty Room, second floor Exhibition galleries, second floor

The Octagon, one of the earliest Federal houses in Washington, is owned by the American Architectural Foundation, which preserves it as a museum of architecture and the decorative arts. The temporary White House during the War of 1812, it is a six-sided structure, despite its name.

THE BUILDING

In 1798, Washington was a rural village with only a few frame houses and unpaved, muddy streets—hardly the major capital city envisioned in Pierre Charles L'Enfant's elaborate plan.

The capital's planned move from Philadelphia to Washington in 1800 sparked a wave of real estate speculation and a small-scale building boom. George Washington, who had selected the site for the new capital, was among those promoting its virtues. He encouraged his friend, Col. John Tayloe III to build a town house in Washington, rather than in Philadelphia.

In April 1797, Tayloe paid Gustavus W. Scott, one of the first purchasers of land in the newly platted Federal City, $1,000 for Lot 8 in Square 170 at the corner of New York Avenue and Eighteenth Street. As designer, he selected Dr. William Thornton, who had won the design competition for the Capitol. Two years later, in April 1799, Thornton wrote George Washington that "Mr. J. Tayloe, of Virginia, has contracted to build a house in the City near the President's Square of $13,000 value." As sometimes happens with architectural estimates, the final cost was more than double that amount.

Thornton, who was born in the West Indies and raised in England, studied medicine in Edinburgh. Although trained as a

The Octagon

physician, Thornton's interests covered many fields, from art, architecture, and astronomy to government and philosophy. He was a self-trained architect, who reportedly studied architecture for just two weeks. Most of his knowledge of architecture came from the handbooks on the subject that were part of eighteenth-century gentlemen's libraries. Benjamin Ogle Tayloe, son of John Tayloe III, wrote of Thornton, "He had a well-earned reputation for letters and taste; he was a wit, a painter, and a poet." Thornton's elegantly simple Federal design for the Octagon is an ingenious solution to the problem of an oddly shaped site.

The house was finished in 1801 and soon became a center of social life and hospitality. A report of 1801 notes that the Octagon was one of only three brick houses in the city. (There were also three made of wood.) And, with its Sheraton and Hepplewhite furnishings largely imported from England, it was clearly one of the most elegant homes in the new capital.

George Washington, James Madison, Thomas Jefferson, James Monroe, John Adams, Andrew Jackson, Stephen Decatur, the Marquis de Lafayette, Henry Clay, and Daniel Webster were among those entertained at the Octagon.

On August 24, 1814, during the War of 1812, the British set fire to the White House, the Capitol, and other government buildings. Dolley Madison fled the White House just before the British arrived, and the Madisons stayed with friends near Langley, Virginia.

The French Minister, Louis Serurier, was living at the Octagon, which he called "the best house in the city," and the French flag was flying over the mansion. During that period, the Tayloes occupied their town house only during the winter.

Serurier sent a message to General Robert Ross, commander of the British troops at the President's House, requesting that the Octagon be spared, since it was the French Embassy. The general agreed, and no damage was done to the Octagon or, in fact, to any other private property.

The following month, with the French minister planning to move to Philadelphia, John Tayloe invited the Madisons to stay at the Octagon while the White House was being restored. The Madisons lived there from September 8, 1814 until March 1815, when they moved to a smaller house at Pennsylvania Avenue and Nineteenth Street. Dolley Madison resumed her *levées* and parties in the Octagon drawing room. And the president set up his office in a second floor study. It was in this room, on February 17, 1815, that Madison signed the Treaty of Ghent, ending the War of 1812.

The first floor stair hall

The Tayloes had fifteen children, including seven who were born at the Octagon. The family continued to occupy the house until Ann Ogle Tayloe died in 1855. The house was then rented to a variety of tenants, including a girls' school and the government hydrographic office. By the turn of the century, the neighborhood was no longer the prime residential area it had once been, and the building had fallen into disrepair. Before the American Institute of Architects (AIA) leased it in 1899, ten tenant families occupied the house. Trash was four-feet deep in the drawing room, fireplaces were boarded up, windows were broken, and paint was peeling from the walls.

In 1902, AIA purchased the building, together with the original stable, smokehouse, and garden, for its headquarters. By 1940, AIA had outgrown the space and added new administrative offices along the eastern property line. Eventually, more space was needed, so those offices were razed and, in 1972, a seven-story, $7 million glass and concrete headquarters building, designed by The Architects Collaborative, was erected. It encloses the garden and focuses on the historic house.

The mansion has undergone extensive rehabilitation since the AIA acquired it. In 1968, when the building was transferred to the AIA Foundation, it was decided to restore it as closely as possible to its original condition. A $3.5 million restoration, currently under way, includes stripping away as many as twenty-seven layers of paint from walls, woodwork, doors, and moldings, duplicating the original paint colors, and restoring the basement to its original configuration as a service area.

FIRST FLOOR

ENTRANCE HALL

You enter a large circular entrance hall with blue-green walls and the original gray-and-white marble floor. The two rare coal-burning stoves, topped with Adamesque urns, are tucked into the same wall recesses they occupied in the Tayloes' day. Coal was more expensive than wood at the time the Octagon was built, and only the wealthiest families had stoves such as these.

The English settee and chairs in the adjoining stair hall are original Tayloe pieces.

Note the ivory "amity buttons" in the mahogany handrail at the foot of the stairway, indicating that the building has been completed and paid for.

The impressive oval staircase curves continuously to the third floor. According to legend, several ghosts occupy the Octagon, including two Tayloe daughters who allegedly died in falls from the third floor stairway after disagreeing with their father about the men they wanted to marry. There have also been reports from time to time of a swaying chandelier, flickering lights, mysterious footprints, unexplained noises, and cooking aromas from the long-unused kitchen.

DINING ROOM

Both the dining room and the drawing room have their original Coade stone mantels, which were made in England about 1800. The Coade factory's product was an exceptionally durable artificial cast stone, similar to terracotta. Unfortunately, the formula has been lost and Coade stone has not been made since around 1836.

The period furnishings include a Scottish Chippendale breakfront filled with Chinese export porcelain, Hepplewhite chairs, and an inlaid Sheraton sideboard in a shallow wall recess. The table settings are changed each month. For example, you might see the table laid for high tea, with a silver tea service and Staffordshire cups and saucers. On another occasion, there might be a three-part Sheffield plateau, once owned by the Tayloes, in the center of the table.

On the wall are profile portraits of Dr. William Thornton and Colonel John Tayloe, painted by French artist Charles de Saint-Mémin in 1805.

Above the mantel is a copy of Edward Savage's well-known painting *The Washington Family*, showing George and Martha

Washington at Mount Vernon with L'Enfant's plan for the Federal city. The original is at the National Gallery of Art.

DRAWING ROOM

This room, to the right of the entrance hall, was the focal point of entertainment in the new capital. Everybody who was anybody in the young republic came here to discuss the news of the day and trade bits of gossip beneath the sparkling English Regency chandelier.

The two fine Gilbert Stuart portraits of *William Thornton* and *Mrs. Thornton* have been loaned by the National Gallery of Art.

TREATY ROOM   SECOND FLOOR

This circular room at the head of the stairs was John Tayloe's study and President Madison's office. Its most important role came in 1815, when the Treaty of Ghent was taken out of the leather-bound box on the table and signed by President Madison, ending the War of 1812. The round English rent table on which the treaty was signed has file drawers marked from A to Z in ivory. In 1897, the table was sold by John Ogle Tayloe to Mrs. A. H. Voorhies of San Francisco. To protect it during the 1906 earthquake and fire, Mrs. Voorhies wrapped the table in bedsheets, turned it on its side, and rolled it away from her home. She later sold the table to the San Francisco AIA chapter for $1,000, and it was returned to the Octagon in 1911.

On either side of the Treaty Room, former bedrooms have been converted into galleries for architecture and design-related exhibitions.

The upstairs parlor, where the Treaty of Ghent was signed.

KITCHEN AND WINE CELLAR   BASEMENT

The original brick floor is laid in a herringbone pattern. Note the large fireplace and oven and the eighteenth-century cooking utensils.

A cupboard holds blue-and-white Canton porcelain, which came to America as ballast in early sailing ships.

Recesses in the adjoining wine cellar held barrels of wine.

OLD EXECUTIVE OFFICE BUILDING

**Pennsylvania Avenue and Seventeenth Street, N.W.
Washington, D.C. 20503
202/395-5895**

METRO	Farragut North or West.
TOURS	By appointment 9 A.M. to Noon Saturday. Write Preservation Office, Room 484, for reservations or call between 9 A.M. and Noon weekdays. Give birth date of each person on tour.
ADMISSION	Free.
HANDICAPPED FACILITIES	Ramp entrance at Seventeenth Street. Elevators available.
AUTHOR'S CHOICE	Indian Treaty Room Executive Office of the President Library Vice President's office West Rotunda

Every now and then, you find a building whose architecture arouses a storm of controversy—feelings of great affection or animosity. Ever since it was built as the State, War, and Navy Building, the Old Executive Office Building (OEOB) has been in that category.

Few structures in Washington are associated with as many historic people and events as this one. OEOB has housed twenty-five secretaries of state, twenty-one secretaries of war, and fifteen secretaries of the navy. And every vice-president since Lyndon B. Johnson has had an office in the building.

Six presidents worked here before winning the White House—Theodore Roosevelt, assistant secretary of the navy, 1897–98; William Howard Taft, secretary of war, 1904–08; Franklin D. Roosevelt, assistant secretary of the navy, 1913–18; Dwight D. Eisenhower, military aide to General Douglas MacArthur, 1933; Lyndon B. Johnson, vice-president, 1961–63, and George Bush, vice-president, 1981–89.

More than a thousand treaties have been signed here.

The Old Executive Office Building

Secretary of War Taft was in his OEOB suite when he received word of his presidential nomination. And in Room 208, Secretary of State Cordell Hull received the Japanese ambassadors on December 7, 1941, the day Pearl Harbor was attacked.

Yet, despite this impressive record, OEOB's history also includes threats to obliterate its exuberant Second French Empire façade and to raze the building completely.

Until June 1985, the building was closed to the public. Now, it is open for prearranged Saturday morning tours. Because of security requirements, you must give the birth date of everyone in your party when you write or call for a reservation.

Tours begin in the Seventeenth Street lobby, opposite G Street, and include the Indian Treaty Room, the State Department and War Department libraries, the Secretary of the Navy's office, and several other restored areas on five floors. Elevators are available for those unable to climb stairs.

HISTORY

Originally, two small brick government office buildings flanked the White House. The Treasury Building, begun in 1798, stood on the east side and a similar structure, begun in 1799 to house the War Department, was located west of the White House. Following a fire in 1800, the building was rebuilt to house the State, War, and Navy Departments. On August 24, 1814, the White House and the two executive office buildings were burned by the British. The executive offices were rebuilt in 1816, according to a Federal-style design by White House architect James Hoban. Two additional office buildings of similar design were constructed in front of the original pair on Pennsylvania Avenue two years later.

With the country growing rapidly, the burgeoning federal bureaucracy soon outgrew these four small buildings. In 1836, work began on a Greek Revival Treasury building designed by Robert Mills, architect of the Patent Office and later of the Washington Monument. In 1852, plans were drawn for a similar building on the other side of the White House, but the Civil War forced cancellation of its construction.

When the war ended, Congress voted to house the State, War, and Navy Departments together on a site west of the White House. In 1870, Secretary of State Hamilton Fish, who was in charge of construction, selected Alfred B. Mullett, supervising architect of the U.S. Treasury, to design a new federal office building "similar in ground plan and dimensions to the Treasury Building."

Fish, who had discovered the Second French Empire style while visiting Europe before the Civil War, shared Mullett's enthusiasm for the new, cosmopolitan architecture. The Renwick Gallery, one of the earliest Second Empire public buildings, had been built across the street from the OEOB in 1859 to house William Wilson Corcoran's art collection. The style, characterized by a mansard roof, pavilions, and rows of columns and pilasters on successive stories, was inspired by the new wing of the Louvre in Paris.

In addition to designing the exterior, Mullett designed the interior of the State Department's south wing. In 1874, he resigned, following a series of disagreements with the new secretary of the treasury. Mullett committed suicide in 1890, and his ghost and that of Hamilton Fish are said to haunt the building. Mullett was succeeded by Richard von Ezdorf, an Austrian architect, who is credited with some of the building's most flamboyant decorative details.

Those who were expecting a Greek Revival building that would complement the Treasury Building were sorely disappointed by Mullett's design. In later years, as Victorian styles fell out of favor and were replaced by Beaux Arts and Neoclassical designs, there was talk of changing the façade. In 1917, John Russell Pope, who later designed the National Gallery of Art West Building, the Jefferson Memorial, and the National Archives Building, sketched a Classical Revival-style exterior. And in 1930, Congress authorized Waddy B. Wood, architect of the Woodrow Wilson house and the Textile Museum, to redesign the building to make it "harmonious generally in architectural appearance with the Treasury Building." Only a last minute contract dispute and financial problems caused by the Depression prevented Mullett's Second French Empire façade from being redesigned.

In 1957, an advisory commission on presidential office space recommended that the Old Executive Office Building be torn down and replaced with a new seven-story office building for the executive office of the president and several other agencies. The report again focused attention on the OEOB, and the controversy between those who wanted the building to remain and those who thought it should be razed continued for several years. Finally, in 1961, officials of the General Services Administration announced that it would "stand indefinitely." Inclusion in the National Register of Historic Places in 1971 and in the District of Columbia Inventory of Historic Sites in 1972 added further protection.

The Navy Department moved out of the building in 1918, and the War Department left in 1938, followed by the State Department in 1947. The White House began to use the space for offices as early as 1939. Ten years later, the Executive Office Building was turned over to the executive office of the president. When a new Executive Office Building was constructed in the early 1960s, this historic structure was given its present name. In addition to presidential staff, the building now houses offices of the vice-president, the National Security Council, the Council of Economic Advisors, and the Office of Management and Budget, among others.

THE BUILDING

Construction began in 1871 and continued, one wing at a time, for seventeen years. When the OEOB was finally completed in 1888, it was the largest office building in Washington. Its size conveyed a sense of stability that was important in the aftermath of the Civil War. The building boasted more than five hundred rooms and nearly two miles of black-and-white marble halls, with eighteen-foot ceilings and four-foot thick granite walls. Because a series of fires had destroyed earlier government buildings, nearly all of the interior detail is of plaster or cast iron, rather than wood. The granite came from quarries near Richmond, Virginia, and in Vinal Haven, Fox Island, Maine.

The building is rectangular, with four wings and two large interior courts separated by a central wing. Soaring, cantilevered staircases with hand-cut granite steps and more

Detail of encaustic tile floor, Indian Treaty Room

than four thousand solid bronze balusters are major architectural features. Each of the 1,314 brass doorknobs bears the insignia of the State, War, or Navy Department, designating the original occupant of the offices. The interior is a vast and wonderful potpourri of columns, pilasters, marble, mahogany, and Minton tile. Research by the OEOB Preservation Office has revealed that areas formerly painted in drab colors were originally richly decorated. The restoration work has begun and is expected to continue for several years.

SOUTH WING

The south wing, completed in 1875, was originally occupied by the State Department. It was the first section of the building to be constructed. (The State Department, whose original building was torn down in 1866 to make room for the Treasury Building, had occupied the D.C. Orphans Asylum until its new home was ready.)

Skylit coffered domes crown the staircases of the north and south wings. The south wing domes have been restored to their original pale green, rust, gold and mauve colors, with a frieze of gold carving against a salmon-colored background.

The four-story library of the Executive Office of the President, originally the State Department's library, was built in 1875 entirely of cast iron. It is notable for the elaborate white cast-iron railings that surround the balconies on the three upper floors. The State Department seal is visible in the two upper-level railings, which appear as delicate as the icing on a cake.

From the time the building opened until approximately 1903, a small museum on the ground floor of the library made this room a popular tourist attraction.

Originally, the library was white with gold-leaf trim. The coved ceiling, of stenciled gold leaf with a blue and gray Greek key design, is the only original decorative painting in the building which has remained untouched. The blue, yellow, brown, and white Minton tile floor is also original. Minton floor tiles, manufactured in England, were a fashionable decorative element in Victorian interior design. Two other libraries of the OEOB, as well as the Capitol, have Minton tile floors.

When the State Department vacated the building in 1947, this space was used for offices and storage. Its library function was restored in 1981 during the Reagan administration, and it is now a general reference library for the White House staff.

EAST WING

Designed for the Navy Department, this wing was completed in 1879. Although most of the Navy moved out in 1918, the secretary of the navy continued to occupy a second-floor office here until 1921.

A massive mahogany desk, flanked by the American and vice-presidential flags, is perhaps the most historic object in the spacious, high-ceilinged vice-president's office. Beginning with Harry S Truman, every vice-president has signed his name inside the top drawer of the desk.

Lyndon B. Johnson was the first vice-presidential occupant. With the exception of Hubert H. Humphrey, whose office was in Room 180, and George Bush, who moved to Room 180

The Indian Treaty Room

when restoration work began near the end of his term, in 1986, all vice-presidents have worked in this historic office.

The intricately designed marquetry floors, Victorian-style chandeliers, and decorative ceiling and woodwork—restored to their original condition in 1987—evoke von Ezdorf's baroque taste.

The east rotunda was restored in 1984, revealing von Ezdorf's 1879 blue-and-white skylight and the original gold and silver moldings, now done in bronze and aluminum powder paint. This rotunda is considered one of von Ezdorf's greatest triumphs, with its red, white, and blue star-shaped lights surrounding an oval skylight. For many years, the skylight had been painted white; during World War II the glass was painted over.

The handsome, two-story Indian Treaty Room was originally the navy department library and reception room. It cost more per square foot than any other room in the building because of its marble wall panels, gold-leaf decoration, and eight-hundred-pound bronze lamps representing War and Peace, Arts and Sciences, Liberty, and Industry. Note that Liberty wears the same type of spiked crown as Frederic Bartholdi's *Statue of Liberty*, which had been designed but was not yet in the New York harbor when this room was created.

Von Ezdorf is credited with the decorations in this elaborate room. Notice the nautical motifs—the shells, seahorses, fish, dolphins, and anchors—worked into the moldings around the Italian marble panels, into the wrought iron railings of the balcony, and scattered throughout the Minton-tiled room. Despite its name, no Indian treaties have been signed here.

Eventually, the Navy Department used this room as a library, rather than for receptions. In 1923, it became a State Department file storage area. Beginning in 1950, it was used for presidential news conferences, and it is now a conference and meeting room.

NORTH, WEST, AND CENTER WINGS

It took ten years to construct the last section of the building, the north, west, and center wings, which were occupied by the War Department.

The north wing domes were completed eight years after the south wing domes, and their stylistic differences result from design changes during the construction period. The central skylights are round, rather than oval, and the coffers are square, rather than octagonal. Research revealed that shades of salmon, green, and tan were the original colors.

Another recently restored space is the west rotunda. Although the original stained glass was removed earlier, the original design has been copied and new glass installed. It resembles a large Tiffany lamp.

Von Ezdorf designed the cast-iron balconies in the small, three-story War Department library of cast iron, electroplated to look like copper and bronze. The decorative metalwork here is the most unusual in the building, with its combination of Classical, Gothic, Moorish, and naturalistic forms. The green, brown, and beige Minton tile floor differs from that of the other OEOB libraries in its mosaic-patterned geometric design. Restored to its original rose and beige tones, this room is now the White House law library.

After Secretary of War William Howard Taft fell down the stairs of one of the wings, brass railings were added to the mahogany railings throughout the building. Until the 1930s, cleaning crews polished the brass railings and the bronze balusters daily, which prompted one scrubwoman to say that the "golden stairs and marble halls looked just like heaven."

ORGANIZATION OF AMERICAN STATES

**Seventeenth Street and Constitution Avenue, N.W.
Washington, D.C. 20006
202/458-3000**

METRO	Farragut West.
HOURS	9 A.M. to 5 P.M. Monday through Friday. Closed Saturday, Sunday, and holidays.
TOURS	Guided tours in English or Spanish by appointment. Call 202/458-3751.
ADMISSION	Free.
AUTHOR'S CHOICE	Statue of Queen Isabella
Tropical patio
Hall of the Americas
Hall of Flags and Heroes

The architectural styles of North and South America blend happily in the House of the Americas, home of the Organization of American States, the oldest international regional organization in the world. Originally called the Pan American Union, its thirty-five member nations represent North, South, Central American, and Caribbean countries.

Designed by Albert Kelsey and Paul Cret, this beaux arts hacienda was built between 1908 and 1910 with funds provided by steel magnate Andrew Carnegie and by the original member states. The land was donated by the U.S. government through an act of Congress.

A statue of Queen Isabella by Spanish artist José Luis Sanchez, a gift from the Institute of Spanish Culture in Madrid, stands outside the main entrance. Since Queen Isabella financed Christopher Columbus's expedition to the New World, her image is an appropriate link between the hemispheres.

Inside, opposite the front door, is a patio covered by a sliding glass roof which protects the tropical atmosphere in winter. The focal point of the patio is a fountain with Aztec motifs, which is surrounded by plants and trees from OAS member states. The lush tropical foliage includes fig, rubber, coffee, and palm trees. Note the stone Aztec figures set into the patio's brick floor.

To the left of the fountain is the Peace Tree, planted by President William Howard Taft in 1910. This fig tree grafted to a rubber plant symbolizes the cultural heritage of the Americas.

Beyond the patio is an art gallery, an adjunct to the Art Museum of the Americas, which features monthly exhibitions of contemporary Latin American artists. Many of these artists are not well known outside of their own countries, and an OAS exhibit provides an excellent opportunity to show their works beyond the borders of their native lands.

On the second floor, you can see the Hall of the Americas and the Hall of Flags and Heroes, filled with busts of the national heroes of the member countries.

RENWICK GALLERY

Pennsylvania Avenue at Seventeenth Street, N.W.
Washington, D.C. 20560
202/357-2700

METRO	Farragut North or West.
HOURS	10 A.M. to 5:30 P.M. daily. Closed Christmas Day.
TOURS	Between 10 A.M. and 1 P.M. Monday through Thursday, by appointment, for groups of five to eight people. Call 202/357-2531.
ADMISSION	Free.
HANDICAPPED FACILITIES	Ramp to lower level entrance on Pennsylvania Avenue at Seventeenth Street. Wheelchairs available.
MUSEUM SHOP	Books on crafts, decorative arts, and design, jewelry and objects relating to the exhibitions. Sales exhibitions of contemporary quality crafts.
SPECIAL EVENTS	"The Creative Screen," a lunchtime film program twice a month on Thursdays. Lectures, concerts, and crafts demonstrations related to exhibitions.
MEMBERSHIP	James Renwick Alliance from $50.
AUTHOR'S CHOICE	Grand Salon, second floor Octagon Room, second floor Sales exhibitions of crafts, museum shop

Washington's first art museum, the Renwick Gallery is a visible reminder of nineteenth-century Washington. Now a curatorial department of the Smithsonian's National Museum of American Art, the gallery presents special exhibitions of contemporary and historical crafts and decorative arts. Its permanent collection features outstanding examples of contemporary American crafts in glass, metal, fiber, clay, and wood.

Wrought iron gates by Albert Paley

HISTORY
In 1859, five years after retiring from the Corcoran and Riggs Bank, William Wilson Corcoran decided to build an art museum to house his collection of paintings and sculpture. He chose James Renwick, Jr., a fashionable architect, for the task. At the age of twenty-seven, Renwick had designed the Smithsonian Institution Building (the "Castle") ten years earlier. Both Corcoran and Renwick had visited the 1855 Paris Exposition and were impressed with the elegance and ornamentation of the new wing of the Louvre, which was built in a style then called Renaissance. Today known as Second French Empire, it is the same architectural style as the Old Executive Office Building across the street.

The Renwick Gallery building, which was designed to be seen on only two sides, has a slate mansard roof and replicas of the original sandstone facings and ornaments. Three corners of the building are topped with pavilions crested with ironwork. To "Americanize" the building, Renwick chose red brick instead of sandstone and crowned the capitals of the

The Corcoran Art Depository, Harper's Weekly, *1869, now the Renwick Gallery of the National Museum of American Art.*

pilasters with ears of Indian corn instead of the traditional acanthus leaves.

Other features of the exterior included niches for statues of "great figures of art" (now replaced with second-story windows), and Corcoran's four-foot-wide portrait medallion and monogram carved into the façade. The inscription "Dedicated to Art" was placed over the entrance.

When the Civil War began in August 1861, the U.S. Army appropriated the partly finished building for the Quartermaster Corps. Records and uniforms were stored there until 1864, when Quartermaster General Montgomery Meigs converted the building from a warehouse to office space.

Corcoran, a Southern sympathizer, went to Europe during this period. In 1869, when the government returned the building to him, he officially established Washington's first art museum, with a nine-man board of trustees. They obtained tax-exempt status for the museum and collected $125,000 from the government in back rent, which was about two-thirds less than Corcoran felt was owed. The building was finished and restored to its original purpose as an art gallery, at a cost of $250,000.

In February 1871, a gala ball to raise construction funds for the Washington Monument celebrated both the official opening of the Corcoran Gallery and George Washington's birthday. President and Mrs. Grant walked across the street from the White House to join hundreds of elegantly dressed guests gathered in the Main Picture Gallery, which was brilliantly lit by 280 gas jets suspended from the ceiling. The decorations included cages of singing canaries.

Two years later, Corcoran donated his private collection, which was worth $100,000, with a $900,000 endowment. Working closely with Renwick on the design of the building, Corcoran commissioned Moses Jacob Ezekiel in Rome to create statues of noted artists for the niches in the façade. (Ezekiel is the sculptor of the Confederate Memorial in Arlington Cemetery.) The eleven artists immortalized were Phidias, Raphael, Michelangelo, Dürer, Titian, da Vinci, Rubens, Rembrandt, Murillo, Canova—and Thomas Crawford, the only American and the man Corcoran considered to be the greatest contemporary sculptor. The statues are now in Norfolk's Botanical Gardens.

A Corcoran School of Art was added in 1889, and the gallery's collection soon outgrew its space. A new Corcoran Gallery was built several blocks away, at Seventeenth Street and New York Avenue, and the collection moved there in 1897. In 1899—and for sixty-five years thereafter—the Renwick building was occupied by the U. S. Court of Claims.

During the 1940s, the decorative ironwork was removed in a wartime scrap-metal drive. President Roosevelt reportedly wanted machine guns placed on the roof of the building to protect the White House, diagonally across the street. When told that there were no machine guns in Washington, he ordered wooden mock-ups of guns placed on the roof instead.

In the late fifties and early sixties, there was talk of tearing down the building, which was considered to be a fire hazard. Air pollution had taken its toll and about ninety percent of the ornamental stonework had deteriorated. Fortunately, instead of razing the building, the Kennedy and Johnson administrations included it in the Lafayette Square restoration project.

In 1965, the building, renamed the Renwick Gallery in honor of its architect, was turned over to the Smithsonian "for use as a gallery of arts, crafts, and design." Hundred-year-old photographs by Mathew Brady provided restorers with details of carved medallions, garlands, and wrought iron railings. Statues of Rubens and Murillo, replicas of the originals, were placed in niches on the west façade. With a combination of New World technology and Old World skills, the building was carefully restored to its original condition and reopened in January 1972.

As Joshua C. Taylor, then director of the National Collection of Fine Arts (now the National Museum of American Art), said at the time, "The extraordinary atmosphere of the building itself makes the museum's principal point: design is not an isolated element but affects all that we do."

THE INTERIOR
Originally the first floor was to have a white marble floor and white staircase in contrast to the colorful exterior. Plans changed, however, and although the white marble floor remained, the grand staircase that you see as you walk through the etched glass front door is made of brownstone and the woodwork simulates dark walnut.

Galleries with twenty- and thirty-foot ceilings on both the first and second floors are used for temporary exhibitions. In the galleries to the left of the main entrance, two pairs of Corinthian columns provide a novel architectural element.

THE GRAND SALON
At the top of the broad red-carpeted staircase is the ninety-foot-long Grand Salon. This opulent gallery with its raspberry walls, tufted velvet settees, porcelain-filled cabinets, and paintings hung in tiers is a re-creation of an elegant salon of the 1870s. When the Grand Salon, or the Main Picture Gallery as it was called, opened to the public in 1874, there were only a few wooden benches in the room. Hanging in several tiers on the walls were 115 paintings from Corcoran's collection "according to no artistic classification."

In the center of the north wall is a full-length portrait of *William Wilson Corcoran* in 1870, with the Renwick Gallery in the background, by William Oliver Stone. This painting and two others—*The Helping Hand* by Émile Renouf and *The Trial of Queen Katherine* by Edwin Austin Abbey—are on loan from the Corcoran Gallery of Art. All of the others belong to the

The Grand Salon

Smithsonian's National Museum of American Art. The landscapes, portraits, and genre scenes mirror the traditional Victorian taste of Corcoran and his contemporaries.

The earliest painting, on the west wall, is *Landscape With Cows and Sheep* attributed to seventeenth-century Dutch artist Jan Both.

THE OCTAGON ROOM

The Octagon Room, which is opposite the Grand Salon, is actually six-sided, rather than eight. It was designed to show off Hiram Powers's sculpture of a nude, *The Greek Slave*—a daring work of art in those prudish, Victorian days. Separate viewing hours were set aside for men and women, and nobody under sixteen was admitted. The sculpture is now at the Corcoran Gallery of Art, and the original plaster model is at the National Museum of American Art along with other works from Powers's studio in Florence.

Today the Octagon Room has a pair of portraits by George Peter Alexander Healy of *Mrs. Albert J. Myer* and *Mrs. Thomas B. Bryan*. Healy is the nineteenth-century artist who was commissioned to paint the first series of presidential portraits for the White House.

The Octagon Room's raspberry walls and tufted velvet settee echo the decor of the Grand Salon. Note the table with a porcelain portrait plaque of Napoleon in the center, surrounded by fourteen smaller plaques of his marshals.

EXHIBITIONS

Ever since the opening show, *Design Is . . .*, which explored the nature of design, the Renwick has become known for presenting the best in historical and contemporary crafts and decorative arts. Exhibitions have included Louis Comfort Tiffany masterworks, the pottery of George Ohr, beads in contemporary American art, new American furniture, and fiber art by Lenore Tawney.

THE COLLECTION
The museum serves as a showcase for the creative work of American craft artists, and a selection from its permanent collection is shown on a rotating basis. Among these noted artists are Albert Paley, Dale Chihuly, Harvey Littleton, Mark Lindquist, Anni Albers, Wendell Castle, and William Harper.

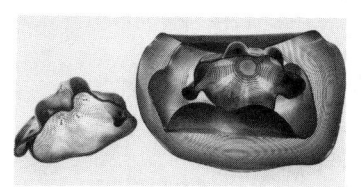

Sea Form, *blown glass by Dale Chihuly*

THE WHITE HOUSE

1600 Pennsylvania Avenue, N.W.
Washington, D.C. 20500
202/456-1414

METRO	Farragut North or West; Metro Center, McPherson Square.
TOURS	10 A.M. to 2 P.M. Tuesday through Saturday, Memorial Day through Labor Day; 10 A.M. to Noon September through May. Closed Thanksgiving, Christmas, and New Year's Day. Also special guided tours 8 A.M. to 10 A.M. Tuesday through Saturday arranged in advance through congressional offices. Entrance at East Gate on East Executive Avenue.
ADMISSION	Free.
HANDICAPPED FACILITIES	Disabled people need not wait in line but go directly to the Northeast Gate on Pennsylvania Avenue. Signed tours for the hearing-impaired by advance reservation. Call TDD 202/456-2216.
SPECIAL EVENTS	Easter egg roll, spring and fall garden tours, Christmas candlelight tours.
AUTHOR'S CHOICE	*George Washington* by Gilbert Stuart, East Room Bellangé furniture, Blue Room Mantel with John Adams inscription, State Dining Room

Pierre Charles L'Enfant had a neat sense of the fitness of things when he designed the city of Washington in 1791. By placing the President's House at one end of Pennsylvania Avenue and the Capitol at the other, he separated the executive and legislative branches, both physically and symbolically.

As a symbol of presidential power, the White House is the only official residence in the world that is open to the public free of charge. And, although in the nineteenth century its rooms were filled with patterned-and-plush Victorian furnishings, the house now is a museum of Americana, reflecting the styles of the early 1800s, the era when it was built.

HISTORY

The President's House was the first public building constructed in Washington. Dublin-trained architect James Hoban won a $500 prize for its design, which was modeled after Irish and English country houses. (Thomas Jefferson, an amateur architect, was among those who entered the competition, with a building whose dome foreshadows Monticello, his home in Charlottesville, Virginia.)

Construction began in 1792 but work proceeded slowly. In November 1800, when John Adams moved in only four months before the end of his term, the house was barely habitable. Abigail Adams hung laundry in the East Room and complained privately to her daughter about the cold, drafty rooms. At that time, Washington was little more than a rural village of 501 households. Moving the capital to Washington

North lawn, the White House

from Philadelphia added 131 bureaucrats to the population in 1800.

Thomas Jefferson, the third president, was the first to spend a full term in the still-unfinished executive mansion. He designed terraces on the east and west sides of the building to provide additional space, and appointed Benjamin H. Latrobe, one of the country's few professional architects, as surveyor of public buildings. By 1803, the first structural problems were detected when a leaky roof caused the East Room ceiling to collapse. Four years later, Latrobe planned a semicircular portico for the south façade. More than twenty years elapsed before the porticoes were finished under Hoban's direction. (South portico, 1824; north portico, 1829.)

Jefferson furnished the White House "in the antique taste," with handsome pieces of Louis XVI and federal design. Under Dolley Madison's stewardship, the President's House began to acquire a reputation for elegance. It was praised as "immense and magnificent," and the Oval Room curtains, which cost four dollars a yard, were considered "superb."

On August 24, 1814, during the War of 1812, British forces entered the city and burned the White House, the government office buildings adjoining it, and the Capitol. Dolley Madison loaded official documents into a carriage, supervised the removal of the Gilbert Stuart painting *George Washington* from its frame, sent her parrot to the French minister for safekeeping, and escaped to the home of friends near Langley, Virginia. That night, a torrential rainstorm quenched the fires and sent the British back to their ships.

The Madisons never returned to the White House. They lived in Col. John Tayloe's home, the Octagon, for a year and then moved into a small house on Pennsylvania Avenue. Hoban rebuilt the mansion, which had been popularly called the White House as early as 1808. The original sandstone walls were white-washed in 1798 and then painted after the reconstruction.

President James Monroe, who moved into the rebuilt house in 1817, selected the furnishings that provide the nucleus of the current White House collection. With $20,000 appropriated by Congress, he purchased furniture from a Georgetown cabinetmaker, and ordered china, silver, clocks, gilded chairs, and sofas from Paris. Some of these original pieces are presently in the White House.

For the first hundred years—until the Theodore Roosevelt administration—presidential offices were located on the second floor of the mansion. A steady stream of officeseekers, petitioners, and lobbyists took its toll on the furnishings. Presidents redecorated the house as their budgets and fashion dictated. Running water was installed in 1833, gas lights in 1849, and electricity in 1891. When relations with Congress were strained, appropriations suffered and redecorating led to congressional debate. Martin Van Buren's defeat in 1840 was traced, at least in part, to criticism of the "regal splendor of the presidential palace."

President James Buchanan replaced Monroe's gilded French furniture in the Oval Room with rococo-revival furnishings that remained throughout most of the Victorian era. In 1882, during the Chester A. Arthur administration, twenty-four wagonloads of "decaying furnishings" were carted off to be sold at auction. The executive mansion was a model of Victoriana, with plush settees, heavy velvet draperies, potted palms, and Tiffany glass.

The addition of the West Wing for offices in 1902 gave presidential families a measure of privacy on the second floor. In the 1902 remodeling, a new heating system was installed, sagging floors were replaced, Jefferson's west terrace was restored, and the east terrace was rebuilt to shelter visitors arriving at the new east entrance. The mansion was officially named the White House during Theodore Roosevelt's administration. For the first time, efforts were made to return the interior of the house to its original appearance. Architects McKim, Mead & White redecorated the State Floor, replacing Victorian tile floors and frescoes with the parquet floors, classical pilasters, and moldings you see today.

Nearly fifty years later, in 1948, after a controversial balcony had been added to the south portico, Mrs. Truman noticed the Blue Room chandelier shaking whenever someone walked on the floor above it. One of the legs of Margaret Truman's piano began to sink into the floor of her room. After engineers found that the carrying timbers of 1817 were splitting under the strain of heating, ventilating, and plumbing additions, a congressional commission ordered the dangerously weakened mansion closed and all of its furnishings, chandeliers, paneling, and plasterwork removed. While the Trumans spent the next three years across the street in Blair House, the White House underwent a complete renovation, with fireproofing, new concrete foundations, and a steel framework installed. All of the historic items were replaced when the Trumans returned to the mansion in 1952.

In 1961, Jacqueline Kennedy appointed a fine arts committee for the White House and began to restore the state rooms to their early nineteenth-century appearance. The Committee for the Preservation of the White House, appointed by President Lyndon B. Johnson in 1964, continued Mrs. Kennedy's efforts to locate objects that had formerly been in the mansion or were similar to the original furnishings in period and quality. Renovation of the State Rooms continued during the Nixon and Ford administrations. President Jimmy Carter was particularly interested in finding objects associated with former White House occupants, and Mrs. Carter added thirty-four American paintings to the collection. Mrs. Reagan refurbished the second- and third-floor rooms, and retrieved many fine pieces of nineteenth-century furniture from storage.

The many paintings and antique furnishings donated by private citizens reflect both an interest in historic preservation and pride in the house that symbolizes American democracy. Traditionally, presidential families, rummaging through storerooms, find different objects appealing. For example, the Lincoln bed was used by the Theodore Roosevelts and President Wilson, but it was consigned to storage by the Tafts and the Hardings. The desk presented to President Rutherford B. Hayes by Queen Victoria, made from the timbers of the British ship, *HMS Resolute*, was placed in the Oval Office by President John F. Kennedy after it was found in a storeroom. It was also used by Presidents Carter and Reagan.

A few statistics are also in order. The White House has 132 rooms and twenty-eight working fireplaces. Since 1800, one president (Grover Cleveland) has been married here and seven presidents have lain in state in the East Room.

TOURING THE WHITE HOUSE

Tickets are required for admission during the Spring, Summer, and Fall—from early March through October—but are not needed at other times of the year. Free tickets are distributed at booths on the ellipse south of the White House beginning at 8 A.M., and it is best to get there early to be sure of admission. These walk-through tours—with White House tour guides available to answer questions—include five rooms on the first floor. Occasionally, if a foreign dignitary is visiting or if a special function is taking place, the White House will be closed to visitors.

One way to avoid long lines of visitors is to ask your senator or congressman to arrange a V.I.P. tour. Reserved weeks or months in advance, depending upon the season, tours of approximately fifty are escorted through the White House at fifteen-minute intervals before the mansion opens to the general public. These guided tours include rooms on the ground floor—the Library, Vermeil Room, China Room, and Diplomatic Reception Room—that are not included on the regular tours.

Your tour begins at the east gate on East Executive Avenue and proceeds through the east wing corridor, lined with portraits of former first ladies, to a glass-enclosed colonnade with displays of White House memorabil. The Jacqueline Kennedy Garden, designed to resemble ar ighteenth-century garden with herbs, roses, flowering shrubs. nd trees can be viewed here.

Portraits of former presidents and their vives are displayed on the walls of the ground floor corridor, with the most recent first ladies' pictures placed on either side of the Diplomatic Reception Room. A large Sheraton-style mahogany breakfront, made in Baltimore around 1800-10, contains presidential china. George Washington's plates are in the center of the top shelf, above a few pieces of Abraham Lincoln's purple-bordered dinner service. Mrs. Benjamin Harrison, whose hobby was painting china, started the collection of porcelain from every presidential administration in 1889. It grew so large that the collection was installed in a special room filled with glass display cases in 1917.

You pass the Library and the Vermeil Room before mounting the stairs to the State Floor.

EAST ROOM

Largest of all the rooms on the first floor, the East Room has been the scene of weddings, concerts, dances, theatrical performances, and memorial services. Abigail Adams hung her laundry here and Teddy Roosevelt used the room for boxing matches. Today, it is best known as the setting for bill signings and award ceremonies.

Thomas Jefferson, who said that the White House was "big enough for two emperors, the Pope, and the Grand Lama," divided the East Room in half, using the south half as living quarters for his secretary, Meriwether Lewis, until the ceiling collapsed in 1803.

Although this was the principal reception room in Hoban's plan, it was not completely decorated until Andrew Jackson's administration, when $9,000 was spent for chandeliers, marble fireplaces, red bordered Brussels carpet, and lemon-yellow wallpaper. The room's outstanding architectural details—its classical pilasters and moldings—date from the 1902 renovation. At that time, Mrs. Theodore Roosevelt selected the gold-and-white color scheme. Red draperies replaced the gold during the Franklin D. Roosevelt administration, but the Truman renovation brought them back in 1952.

The Gilbert Stuart portrait *George Washington*, saved by Dolley Madison during the British burning in 1814, hangs on the east wall and is the only object known to have been in the mansion since 1800. Other portraits include *Martha Washington* by E. F. Andrews, *William McKinley* by Harriet S. Murphy, and *Theodore Roosevelt* by John Singer Sargent.

The grand piano, with its gold eagle supports, was the three-hundred-thousandth Steinway manufactured. Donated in 1938, it replaced the gold piano that is now in the National Museum of American History's First Ladies Hall.

George Washington
by Gilbert Stuart

GREEN ROOM

Although Thomas Jefferson used this room as a dining room—"with a canvas floor cloth, painted Green"—it has been a parlor since the Madison administration. The Monroes decorated it with green silks and played card games here. The Italian marble mantels in the Green and Red Rooms, which were moved from the State Dining Room in 1902, are the only mantels on the State Floor that date from Hoban's 1817 restoration.

Furnished as an informal sitting room, with moss green watered-silk walls, much of the furniture here was made in New York between 1800 and 1815, including some in the workshop of the cabinetmaker Duncan Phyfe.

John Adams's 1785 Sheffield silver coffee urn and Dolley Madison's French silver candle sticks (purchased from President Monroe in 1803) stand on a table in front of a Duncan Phyfe sofa. The nineteenth-century, cut-glass-and-ormolu chandelier is French. One of the handsomest items in the room is the soft green-and-brown, twentieth-century copy of a Turkish Hereke carpet.

A pair of early nineteenth-century English silver Argand lamps on worktables flanking the fireplace have tubular wicks that burned brighter and cleaner than candles or other lamps of the period. Over the mantel, David Martin's *Benjamin*

Franklin, painted in London in 1767, shows Franklin reading a document beside a bust of Isaac Newton.

The Sheraton secretary-bookcase on the south wall, filled with early nineteenth-century green Fitzhugh Chinese export porcelain, is attributed to Duncan Phyfe. Above it hangs *Lighter Relieving a Steamboat Aground*, painted in 1847 by George Caleb Bingham. *Independence Hall in Philadelphia* by Ferdinand Richardt was found over a hundred years later in Hyderabad, India. It was restored and presented to the White House in 1963.

Other noteworthy paintings include *President John Quincy Adams* and *Mrs. Adams* by Gilbert Stuart and *The Mosquito Net* by John Singer Sargent.

BLUE ROOM

This formal oval reception room—Hoban's "elliptic saloon"— is graced with several examples of the gilded furnishings President Monroe purchased from Parisian cabinetmaker Pierre-Antoine Bellangé. In 1817, President Monroe ordered mahogany furniture for the executive mansion, but received gilded pieces instead, with the comment that "mahogany is not generally admitted in the furniture of a Saloon, even at private gentlemen's houses." Legend has it that Bellangé had been unable to sell the gilded furniture in his shop and decided to ship it to the unsuspecting Americans. Other stories say that Monroe's agents knew what they were buying in France. Although most of the thirty-eight Bellangé chairs were sold at auction in 1860, seven chairs and a sofa, covered in blue silk with a gold eagle design copied from the original fabric, have been returned to this room.

Armchair by Pierre-Antoine Bellangé, purchased in Paris for the Blue Room, 1817.

President Van Buren started the tradition of blue upholstery in the Blue Room in 1837. From the 1880's through the early twentieth century, the walls were covered in various shades of blue fabric ranging from robin's egg to steel blue. In 1962, the walls were covered with blue-bordered, cream-colored satin. The room was redecorated in 1972 with blue satin draperies copied from an early nineteenth-century French design. The off-white wallpaper, adapted from an 1800 French Directoire paper, has a classically inspired frieze of blue and gold at the chair rail and the ceiling.

The pair of Sèvres porcelain vases on the mantelpiece were purchased by Monroe for the "Card Room," now the Green

The Blue Room

Room. Made around 1800, they are decorated with scenes of Passy, the Parisian suburb where Benjamin Franklin lived while he was minister to France. A figure of Hannibal, who fought the Romans in 218 B.C., is prominently featured on the bronze-doré mantel clock, also purchased by Monroe.

John Tyler by George P. A. Healy over the sofa is considered his best in the series of congressionally commissioned presidential portraits. Other paintings include a 1793 portrait *John Adams* by John Trumbull, *James Madison* by John Vanderlyn, *James Monroe* by Samuel F. B. Morse, Rembrandt Peale's *Thomas Jefferson* and *William Howard Taft* by Anders Zorn.

The second Mrs. John Tyler (Julia Gardiner Tyler) received guests in the Blue Room while standing on a raised platform. She was assisted by a "court" of twelve maids of honor—six on each side.

In 1886, President Cleveland married Frances Folsom in the Blue Room, and the wedding of Eleanor Wilson and Secretary of the Treasury William Gibbs McAdoo took place here in 1914.

Traditionally, the White House Christmas tree is placed in the center of the room each year.

RED ROOM

This room—originally "the President's Antichamber"—contains furniture crafted in New York between 1810 and 1830. Especially noteworthy is a secretary-bookcase attributed to Charles Honoré Lannuier, a French cabinetmaker who settled in New York, where he helped to popularize the elegant American Empire style. Other Lannuier pieces include a mahogany sofa table near the fireplace and a *gueridon*, a small, round table opposite it—the most important American Empire piece in the White House. The table top is fashioned of marble in a geometric design, and the legs are topped with bronze-doré female heads.

This was Dolley Madison's "Yellow Drawing Room," the setting for her fashionable Wednesday evening receptions. During the Polk and Tyler administrations, it was called the "Washington Parlor" because it contained Gilbert Stuart's *George Washington*, now in the East Room.

In 1971, the room was redecorated in the American Empire style adopted during the Kennedy administration remodeling. The walls have been covered with cerise satin bordered with a gold scroll design, with the same colors repeated in the damask upholstery fabric. The gold satin draperies with gold-and-red fringe and red damask valances are based on a nineteenth-century design.

Notice the Italian marble mantel with caryatids, which dates from the mansion's 1817 restoration. The Louis XVI musical clock on the mantelpiece was a gift from French President Vincent Auriol in 1952. It stands between a pair of Washington and Lafayette commemorative porcelain urns, manufactured in France in the nineteenth century.

An American Empire music stand near the fireplace holds sheet music for "President Jackson's Grand March." During the nineteenth century, this room often served as a music room for presidential families.

In 1804, Gilbert Stuart painted Dolley Madison, seated in a red chair. It is possible that the painting hung here during the Madison administration and was rescued during the fire of

1814. In the portrait of *Angelica Singleton Van Buren* by Henry Inman over the mantel, a marble bust of her father-in-law, President Van Buren, can be seen in the background. The same sculpture by Hiram Powers is placed above the secretary, on the wall between the windows.

Visitors sometimes mistake the buckskin-clad *John James Audubon* for Daniel Boone. Audubon was painted by Scottish artist John Syme in Edinburgh in 1826. Other paintings to note are Albert Bierstadt's *The Rocky Mountains* and *Rutherford B. Hayes* by George P. A. Healy. Hayes took the oath of office in the Red Room on a Saturday in 1877, because the inaugural day fell on Sunday.

STATE DINING ROOM

The pensive portrait of *Abraham Lincoln* over the mantel was painted by George P. A. Healy in 1869. It was presented to the White House in 1939 by the widow of Lincoln's son, Mrs. Robert Todd Lincoln. Carved into the mantel is a quotation from a letter John Adams wrote to his wife in November 1800, "I pray Heaven to bestow the best of blessings on this house and all that shall hereafter inhabit it. May none but honest and wise men ever rule under this roof."

The State Dining Room can accommodate 140 guests at official luncheons and dinners. Andrew Jackson was the first president to call it the State Dining Room. In earlier years, it had served as a drawing room, dining room, office, and cabinet room.

In the 1902 renovation, when the two marble mantels were removed, a single large fireplace was built in the west wall. The interior was modeled after that of a late eighteenth-century neoclassical English house, with cornices, paneling, and Corinthian pilasters.

President Theodore Roosevelt had bison heads carved in the new stone mantel, a stuffed moose head was hung over the fireplace, and other big-game trophies were placed around the room.

The 1952 Truman renovation preserved the 1902 woodwork and replaced the bison mantel with one of black marble. In 1962, a reproduction bison mantel was installed.

The walls were painted celadon green during the Truman renovation. The decorative scheme of white walls and gold draperies was selected during the Kennedy administration.

The mahogany dining table holds a bronze-doré centerpiece purchased by President Monroe in 1817. It includes seven mirrored sections and measures thirteen feet six inches when fully extended.

CROSS HALL

Portraits of recent presidents hang in the Cross Hall, adjacent to the state rooms. Furnishings include a Bellangé pier table and a pair of French mahogany settees.

NORTH HALL AND NORTH PORTICO

The scarlet-coated U.S. Marine Band frequently performs in the North Hall during White House receptions and dinners.

After your tour, as you leave the White House through the colonnaded North Portico, notice the elaborate carving over the fanlight of the door. This is part of the original late-eighteenth-century stonework.

The Textile Museum

DUPONT/KALORAMA

ANDERSON HOUSE

The Society of the Cincinnati
2118 Massachusetts Avenue, N.W.
Washington, D.C. 20008
202/785-2040

METRO	Dupont Circle.
HOURS	*Museum;* 1 P.M. to 4 P.M. Tuesday through Saturday. *Library:* 10 A.M. to 4 P.M. Monday through Friday. Closed legal holidays.
TOURS	Group tours by appointment 9:30 A.M. to 4 P.M. Monday through Saturday.
ADMISSION	Free.
HANDICAPPED FACILITIES	First floor accessible to the disabled; elevator to second floor.
SPECIAL EVENTS	Free concerts 12:30 P.M. second and fourth Wednesday, October through May, and 2:30 P.M. usually second Saturday of each month.
SPECIAL FACILITIES	Harold Leonard Stuart Reference Library with 30,000 volumes on the American Revolution and related subjects.
AUTHOR'S CHOICE	Collection of miniature soldiers Seventeenth-century tapestries Revolutionary War portraits and memorabilia

The flag flying at the entrance is the first visible hint of the building's function. Its blue-and-white stripes and thirteen-star circle represent the Society of the Cincinnati, the oldest patriotic organization in the world. As society headquarters, Anderson House contains an extensive collection of books, documents, portraits, and memorabilia relating to the Revolutionary War period.

It is also a fifty-room historic house museum, recapturing an opulent way of life enjoyed by a privileged few during the early years of the twentieth century.

HISTORY

Larz Anderson III was a foreign service officer and the great grandson of Col. Richard Clough Anderson, aide-de-camp to General Lafayette in the American Revolutionary War.

In 1893, after serving as first secretary of the American embassy in Rome, he married Boston heiress Isabel Weld Perkins. Both were interested in the Society of the Cincinnati, an organization composed of the direct male descendants of officers who had fought in the war for independence. Anderson was a member for forty-three years. In planning their town house in Washington, they decided to incorporate this interest into certain design elements. The emblem of the society is carved into the pediment over the front door, and a mural in one of the rooms shows George Washington presenting a diploma of the society to General Lafayette.

Anderson served as ambassador to Belgium in 1911, followed by a similar appointment to Japan from 1912 to

The membership badge of the Society of the Cincinnati, designed by Pierre Charles L'Enfant.

1913. The house, filled with antique French and English furniture, reflects the Andersons' many years of foreign travels. They collected Oriental porcelains, screens, lacquerware, carvings, and other objets d'art.

After his retirement, Anderson sometimes lent his palatial home to the federal government to entertain dignitaries from abroad. In 1931, the house was occupied by the visiting king and queen of Siam.

Anderson bequeathed his home to the Society of the Cincinnati when he died in 1937. In addition to serving as the society's headquarters, it is sometimes used for high-level official entertaining by the federal government and foreign ambassadors. With only one exception, every president of the United States since William Howard Taft (a personal friend of the Andersons) has been entertained here. Foreign guests included Nikita Krushchev, West German Chancellor Konrad Adenauer, Egyptian President Anwar Sadat, and the Shah of Iran.

Anderson House

THE SOCIETY OF THE CINCINNATI

In April 1783, General Henry Knox, George Washington's chief of artillery, proposed that the officers who were soon to be demobilized form a fraternal patriotic organization. The following month, a charter (called the Institution) was developed and sent for approval to the officers of each of the thirteen original states. By the end of 1783, they had adopted the charter and had formed thirteen state societies.

About twenty-four hundred officers joined as "Original Members." The original members were officers in the regular Continental army or navy or those who served with the French forces under General Rochambeau and Admiral deGrasse from 1775 to 1783. Although rules may differ in various state societies, membership generally passes to the eldest son of the descendants of the original members. Descendants of officers who were qualified but did not join originally are also eligible for membership.

French officers in Rochambeau's army and de Grasse's fleet were also invited to join the society, in recognition of their important role in gaining American independence. The French society was formed in 1784, under the patronage of King Louis XVI. It was destroyed by the French Revolution in 1792, and many French members lost their lives in the Reign of Terror that followed. Nearly 150 years later, the French society was reconstituted, becoming the fourteenth state society in 1925. More than two hundred members of the society's present membership of thirty-three hundred belong to the French society.

George Washington was the first president general—an office he held for sixteen years, until his death in 1799. Alexander Hamilton served as the second president general for the next five years.

Pierre Charles L'Enfant designed the membership badge of an eagle surmounted by a laurel wreath. The society's blue-and-white colors symbolize the association between the United States and her revolutionary ally, France.

The founders of the society, who were schooled in Latin and Greek, were familiar with the history of Lucius Quinctius Cincinnatus. A Roman born around 519 B.C., Cincinnatus was twice appointed dictator, and, each time after routing Rome's enemies and quelling civil disturbances, he retired from public life to become a farmer. The society symbolized the return to private life of Washington and his officers.

In 1790, Major General Arthur St. Clair, a member of the society from Pennsylvania and the first governor of the Northwest Territory, named a small settlement on a bend of the Ohio River "Cincinnati." The name was chosen partly to honor the former officers who settled there after the Revolutionary War.

THE HOUSE

Designed by the Boston architectural firm of Little and Brown, the house was built between 1902 and 1905 at a cost of $800,000. A dozen rooms, most furnished as they were when the Andersons lived here, are open to the public.

Upon entering, visitors are given a notebook with a self-guided tour of each room. The foyer, with its marble bust of Washington and flags representing the United States of America and the Society of the Cincinnati, establishes the patriotic theme of the museum.

The first floor contains the society's permanent collection of portraits by Gilbert Stuart, John Trumbull, George Catlin, and other artists, and temporary exhibits of Revolutionary War memorabilia, often including the society's large collection of miniature soldiers. The great hall, which is sixty feet long, thirty feet wide, and thirty feet high, boasts a cantilevered "flying" staircase leading to a musicians' gallery.

A grand marble staircase leads to the second floor. Among notable treasures here are Henry Siddons Mowbray's murals in the Key Room (so-called because of the Greek key motif in the marble floor), and the seventeenth-century Brussels tapestries in the dining room. The tapestries were a gift from French King Louis XIII to Cardinal Barberini, the Pope's representative at the French court. The dining room walls are panelled, with carvings designed especially for this room in the style of eighteenth-century English carver Grinling Gibbons. A striking portait of *Isabel Anderson* by Cecilia Beaux, showing her in 1896 as a beautiful, wasp-waisted woman, hangs in the dining room.

In the Olmsted Gallery, filled with souvenirs of the Andersons' travels in the Far East, you can see the gold-encrusted uniform and plumed hat Anderson reportedly designed for his assignment as ambassador to the Belgian court in 1911. An accompanying photograph shows the man who lived in this splendid marble palace as a mustachioed ambassador in full regalia.

BARNEY STUDIO HOUSE

2306 Massachusetts Avenue, N.W.
Washington, D.C. 20008
202/357-3111

METRO — Dupont Circle, Que Street Exit.

TOURS — By reservation only 11 A.M. and 1 P.M. Wednesday and Thursday; 1 P.M. the second and fourth Sunday of each month, October through June. Closed July through September. Group size limited to thirty per visit.

ADMISSION — Free.

AUTHOR'S CHOICE — Alice Pike Barney's pastel portraits
Changing exhibitions relating to Alice Pike Barney

Barney Studio House is Washington's best-kept secret.

Alice Pike Barney, who occupied the house for twenty-two years, revitalized Washington's cultural life at the turn of the century. A multifaceted, free-spirited woman, she was a talented artist, dramatist, and producer, as well as an activist, philanthropist, and social leader.

Barney was the major benefactor of the Neighborhood Settlement House, now the Barney Neighborhood House, and a founder of the Sylvan Theatre on the Washington Monument grounds, the first federally supported outdoor theater. She helped to preserve urban parklands as a member of the Rock Creek Citizens Committee. A supporter of women's suffrage, she urged her congressional friends to approve the duty-free importation of works of art—a law that aided the development of great pre-World War II art collections. And she provided financial support for less fortunate artists, including Elizabeth Nourse and Edwin Scott.

In short, Alice Barney was a genteel Bohemian with a social conscience.

Born in Cincinnati, Ohio, in 1857, Barney learned about the arts and the social responsiblity that goes with wealth from her father, Samuel N. Pike. Pike, a millionaire businessman, built Cincinnati's first opera house in 1859 and the Grand Opera House in New York in 1868.

In 1874, two years after her father's death, Barney went to Europe with her mother and sisters. In London, she met adventurer Henry Morton Stanley, who was preparing to leave on an expedition to Africa. Stanley fell in love with the vivacious seventeen-year-old, and they signed a marriage contract. In her honor, he named the forty-foot boat in which he explored the Congo *Lady Alice*, as well as the *Lady Alice Rapids* near Stanley Pool.

Despite the marriage contract with Stanley, she married Albert Clifford Barney, a staid Ohio millionaire, in 1876. For the next dozen years, the Barneys and their two daughters, Natalie and Laura, divided their time among Cincinnati, New York, and Europe. She enrolled in a painting class in Paris in 1886, while her daughters were attending a French boarding

Self-Portrait With Hat and Veil, *pastel by Alice Pike Barney*

school. The following year, while studying with John Singer Sargent's teacher, Charles Émile Augustus Carolus-Duran, one of her paintings of Natalie was accepted by the Salon des Beaux Arts in Paris.

In 1889, Albert Barney built a mansion on Rhode Island Avenue near Scott Circle, and the family moved to Washington. Alice Barney painted every day, despite an active social schedule and her husband's disapproval. In 1898, she returned to Paris as a student of James McNeill Whistler, who became a close friend. Her pastel portraits were favorably compared with those of artist Elihu Vedder. Returning to Washington in 1901 for a one-woman exhibition at the Corcoran Gallery of Art, she began planning Studio House as a combination home, art studio, and salon.

After Albert Barney died in 1902, she was free to complete the house as she pleased. Studio House became the setting for plays, concerts, lectures, poetry readings, and dance performances. *Washington Society* magazine called it the "meeting place for wit and wisdom, genius and talent, which fine material is leavened by fashionable folk, who would like to be a bit Bohemian if they only knew how, with the result that Mrs. Barney's entertainments, her dinners, luncheons, teas, receptions have a piquant and unusual flavor different from any other attempted here."

Alice Barney was fascinated by the artistic and intellectual life of Paris and felt that Washington's cultural life suffered by comparison. "What is capital life after all?" she asked. "Small talk and lots to eat, an infinite series of teas and dinners. Art? There is none."

To fill the cultural vacuum, Alice Barney wrote, directed, and produced plays and pageants, often designing the costumes and sets as well. The performers were chosen from among her circle of friends. Guests included President Theodore Roosevelt, members of the diplomatic corps, and, on at least one memorable occasion, actress Sarah Bernhardt, who was carried on a litter by four liveried footmen.

After seeing Isadora Duncan dance in Paris, she often included "exotic dances" in her programs. In 1906, Barney sponsored Ruth St. Denis's Washington debut in a fanciful Indian temple dance, *Radha*, which featured incense and flowing veils. And, at the request of ballerina Anna Pavlova, she wrote the scenario and designed the sets and costumes for a one-act ballet in which Pavlova toured the country in 1915.

Ten thousand people attended Barney's presentation of an allegorical tableau on the grounds of the Washington Monument in 1915, which led to the establishment of the Sylvan Theatre two years later.

In 1924, Barney moved to Los Angeles, where she founded the Theatre Mart, a showcase for young actors and playwrights. In 1927, she received the Drama Critics' Award for her play, *The Lighthouse*. Her last one-woman art exhibition was mounted at a Los Angeles gallery in 1930, and her final production was a mime-ballet with the Los Angeles Symphony Orchestra at the Hollywood Bowl in 1931. Barney died while attending a concert in Los Angeles in October 1931. Her tombstone in Dayton, Ohio, is inscribed simply, "Alice Pike Barney, The Talented One."

Her daughters, Laura, a sculptor, and Natalie, a writer, gave a collection of Alice Barney's works and those of artists she had befriended to the Smithsonian Institution in the 1950s. They donated Studio House in 1960. Administered by the National Museum of American Art, it was renovated and opened to the public in November 1979.

STUDIO HOUSE
The second house to be built on Sheridan Circle, then outside the city limits, this was one of Waddy B. Wood's earliest residential commissions. The young, largely self-taught architect later designed the Woodrow Wilson House and the Textile Museum, and became president of the Washington branch of the American Institute of Architects.

Wood designed a rather small Mediterranean-style house with a buff-colored stone and stucco exterior and a red tile roof. Alice Barney's motto, "To overcome disappointment with work," is in a mosaic plaque in Latin set into the façade, and is also visible on the wall of the first-floor hall.

After entering the ground floor, where Barney parked her small electric car, visitors mount a flight of stairs to the first floor. Five rooms are open to the public on the first and second floors.

On the first floor are the reception room, dining room, and the library, which is now used for special exhibitions. The second floor contains the East and West Studios.

RECEPTION ROOM — FIRST FLOOR
In Alice Barney's day, the entire house was like a stage set that served as a backdrop for her flamboyant personality. Invitations were eagerly sought to attend performances presented on her stage, the raised area at the end of this reception room.

A pastel self-portrait, painted by Barney around 1895, hangs over the stone fireplace, flanked by a pair of metal sconces that had been in her California home. Nearby is a bust of Ellen Goin Rionda, Barney's niece, by Laura Barney.

Barney sketched portraits of her friends, including Whistler, Gilbert K. Chesterton, and George Bernard Shaw. Her pastel portrait of Whistler hangs in this room.

DINING ROOM
Although she was only five feet tall, Alice Barney preferred massive neo-Gothic furnishings, rather than more delicate styles. She purchased the Italian Renaissance-influenced furniture now in this room from the Cincinnati studio of Henry Fry—one of the foremost American exponents of the arts and crafts movement—and the Indian-style rug was woven specifically to fit the floor space.

A silver-plated tea service on the breakfront and silver-plated and brass trays on the plate rail are original.

The light fixtures, which are original, are reminiscent of Tiffany glass. The stenciled design above the plate rail was reproduced from early photographs of the house.

HALL — SECOND FLOOR
Hand-blown light fixtures similar to those in the dining room are on the walls. On a table in the center of the hall is a nineteenth-century reproduction of a German Renaissance marriage chest. Barney believed in mixing antiques with

reproductions, and diamond jewelry with paste copies. All that mattered was the dramatic effect.

The West Studio

WEST STUDIO

Barney spent nearly every morning at her easel in the West Studio, painting portraits of her family, friends, and acquaintances. When a model was not available, she painted self-portraits, such as the *Self-Portrait in Painting Robe*, a 1904 oil, on the easel.

Working there, she may have glanced occasionally at the quotation from Goethe inscribed on the base of the musicians' gallery: "The highest problem of art is to cause by appearance the illusion of a higher reality."

On the walls are paintings by Barney and her friends, including a Parisian scene by Edwin Scott, who was known in France as the dean of the American Expressionists; Barney's pastel protrait *Madame Inez Dreyfus Cordozo*, Laura Barney's mother-in-law, and a life-size portrait of Alice Barney by Hubert Vos.

The neo-Gothic chair with a carved sunburst design was made by students at the Neighborhood Settlement House, which was organized to bring industrial arts training and recreational opportunities to poor people in Southwest Washington.

EAST STUDIO

Originally furnished in Louis XV style, this feminine room was used for meetings of women who were active in drama, art, and charity groups. The floor-to-ceiling mirror is an unusually good example of Barney's use of mirrors to give the impression of larger space, a technique found elsewhere in the house.

FONDO DEL SOL

**Visual Art and Media Center
2112 R Street, N.W
Washington, D.C. 20008
202/483-2777**

METRO	Dupont Circle.
HOURS	12:30 P.M. to 5:30 P.M. Tuesday through Saturday.
TOURS	Group tours in English, Spanish, and French by appointment.
ADMISSION	Free.
SPECIAL EVENTS	Film and video programs with art exhibitions; video every Saturday; Caribbeana Arts Festival in September.
SPECIAL FACILITIES	Video production and editing facilities.
MEMBERSHIP	From $30.
AUTHOR'S CHOICE	Special exhibitions

Fondo del Sol Visual Art and Media Center

Washington's only bilingual, artist-run museum, the Fondo del Sol Visual Art and Media Center sponsors a variety of programs designed to promote Hispanic, Afro-American, Native American, and Caribbean cultural groups. Fondo del Sol, which means depth of the sun, is an artist-operated, nonprofit organization receiving support from individuals, foundations, and the government.

The center was founded in 1973 by a group of South, Central, and North American writers and artists who wanted to increase the understanding and appreciation of the artistic heritage of the Americas.

From 1973 to 1977, Fondo del Sol artists worked primarily with Latino youth and students in bilingual schools. After opening the Visual Art Center in this town house near Dupont Circle in 1977, Fondo del Sol, in cooperation with the National Collection of Fine Arts, organized the first international touring exhibition of contemporary Latino, Chicano, and Puerto Rican artists. Entitled "Roots and Visions/Riaces Antiguas, Visiones Nuevas," the exhibit was shown in ten U.S. museums from 1977 to 1979 and in Mexico City's Palacio de Mineria from 1980 to 1981.

Since 1977, approximately 250 exhibitions and programs have been presented, featuring the work of nearly five hundred artists of Hispanic, Caribbean, Native American, and Afro-American heritage. Selections from the museum's permanent collection of Santos, pre-Columbian, folk, and contemporary Hispanic, North, and Latin American art are shown periodically.

The Fondo del Sol Media Center, which opened in 1978, produces, distributes, and exhibits videotapes, films, and television documentaries focusing on various ethnic groups. A videotape and film archive documents the work of individual artists and cultural events.

Each September, Fondo del Sol, in cooperation with a

Washington radio station, sponsors a Caribbeana Arts Festival. Thousands of people flock to the 2100 block of R Street and Rose Park in nearby Georgetown for the music, dances, crafts, food, film, and poetry of the Caribbean.

In 1983, Fondo del Sol joined with six other museums to found the Dupont-Kalorama Museum Consortium. The group includes Anderson House, Barney Studio House, the Historical Society of Washington, D.C., the Phillips Collection, the Textile Museum, and the Woodrow Wilson House. All of those museums are located in buildings that were formerly private homes, whose architecture ranges from Georgian Revival and Spanish to Victorian and Beaux Arts styles.

The Dupont-Kalorama Museum Walk, held on the first Saturday in June, provides an opportunity to visit the museums and to stroll through this historic district. The streets clustered around Dupont Circle, first developed in the 1870s, became a fashionable residential area of embassies and large homes by the 1920s. In 1884, the circle was named in honor of Admiral Samuel F. Dupont. A bronze statue of Admiral Dupont was replaced in 1921 by the present marble fountain, which was designed by Daniel Chester French, sculptor of the statue of Abraham Lincoln at the Lincoln Memorial.

The area adjacent to Dupont Circle, known as Kalorama, was the country estate of Joel Barlow, a poet, diplomat, and friend of Thomas Jefferson. Barlow called his estate Kalorama, or "beautiful view" in Greek. The residential neighborhood, which developed between approximately 1890 and 1920, is noted for its fine Georgian Revival houses. Presidents Taft, Wilson, Harding, and Hoover lived in Kalorama.

HISTORICAL SOCIETY OF WASHINGTON, D.C.

Heurich Mansion
1307 New Hampshire Avenue, N.W.
Washington, D.C. 20036
202/785-2068

METRO	Dupont Circle.
HOURS	*House*: Noon to 4 P.M. Wednesday through Saturday. *Library*: 10 A.M. to 4 P.M. Wednesday, Friday, and Saturday. *Exhibition gallery*: 10 A.M. to 4 P.M. Wednesday through Saturday. *Victorian garden*: 11 A.M. to 3 P.M. Monday through Friday.
TOURS	Walk-in tours upon arrival. Group tours for 10 or more by appointment.
ADMISSION	Exhibition gallery and library free. House tours $3, adults; $1.50, senior citizens; members and students under 18 free.
HANDICAPPED FACILITIES	Elevator with ground level access.
MUSEUM SHOP	Washington, D.C. books, monographs, maps, and prints.
SPECIAL EVENTS	Lectures, tours, workshops on Washington, D.C. history; annual conference on D.C. historical studies.
SPECIAL FACILITIES	Library containing documents and photographs relating to the history of Washington.
MEMBERSHIP	From $35.
AUTHOR'S CHOICE	The library German breakfast room

Combine an immigrant's dream of success with memories of his childhood, add plenty of money and a passion for the latest Victorian fashions, and the result is the Heurich (pronounced High'-rick) Mansion.

This imposing four-story, brownstone and brick building at the corner of Twentieth Street and New Hampshire Avenue is the headquarters of the Historical Society of Washington, D.C. (formerly the Columbia Historical Society), founded in 1894 to document and preserve the history of the District of Columbia.

HISTORY

Christian Heurich, an immigrant German brewer and businessman, settled in Washington in 1872. By 1891, his business was so successful that he began planning both a thirty-one-room mansion near Dupont Circle and a modern brewery in Foggy Bottom, near the site of the present Kennedy Center.

In 1899, Heurich married his third wife, Amelia Louise Keyser, who was the niece of his first wife and the mother of his four children. A close-knit family, they weathered such personal and business vicissitudes as the anti-German

The Historical Society of Washington, D.C.

sentiment of World War I and Prohibition in the 1920s. Prohibition meant the end of beer sales, so Heurich invested in real estate, buying properties downtown, in Georgetown, and near Tenley Circle in northwest Washington.

Heurich died in 1945 at 102. His widow bequeathed the house to the Historical Society in 1956.

THE HOUSE

Architect John Granville Meyers designed what is perhaps the city's first fireproof residence. The turreted Romanesque Revival mansion, built 1892-94, was also Washington's first single-family residence to be constructed with poured concrete.

Heurich hired German-Americans to design the elaborate interior. The Washington firm of August Grass carved the oak and Philippine mahogany woodwork; the New York interior design firm of Charles H. Huber Brothers was in charge of the decorating. Virtually every inch of wall and ceiling surface is painted, plastered, stenciled, or carved. The house, which contains the furnishings of its original owners, is considered to be one of the most authentic late nineteenth-century buildings in the country.

The general impression is that of an exuberant turn-of-the-century version of a Medieval European castle—a style that has been dubbed "beer barrel baronial" by architectural historian Richard Howland. In the entrance foyer, a suit of armor stands near a marble staircase that boasts a bronze and brass banister rarely found in a private home. In the museum shop to the left of the entrance, originally Heurich's reception room, is one of the house's twelve ornately carved mantelpieces.

Other rooms leading from the foyer include a formal parlor furnished in damask and gilt, a conservatory with a fountain in memory of a daughter who died in infancy, and a music room barely large enough to accommodate its gilt grand piano, with a musicians' gallery above it.

In the dining room—a mixture of red plush, silver, and carved oak furniture created especially for this setting—the eighteen Jacobean-style chairs were filled with Heurich relatives and guests every Sunday. Other meals were taken downstairs in the German breakfast room. If the rest of the house seems forbiddingly formal and ornate, the German breakfast room is one place where you can imagine the owner in his shirt-sleeves, quaffing a few samples from the Heurich Brewery. Carvings based on historical figures from Heurich's native village in Thuringia decorate the furniture. The wine bottles painted on the ceiling and the mottoes in praise of beer on the walls carry out the "rathskeller" atmosphere.

The Heurichs generally spent June and July at their country home in Prince Georges County and traveled to Europe every August to escape the heat of Washington summers. Many of the objets d'art throughout the house, such as the porcelain urns, paintings, and statues, were probably souvenirs of their European travels.

A carriage house was built in 1902, and a home office wing was added in 1914. Heurich's first floor office is now a gallery for exhibitions on Washington, D.C., history.

A desk that is clearly one of a kind can be seen in the Reception Room. Formerly in Heurich's office, the desk was reportedly made for General Ulysses S. Grant by an admirer in the Montana Territory, but Grant refused to accept it. A three-sided contraption of mixed woods, it combines drawers, secret storage space, and sliding panels in a unique arrangement topped with antlers and the date "1872."

THE LIBRARY

The third and fourth floors house the library of the Historical Society of Washington, D.C. The library includes approximately fifteen thousand books and pamphlets; more than two hundred maps; two thousand nineteenth- and twentieth-century paintings, prints, and drawings, and more than one hundred thousand photographs and slides, including three thousand glass-plate negatives and lantern slides. There are also manuscripts, city directories from 1822 to 1967, land records and deeds, and the correspondence of early residents and land speculators.

THE PHILLIPS COLLECTION

1600 Twenty-first Street, N.W.
Washington, D.C. 20009
202/387-2151
202/387-0961 recorded information

METRO Dupont Circle, Q Street Exit.

HOURS 10 A.M. to 5 P.M. Monday through Saturday; Noon to 7 P.M. Sunday.

TOURS Free introductory tours at 2 P.M. Wednesday and Saturday. Group tours available in English, French, or Spanish by appointment at $7 per person for 45-minute gallery tour, $4.50 for senior citizens; $6 per person for 15-minute orientation, $3.50 for senior citizens.

ADMISSION Voluntary contributions suggested Monday through Friday. $5, adults; $2.50, students and senior citizens 62 and over, Saturday and Sunday. Members and children 18 and under, free.

HANDICAPPED FACILITIES Ramp entrance on Hillyer Court. Accessible to the disabled.

FOOD SERVICE Café at the Phillips Collection, 10:45 A.M. to 4:30 P.M. Monday through Saturday; Noon to 6:15 P.M. Sunday.

MUSEUM SHOP Art books, catalogs, postcards, posters, notecards, toys, and Washingtoniana.

SPECIAL EVENTS Gallery talks, 12:30 P.M. first and third Thursdays. Concert series 5 P.M. Sunday, September through May. Lectures, classes, and films. Annual Dupont Kalorama Museum Walk Day, first Saturday in June.

MEMBERSHIP Individual memberships from $35; corporate memberships from $2,500.

AUTHOR'S CHOICE
The Luncheon of the Boating Party by Auguste Renoir
The Repentant Peter by El Greco
Dancers at the Bar by Edgar Degas
Self-Portrait by Paul Cézanne
The Palm by Pierre Bonnard
The Road Menders by Vincent Van Gogh
Paul Klee paintings
Mark Rothko paintings

If you were to take a poll to determine the museum that has had the greatest historical impact on the artistic life of Washington, chances are the Phillips Collection would be the winner.

In this city of world-class museums, the Phillips occupies a unique position as America's first museum of modern art. Yet, for many years, it was relatively unknown to visitors and Washingtonians alike. Fortunately, that has changed as, increasingly, this intimate museum has been "discovered."

The local artistic community has always had a special relationship with the Phillips. Until well into the 1950s, it was the only museum in Washington where you could regularly see twentieth-century modern art. Noted art historians lectured, and, during the 1930s, art classes were held there. In addition to selecting art for the permanent collection, museum founder Duncan Phillips aided artists by purchasing the works of students and emerging artists for his "encouragement collection."

As artist Jacob Kainen wrote, "In the 1950s, the gallery's collection and its special exhibitions inspired the advanced artists who were centered in the Washington Workshop a few blocks away. Kenneth Noland spent many hours examining the great Klee collection. Morris Louis was impressed by the large abstract works of Augustus Vincent Tack, who is still unrecognized outside of the Phillips. Gene Davis paid particular attention to the Rothko room, with its luminous canvases made up of large color areas. Everybody was enchanted by the magnificent Bonnards."

Although other Washington area museums now show modern art, the pioneering Phillips is still a special place. "A painting seems to have more meaning there," Kainen said.

HISTORY

Duncan Phillips, the grandson of a founder of the Jones and Laughlin Steel Company, began collecting and writing about art after graduating from Yale University in 1908. While still an undergraduate he wrote an article for the *Yale Literary Magazine* on "The Need for Art at Yale," deploring the lack of courses in art history and appreciation. His first book, *The Enchantment of Art*, was published in 1914. Phillips and his brother, James, persuaded their parents to form a small family collection, setting aside $10,000 each year for the purchase of art works.

The death of his father, Major Duncan Clinch Phillips, in 1917, followed by James's death fifteen months later, had a profound influence on Phillips. He decided to establish a museum in the family home on Twenty-first Street near Dupont Circle as a memorial to his father and brother. Phillips wanted his museum to be "a joy-giving, life-enhancing influence, assisting people to see beautifully as true artists see."

In the next few years, the collection grew to include some 240 paintings, and, in the fall of 1921, two rooms of the Phillips Memorial Gallery were opened to the public. Shortly before the opening, Phillips married Marjorie Acker, a talented artist. Mrs. Phillips became associate director in 1925, and

Marjorie and Duncan Phillips in the main gallery of the Phillips Memorial Gallery, circa 1922.

when her husband died in 1966, she succeeded him as director. Their son, Laughlin, assumed the directorship in 1972 with Mrs. Phillips remaining a trustee and director emeritus until her death in 1985 at ninety years old. Laughlin Phillips retired in 1992.

From the beginning, Duncan and Marjorie Phillips had a unique vision. At a time when few collectors were purchasing the works of twentieth-century artists, they focused their attention on contemporary art. They also sought out works by earlier masters who had influenced modern painters. Relying on their own taste and judgment—not that of art dealers and other experts—they selected and donated to the museum most of the twenty-five hundred works in the collection today.

THE BUILDINGS
Duncan Phillips's father, Major Duncan Clinch Phillips, built the Georgian Revival brownstone house in 1897 when he moved to Washington from Pittsburgh. It was designed by Hornblower and Marshall.

Entering the museum is like walking into a handsome private home filled with Oriental rugs, beautiful paintings, and comfortable chairs and sofas. The informal, homelike atmosphere is underscored by the presence of artists and art students in the galleries instead of uniformed guards.

To the left of the foyer are the reception room and the drawing room. The dining room is on the right and beyond it is the music room which was added in 1907. Since 1941, free Sunday afternoon concerts have been presented in the Renaissance-style music room with its vaulted ceiling, dark oak paneling, and superb paintings.

A second floor was added above the music room in 1920, and, three years later, a fourth story was built onto the original part of the house by McKim, Mead, and White. The collection grew so large that in 1930 the Phillips family converted the entire residence into a museum and moved to another home.

In 1960, architects Wyeth and King designed an annex and a glass-enclosed connecting bridge between the two buildings, and the museum was given its current name, the Phillips Collection. A bas-relief of a bird in flight, adapted from one of Duncan Phillips's favorite engravings by Georges Braque, is mounted over the front door of the new wing. Carved in brown granite, it is the work of Pierre Bourdelle, son of the sculptor Antoine Bourdelle.

A major renovation of the museum was completed in 1989, under the direction of Arthur Cotton Moore/Associates. In Phase I, completed in 1984, new wiring, air-conditioning, handicapped access to all areas of the museum, and security systems were installed, in addition to new office space, an elevator, and a café. In Phase II, several floors were added to the 1960 annex, resulting in fifty percent more gallery space with an entire floor for temporary exhibitions; an education-orientation space, and increased storage and handling space. The renovated and expanded Goh Annex was named in honor of Mr. and Mrs. Yasuhiro Goh, the major donors to the building project.

Until 1980, the museum was supported by an endowment left by Duncan Phillips. In 1981, the Phillips Collection began raising funds for the renovation of its facilities, as well as to expand its curatorial and educational activities. In 1982, the museum received a $500,000 challenge grant from the National Endowment for the Arts, and in 1983 it initiated a corporate membership program, followed by a patrons membership program in 1984 and other categories of membership in 1986.

THE COLLECTION

The Phillips Collection is best known for its superb paintings by the French Impressionists, Post-Impressionists, and American modernists. Although the collection is devoted primarily to European and American art of the late nineteenth and early twentieth centuries, it also includes outstanding examples of Old Master paintings.

Phillips recognized the historical traditions of art and wanted his collection to be "a gallery of modern art and its sources." He understood the connection between the moderns and El Greco, for example, whom he called "the first impassioned expressionist." He considered the early sixteenth-century artist Giorgione to be "the inventor of romantic landscape as an end in itself." And Jean-Baptiste Siméon Chardin, an eighteenth-century artist whose *Bowl of Plums* he acquired in 1920, appealed to him as the first truly modern painter. He believed that Chardin was "the first to accept and explore the complexity of visual appearance."

When Phillips found an artist whose work he admired, he collected "exhibition units" that provided miniature retrospectives of his favorites. He was especially responsive to color, so it is no coincidence that the Phillips Gallery was the favorite gathering place of Washington Color School painters during the 1940s and 1950s.

Phillips was not afraid to make mistakes in developing his collection. "There are fashions in painting and they affect market values," he said, "but the market values and artistic values do not always coincide, and I am interested only in artistic values."

His aim was "not merely to exhibit but also to interpret beauty in art whatever the manifestation and to gradually popularize what is best, more particularly in modern painting, by novel and attractive methods of exhibition."

In addition to his early enthusiasm for the French Impressionists, Phillips was among the first to appreciate such American modernists as Georgia O'Keeffe, John Marin, Marsden Hartley, and Milton Avery. He was both a friend and a patron of Karl Knaths, Augustus Vincent Tack, and Arthur G. Dove.

In addition to collecting, Phillips was a perceptive and articulate critic whose writings helped to promote an understanding of art. He wrote *A Collection in the Making* in 1926 and *The Artist Sees Differently* in 1931. In 1937, he expanded an early essay on Giorgione into a book, *The Leadership of Giorgione*, which art historian Bernard Berenson called "by far the best book" on the subject that had appeared in decades.

On a trip to Europe in 1923, Duncan and Marjorie Phillips had lunch in Paris with Joseph Durand-Ruel, the son of art dealer Paul Durand-Ruel. Mrs. Phillips later recalled that Renoir's *The Luncheon of the Boating Party* was hanging across the room and they could hardly take their eyes from the painting. They purchased it soon afterward for $125,000. The

The Luncheon of the Boating Party by Pierre Auguste Renoir

painting became the cornerstone of their collection and helped to establish the reputation of the museum. Considered to be the finest work in Renoir's long career, the painting shows a lighthearted group of Renoir's friends lunching at the Fournaise restaurant on an island in the Seine near Paris.

Phillips liked to move paintings from gallery to gallery, finding new enjoyment in seeing how the pictures related to each other in different settings. And, by showing collection units together, he could study an artist's development at various stages. He was also extremely generous in lending paintings for temporary exhibitions throughout the world. This policy continues today, with new paintings frequently brought out of storage and rehung, and pictures shifted to different locations or loaned for temporary exhibitions in other cities.

Between 1979 and 1989—while renovations were underway—the museum's best-known paintings were sent on three major tours. They traveled across North America, to Japan, and to Australia, England, Germany, and Spain. Revenues from these exhibitions helped to finance the renovation project.

The galleries on the ground floor of the main building usually contain the earliest works in the collection—*The Hour Glass*, attributed to Giorgione, Chardin's *A Bowl of Plums*, El Greco's *The Repentant Peter*, and Francisco José de Goya's version of the same subject. (It is interesting to compare Goya's Peter, who has the craggy face of a peasant, with El Greco's ascetic likeness.)

Also on the ground floor are such gems as Edouard Manet's *Ballet Espagnol*, Vincent Van Gogh's *The Road Menders*, Edgar Degas's *Dancers at the Bar*, *The Small Bather* by Jean-Auguste-Dominique Ingres, and Honoré Daumier's *Three Lawyers*, one of Phillips's earliest and most treasured paintings, which he acquired in 1920.

The Repentant Peter by El Greco

The Phillips collection includes units of from five to thirty works each by Bonnard, Braque, Cézanne, Daumier, Dove, Klee, Knaths, Kokoschka, Marin, Prendergast, Rothko, Rouault, Ryder, and Tack.

The Bonnard holdings are particularly impressive. Attracted by Bonnard's mastery of color, Phillips purchased his first painting by the artist in 1925. During the next thirty years, he acquired fifteen additional oils, as well as numerous lithographs and drawings. The museum now has the largest

The Road Menders
by Vincent van Gogh

collection of Bonnard's works in the United States. Among the finest paintings are *The Palm*, *Circus Rider*, *The Open Window*, *The Riviera*, *Early Spring*, and *Woman With Dog*.

Other gems in the collection include four Rothko paintings in their own gallery; a group of charming Klee paintings shown together; Cézanne's *Self-Portrait*, *Mont Sainte-Victoire*, and *Provençal Landscape Near Les Lauves*; Henri Matisse's *Studio, Quai St. Michel*; John Sloan's *The Wake of the Ferry II*; Edward Hopper's *Sunday*, and *Miss Amelia Van Buren* by Thomas Eakins. In the latter painting, Eakins was more concerned with capturing the character of his subject, than with creating an exact likeness. When he painted her, Amelia Van Buren was a young, full-faced blonde girl. As she grew older, however, she bore a strong resemblance to the gray-haired woman in the painting.

At least one of Marjorie Phillips's paintings is usually on view. Look for *Night Baseball*—one of her best—which shows Joe Di Maggio at bat for the New York Yankees in a game with the former Washington Senators. Phillips was an avid baseball fan but his wife was more interested in sketching than in watching the game. A New York art dealer tried to buy the painting for the Baseball Hall of Fame in Cooperstown, New York, but Phillips refused to part with it.

In describing the collection, Duncan Phillips wrote that it "has been the creation of two artists who love painting very much, my wife Marjorie Phillips and myself. It has been our wish to share our treasures with all open-minded people. We enjoy many ways of seeing and painting, none of which we claim to be the only right way. Our catalog reveals a catholicity of taste and multiplicity of interests."

It is that scope and breadth, as well as the personal vision of its founder, that makes the Phillips Collection one of the great, not-so-secret treasures of Washington.

TEXTILE MUSEUM

2320 S Street, N.W.
Washington, D.C. 20008
202/667-0441

METRO	Dupont Circle, Q Street Exit.
HOURS	10 A.M. to 5 P.M. Monday through Saturday; 1 to 5 P.M. Sunday.
TOURS	Highlight tours Tuesday and Wednesday 1:30 P.M.; Sunday 2 P.M. September–May. Also youth and group tours by appointment.
ADMISSION	Free; suggested contribution (nonmembers) $5.
HANDICAPPED FACILITIES	Accessible to the disabled. Elevator available. Advance notice suggested.
MUSEUM SHOP	Textile and rug related books, and special gifts.
SPECIAL EVENTS	Lectures, workshops, films, demonstrations, rug conventions, symposia. Saturday morning rug appreciation programs, when visitors bring in carpets for analysis by local experts; conservation consultations and Eastern Hemisphere curatorial consultations first Wednesday of every month.
SPECIAL FACILITIES	Arthur D. Jenkins Library open 10 A.M. to 5 P.M. Wednesday through Friday; 10 A.M. to 1 P.M. Saturday; other times by special arrangement. More than 13,000 books and periodicals relating to the textile arts.
MEMBERSHIP	From $25.
AUTHOR'S CHOICE	Wide variety of changing exhibitions

If you like Oriental rugs and beautiful, historic textiles, you will enjoy this jewel of a museum, which is one of the few in the world devoted entirely to the exhibition and study of textiles. No other institution can match the Textile Museum's world-class collection of pre-Columbian, Peruvian, Egyptian, and Islamic textiles and Oriental carpets. The collection includes more than twelve thousand textiles and fourteen hundred rugs.

The museum, a private, nonprofit institution founded by George Hewitt Myers in 1925, is housed in two adjoining buildings, known as the Residence and the Museum.

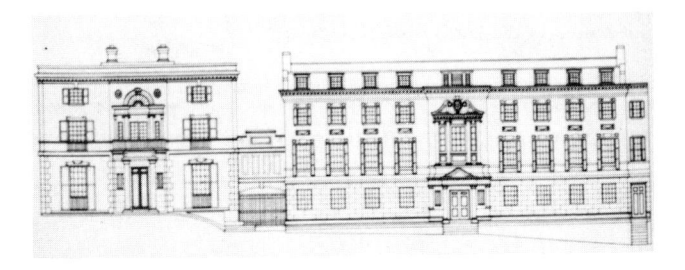

HISTORY
Myers began his collection in 1898 when he purchased an Oriental rug for his dormitory room at Yale —one of several

he bought in the late 1890s. When Myers learned that his rugs incorporated design elements found in even earlier examples, he embarked on a study of the history and aesthetics of rugs and textiles. Soon he evolved from a casual collector to a connoisseur.

Myers said, "When I first bought a few rugs in the 1890s, I had no thought of buying several thousand. One thing led to another, and the only underlying thought, if any, was to find out what went before a certain piece to make it as it was."

The half-brother of John Ripley Myers, cofounder of Bristol-Myers Pharmaceutical Company, Myers was involved in a number of other business ventures, including several relating to forestry, his major field of study. He developed a forestry and pulpwood business in Georgia and bought eight thousand acres of forest land in New Hampshire and Connecticut, most of which he later donated to the Yale University Forestry School.

A multifaceted personality, Myers collected original manuscripts of prose and poetry, as well as Robert Louis Stevenson's letters and first editions, which are now in the Yale University Library. Some of his pre-Columbian gold figurines are now part of the Dumbarton Oaks collection.

In 1913, John Russell Pope, architect of the National Archives building, the Jefferson Memorial, and the National Gallery of Art West Building, designed a handsome Georgian-style brick house for Myers at 2310 S Street. In designing the house, Pope explained to his client that he envisioned "a Southern Colonial house of the best type" that would have "a certain amount of dignity" and yet be very informal.

The textile collection was housed next door, at 2320 S Street, in a house designed in 1908 by architect Waddy Wood (who also designed the Woodrow Wilson House at 2340 S Street). Myers believed that his collection should be available for study by scholars and the public, so he opened his museum in 1925 with 275 rugs and sixty textiles. Myers initiated many of the museum's present programs of exhibition, publication, conservation, and education, and established the first conservation laboratory for ancient textiles. He traveled throughout the world, lecturing and collecting, and brought together a network of scholars, authorities, and collectors. When Myers died in 1957, the museum had 480 rugs and 3,500 textiles.

The museum was remodeled in 1980, and the entrance was moved to its current location at the Myers residence at 2320 S Street. The museum shop to the left of the entrance was once the handsomely paneled library of the Myers home.

THE COLLECTIONS

An enclosed passageway to the right of the entrance leads to the museum. Selections from the permanent collection and loan exhibitions are displayed in galleries on the first and second floors. Exhibitions have included Guatemalan textiles, Armenian rugs, and *fukusa*, traditional Japanese gift covers.

The museum's holdings include classical and court textiles of the Middle East; classical carpets; Peruvian pre-Columbian textiles; Eastern Hemisphere ethnographic rugs; Western Hemisphere ethnographic textiles; Southeast Asian textiles; Navajo rugs; quilts; and Persian textiles and rugs.

The collections reflect Myers's personal tastes and are evenly divided between the Old and New Worlds.

CLASSICAL AND COURT TEXTILES OF THE MIDDLE EAST

Myers was intrigued with the similarity of designs found, for example, in Ottoman Turkish and Greek Island embroideries, as well as in needlework from central Asia.

When he visited Egypt in 1930, he began to acquire textile fragments from archaeological sites that he believed would shed light on historical understanding of ancient periods. From one dealer in Cairo, over a twenty-five-year period, he bought three similar rug fragments, woven in Akhmin, Egypt, in 818-19 A.D. In 1946 and 1947 he bought fragments of a fourth-century Egyptian curtain featuring medallion portraits of Dionysus, and a sixth-century Egytian tapestry fragment with scenes of animals and human figures.

Medallion with head of Dionysus, 4th century

Under Myers's guidance, the museum became the leading center for the study, analysis, cleaning, and preparation of archaeological textiles. And the museum's Greco-Roman, Coptic, and Islamic materials from Egypt form an unparalleled collection.

CLASSICAL CARPETS

As Myers's knowledge increased, his interests turned from the semi-antique and tribal rugs he originally collected to Classical carpets. He was constantly searching for the origins of textile designs and tried to acquire examples that would illustrate all stages in the process of an evolving tradition.

Like other collectors, he sometimes made mistakes. As he wrote in 1931, "The first sight of a tattered old Ghiordes (Gordes) threw the spotlight of authenticity upon two or three of (my) earliest purchases, which had proved to be modern examples of this weave which had received an effective application of pumice-stone and elbow grease."

As a scholarly collector, Myers acquired many fragments of Classical carpets, merely to document important traditions, particularly those of Mughal India and Safavid Iran. He acquired one of the world's best collections of fifteenth-century Spanish and Mamluk carpets, including many of the finest surviving examples—in scope and in quality—of complete carpets. For example, the museum owns two of only ten known fifteenth-century Spanish armorial rugs. And the collection of "Dragon" rugs from the Caucasus is equally outstanding.

PRE-COLUMBIAN PERUVIAN TEXTILES

The textile tradition was fully developed in Peru by 600 B.C., the date of one of the earliest pieces in the museum's collection. It continued until the Spanish conquest in 1532 and, in some areas, has continued into modern times. Textiles of cotton, found near the coastline, and animal hair, such as alpaca, located at the higher elevations of the Andes, were used to create clothing and wall hangings woven on simple looms. Fabrics have been preserved through the centuries primarily by being buried in the dry desert sands along the Pacific coast.

The collection of pre-Spanish and Colonial Peruvian textiles in the museum is superb. George Hewitt Myers believed that objects such as the Huari-style tunics were comparable to textiles preserved in the Egyptian desert. In addition, Alan R. Sawyer, the museum's director during the 1960s, specialized in pre-Columbian Peruvian textiles and encouraged the growth of this area of collecting. (Other pre-Columbian textiles are in the Dumbarton Oaks collection.)

EASTERN HEMISPHERE ETHNOGRAPHIC RUGS

During his lifetime, George Hewitt Myers acquired fewer than a dozen flatweave village and tribal rugs, although the first rugs he collected were nineteenth-century examples of this type of carpet. Aesthetics appealed to him more than the cultural context of tribal and ethnographic materials.

In recent years, the Textile Museum has helped to focus attention on flatwoven rugs and tribal weaving, and many examples have been donated since Myers's death. Some, such as a nineteenth-century Iranian Gabbeh rug purchased by Myers in the 1890s, are like modern hard-edge paintings, with simple, geometric designs.

WESTERN HEMISPHERE ETHNOGRAPHIC TEXTILES

In many parts of the Americas, native weaving traditions dating back to pre-Spanish times continue to the present day. For example, in the Andes mountains of Peru and Bolivia, alpaca hair and sheep's wool are woven in a variety of complex techniques. At slightly lower elevations, in the mountains of Guatemala and Mexico, local cotton, wool, and silk are combined to produce intricately patterned textiles. Mexican tapestry-woven serapes and North American Indian pieces are also in the museum's collection. These traditions are direct descendants of the pre-Spanish ones that interested Myers.

SOUTHEAST ASIAN TEXTILES

In contrast to his contemporaries who collected silks and metallic textiles from Indonesia, Myers preferred somber, dark cotton ikats from the small islands in the eastern part of the archipelago. The Textile Museum owns pieces from Indonesia, Malaysia, Burma, Thailand, Taiwan, and Laos, including many that are irreplaceable today.

Cotton palepai (ceremonial hanging), Indonesia, South Sumatra, circa 1900.

WOODROW WILSON HOUSE

**2340 S Street, N.W.
Washington, D.C. 20008
202/387-4062**

METRO	Dupont Circle.
HOURS	10 A.M. to 4 P.M. Tuesday through Sunday. Closed Thanksgiving, Christmas, and New Year's Day.
TOURS	Periodically throughout the day. Group tours, with food and beverages available, by appointment.
ADMISSION	$4, adults; $2.50, students and senior citizens; free, members of the National Trust for Historic Preservation and children under 7.
HANDICAPPED FACILITIES	First floor accessible to the disabled.
MUSEUM SHOP	Books, postcards, posters, jewelry, handcrafts, toys, and gifts.
SPECIAL EVENTS	Christmas open house; Armistice Day celebration; Kalorama House Tour.
MEMBERSHIP	Friends of the Woodrow Wilson House membership from $25.
AUTHOR'S CHOICE	Woodrow Wilson's bedroom The library Gobelins tapestry presented by French ambassador Restored 1920s kitchen

In 1920, Mrs. Woodrow Wilson began looking for a house in Washington where she and President Wilson could retire at the end of his second term. After considerable searching, Mrs. Wilson found this red brick Georgian Revival town house on S Street, a short distance from Massachusetts Avenue's Embassy Row. It appealed to her as "an unpretentious, comfortable, dignified house, fitted to the needs of a gentleman's home." The house had been designed in 1915 by architect Waddy B. Wood for Henry Parker Fairbanks. (Wood also designed the Textile Museum next door at 2320 S Street.)

One mid-December day, the president insisted that his wife attend a concert and when she returned, he gave her the deed to the property. Friends had helped to raise the $150,000 purchase price. The following day, the Wilsons visited the house and the president—telling her this was an old Scottish custom—gave his wife a small piece of sod from the garden, representing the land, and a key to the front door, representing the house.

When the Wilsons moved into the house in March 1921, they installed an elevator and a billiard room, built a brick garage with a large porch over it, and placed iron gates at the entrance to the driveway. Additional shelves were built in the library to hold most of the president's eight-thousand volume collection.

Woodrow Wilson is the only former president to have made

his retirement home in the nation's capital. He lived here quietly, receiving both international leaders and prominent Americans.

Three years after leaving the White House, Woodrow Wilson died in this house on February 3, 1924, and was buried in the Washington National Cathedral. Mrs. Wilson continued to live here, carefully preserving the house and its presidential mementoes. When she died in 1961, the house and its contents were bequeathed to the National Trust for Historic Preservation. The house became a National Historic Landmark in 1965. Approximately ninety percent of the items now in the house belonged to the Wilsons at the time they lived here.

FIRST FLOOR

During the Wilson era, there were separate reception rooms for men and women on the first floor. The latter is now an office, but visitors can still see the room the Wilsons called the "dugout," where Edith Bolling Wilson's brother, Randolph Bolling, worked as the former president's personal secretary. Books on the shelves—*Celebrated Female Sovereigns*, *How To Keep Household Accounts*, *Working Girls in Evening Schools* and *A Laugh a Day Keeps the Doctor Away*—probably belonged to Mrs. Wilson or her brother. A baseball used in a 1918 Army-Navy game in London and signed by King George V of Great Britain is on the mantelpiece, as it was when President Wilson, an avid sports fan, was alive.

Among the photographs and memorabilia of Wilson's early days is a portrait of his first wife, Ellen Axson Wilson, who died in 1914. Be sure to see the old Hammond typewriter which the former President carried with him on his travels. He used it to draft the Versailles Peace Treaty in 1919.

At the top of the stairs stands the hand-cranked Victrola on which the Wilsons listened to the Scottish ballads of Harry Lauder and the operatic arias of Enrico Caruso.

DRAWING ROOM

SECOND FLOOR

The drawing room contains many of the gifts presented to President Wilson by foreign leaders, including framed photographs of Britain's King George V, Queen Mary, and the Prince of Wales. A wall-size Gobelins tapestry woven in France and presented by a former French ambassador, which hung in the White House during the Wilson administration, is displayed over the sofa. Presidents are no longer permitted to keep gifts from other governments, but in the 1920s there were no such restrictions.

A portrait of Mrs. Wilson, dressed in her favorite shade of purple, hangs over the mantelpiece. It is a copy of the painting by A. Muller Ulrey that hangs in the White House. Another family portrait by Robert Vonnoh shows Ellen Axson Wilson and her three daughters having tea.

Occasionally, the former president stood at the drawing room window, leaning on his cane, to greet the crowds that gathered in the street below on Armistice Day, November 11, and on his birthday, December 28.

LIBRARY

This is the room in which the scholarly twenty-eighth president spent most of his time, surrounded by the books he loved. His own books are now in the Library of Congress, a gift of Mrs. Wilson. Biographies of Wilson and his contemporaries, books and magazines of the era, and a leather-bound set of the former president's writings—a wedding gift from the Guatemalan ambassador—are on the shelves. The large high-backed chair in front of the bookcases was used by President Wilson at cabinet meetings in the White House.

Sometimes, Wilson took his meals here, seated in a worn velvet armchair. His wife read detective stories, biographies, and magazine articles to him, and they played double solitaire in front of the fireplace. Wilson was a fan of screen star Mary Pickford, and her husband, actor Douglas Fairbanks, gave him a movie projector. Every Sunday a Georgetown theater owner brought the Wilsons new films to watch.

Edith Bolling Wilson traced her ancestry back to Pocahontas, the Indian princess who married English settler John Rolfe in Jamestown, Virginia, in 1614. Framed photographs of Rolfe and other Bolling ancestors line the wall near the fireplace.

The library

SOLARIUM

Large windows overlooking the garden and an interior window to the staircase—a favorite architectural device of Waddy Wood—are highlights of this plant-filled room.

DINING ROOM

The dining room boasts an exquisite Brazilian rosewood dining table and silver Tiffany candleholders trimmed with burgundy-colored fringe. President Wilson insisted on wearing a dinner jacket whenever he dined in this room.

Mrs. Wilson and some of her friends stitched the needlepoint chair seats whose grape-leaf design is worked in soft tones of rose and burgundy. The First Lady's portrait over the mantelpiece was painted by Seymour M. Stone in 1920.

PRESIDENT WILSON'S BEDROOM

THIRD FLOOR

It appears as if the president has just stepped out for a moment. His robe is carefully folded on a rocker next to the bed and shaving utensils are laid out nearby. To ease the transition from public to private life, Mrs. Wilson attempted to reproduce the president's White House bedroom, even ordering a bed the same size as the Lincoln bed in which he used to sleep.

In the closet are the president's tailcoats, overcoats, and a handsome "wombat coat," a gift from the Australian government. Wilson wore the heavy brown fur coat when he went to Europe to attend the peace conference in 1919. A set of wooden-shafted golf clubs stands near his walking sticks, a reminder of his once active and sports-filled life.

Ellen Axson Wilson and Her Daughters by Robert Vonnoh

The brass shell casing on the mantelpiece is a memento of the first shot fired by American doughboys in World War I. And a sketch of the retirement house the Wilsons had hoped to build hangs on the wall.

MRS. WILSON'S BEDROOM

A fireplace and comfortable armchairs give this room a warm, inviting look. The sewing machine in front of the window is the one on which Mrs. Wilson made items for servicemen during World War I.

Beside her bed is a 1930s Atwater Kent radio. Her appointment book for 1924, the year of the president's death, is on a table nearby. Portraits of Pocahontas hang on the wall and a statue of the Indian princess stands on the desk.

According to legend, a handmade rug that included a view of Niagara Falls was on the floor when the Wilsons lived here. One day, when a friend called the former president to inquire about his health, he replied, "I must be better. I walked over Niagara Falls this morning."

NURSE'S ROOM

While on duty, the nurse who took care of the partially paralyzed former president stayed in this simple, rather Spartan room that opens onto a large balcony overlooking the garden.

KITCHEN AND PANTRY

BASEMENT

Here are the well-stocked kitchen and pantry of a typical upper-middle-class Washington home of the 1920s. A large cast-iron coal and gas stove, separate sinks for washing vegetables and dishes (including an unusual nickel-plated sink to prevent the chipping of dishes), a dumbwaiter to carry food upstairs to the dining room, and gelatin molds, cookie cutters, cookie sheets, and an early toaster are here—plus Campbell soup cans, Dole pineapple, Kellogg's Rice Krispies, Rinso, and Ivory soap flakes in their original 1920s containers.

BILLIARD ROOM

Now used for meetings and visitor orientation, this was formerly the Wilsons' billiard room. The walls are covered with rotating exhibitions of World War I posters, including *Our Boys Need Sox*, *Knit Your Bit*, and *Beat Back the Hun With Liberty Bonds*.

Dumbarton House

GEORGETOWN AND UPPER NORTHWEST

DUMBARTON HOUSE

National Society of the Colonial Dames of America
2715 Que Street, N.W.
Washington, D.C. 20007
202/337-2288

METRO	Dupont Circle
HOURS	9:30 A.M. to 12:30 P.M. Monday through Saturday. Closed holidays.
TOURS	Afternoon group tours by appointment.
ADMISSION	$3, adults; $2, students and senior citizens; children under 12, free. Group rates available.
HANDICAPPED FACILITIES	First floor and garden accessible to the disabled; access to upper floor by elevator.
AUTHOR'S CHOICE	*The Stoddert Children*, Charles Willson Peale Washington family memorabilia

Dumbarton House is a nineteenth-century oasis on a busy Georgetown street. It is filled with handsome Federal furnishings, whose quality and historic associations may surprise you. A quilt top made by Martha Washington, her granddaughter's china, and baby dresses purchased by Dolley Madison are just a few of the unexpected treasures preserved behind the mansion's imposing brick walls.

HISTORY

The land was originally part of the Rock of Dumbarton, a large tract patented by Ninian Beall in 1703. (Dumbarton Oaks was also part of this tract.) Beall's grandson, Thomas Beall, sold the four-and-a-half-acre lot to Peter Casenave in 1796. Two real estate speculators, Uriah Forrest and Isaac Pollock, owned the land before Samuel Jackson purchased it in 1798 and began building the present Dumbarton House. Three other owners followed in rapid succession before Comptroller of the Currency Gabriel Duvall sold the property in 1805 to Joseph Nourse, registrar of the U.S. Treasury. Robert Mills, a young architect who later designed the Old Patent Office Building, the Washington Monument, and other government buildings, was a paying guest during this period.

In 1813, the house was purchased by Charles Carroll, who called the property Bellevue.

Dumbarton House

The house changed ownership three times between 1820 and 1928, when it was acquired by the National Society of the Colonial Dames of America as its national headquarters. It is furnished with family heirlooms and gifts donated by members and friends of the society.

THE BUILDING

Although there are no records to indicate who designed Dumbarton House, experts have pointed out similarities between its façade and Woodlawn Plantation near Mount Vernon, designed by William Thornton in 1800. Dumbarton House, like the Octagon, is a good example of Federal architecture and design. The Georgian style has been softened by the use of curving arches and rounded bays.

When Que Street was extended in 1915, the house was moved a hundred yards north to its present location. The main section of the building was placed on rollers and moved a few feet each day, powered by a single sturdy, white horse. The two wings, which had no basements, could not be moved intact and were rebuilt on a new foundation.

In 1932, various early twentieth-century Georgian embellishments were removed, and the house was restored to its original Federal appearance by architects Horace W. Peaslee and Fiske Kimball.

An underground meeting room with an adjacent terrace, a ramp for disabled visitors, and an elevator were added during an extensive renovation of the building, which began in November 1990. In addition, all of the rooms were repainted and refurbished.

THE COLLECTION

Designed around a wide center hall, eight rooms are open to the public—four each on the first and second floors. Most of the furnishings date from the Federal period, approximately 1790 to 1830, with the exception of a few Chippendale pieces that are earlier. All of the floors in the house are original.

BLUE PARLOR   FIRST FLOOR

The formal drawing room to the right of the entrance hall takes its name from the pale blue damask fabric used to cover the Sheraton mahogany chairs. All of the mantelpieces in the house were installed during the 1932 restoration. This one dates from the late 1790s and combines neoclassical urns and garlands with a row of pineapples, the symbol of hospitality. A pair of Hepplewhite fire screens flanking the fireplace shielded ladies' faces from the heat. Fire screens were essential because eighteenth-century cosmetics had a wax base that tended to melt when exposed to heat.

Notice the "lolling chair," or Martha Washington armchair, next to the fireplace. Although the high-backed style was no longer fashionable in England after the 1740s, cabinetmakers continued to produce these chairs for the American market.

LIBRARY

Across the hall from the blue parlor, this room and the adjoining dining room retain their original 1800 plaster cornice moldings. The gentleman's reading chair, of Maryland origin, is an adaptation of a cockfight chair. Its owner sat backward reading, in this case, a 1792 *Book of Common Prayer* placed on the bookrest attached to the back of the chair. A pair of candlesticks fastened to the chair provided illumination.

A Chippendale mahogany breakfront contains such books as a 1792 edition of the *Encyclopedia Brittanica* and an 1808 first edition of Chief Justice John Marshall's *Life of George Washington*. Other furnishings include a John Garland bracket clock, which was an early alarm clock; a Chippendale secretary with rare brass inlays, and a Chippendale carved and gilded looking glass topped with a "liver bird," an imaginary bird symbolic of Liverpool, England. Like other looking glasses in the house, it was made in two sections to avoid the heavy taxes on glass imposed by the English before the American Revolution. Looking glasses were flat; mirrors—such as one in the front hall formerly owned by Chief Justice John Marshall—were convex.

DINING ROOM

The dining room, with its rounded bay and elaborate plaster cornice, is elegant and well proportioned.

Charles Willson Peale's 1789 portrait of the three children of Benjamin Stoddert, John Adams's secretary of the navy, hangs over a Maryland sideboard. In the background is the earliest known painted view of Georgetown harbor, with ships, tobacco warehouses, and Roosevelt Island.

The mantelpiece, decorated with eagles and a carving of the warship *Constitution*, came from the home of former Chief Justice John Marshall.

The Sheraton chairs and banquet table are from Massachusetts. The French silver plateau in the center of the table is similar to one in the White House State Dining Room.

James Sully, painted by his brother Robert, hangs above the mantel. Both Sullys, along with their better known uncle, Thomas, were portrait artists.

As you leave the dining room, notice the corner cupboard in the hall containing part of Eliza Custis Law's Chinese export porcelain dinner service. In 1795, Eliza Parke Custis, Martha Washington's granddaughter, married Thomas Law, a wealthy real estate speculator. The couple separated soon afterward, when Law returned to his native England. In 1804, Eliza Custis Law became the first woman to be divorced in Washington. Fortunately, George Washington had recommended a prenuptial agreement that protected her Custis inheritance.

MUSIC ROOM

This room, with its projecting bay and rather splashy rose-and-green wallpaper (a reproduction of a handpainted French paper) is considered to be the most beautiful one in the house.

A *Portrait of a Lady*, attributed to Allan Ramsey, court painter to King George III, hangs above a London piano of the late 1700s. A carved-and-gilded harp and a lyre-shaped Sheraton music stand are nearby. The cobalt blue glass chandelier was crafted in Russia in the late eighteenth century.

Hanging over the mantel is a painting by an unknown folk artist of Lawrence and Harriet Washington, the niece and nephew of George Washington. Titled *The Troublesome Generation*, the painting depicts the little girl with a mischievous look, but the boy wears a small silver medallion engraved with the word "spelling" and holds an English reader under his arm.

HALL

In colonial America, closets were taxed as extra rooms, so cupboards and linen presses were used instead. The handsome Chippendale mahogany linen press holds a quilt top Martha Washington made by sewing strips of dress fabric together with infinitesimal stitches. The quilt border was added by Eliza Custis Law. (The thrifty Mrs. Washington also made a purse, using scraps of her husband's uniform and old dresses. It can be seen at the National Museum of American History.)

SECOND FLOOR

BLUE PARLOR CHAMBER

The bedrooms are furnished with Sheraton mahogany four-poster beds of the same size as those carried on military campaigns of the period. This room, directly above the blue parlor, is decorated with pale yellow walls and a blue-and-white floral toile de Jouy upholstery and drapery fabric.

On the bed is a white muslin dress owned by Martha Washington and remade to fit her granddaughter, Eliza Custis Law.

LIBRARY CHAMBER

An Aubusson rug echoes the pale pink walls in this feminine room. The mantelpiece boasts an unusual decorative motif, in addition to the traditional pineapples and garlands. The quiver of arrows, bow, and torch tied together is said to symbolize fidelity and marital happiness.

In addition to two handsome bird's eye maple chests from New England, an applewood traveling medicine chest provides space for herbals, medicines, and cosmetics.

DINING ROOM CHAMBER

The bed hangings and wing chair are covered in red-and-white toile de Jouy, a fabric made popular by Thomas Jefferson upon his return from France. The "Discovery of America" pattern includes American Indians, French soldiers, sailing ships, and coconut trees, which the French thought grew in Boston.

Martha Washington's traveling cloak of olive green padded and quilted silk is displayed on a mannequin. The dimensions indicate that Mrs. Washington was considerably smaller and less buxom than she usually appears in contemporary portraits.

The windows are hung with Venetian blinds, which were invented in the 1760s to keep out the sun and provide ventilation.

MUSEUM ROOM

Period clothing, silver, china, crystal, and other mementoes are stored in drawers and displayed in vitrines here.

The carefully preserved clothing includes embroidered baby dresses ordered from Paris by Dolley Madison as a gift to Mrs. Thomas McKean, Jr., daughter-in-law of a signer of the Declaration of Independence. They look as fresh and new as if they had just been made.

In addition to a selection of early silver, porcelain, and crystal, you can see Martha Washington's jewelry, George Washington's silver camp tumbler, and the silver seal he used on wax for letters and documents.

DUMBARTON OAKS

1703 Thirty-second Street, N.W.
Washington, D.C. 20007
202/338-8278

METROBUS — Numbers 30, 32, 34, 36, D2, D4 and M12 come within two blocks of garden entrance.

HOURS — April through October: *Museum*, 2 to 5 P.M. Tuesday through Sunday; *gardens*, 2 to 6 P.M. daily except during inclement weather; November through March: 2 to 5 P.M. Both closed on national holidays and Christmas eve.

TOURS — Tours for educational groups by appointment. Call 202/342-3212.

ADMISSION — Free to museum, tax-deductible contributions suggested. April through October: gardens $2, adults; $1 senior citizens and children; November through March: free. Senior citizens free on Wednesdays.

MUSEUM SHOP — Postcards, notecards, slides, books on Byzantine and pre-Columbian art and landscape architecture. Reproductions of pre-Columbian and Byzantine jewelry.

SPECIAL EVENTS — Lectures, seminars, and concerts.

AUTHOR'S CHOICE —
The music room
The pre-Columbian collection
The gardens

Dumbarton Oaks is an extraordinary museum. Really three museums in one, its collections are elegantly displayed on sixteen rolling acres in Georgetown.

The Byzantine art collections reflect the interests of Mr. and Mrs. Robert Woods Bliss, the last private owners of Dumbarton Oaks. In addition, Mr. Bliss was among the earliest collectors of pre-Columbian art, and Mrs. Bliss was a connoisseur of gardens and landscape architecture.

Robert Bliss's widowed father married Mildred Barnes's widowed mother in 1894, when the children were eighteen and fourteen respectively. Mrs. Bliss was the heiress to the Fletcher's Castoria fortune, and both were independently wealthy.

The Blisses were scholarly collectors, so it is appropriate that, in donating Dumbarton Oaks to Harvard University in 1940, they established the Dumbarton Oaks Research Library and Collection.

In 1944, the house gave its name to two international conferences that laid the groundwork for the establishment of the United Nations.

Dumbarton Oaks

HISTORY

The land dates back to a royal patent granted in 1703 to Col. Ninian Beall, one of the original settlers of Georgetown. Beall named the property the Rock of Dumbarton, in tribute to a famous outcropping, topped by a castle, near Glasgow on the River Clyde in his native Scotland.

Ninian Beall's grandson sold twenty acres of the land to William Hammond Dorsey in 1800. Dr. William Thornton may have been involved in the design of Dorsey's house (now part of Dumbarton Oaks), because the Dorsey and Thornton families were good friends and neighbors. In 1805, Dorsey, a real estate speculator heavily in debt, sold the Rock of Dumbarton to Robert Beverley for $15,000. Beverley added the brick orangery east of the house.

The property changed hands—and names—several times in the next 120 years. During the post-Civil War era, the house acquired a round tower, an octagonal cupola, and a mansard roof in the then-fashionable French Second Empire style. Later owners turned the attic into a 200-seat theater for amateur theatricals, with a stage and "royal box" for V.I.P.s such as President Taft and inventor Alexander Graham Bell. At various times, the house was called Acrolophus, Oakly, Monterey, and The Oaks.

Mr. and Mrs. Bliss, who bought the property in 1920, added the gardens and restored the house—renamed Dumbarton Oaks—to its Federalist lines of 1800.

Robert Woods Bliss was a career foreign service officer who dreamed of having a "country house in the city." The Blisses moved into Dumbarton Oaks in 1933, when Robert Bliss retired from the diplomatic service, but lived there only seven years. Even before retirement, they had decided to turn their home into a research center administered by Harvard.

They had added a music room in 1929, and a wing to house their Byzantine collection in 1940. After building this wing, they gave the house, the gardens, and the collections to Harvard. About twenty-seven heavily wooded acres were given to the National Park Service to create Dumbarton Oaks Park.

After Dumbarton Oaks was transferred to Harvard, the Blisses moved to Montecito, California, and continued to contribute to the collections. They returned to Washington in 1942. In the early 1960s, Mrs. Bliss underwrote the cost of the wing for the pre-Columbian collection, designed by architect Philip Johnson, and the Garden Library wing, designed by Frederick Rhinelander King.

BYZANTINE COLLECTION

THE MUSEUM

The Blisses' interest in Byzantine art was spurred by an international loan exhibition they saw in Paris in 1931. In building their collection, their aim was to acquire the finest examples available of each period and each medium. The result is one of the world's greatest Byzantine collections.

The Byzantine Collection is the oldest publicly exhibited part of Dumbarton Oaks, yet it has the newest gallery. Completed at the end of 1989, the Courtyard Gallery now contains works of art that were created in cultures either chronologically earlier than the Byzantine Empire (330–1453 A.D.) or contemporary to it but located on its frontiers. Objects of the Greek and Roman periods are highlighted, including exquisitely detailed small-scale bronzes; large-scale sculpture, such as a second-century bronze horse from South Arabia, and a portrait head of Menander, a noted Greek playwright. The Courtyard also displays small decorative and functional objects, such as nomadic bronzes from different parts of Asia, lamps from Egypt, carvings in ivory, wood, and semi-precious stones, and several mosaic pavements from villas in Antioch. A small gallery devoted to Byzantine and Islamic textiles showcases garment decorations, parts of curtains, and wallhangings in wool, linen, and silk.

The Byzantine Gallery presents the luxury arts of the Empire, along with a few choice objects from the western medieval and Islamic traditions. Byzantine art is divided into three periods extending from the fourth to the fifteenth centuries: *Early Byzantine*, from 330 A.D., when Constantine the Great, the first Christian Roman Emperor, transferred his capital to Byzantium (renamed Constantinople in his honor), until the beginning of Iconoclasm in 726 A.D.; *Middle Byzantine*, from 843 A.D., when icons were restored, until the crusaders' conquest of Constantinople in 1204, and *Late Byzantine*, from the recovery of the capital by the Palaeologan rulers in 1261 to its capture by the Turks in 1453.

The collection is organized by period and medium. Four cases hold ecclesiastical and secular silver, including chalices, patens, lamps, bookcovers, plates, and an altar fan with a border of stylized peacock feathers. Don't miss the great silver-gilt paten with the Communion of the Apostles represented in repoussé. Found in Syria, it was made between 565 and 578 A.D.

Rings, necklaces, earrings, bracelets, and pendants of gold and semi-precious stones are displayed in several cases. Some of the pieces—fifth-century Roman drop earrings with flawless sapphires and a heavy gold seventh-century Egyptian bracelet with two panthers, for example—would not be out of place if worn today. A gold necklace from Egypt with links of paired ducks has been reproduced for sale in the museum shop.

The exquisite fifth- or sixth-century amethyst intaglio with a standing figure of Christ was a gift to the museum from the Blisses in honor of their forty-fifth wedding anniversary. The gift also commemorated the death of their friend Royall Tyler, a noted Byzantine scholar.

Although Byzantine art is primarily religious, its anonymous artists and craftsmen are noted for the ornamentation of everyday objects, such as belt buckles and carved boxes. In the latter category, note the elaborately carved ivory casket, dating from the tenth to the eleventh century, which depicts huntsmen with bows and arrows and warriors with swords and shields.

Also note the marble relief icon of the interceding Virgin. It was carved in the eleventh century on the back of a marble slab originally used in early Byzantine times. Nearby is a late thirteenth-century Macedonian icon of Saint Peter which—unlike most Byzantine paintings—is strikingly realistic. An unusual detail is the cord around his neck holding the saint's attributes, the Keys to the Kingdom of God. Also from the late period are two exceptional miniature mosaic icons. One, showing the martyrdom of forty Christian Roman soldiers on a frozen lake, is a precursor of the more emotional style of the Italian Renaissance; the other represents an austere "portrait" of the early Byzantine patriarch and saint John Chrysostom.

PRE-COLUMBIAN ART

In Paris in 1914, Robert Woods Bliss bought an Olmec jadeite figure of a man. At that time, the works of the indigenous peoples of the Americas might be found in ethnographic or natural history museums but they were not considered "art." Bliss was one of the first to recognize the aesthetic qualities of these objects. He built his collection carefully for nearly fifty years after making that first purchase in Paris.

In 1947, through his friendship with the director and the chief curator of the National Gallery of Art, Bliss was offered the opportunity to display his collection in a ground floor area of the gallery. During the next fifteen years, while the collection remained on loan, it provided an introduction to pre-Columbian art for thousands of visitors. With the death of Robert Bliss in 1962, plans were made for the pre-Columbian collection to be installed at Dumbarton Oaks, in accordance with his bequest.

A new wing, north of the Byzantine Collection gallery, was designed by Philip Johnson and opened in 1963. It is impossible to imagine a more attractive or appropriate setting for the collection than Johnson's gem of a museum. It consists of eight circular glass pavilions built around a fountain in a natural wooded environment. Arranged geographically and chronologically according to cultures, the objects are displayed in transparent and translucent cases and pedestals that add to the light, airy quality. The contrast of textures, with marble walls, teak floors, and lush green foliage, enhances the visual experience.

The collection includes objects from the major cultures of Mexico and Central and South America. It is not a comprehensive survey of Western Hemisphere art before the arrival of Columbus. Rather, the collection highlights the finest work in various media, including gold, stone, and jade, created from their beginnings to the Spanish Conquest in the early sixteenth century.

ENTRANCE, ROOM VIII

This introductory gallery is devoted to the art of the Aztecs, the people encountered by Hernando Cortés in Tenochtitlan (now Mexico City) in 1519. In the highly developed Aztec civilization, the death head was a frequent artistic motif. That accounts for the necklace of miniature gold skulls with turquoise eyes and jaws that are hinged to move, and the necklace of skulls in shell and hematite, worn by powerful warriors, merchants, and nobles.

ROOM I

Objects from the Classic period (300 - 600 A.D.) in Teotihuacan in the valley of Mexico are displayed, including a mural in tones of red, green, and black that depicts a mythological creature. The fresco technique used on the murals in palaces was also used to decorate pottery vessels.

The goddess Tlazolteotl in the Act of Childbirth, *aplite with inclusions of garnets, Aztec, Mexico.*

ROOM II

The Olmec civilization, which flourished in southern Veracruz and Tabasco from about 1200 to 300 B.C., is Mexico's earliest known civilization. The collection includes objects of jade and serpentine dating from about 1100 to 500 B.C. A special favorite is the pendant in the form of a reclining man, whose relaxed pose is reminiscent of a guest at a Roman banquet.

ROOMS III AND IV

Onyx and marble bowls, turquoise and jade masks, and carved pottery were created by the Mayans in eastern Mexico and northern Central America between 300 and 900 A.D.

The art of this highly developed civilization was sensitive

and realistic. Note, for example, the couple embracing and the small figure inside the petals of a flower.

The polychrome vases, placed in noblemen's tombs, portray mythical events, while the three limestone relief panels commemorate events in the lives of actual rulers.

ROOM V
During the Classic period, from 300 to 900 A.D., the residents of central Veracruz made stone objects such as the yokes, palmas, and hachas seen here. The U-shaped yokes, including one elaborately carved version, were probably stone re-creations of the heavy belts worn during the ceremonial ball game. The thin stone heads known as hachas, or axes, and the palmas, or palmette stones, were functional and ceremonial as well as decorative. They may have been placed on top of the yoke at the waist or may have been used as markers on the ball court.

ROOM VI
These exquisite necklaces, earrings, and pendants of cast and hammered gold and jade were produced in Central America. Particularly outstanding are jade pendants fashioned in Costa Rica between 500 and 700 A.D., ranging in color from the palest green to a deep blue-green. From Costa Rica, Panama, and Colombia come intricately cast figures of man and beast—a turtle, birds, and a delightful pair of miniature animals linked by the stick they carry in their mouths.

ROOM VII
Gathered together here are objects from South America, including repoussé gold ornaments made by the Chavin, Peru's earliest great culture, in about 900 to 200 B.C.; Moche and Nazca pottery (200 to 600 A.D.), and a spectacular Huari mirror of shell, pyrites, and turquoise dating from 650 to 900 A.D.

TEXTILE FOYER
Textiles from the Chavin, Paracas, Nazca, Huari, Chimu, and Inca cultures of Peru are displayed in the foyer adjoining the pre-Columbian galleries.

MUSIC ROOM
Added to the house in 1929, the Music Room is furnished in Renaissance style, with Spanish, French, and Italian furniture of the fifteenth to the seventeenth century, and fifteenth- and sixteenth-century Flemish tapestries on the walls.

The carved stone chimney piece came from the sixteenth-century Château de Théoban in southwest France. The oak parquet floor was made in France in the eighteenth century, and two seventeenth-century Spanish bronze lamps hang from the ceiling. The ceiling, incidentally, was copied from a painted wooden ceiling in the Château de Cheverny, a sixteenth-century castle in the Loire Valley.

The most important painting in the room is a late El Greco, *The Visitation*, painted in 1610, which hangs near the entrance.

In this room, Igor Stravinsky—whose autographed photograph is on a table near the fireplace—conducted his "Concerto in E Flat," known as the "Dumbarton Oaks Concerto." The Blisses commissioned the piece in 1938 to commemorate their thirtieth wedding anniversary.

The music room

Composers François Poulenc and Aaron Copeland also conducted their compositions here. Other concerts have featured Joan Sutherland, Leontyne Price, Alexander Schneider, Wanda Landowska, Ralph Kirkpatrick, and Rudolph Serkin. The Blisses' friend, Polish pianist and statesman Jan Paderewski performed here and autographed the grand piano that stands near the entrance to the Music Room.

Since 1946, the Friends of Music at Dumbarton Oaks have presented chamber music concerts in this room.

Although musical history has been made here, the Music Room is best known for another historical role. In 1944, meetings were held at Dumbarton Oaks to discuss the formation of an international organization to promote peace and security. Plenary sessions were held in the Music Room, and the proposals developed here were later incorporated into the charter of the United Nations.

THE GARDENS

Dumbarton Oaks is surrounded by nearly sixteen acres of lawns and gardens, including ten acres of formal gardens, nine fountains, and eleven pools. The gardens were designed by Mrs. Bliss and Beatrix Farrand, a noted landscape gardener.

In 1920, when the Blisses purchased Dumbarton Oaks, the grounds had been neglected, with cowpaths leading to various farm buildings. As an admirer of gardens in England, France, and Italy, Mrs. Bliss believed that gardens are, in effect, outdoor living rooms and should provide areas for family living or entertaining. She also wanted to vary the plantings, so that there would be blooms virtually year-round. The most formal parts of the garden are near the house. The designs, materials, and plantings become progressively informal as the gardens extend down the northern and eastern slopes.

All of the decorative Swedish wrought ironwork was designed by Beatrix Farrand and her successors. The lyre motif reflects the Blisses' interest in music. The stylized sheaf of wheat, found in both decorative ironwork and in the Pebble Garden, is a subtle reflection of the Bliss coat of arms, "Quod Severis Metes"—"As you reap, so shall you sow."

The major work on the gardens took twenty years, from 1921 to 1941, although Mrs. Bliss continued to make changes. The Pebble Garden, designed by Ruth Havey, replaced the tennis court in the early 1960s.

In spring, masses of azaleas, forsythia, wisteria, dogwood, lilacs, cherry trees, and bulbs are in bloom. During the summer, roses, magnolias, gardenias, and perennials can be seen, and chrysanthemums bloom in late September and October. In addition, there is an herb border with thyme, parsley, mint, basil, and rosemary.

OLD STONE HOUSE

**3051 M Street, N.W.
Washington, D.C. 20007
202/426-6851
202/426-6835 TDD for hearing-impaired visitors**

METRO	Foggy Bottom.
METROBUS	Numbers 30, 32, 34, 36.
HOURS	9 A.M. to 4:30 P.M. Wednesday through Sunday. Closed Thanksgiving, Christmas, and New Year's Day.
ADMISSION	Free.
HANDICAPPED FACILITIES	Ground floor accessible to the disabled. Sign language interpreter available for the hearing impaired.
SPECIAL EVENTS	Woodcraft demonstrations; spinning demonstration on request.
AUTHOR'S CHOICE	Kitchen Dining room Garden

This simple stone house, the oldest surviving building in Georgetown, provides a glimpse of middle-class life in eighteenth-century Georgetown.

HISTORY

After a local warehouse was officially designated for the inspection of tobacco in 1747, the port of Georgetown became a bustling center of commercial activity. Cabinetmaker Christopher Layman moved there from Pennsylvania and began building this house in 1764 on parcel number three of the original tract. Layman lived and worked in the one-room structure.

After Layman's death in 1765, Cassandra Chew, a neighbor, bought the house and occupied it with her two daughters.

The Old Stone House

Chew added the kitchen in 1767 and additional rooms upstairs in the 1770s. The paneling and the Adam mantel in the dining room came from her original home on Greene (now Twenty-ninth) Street, and date from approximately 1758.

Eventually, the Chews moved to the west end of town. The house remained in the family until the early 1800s, when it was occupied by Chew's older daughter and her six children.

Through the years, several business establishments were located here, including a tailor, clockmaker, printer, cobbler, glazier, and goldsmith. Before the National Park Service purchased the property in 1950, it had been a used car lot. The building and grounds were restored, five rooms were furnished, and the house was opened to the public in 1960.

TOURING THE HOUSE

The beams in the kitchen, the thick stone walls, the floors, and the paneling throughout the house are all original.

The ground floor contains the shop and the kitchen. Park interpreters are here to answer questions and to demonstrate how to spin wool. A herringbone-patterned brick floor, large working fireplace, and a spinning wheel add a homey touch to the kitchen.

In the handsomely paneled dining room upstairs, fragments of dishes, ranging from salt-glazed stoneware and English earthenware to Chinese export porcelain, are displayed in a cupboard. Found by archaeologists excavating the ground floor, they date from approximately 1760 to 1810.

A fine eighteenth-century mantel by Robert Adam is the main attraction in the front parlor. The second and third floor bedrooms are simply furnished, with woven coverlets on the beds.

A brick courtyard off the kitchen leads to a garden with fruit trees and seasonal plantings. In the eighteenth century, livestock were kept here and a kitchen garden flourished on a small plot of ground.

The garden is a quiet oasis in the middle of Georgetown, attracting both tourists and local passersby.

A spinning demonstration

TUDOR PLACE

**1644 Thirty-first Street, N.W.
Washington, D.C. 20007
202/965-0400**

METROBUS	30, D2, and D4.
TOURS	10 A.M., 11:30 A.M., 1 P.M. and 2:30 P.M. Tuesday through Saturday.
ADMISSION	$5 donation.
HANDICAPPED FACILITIES	Accessible to the disabled, except those confined to wheelchairs. Gravel paths somewhat difficult to maneuver. Call in advance to make special arrangements.
AUTHOR'S CHOICE	The portico Boxwood gardens

Here is another well-kept Washington secret. Shielded from public view by tall trees and ancient boxwood, this historic house was occupied by six generations of a family that traces its roots to Martha Washington. There are ties to the Marquis de Lafayette and Robert E. Lee, as well. And the gardens are a special delight.

HISTORY
The property was originally part of the Rock of Dumbarton, a tract of land patented by Ninian Beall in 1703.

In 1805, Thomas and Martha Parke Custis Peter bought eight acres, encompassing the entire block from Thirty-first to Thirty-second Street and from Q to R Street. Martha, the granddaughter of Martha Washington, used her eight-thousand-dollar inheritance from George Washington to pay for the land.

Thomas Peter's father, Robert, was the first mayor of Georgetown and one of sixteen landowners in the new Federal City. Successive generations of the family lived here until 1984. The last owner, Armistead Peter III, bequeathed the house and garden to Tudor Place Foundation, which opened it to the public in 1988. The grounds now cover five-and-a-half acres.

The house, with its Washington family memorabilia, reflects the economic and social life of Georgetown. And the furnishings mirror the decorative tastes of the eighteenth, nineteenth, and twentieth centuries.

THE BUILDING
Dr. William Thornton, architect of the U.S. Capitol and a good friend of the Peter family, designed a neoclassical house that incorporated two small buildings, a residence to the west and a stable and carriage house to the east, that had been built on the property in the 1790s. The most spectacular feature of his five-part design is a round, two-story, Doric-columned pavilion at one end of the saloon, or entrance hall. The building was completed in 1816.

FIRST FLOOR
SALOON
In the eighteenth century, the "saloon" was the room where one greeted guests. Today, it might be referred to as the

Tudor Place

entrance hall. Notice Thornton's unique, neoclassical portico, which is half inside and half outside this spacious, high-ceilinged room. Instead of doors, the casement windows—with their original glass—provide access to the outdoors. The finely detailed plasterwork and woodwork here and in the adjoining parlors are original.

Thomas Peter, an executor of Martha Washington's estate, bought some of her furniture and objets d'art after her death. Here, for example, are a tea table, a Chinese export punch bowl, and gilded wall brackets that had been at Mount Vernon. The piano was made in England for Thomas Peter's brother.

The chandelier—a Victorian gasolier—was installed by Thomas and Martha Peter's daughter, Britannia, who lived here from 1815 until her death in 1911. Gas lighting was an innovation during her lifetime.

DRAWING ROOM

The Peter family received General Lafayette in this room during his triumphal tour of the United States in 1824. Martha and Thomas Peter's daughter, America, married a member of Lafayette's honor guard, Army Captain William G. Williams, whom she met during Lafayette's visit.

The Louis XVI marble-and-gilt mantel clock seen here was made in about 1795 and showed days, months, and signs of the zodiac. The fireplace, which is original to the house, has an unusual carving of Father Time with a broken scythe. The implication is that time stands still at Tudor Place.

Among the family portraits hanging here, perhaps the most interesting are a portrait of America Peter with her son, Laurence, by William G. Williams, and an engraving of George Washington from a John Trumbull painting, which was bequeathed to Martha Peter by Martha Washington.

PARLOR

This elegant, gold parlor across the saloon from the drawing room contains many items that were formerly at Mount Vernon. Notice, for example, the three cabinets filled with Sèvres and other French porcelain and a pair of brass andirons that were originally in George Washington's bedroom.

Late-nineteenth-century Sèvres urns and a seventeenth-century English clock stand on the simple, classically designed Federal mantelpiece.

Martha and Thomas Peter's daughter, Britannia, inherited Tudor Place in 1854. When the Civil War began, Britannia was in Virginia with her daughter. When rumors reached her that

Martha Peter by Robert Edge Pine, copied by Armistead Peter III

the Union Army was planning to requisition her house, the enterprising Britannia returned to convert her home into a boardinghouse for Union officers. Britannia later told her grandson that she was aware of her lodgers' sentiments, but "Before me they never discussed the war and showed me every consideration."

Family portraits lend an intimate touch to this room. Notice especially portraits of Thomas Peter and his wife, Martha Custis Peter; John Custis IV, her great grandfather; a self-portrait of Armistead Peter III in his World War II uniform, and photographs of Britannia Peter Kennon and her grandchildren.

The large desk belonged to Francis Scott Key, a law partner of Thomas Peter's nephew and author of "The Star-Spangled Banner."

DINING ROOM

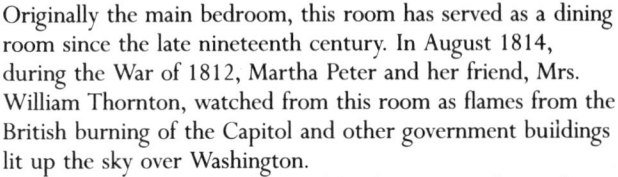

Originally the main bedroom, this room has served as a dining room since the late nineteenth century. In August 1814, during the War of 1812, Martha Peter and her friend, Mrs. William Thornton, watched from this room as flames from the British burning of the Capitol and other government buildings lit up the sky over Washington.

The six Philadelphia Chippendale chairs covered in red damask belonged to George Washington, and were used in Philadelphia when it was the first capital. The chandelier is original, and has not been converted to electricity.

Armistead Peter's 1925 portrait of his first wife, Caroline, wearing a green hat, hangs in this room. Caroline Peter was the stepdaughter of sculptor Paul Bartlett, some of whose works can be seen in the library.

The dining room

HALL

Highlights include an eighteenth-century *demi-lune* table, and an English hall clock with an unusual step-bonnet top. A large portrait of Leonard Calvert, brother of the first Lord Baltimore, hangs here.

SECOND FLOOR

BRITANNIA PETER'S BEDROOM

Britannia Peter's husband was the commandant of the U.S. Navy Yard. Unfortunately, he was killed when a cannon accidentally exploded during a boating party two years after their marriage.

Britannia's traveling trunk, which was made on High Street—now Wisconsin Avenue—in Georgetown, stands at the foot of her bed. The Windsor chair was originally owned by Robert Peter. The wing chair in which Britannia died stands near the window.

Family mementoes help to personalize the room. Notice, for example, the Mathew Brady photograph of Britannia's husband; the framed photograph of her favorite servant; several oil paintings by Armistead Peter III, and Britannia's crystal and silver bowl, which has always held lemon drops.

ROBERT E. LEE BEDROOM

Martha Custis Peter's cousin, Mary Anna Randolph Custis, the daughter of George Washington Parke Custis, married Robert E. Lee and lived at her ancestral home, Arlington House, across the Potomac in Virginia. When Robert E. Lee paid his last visit to Washington, he stayed in this room with its four-poster mahogany bed. Lee's portrait hangs above the mantel.

America and Britannia Peter were close to their Lee cousins. According to legend, they sometimes signaled to the girls at Arlington House by waving white petticoats from the window here. During the Civil War, Britannia Peter stored two wagonloads of the Lees' belongings from Arlington House in her attic.

Brittania's daughter—also named Martha Custis —married her cousin, Dr. Armistead Peter. Their portraits are here.

CHILDREN'S ROOM
Here are a doll's brass bed, a child-size rocker and Windsor settee, teddy bears, and a miniature greenhouse that must have delighted several generations of children in the Peter family.

UPSTAIRS HALL
There is a particularly good view of the boxwoods and the flower knot garden from the window on the landing here.

The chest-on-chest, with its rare eighteenth-century waxwork on top, was originally in George Washington's bedroom. The nineteenth-century Baltimore side chairs belonged to Thomas and Martha Peter. Don't miss the photograph of Britannia Peter in her wheelchair, accompanied by her great-grandson, Armistead Peter III. Together, they represent family continuity at Tudor Place from 1815 to 1983.

LIBRARY   FIRST FLOOR
This part of the house dates back to the 1790s. It was, at various times, a stable and carriage house, Dr. Armistead Peter's medical office, and a storage area. In 1960, Caroline and Armistead Peter III, converted it into the present library.

Caroline's mother, Suzanne, was a friend of the noted portrait painter, Cecilia Beaux, whose portrait of Caroline is here.

Some of the furniture is particularly noteworthy. The handsome secretary, made in Washington or Alexandria around 1800, contains books from the Peter family library.

Notice the framed photograph atop the Chinese chest. It is a picture of the Peters' ancestral home in Lanarkshire, Scotland.

GARDENS
The sense of continuity you feel at Tudor Place, with its multigenerational furnishings, is especially evident in the gardens. Here, damask and moss roses planted by Martha Peter still bloom.

During the Civil War, before Britannia Peter returned to rescue her property, the boxwoods in the flower knot garden, located on the north side of the house, were severely damaged.

The elaborate design of plants and flowers was lost until Armistead Peter III found its duplicate in 1923. A James River Garden Club publication described the Virginia garden of one of his relations. Jane Peter Beverley had copied Tudor Place's flower knot garden at her estate, Avenel, in the early nineteenth century. Peter used cuttings from the original plants to re-create the flower knot. A box circle and a bowling green are also on the north side; a neatly manicured lawn with shrubbery borders rolls away from the portico on the south side.

Some of the trees are as old as the house. A weeping boxwood on the south lawn was transplanted from Mount Vernon.

HILLWOOD

4155 Linnean Avenue, N.W.
Washington, D.C. 20008
202/686-8500
202/686-5807 reservations

METRO — Van Ness (one mile).

HOURS — 9 A.M. to 5 P.M. Tuesday through Saturday; tours by reservation only. Gardens open 11 A.M. to 3 P.M., reservations not required.

TOURS — Two-hour guided tours for twenty-five people each at 9 A.M., 10:30 A.M., Noon, and 1:30 P.M. Special interest tours. Tours conducted in Russian, French, Italian, Dutch, and Greek by special arrangement.

ADMISSION — $10 for house, auxiliary buildings, and gardens; $2 for gardens and auxiliary buildings only. Pets and children under 12 not admitted.

HANDICAPPED FACILITIES — Wheelchairs available.

FOOD SERVICE — Café open 10 A.M. to 5 P.M.

MUSEUM SHOP — Items related to museum collections, including porcelains, books, Russian folk art, costume jewelry, decorative boxes, and American Indian pottery. Open 10:30 A.M. to 5 P.M. Greenhouse sells plants from 10 A.M. to 4 P.M.

SPECIAL EVENTS — Lecture programs in spring and fall.

AUTHOR'S CHOICE —
Two Russian imperial Fabergé Easter eggs, Icon Room
Gold chalice of Catherine the Great, Vestment Hall
Russian imperial bridal veil, Lace Wing
Catherine the Great dinner services, Russian Porcelain Room

Hillwood is a red brick mansion surrounded by twenty-five acres of manicured lawns and gardens in one of Washington's most exclusive residential areas. The forty-room house is filled with the most comprehensive collection of Russian decorative arts outside the Soviet Union, as well as a spectacular collection of eighteenth-century French furniture, tapestries, and objets d'art. As if that were not enough to lure visitors, there is also a small but choice collection of American Indian art.

HISTORY

Hillwood is the creation of Marjorie Merriweather Post, the only child of Charles W. Post, founder of the Post Toasties fortune (now General Foods). Mrs. Post, who was born in 1887, had four husbands, Edward B. Close (father of her daughters Adelaide and Eleanor), Edward F. Hutton (father of actress Dina Merrill), Joseph E. Davies, and Herbert A. May. After her divorce from May in 1964, she resumed using her maiden name. A shrewd businesswoman, generous philanthropist, and gracious and popular hostess, Mrs. Post was, most importantly, a monumentally acquisitive collector.

Marjorie Merriweather Post
by Douglas Chandor

Joseph Davies's assignment as ambassador to the Soviet Union from 1936 to 1938 came at a most opportune time. For years, Mrs. Post had been collecting eighteenth-century French decorative arts for her Long Island and New York City homes. Her summer home in the Adirondacks was filled with American Indian art and artifacts. Finding herself in the Soviet Union at a time when the Russians, in need of hard currency, were disposing of imperial and church treasures—some priced at only five cents a gram—she bought scores of chalices, icons, porcelains, and paintings. Through the years, her interest in Russian art continued.

When she died in 1973, Mrs. Post bequeathed Hillwood to the Smithsonian Institution. Three years later, the Smithsonian, concerned about the high cost of maintenance, returned Hillwood to the Marjorie Merriweather Post Foundation of the District of Columbia, which opened the museum to the public in 1977.

TOURING THE MUSEUM
A half-hour orientation film narrated by Mrs. Post's daughter, actress Dina Merrill, is presented in the Visitors Center.

Twenty-five visitors are included in each tour group, which is then divided into three smaller groups. As a result, there are only about eight people at a time, accompanied by a guide, in each room.

Visitors see the rooms on the first and second floors, as well as the C.W. Post Wing, the Russian dacha, the Indian building, the greenhouse, and the gardens.

THE HOUSE AND GROUNDS
Mrs. Post bought Hillwood after her divorce from Ambassador Davies in 1955. The main house, built in 1926, was remodeled extensively to make it more suitable for entertaining and to accommodate her collections.

There are rose gardens, a formal French garden, a Japanese garden, and a Friendship Walk. The estate is planted profusely with azaleas, rhododendrons, dogwoods, and holly.

FRONT HALLWAY
The opulent tone of the collection is established as soon as you enter the two-story-high reception hall with its marble floors

South façade, Hillwood

and floor-to-ceiling portraits of Russian tsars and tsarinas. A mammoth Russian rock crystal chandelier from an imperial palace sparkles overhead. Opposite the front door, at the entrance to the library, is a commode by Jean-Henri Riesener with marquetry designs of birds and flowers. A similar piece is in Windsor Castle.

A large portrait of Catherine the Great attributed to Levitski, one of the best native-born Russian portrait painters of the eighteenth century, dominates the stair wall. Catherine the Great, who ruled Russia from 1762 to 1796, is surrounded by portraits of other rulers, including her predecessor, Elizabeth I, founder of the Imperial Russian Porcelain Factory. Several other imperial portraits are on the opposite wall, including the last tsar and tsarina, Nicholas II and Alexandra, whose reign ended with the 1917 Russian Revolution.

ICON ROOM

Some of the rarest Russian art treasures are in this small room. On the right, a glass case on a malachite and ormolu table holds the imperial nuptial crown, encrusted with three hundred carats of diamonds. Made in 1840, it was worn at the weddings of the last three tsarinas, and is the only piece of Russian imperial regalia housed in a collection outside the Soviet Union.

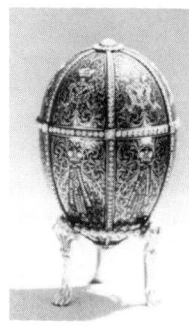

Also in this case is an ornate pink enamel and gold Russian imperial Easter egg by Carl Fabergé. A gift from Tsar Nicholas II to his mother in 1914, the egg contained a surprise—a miniature sedan chair. Years later, the egg was a gift to Mrs. Post from her daughter, Eleanor.

A glass case across the room holds the only other imperial Easter egg in the collection. It is blue enamel, decorated with gold and diamonds by Fabergé, and was a gift from Tsar Alexander III to his wife, Maria Fyodorovna, in 1892. Carl Fabergé, the court jeweler and goldsmith, was renowned for his delicate and imaginative workmanship. Fabergé created fifty-four imperial Easter eggs, beginning in 1885, when Alexander III commissioned one as a surprise gift for his wife. After Alexander's death, his son Nicholas II continued the tradition, ordering two eggs each year, one for his mother and the other for his wife. There are about ninety Fabergé objects at Hillwood, including Easter eggs, picture frames, patch boxes, silver candlesticks, and presentation boxes.

Imperial Easter egg by Fabergé

To the left of the entrance, a glass display case contains most of Mrs. Post's collection of gold and silver chalices, made for the Russian Orthodox Church from the seventeenth to the early nineteenth century. When Mrs. Post first found the chalices in a Moscow shop, they were so tarnished that they appeared to be pewter. After one piece was cleaned at the embassy, it was found to be of silver gilt decorated with miniatures and gemstones from the Ural Mountains. The gold chalice in this case, sparkling with diamonds and rubies, was crafted in Moscow in 1824, a gift to the Kazan Cathedral in Saint Petersburg.

On the far wall is an unusual cabinet of ebony, ormolu, and lapis lazuli, which was a twenty-fifth wedding anniversary gift to Grand Duke Konstantin and his wife, Princess Alexandra, in 1873. Their portraits are inside the doors. The cabinet holds a collection of silver gilt *kovshi*, a vessel originally designed for ladling beer, and shaped somewhat like a bird. *Kovshi*, presented to various Russians as a reward for outstanding service to the country, can also be seen in the case with the blue Fabergé egg.

In keeping with the theme of the room, many Russian icons are on the walls and in vitrines. The oldest is a seventeenth-century icon of St. George.

There are also eighteenth- and nineteenth-century boxes of niello work on silver. The niello technique involves rubbing an alloy which includes sulfur into lines incised on a piece. The design then turns black when the piece is fired.

ICON ROOM/LIBRARY/PASSAGEWAY

Vitrines contain examples of Russian porcelain figurines and cups and saucers from the eighteenth and nineteenth centuries. Landscapes and portraits of Tsar Nicholas II are on the walls.

LIBRARY

Over the mantelpiece, a portrait of C.W. Post by Sir Oswald Birley looks out on the English-style library. Across the room is a portrait of Mrs. Post's mother.

A Waterford crystal chandelier sparkles above a collection of antique English furniture, including several miniature pieces that may have been salesmen's samples.

Family photographs in Chinese jade frames give the room a cozy feeling, an impression enhanced by viewing the bed in which Scampi, Mrs. Post's miniature schnauzer, slept. (He is now buried on the grounds of Hillwood.) In keeping with the decor of the house, Scampi's bed is an early nineteenth-century French canopied pink bower.

LIBRARY/DINING ROOM PASSAGEWAY

In the passageway connecting the library and dining room are cups and saucers made at the Imperial, Gardner, Popov, and Novyi porcelain factories during the eighteenth and nineteenth centuries, as well as Russian commemorative glassware.

DINING ROOM FOYER

The foyer adjoining the dining room contains part of Mrs. Post's collection of Sèvres porcelain, including pieces in turquoise or bleu celeste, yellow, and apple green. Much of it was made for the French aristocracy in the eighteenth century.

DINING ROOM

Part of the French Regency oak paneling in this room came from an old Paris house. According to legend, the nineteenth-century Aubusson carpet was a gift from the French court to Emperor Maximilian and Empress Carlota of Mexico.

Note the pair of lapis lazuli and ormolu candlesticks near the mantelpiece, made about 1800. Formerly in a St. Petersburg palace, they were a gift from a group of Mrs. Post's friends on her eightieth birthday, March 15, 1967.

The dining room table, with all of its leaves extended, can seat thirty people. It was made in Italy in 1927 for Mar-a-Lago, Mrs. Post's home in Palm Beach. Eleven different stones, ranging from marble and alabaster to jasper and lapis lazuli, are worked into the mosaic designs. The table settings are changed periodically. You might see Venetian lace place mats and napkins, Sèvres porcelain, Val Saint Lambert crystal,

Gorham silver, and a silver Tiffany centerpiece and candelabra—as if a banquet were to begin at any moment.

BREAKFAST ROOM
This charming little plant-filled room with its damask-covered gilt chairs seems far too elegant for anything as mundane as bacon and eggs. The Russian glass and ormolu chandelier, made in the 1780s, came from the Catherine Palace at Tsarskoe Selo near St. Petersburg and is said to have hung in the bedroom of Catherine the Great.

A portrait of Mrs. Post's daughter Dina Merrill as a child hangs on the wall.

The breakfast room

PASSAGEWAY TO THE PAVILION
Wall vitrines in the passageway leading to the pavilion display Chinese carvings and snuff bottles of varicolored jade, rose quartz, lapis lazuli, turquoise, malachite, rock crystal, ivory, amber, and coral.

PAVILION
This room was used for square dances and movies.

A large painting of an imaginary seventeenth-century Russian wedding party, *The Boyar Wedding* painted in 1883 by Konstantin Makovski, dominates the room.

Handsome pieces made of malachite from the Ural Mountains are placed throughout the room. Note particularly the malachite candelabra and tazza or compote.

FRENCH DRAWING ROOM
This room is furnished in the style of Louis XVI, with wood paneling from a French château and three tapestries woven at Beauvais after cartoons by François Boucher. The large one, dated 1736, is from a series called *Fêtes of the Italians*. The two smaller tapestries across the room are from a series based on *Loves of the Gods* and represent *Bacchus and Ariadne* and *Jupiter and Antiope*.

A portrait of French Empress Eugénie, painted in 1857 by Franz Wintherhalter, hangs over the mantel in its original frame.

The two sofas and eight chairs are covered in tapestries woven at Gobelins, commissioned by Louis XVI and Marie

Antoinette as a gift to Prince Henry of Prussia, brother of Frederick the Great.

The rolltop desk, made by David Roentgen around 1770, was one of Mrs. Post's earliest purchases of eighteenth-century furniture. The marquetry in various types of wood and mother-of-pearl represents the arts and sciences. (In the Hillwood orientation film, Dina Merrill recalls finding secret compartments in this desk as a child.) The swivel desk chair is by the cabinetmaker C. Sené and bears the mark of the household of Marie Antoinette.

Among the objets d'art displayed in vitrines throughout the room are a diamond-studded Order of the Golden Fleece, the highest order of the Hapsburg Empire, and a miniature of Mrs. Post in an exquisite gold Fabergé frame.

RUSSIAN PORCELAIN ROOM

A pair of vases made by the Imperial Russian Porcelain Factory flank the doorway. They were a gift from Mme. Molotov, wife of the Soviet premier, when Ambassador and Mrs. Davies left the Soviet Union in 1938.

In the center of the floor is an unusual marquetry design representing the Russian imperial eagle. It was created by Philipp Rimmler in 1957 with forty-six different woods.

The room was designed to hold Mrs. Post's collection of Russian porcelain, especially the four dinner services commissioned by Catherine the Great from the Francis Gardner Factory in 1777 and 1783. These were each used once a year for a dinner at the Winter Palace for the knights of the four imperial orders. The boldly patterned designs reflect the badges and ribbons of each order. Included are the service for the Order of Saint Vladimir, with a black-and-red ribbon design; the Order of Saint George service with an orange-and-black ribbon; the Order of Saint Andrew service with a blue ribbon design, and the service for the Order of Saint Alexander Nevskii with its red ribbon design.

The earliest pieces in the room are part of the personal dinner service made for Elizabeth I in the late 1750s. Oddly enough, the trellis design of pink rosettes appears to be quite modern.

On the walls, above the vitrines, are a group of Russian "bread and salt" dishes, traditionally presented to an important visitor as a symbol of hospitality.

PANTRY AND KITCHEN

Mrs. Post's porcelain collection was so large that she could have dinner and lunch served for two weeks without duplicating the table settings. Some of her dishes are in the cupboards.

In an adjoining linen closet, tablecloths and napkins are stored in plastic cases, neatly tied with ribbons. Mrs. Post was especially fond of Belgian and Italian lace, which she collected on her travels.

The only thing lacking in the large, fully equipped kitchen is a dishwasher. All dishes were washed and dried by hand.

VESTMENT HALL

Formerly the staff dining room, this room now contains velvet and brocade robes made for the Russian Orthodox Church. In the center of the room is a spectacular gold chalice encrusted with diamonds and carved stones by Iver W. Buch. It was commissioned by Catherine the Great in 1791 and was presented to the Alexander Nevsky Monastery in St. Petersburg.

An alcove adjoining the Vestment Hall contains Russian furniture and small paintings and engravings of Russian scenes.

SECOND FLOOR

HALLWAY
A display case holds a gold-and-black porcelain tea set ordered by Catherine the Great for her favorite, Gregory Orlov, who organized the coup that placed her on the throne in 1762.

There is also a portrait of Mrs. Post wearing a cabochon emerald brooch and necklace. The necklace, along with most of Mrs. Post's other historical jewelry, is now in the National Museum of Natural History.

MRS. POST'S BEDROOM
A 1790 painting of *The Beloved Child* by Marguerite Gérard, a pupil of Fragonard, hangs in the hall leading to the bedroom.

Mrs. Post's bedroom is decorated in Louis XVI style in soft tones of pink and gold. An oval marquetry table with Sèvres porcelain plaques was made in 1790 by the famed French cabinetmaker Lannuier. The pair of chairs flanking this table were made by Delaissement in 1780. The rolltop desk in the corner, of marquetry and ormolu, is a late eighteenth-century piece by Conrad Mauter. A collection of small objects in dark green bloodstone, Mrs. Post's birthstone, is in a table vitrine. Lace pillows on the loveseat and lampshades made with antique lace add a feminine touch.

In an adjoining dressing room, a closet holds dozens of pairs of silk evening shoes, dyed to match Mrs. Post's gowns.

ADAM BEDROOM
This guest room carries out the neoclassic Adam style, from the molded plaster ceiling to the oval pattern of the rug. Blue-and-white jasper ware by Wedgwood provides decorative accents.

LIBRARY
The library decor is English. A mid-eighteenth-century Chippendale card table with its original needlepoint top is one of the most important pieces of English furniture in the house.

ENGLISH BEDROOM
This room features an eighteenth-century Chippendale four-poster canopy bed, an eighteenth-century chest on chest, and a handsome early nineteenth-century Sheraton tambour-front desk from New England.

LACE WING
Several small rooms in the former service area of the mansion have been remodeled to create a setting for many of Mrs. Post's gowns, jewelry, and accessories, as well as her lace collection. The gowns on display span the period from the early 1900s to the 1960s.

When Mrs. Post entertained, she often used many of the lace tablecloths, place mats, and runners displayed here. Her lace collection also includes an eighteenth-century Belgian woman's cap and a deep flounce made in France in the seventeenth century.

The most spectacular object on view, however, is the Hapsburg wedding veil, which was worn by Princess Stephanie of Belgium at her wedding to Crown Prince Rudolph of Austria in 1881. The Belgian lace veil, with the Hapsburg double eagle and twenty-one shields of Belgian and Austrian regional coats-of-arms woven into the design, is 123 inches long and 100 inches wide. Currently on loan from the Smithsonian, the veil was purchased by Mrs. Post in 1925. Her daughter Adelaide wore it when she was married in 1927.

FOLK ART ROOM

When Mrs. Post was alive, her social secretary's office was here. Now the room contains examples of Russian folk art, including painted wooden *kovshi*, papier-mâché boxes, Soviet porcelains, and paintings. Several of the paintings were acquired while the then-Mrs. Davies lived in the Soviet Union during the 1930s.

C.W. POST WING

If Mrs. Post's collections seem rather feminine, the collection of her father, C.W. Post, is just the opposite. Housed in a converted garage, his turn-of-the-century furniture, paintings, and objets d'art acquired in Europe and the United States reflect the eclectic taste of a late-Victorian businessman.

Scattered around the rooms are such disparate objects as suits of armor, an eighteenth-century sleigh, a letter and autographed picture from poet Walt Whitman, Post's double-sided desk (with sample cereal ads on top), Renaissance-style chairs, bronze sculptures, and paintings.

INDIAN BUILDING

This building, designed by architect Sarah O'Neil Manion in 1983, houses nearly two hundred objects from Mrs. Post's extensive collection of American Indian artifacts, formerly kept at Topridge, her summer home in the Adirondacks. Mrs. Post bequeathed the collection to the Smithsonian, and the objects here are on a long-term loan to Hillwood.

The award-winning architecture of the building reflects the rustic nature of the camps built in upstate New York early in this century. The wood, used both for the interior and exterior, provides a simple and appropriate background for the Indian crafts on display.

The collection includes Navajo blankets, leather moccasins, beadwork, basketry, and Hopi, Acoma, and Santa Clara pottery. Don't miss the rare Apache playing cards of tanned and painted hide. They date from the early 1900s and show suits of coins, swords, cups, and clubs, instead of today's clubs, diamonds, hearts, and spades.

DACHA

Built in 1969, this adaptation of a Russian peasant house was designed to house the collection of Russian art given to Hillwood by Mme. Augusto Rosso, whose husband was the ambassador from Italy to the Soviet Union from 1936 to 1941. It is a log structure with colorful carvings around the windows and door.

WASHINGTON DOLLS' HOUSE AND TOY MUSEUM

5236 Forty-fourth Street, N.W.
Washington, D.C. 20015
202/244-0024; 202/363-6400

METRO	Friendship Heights.
HOURS	10 A.M. to 5 P.M. Tuesday through Saturday; Noon to 5 P.M. Sunday. Closed Thanksgiving, Christmas, and New Year's Day.
TOURS	Group tours by appointment.
ADMISSION	$3, adults; $2, senior citizens; $1, children under 14.
MUSEUM SHOP	Dolls' houses and their furnishings; toys, books, postcards; doll house building and wiring supplies. Antique toys on consignment.
SPECIAL EVENTS	Antique train runs on request.
SPECIAL FACILITIES	Edwardian Tea Room available for birthday parties. Also, luncheons and tea parties, by contract, combined with special tours for groups of twelve or more.
AUTHOR'S CHOICE	Nineteenth-century Mexican mansion Working antique train The "shopwindowful of shops" Antique doll collection Exhibit of zoos and Noah's arks

A dolls' house handmade in the 1880s

Tucked between a bank and a shopping mall, near some of Washington's most fashionable stores, is a unique museum of nostalgia. The Washington Dolls' House and Toy Museum is the only museum in the nation's capital devoted entirely to dolls' houses, dolls, antique toys, and miniature shops.

With the exception of a small group of dolls donated by a California collector, all of the carefully researched objects on display come from the collection of Flora Gill Jacobs, an author and internationally recognized authority on dolls' houses. Special rotating and seasonal exhibitions are drawn from her vast collection.

Mrs. Jacobs, who bought her first dolls' house in 1945 while researching *A History of Doll Houses*, eventually acquired more than a hundred authentically furnished miniature houses, shops, stables, schools, and churches, as well as antique toys and games. She opened this museum in 1975, when the collection began to overflow her home. Most of the items are from the nineteenth century, but the collection also includes several eighteenth-century Nuremberg kitchens equipped with tiny pewter plates, copper pots, and earthenware bowls. The most modern dolls' house in the collection is a 1932 white clapboard "colonial" with workable doors, shutters, and electric lights that can be turned on and off.

Children enjoy tolling the bell of a miniature schoolhouse

and turning the reel of an 1884 toy to see pictures of the U.S. Capitol, the White House, and every president up to Chester A. Arthur.

It is adults, however, who return time and again for glimpses of a bygone era. As Mrs. Jacobs points out, dolls' houses reflect the social history of their times. In addition to mirroring architectural styles, dolls' houses reveal how people lived and worked, what they wore, and what pastimes they enjoyed. Here is the world in microcosm. Here are extended Victorian doll families, complete with servants, pets, and elaborate household furnishings. Here are the ubiquitous dogs, cats, and canaries; one Lilliputian home even includes a cage with a pet squirrel. A group of miniature Noah's arks is a reminder that children, forbidden to play on the Sabbath, could use these "Sunday toys" as a form of bible study.

The collection includes a rare early nineteenth-century toy shop from Switzerland; the Tiffany-Platt House, an imposing town house said to have been built for a member of New York's Tiffany family around 1860; a six-story dolls' apartment house from New Jersey, dated 1903; a "street" lined with houses by R. Bliss Manufacturing Company, a famed turn-of-the-century toymaker, and a post-Civil War mansion of "sandstone" construction in the fashionable French Second Empire style.

One of the most elaborate houses is a miniature mansion from Puebla, Mexico, with a 1920s Paige automobile parked in its driveway. Seven feet tall and six feet wide, the fully furnished house includes a tower with a working clock, a glass-enclosed elevator, a dove cote, and a chapel. The 1890 façade, which is French with some Moorish features, reflects many full-sized mansions built in Mexico during the mid-nineteenth-century reign of French emperor Maximilian.

A group of East Baltimore row houses with white steps, made by firemen during their leisure hours, was designed to be exhibited in a Christmas garden during the holiday season. Another Victorian dolls' house, built for five Bel Air, Maryland, sisters in the 1880s, was also part of a Christmas garden at the base of the family's Christmas tree.

Not content merely to show how people lived in the last century, the museum gives glimpses of how they worked. There are turn-of-the-century milliner's shops, schoolrooms, an English butcher's shop, and two German kitchens that served as educational toys.

Other toys include zoos, circuses, and a rare version of Teddy Roosevelt on safari. There is a windup musical tea party with a piano player who performs while the ladies raise their tea cups. And a small but choice collection of antique dolls includes several "long-faced Jumeaus." These nineteenth century French dolls, made by Emile Jumeau, are extremely rare.

Mrs. Jacobs, who considers dolls' houses to be mirrors of the past, believes that preserving the small buildings of this bygone world is as important as saving the full-sized structures they reflect. She thinks that practically everything made in full size has also been created in miniature.

Mrs. Jacobs has unearthed postage stamp-size books and spectacles with which to read them; dolls' dolls and tiny doll carriages; pianos and violins with sheet music; tennis rackets, birdcages and a pet carrier with a pup inside; a tiny Victorian coffin; potted holly and daffodil plants and plant stands; and enough cooking and serving accoutrements to take care of a regiment of dolls for a decade.

Detail of an early 20th-century circus by Schoenhut of Philadelphia

*The cupola of Mount
Vernon*

MARYLAND AND VIRGINIA

CLARA BARTON HOUSE

5801 Oxford Road
Glen Echo, Maryland 20812
301/492-6245

METROBUS	N5 and N8.
HOURS	10 A.M. to 5 P.M. daily.
TOURS	Upon arrival. Tours for groups and those with special needs by appointment.
ADMISSION	Free.
HANDICAPPED FACILITIES	First floor accessible to the disabled.
MUSEUM SHOP	Books relating to Clara Barton and the nineteenth century, Victorian homes, women's history, and guidebooks.
SPECIAL EVENTS	Exhibits, concerts, films, and Victorian-era demonstrations.
SPECIAL FACILITIES	Picnic facilities available at adjacent Glen Echo Park.
AUTHOR'S CHOICE	Restored American Red Cross office, first floor "Lantern" room, third floor

A visit to the Clara Barton House sweeps away misconceptions about the founder of the Red Cross and leaves you with greater awareness of an exceptional woman.

Because of her relief efforts, many people assume that Clara Barton was a nurse. She was not. Her public role as a kindhearted, compassionate angel of mercy overshadowed the private image of a complex woman who was insecure and often depressed. Frequently overlooked in the emphasis on her humanitarianism is the fact that Barton was also an early, vocal supporter of women's suffrage, prison reform, and civil rights. She lived the last fifteen years of her life in this large, rather plain Victorian house, which served as the first permanent headquarters of the American Red Cross.

HISTORY

Clara Barton, born in North Oxford, Massachusetts, in 1821, acquired a strong sense of duty from her father, who had fought in the post-Revolutionary Indian Wars. For eleven years, beginning in 1839, she taught school in North Oxford. In 1852, she established a free school in Bordentown, New Jersey. Such schools were considered to be a form of charity and were rare. Barton's school obviously filled a need because enrollment jumped from six to six hundred in one year. When a man was appointed principal, with her as his assistant, she resigned. After developing one of the first in a lifelong series of nervous illnesses, Barton moved to Washington in 1854, hoping to improve her health and "do something decided" with her life.

In Washington, Charles Mason, the commissioner of patents, hired her as a clerk. Although women had previously been employed by the federal government, it was considered

Clara Barton, founder of the U.S. Red Cross Society

improper for men and women to work together in the Victorian era. Clara Barton was the only female government employee at that time. In 1856, when James Buchanan became president, she lost her job, but regained it in 1860.

Barton was working at the Patent Office when the Civil War began in 1861 and when the Massachusetts Sixth Regiment, which included many friends and former students, arrived in Washington. When the Massachusetts volunteers were attacked by southern sympathizers as they passed through Baltimore, Barton, concerned about her "boys," went immediately to their temporary quarters in the Senate Chamber of the Capitol. Six of the men had been killed, and she found the troops in need of basic necessities. After providing as much as she could, she wrote to their families requesting supplies.

As boxes arrived with blankets, candles, and preserved fruits, Barton's home began to resemble a warehouse. For a year, she continued to solicit and stockpile supplies. As the war dragged on, however, she was no longer content merely to visit hospitals and invalid camps. Determined to help on the battlefield, she obtained permission to join General Burnside's division at the front.

In 1864, Barton was appointed supervisor of nurses for the Army of the James, responsible for organizing hospitals and supervising the daily operation of camps for wounded soldiers. The following year, she spearheaded an effort to locate more than twenty-two thousand missing soldiers. She also worked to establish a national cemetery at Andersonville, Georgia, the site of a former Confederate prison for Union army soldiers.

During the war, Barton was an indefatigable worker. Afterward, however, when she was no longer occupied with urgent relief work, no longer needed and admired, her nervous ailments returned. Following an apparent nervous breakdown in 1869, she sailed for Europe.

During her travels abroad, Barton learned, for the first time, of the work of the Red Cross, which had been established as a result of the Geneva Convention of 1863. The United States had not yet accepted the international treaty protecting civilians and the wounded in wartime, and Barton decided to work for its ratification.

When Barton took the popular "water cure" for her depression at a sanitarium in Dansville, New York, she met Julian Hubbell, a chemistry teacher twenty-five years her junior. Following her advice, Hubbell switched from chemistry to medicine in order to help her with the planned relief organization. In the late 1870s, as her health improved, Barton participated in women's suffrage conventions and began trying to establish the Red Cross in the United States. Her flair for publicity helped to gain support for ratification of the Treaty of Geneva, and led to its final approval by the Senate in 1882.

By this time, Clara Barton was sixty years old and president of the American Association of the Red Cross, which had been organized the previous year. She established the first local Red Cross chapter in Dansville, New York. During the next few years, her fledgling organization helped victims of floods, tornadoes, an earthquake, and yellow fever. Relief efforts peaked during the Johnstown, Pennsylvania, flood of 1889, in which six thirty-room Red Cross hotels were built for survivors of the disaster.

In 1890, two brothers, Edward and Edwin Baltzley,

established a branch of the National Chautauqua, an organization that promoted education and productive recreation, at Glen Echo, Maryland, on the outskirts of Washington. Believing that Clara Barton's presence would attract others to their new residential community, they gave her a plot of land and offered to build a house that could serve as Red Cross headquarters.

Using some lumber from the Johnstown buildings, Dr. Hubbell supervised construction of a building modeled along the lines of the Red Cross shelters. Barton and Hubbell moved into the house in the summer of 1891, but the daily, three-hour carriage rides to Washington were so tiring that the building was used as only a warehouse. However, when electric trolleys came to Glen Echo in 1897, cutting the transportation time, Barton remodeled the house and moved in again.

In addition to Barton and Hubbell, the thirty-five-room house was home to as many as twenty-five volunteers and a steady stream of visitors. The household was relatively self-sufficient, with a cow, chickens, fruit trees, and a vegetable garden to provide food. Barton, who had been decorated by many foreign governments, frequently wore her medals while milking the cow or weeding the garden. "It does brighten up an old dress," she said.

In 1898, the seventy-six-year-old Barton went to Cuba during the Spanish-American War. During the next few years, criticism mounted over her management of the Red Cross. She had always merged her personal and professional life, and the financial accounts were hopelessly tangled. Younger members felt that she was too old to continue day-to-day operations. Finally, in 1904, after President Theodore Roosevelt withdrew from her board of directors in support of her opposition, Barton resigned as president of the American National Red Cross. She was succeeded by Mabel T. Boardman, who served as administrative head of the organization for the next forty years.

A petite woman with coal-black dyed hair, Barton refused to admit that her skills were diminishing as she was growing older. The following year, at eighty-three, she founded the National First Aid Society, designed to teach life saving skills.

Barton died in 1912 at the age of ninety and bequeathed the Glen Echo house to Hubbell. He and two friends formed the Clara Barton Memorial Association and planned to convert the house into a memorial. However, the organization was soon beset with financial difficulties.

Near the end of her life, Barton and Hubbell had become interested in the occult. After Barton's death, Mabelle Rawson Hirons, an acquaintance from North Oxford, claimed that Barton had contacted her in a séance and told her to take charge of the Glen Echo house. Hubbell signed over the property to Hirons, who later evicted him and began renting rooms and selling Barton's furnishings. After a lengthy court battle, Hubbell regained the house. He died in 1929 and left the house to his nieces, Rena and Lena Hubbell, who converted it into an apartment building. The property changed hands again a couple of times and, by 1963, it was owned by the four Frank sisters. As they were quite elderly and unable to keep up the large house, they decided the time had come to sell. The women turned down a $50,000 offer from the amusement park next door because they were afraid that the house would be torn down to make room for a parking lot. They agreed to sell the house for $35,000 to anyone who would promise to save it.

A group of Red Cross volunteers in Montgomery County, Maryland, formed the Friends of Clara Barton and began a fund-raising campaign to buy the property. By the July 1963 deadline, the group had managed to raise only $800 of the $1,000 needed for the down payment. During a meeting with the owners to try to arrange an extension, the lawyer for the amusement park arrived with a check for $50,000. In a scene reminiscent of a silent film melodrama, a Friend rushed in with a $200 check. The Frank sisters accepted the lower offer and returned the $50,000 check to the lawyer.

Continuing their fund-raising efforts, the Friends bought original Barton furnishings from the Frank sisters and made much-needed repairs to the house. By 1975, they had paid off the mortgage and deeded the property to the National Park Service. The group disbanded a few years later and used their remaining funds to furnish the Red Cross offices in the house.

THE BUILDING

When the house was remodeled in 1897, its stone façade was removed and the frame building was painted yellow.

The balconies surrounding the central stair hall, which are reminiscent of a Mississippi River steamboat, were inspired by hotels of the period.

The first floor hall is lined with deep closets designed to store disaster relief supplies. (There are thirty-eight similar built-in closets in the house.) To the left of the entrance is a formal parlor with American and Red Cross flags. Barton was fond of flags, and, when she lived there, the entrance hall was lined with flags of countries where the Red Cross had chapters. An American flag flew from the top of the house, and a Red Cross flag was on a standard on the front of the house.

At the far end of the hall, the original Red Cross offices and the dining room have been restored. You can see where Barton worked and the small backless chair she used. Proud of her posture, she could sit ramrod straight on the uncomfortable chair for hours. In the adjoining office are a graphophone, an early machine for recording messages, typewriters, and a letter press.

Research has indicated that Barton and Hubbell used cloth and old newspapers as insulation in the walls. The original cloth-covered ceiling is visible in the first floor hall.

Barton's second floor corner bedroom and her adjoining sitting room overlook the C & O Canal and the Clara Barton Parkway. The parkway was not built at the time, and Barton could stroll down her lawn to the canal. She did not care for the noise made by the roller coaster in the nearby amusement park, however.

Eight other bedrooms on the second and third floors, used by guests and volunteers, are furnished quite simply, as they would have been at the turn of the century. The most interesting is a "lantern" room on the third floor, which appears to be suspended under the eaves without any visible support for the floor.

The house is currently being restored, room by room, to re-create its appearance during the period from 1897 to 1904, when it served as both Clara Barton's home and the headquarters of the American Red Cross.

NATIONAL CAPITAL TROLLEY MUSEUM

Bonifant Road
Wheaton, Maryland
301/384-6088

TO REACH — Take Capital Beltway north to Georgia Avenue (Route 97) north. Follow Georgia Avenue to Layhill Road (Route 182). Go right on Layhill two miles, right on Bonifant Road to museum on left.

HOURS — Noon to 5 P.M. Saturday and Sunday. Also, Memorial Day, July 4, and Labor Day. Last ride at 4:30 P.M. Open Noon to 4 P.M. Wednesday during July and August. Closed December 15 through January 1.

TOURS — Group tours by appointment.

ADMISSION — Free. Trolley fares $2, adults; $1.50, children under 18. Free, children under 2.

MUSEUM SHOP — Books, postcards, trolley souvenirs.

SPECIAL EVENTS — Lectures, films, "Trolley Car Spectacular" third Sunday in April and September.

MEMBERSHIP — From $25.

AUTHOR'S CHOICE — *Washington Trolleys Rediscovered* slide program
Antique trolley cars

The clang-clang-clang of the trolley is more than just a memory in suburban Maryland. Thanks to a dedicated corps of volunteers, it is now possible to enjoy a slow, bouncy ride through the Maryland countryside aboard an antique trolley.

In the visitors' center, which is built to resemble an old-fashioned railroad station, a brief slide program tells the history of Washington, D.C., trolleys. In addition to seeing the photographic exhibits and memorabilia, visitors can push a button and operate a model streetcar.

HISTORY

Horse cars were introduced during the Lincoln administration to accommodate the influx of people who came to Washington during the Civil War. Horses were replaced, first by cable cars and then by electric cars. In the early days, open-sided cars with straw on the floor were used in spring and summer, and closed cars operated during the winter. From 1892 to 1913, mail was sorted aboard U.S. mail cars operating between Georgetown and the Navy Yard.

Streetcar service ended in Washington on January 28, 1962, a hundred years after it began. Many of the Washington cars were sent abroad and operated until recently in Barcelona, Spain, and Sarajevo, Yugoslavia. Others were rebuilt and are used to shuttle visitors between a parking lot and offices in Fort Worth, Texas.

Three cars from the collection of the National Capital Trolley Museum

THE COLLECTION

The museum's collection comprises fourteen cars, not all of which are in operating condition. They include Number 522, a little orange car built in 1898, which served as a rail grinder work car in Washington; Berlin Car 5954, built in 1924 and used during flower festivals in Karlsruhe, Germany; Sweeper 07, built in 1899, and Sweeper 026, built in 1905, responsible for clearing snow from Washington tracks until 1962, and Car 1053, an experimental streamliner, built in 1935, which once ran along Wisconsin Avenue through Georgetown to Pennsylvania Avenue.

All of the historic cars—including some not normally operated for the public—are brought out of the carbarns twice a year, in April and September, for the "Trolley Car Spectacular."

The museum, which opened in 1969, is especially popular with children and railway buffs. A nonprofit corporation operating under a contract with the Maryland-National Capital Park and Planning Commission, the museum is located on a ten-acre tract in Northwest Branch Regional Park. Volunteers laid the tracks, restored the cars, and are entirely responsible for the operation of the museum.

STABLER-LEADBEATER APOTHECARY SHOP

105-107 South Fairfax Street
Alexandria, Virginia 22314
703/836-3713

METRO King Street. Transfer to bus to Old Town.

HOURS 10 A.M. to 4 P.M. Monday through Saturday; Noon to 4 P.M. Sunday.

ADMISSION $1 donation.

MUSEUM SHOP Collectibles sold on consignment for the benefit of the museum; books, notecards, posters.

AUTHOR'S CHOICE Mrs. Washington's letter to Edward Stabler
Robert E. Lee's chair
Collection of historic bottles

This was George Washington's neighborhood apothecary shop, and, as the nation's oldest continuously operated drugstore, it was also frequented by Robert E. Lee and other distinguished Virginians.

It is reportedly the only business establishment in the country that served both Washington and Lee.

HISTORY
The red brick building, which is currently undergoing renovation, was constructed in 1775. Its first occupant was a silversmith.

Edward Stabler opened an apothecary shop in 1792, and members of his family continued the business here for 141 years. You can still see the original drawers that once contained an array of medicinal herbs and potions.

The interior of the building was modernized in the Gothic Revival style in the 1850s.

THE COLLECTION
In 1933, Mr. and Mrs. L. Manuel Hendler of Baltimore, Maryland, bought a collection of bottles which is considered to be the finest American collection of eighteenth- and nineteenth-century medicinal bottles in their original state.

The Stabler-Leadbeater Apothecary Shop

The bottles were given to the Landmarks Society of Alexandria in 1948.

Since many customers were unable to read in the eighteenth century, color was an important means of identification. Poison was put in colored bottles that were roughened so that their contents could be recognized, even in the dark. Jars filled with colored liquids were placed in the windows to identify it as an apothecary shop, since servants, who often were illiterate, were sent to town with lists of items to purchase there.

Many bottles and other artifacts were unearthed by Alexandria archaeologists in excavations of two wells and part of the basement's dirt floor in 1982 and 1985. During the 1880s and early 1900s, the wells were filled with discarded medicine bottles, syringes, test tubes, ointment jars, and perfume vials.

The museum has the cluttered look of a typical one-room apothecary shop. In addition to the bottle collection, old account books and historic documents are on view. An 1802 letter to Stabler from Mrs. Washington requests "one quart bottle of his best castor oil and the bill for it." Other letters came from George Mason and Robert E. Lee, who bought the paint for Arlington House here.

Lee apparently enjoyed visiting at the shop when he came to Alexandria from his home at Arlington House. Note the wooden chair frequently used by Lee.

In October 1859, Lee was standing at the marble-topped counter, talking with Leadbeater, when he received sealed orders from General Winfield Scott directing him to capture abolitionist John Brown at Harper's Ferry. Scott's messenger had gone to Arlington House and was told that he could probably find Lee at the apothecary shop. Lee read the message and reportedly told Leadbeater, "I am afraid this is only the beginning of more serious trouble."

Religious scruples kept Leadbeater from joining the Confederate army. He was also unwilling to submit to the edict requiring businesses to close unless all clerks took an oath of loyalty to the Union. Despite this law, Leadbeater's shop remained open because Union sympathizer Lewis Mackenzie, a local justice of the peace, would not trust anyone but Leadbeater to fill his prescriptions—an opinion reportedly shared by Alexandria's mayor, as well.

ARLINGTON HOUSE

The Robert E. Lee Memorial
Arlington National Cemetery
Arlington, Virginia 22211
703/557-0613

MAILING ADDRESS
Care of National Park Service
George Washington Memorial Parkway
Turkey Run Park
McLean, Virginia 22101

METRO	Arlington Cemetery.
HOURS	April through September: 9:30 A.M. to 6 P.M.; October through March: 9:30 A.M. to 4:30 P.M. daily. Closed Christmas and New Year's Day.
TOURS	Self-guided tours all year. Group tours October through March. Special tours for the blind and hearing-impaired by appointment.
ADMISSION	Free.
HANDICAPPED FACILITIES	Wheelchair lift adjacent to the conservatory of the house. First floor accessible to the disabled.
BOOK STORE	Books about Lee and the Civil War.
SPECIAL EVENTS	Annual observances of Robert E. Lee's birthday January 19 and wedding anniversary June 30. Special Christmas events, with the house decorated as it would have been just before the Civil War.
SPECIAL FACILITIES	Small museum with Lee memorabilia.
AUTHOR'S CHOICE	White parlor, first floor Painting studio, first floor Playroom, second floor

Arlington House, high on a hill overlooking Washington, is a link in the area's chain of historic associations that began with George Washington and continued into the nineteenth century. The handsome Greek Revival house, built by Martha Washington's grandson, served as home to Robert E. Lee and his family for thirty years, and is filled with Lee and Custis memorabilia.

HISTORY
When John Parke Custis, Martha Washington's son by her first marriage, died of camp fever at Yorktown in 1781, the Washingtons raised his two youngest children. George Washington Parke Custis and Eleanor Parke (Nelly) Custis were known as the "children of Mount Vernon."

In 1802, George Washington Parke Custis began building Arlington House on 1,100 acres, which his father had purchased in 1778. The rolling hills and farmlands comprise present-day Arlington National Cemetery and Fort Myer. Custis was a painter, playwright, and orator. Always hospitable,

Arlington House

Custis opened his home to visitors. Picnickers arriving by ferry from Washington were allowed to use part of the grounds. He even provided tables and benches.

Martha Washington died that same year, and Custis inherited many of her personal possessions and most of the contents of Mount Vernon. Arlington House—named in honor of the Custis family's first home on Virginia's Eastern Shore—was to contain what George Custis called the "Washington Treasury."

Two years later, at the age of twenty-three, Custis married Mary Lee Fitzhugh. In 1831, Mary Anna Randolph Custis, their only child to survive infancy, married her childhood friend, Lieutenant Robert E. Lee, a West Point graduate. Although Arlington House belonged to Mary's parents, it became the Lees' home, as well. Six of the seven Lee children were born here.

Lee served in the Mexican War from 1846 to 1848. He was appointed superintendent of the U.S. Military Academy in 1852.

When George Washington Parke Custis died in 1857, Arlington House was bequeathed to Mrs. Lee during her lifetime and afterward to their eldest son, George Washington Custis Lee. As executor, Robert E. Lee took a two-year leave of absence from the army to repair and improve the estate, which had become badly run down. Lee described his hilltop home as "a house that any one might see with half an eye." He once wrote that "my affections and attachments are more strongly placed [there] than at any other place in the world."

Lee was in Texas in February 1861. He had received orders to report to Washington and was preparing to leave when that state seceded from the Union. Hoping that the Union would survive, Lee accepted a commission, signed by President Abraham Lincoln, promoting him to full colonel in command of the First Cavalry of the United States.

Virginia seceded April 17, 1861, but the news did not become public in Washington until two days later. On April 18, in an effort to retain the loyalty of southern officers, Secretary of War Simon Cameron authorized Francis P. Blair, Sr., to offer Lee command of the army to be organized to invade the seceding states but Lee declined.

In making this decision, Lee chose to join his beloved state of Virginia, rather than remaining in the U.S. Army and fighting against his family and home.

Two days later, the governor of Virginia offered Lee command of Virginia's military and naval forces and a commission as major general. He accepted and never returned to Arlington.

About three weeks later, Mrs. Lee received word from a cousin who worked in General Scott's office that President Lincoln was planning to move troops into Virginia. She packed wagonloads of possessions but still was forced to leave many things at Arlington. Mrs. Lee fled south, staying with various relatives in Virginia.

Meanwhile, Union officers in charge of defending Washington made the mansion their headquarters. Later in the war, most of the Washington furnishings stored at Arlington were sent to the Old Patent Office Building for safekeeping. However, some of the Washington heirlooms and Custis and Lee possessions were taken by the occupying troops.

During the war, Congress passed a law requiring that property in areas occupied by Union forces be taxed. The local tax collector required that the legal owners personally appear to pay the tax. Mrs. Lee, a semi-invalid, arranged for a cousin to pay her ninety-two-dollar tax and the five percent penalty, because she was unable to make the trip from behind the Confederate line. The government refused to accept payment from anyone but Mrs. Lee as owner, confiscated the property, and offered it for sale at a public auction. There were no bidders except the government, which took title to the estate. In 1864, two hundred acres were set aside as a military cemetery, which later became the nucleus of Arlington National Cemetery.

After the war, Lee became president of Washington College (now Washington and Lee University) in Lexington, Virginia. He died there in 1870. His son, George Washington Custis Lee, sued the federal government and recovered Arlington House in 1882. By that time, however, hundreds of graves surrounded the house, and Lee agreed to sell the property to the government for $150,000.

For many years, the mansion was used as offices and living quarters for the cemetery superintendent. In 1925, the War Department began to restore the house, and, in 1933, it was transferred to the National Park Service. It was designated a memorial to Robert E. Lee in 1955. The house is currently being restored to its appearance just before the Civil War, with original furnishings and objects of the period.

In 1909, the body of Pierre Charles L'Enfant was moved to the lawn in front of the portico, on a hill overlooking the city he planned in 1791.

The grave site of Pierre Charles L'Enfant on the front lawn

THE HOUSE

George Hadfield, a young English architect who helped to construct the Capitol, designed the house, which probably was modeled after the temple of Theseus at Athens. Built of brick covered with stucco, the north wing was constructed in 1802 and the south wing was added by 1804. The center section and the sixty-foot-long portico were completed in 1818. The foundation stone and timber came from the estate. Native clay provided the bricks for the house and for the eight massive Doric columns of the portico, which were originally painted to resemble marble.

In 1824, when General Lafayette visited Arlington House, he pronounced the scene across the Potomac, which was visible from the portico, "the finest view in the world."

From 1818 until the white parlor was completed in 1855, the room to the right of the entrance was the main parlor. (The wide center hall also served as a parlor during the summer, with the doors kept open to catch a breeze.) Mary Anna Randolph Custis, attended by six bridesmaids, married Robert E. Lee in the main parlor on June 30, 1831.

When General Lee was at home, he often picked roses in the garden and brought them to the breakfast table for his wife, daughters, and any female guests. The dining room table is set with nineteenth-century blue-and-white Canton china, silver, and glassware owned by the Lees.

The white parlor across the hall—so called because of its white walls—was unfinished and used for storage for nearly forty years. The room was completed in 1855, when the Lees acquired the twin Carrara marble mantels and the rather formal Victorian furniture upholstered in red velvet. Hanging above the two mantels are a portrait of *Mary Custis Lee*, painted when she was twenty-nine years old, and the only painting in the house of *Robert E. Lee*. Unlike Lee's more familiar, bearded portraits, this one (a copy of a William West painting in the collection of Washington and Lee University) shows him as a clean-shaven, thirty-one-year-old man.

Custis's painting studio, originally designed as a parlor, was used by Mrs. Lee as a morning room after 1855. Custis's monumental painting of *The Battle of Monmouth*, *New Jersey* shows Washington and his troops, with Mollie Pitcher loading a cannon in the background. While they were living at Mount Vernon, Washington reportedly regaled the young Custis children with stories about that military engagement. After Mrs. Lee was forced to leave Arlington House during the Civil War, a cousin—a member of the Peter family of Georgetown—took some of the remaining furnishings for safekeeping. The cousin rolled up the large canvas and stored it at her home in Georgetown, where it remained for more than a hundred years. In 1976, the painting was returned to Arlington House as a Bicentennial gift.

Like her father, Mrs. Lee was also a painter. Although Custis specialized in patriotic battle scenes, Mrs. Lee chose more tranquil subjects. Two of her seascapes—copies of eighteenth-century French paintings—hang on the wall near the windows. Because she suffered from rheumatoid arthritis, a bed was placed in this room so that she could rest occasionally.

The conservatory, or "camellia house," was originally an open porch. After it was enclosed, it was used to protect plants during the winter.

Bedrooms on the second floor open onto a spacious hall. In the master bedroom, Lee paced the floor the night of April 19, 1861, before deciding to honor family ties to Virginia and resign his U.S. Army commission.

Christmas decorations

Only the oldest daughter, Mary, had her own room, which she frequently shared with a favorite cousin, Martha Williams. The three boys, Custis, William Henry Fitzhugh (Rooney), and Robert, Jr., shared a room, as did the three younger girls, Annie, Agnes, and Mildred.

The children's playroom, which also served as the girls' dressing room, is filled with pint-sized furniture, dolls, and toys of the nineteenth century. A miniature china cupboard was a gift to Mrs. Lee from her aunt, Nelly Custis.

CARLYLE HOUSE

121 North Fairfax Street
Alexandria, Virginia 22314
703/549-2997

METRO	King Street.
HOURS	10 A.M. to 4:30 P.M. Tuesday through Saturday; Noon to 4:30 P.M. Sunday.
TOURS	On the hour and half-hour, beginning at 10 A.M. Tuesday through Saturday and Noon Sunday. Last tour 4 P.M.
ADMISSION	$3, adults; $2, groups; $1, children 11 to 17.
HANDICAPPED FACILITIES	Elevator to first floor. Second floor not accessible.
MUSEUM SHOP	Books, china, glassware, and other gift items.
SPECIAL EVENTS	Lectures, exhibits, eighteenth-century special events.
MEMBERSHIP	Friends of Carlyle House membership from $15.
AUTHOR'S CHOICE	George Washington's plan of Alexandria, ground floor Master bedroom, first floor

Carlyle House, built by a founder of Alexandria, was the scene of a historic meeting between British General Edward Braddock and five colonial governors—a meeting that led indirectly to the Revolutionary War.

HISTORY

John Carlyle, a native of Dumfries, Scotland, and Carlisle, England, was twenty-one years old when he came to Virginia in 1741 as a factor, or business agent, for William Hicks, an English merchant. Like many other Scotsmen who were Alexandria's original settlers, Carlyle was a shrewd, hardworking businessman. He traveled throughout Virginia and Maryland as Hicks's representative, selling goods from abroad and arranging the shipment of colonial products to England, Scotland, and the West Indies.

When the town held an auction of lots in July 1749, Carlyle bought lots number 41 and 42, two of the choicest and most expensive half-acre properties on the waterfront. Located at the corner of Fairfax and Cameron Streets, across from the market square, Carlyle's land was in the heart of what soon became a flourishing seaport town.

As a member of Alexandria's board of trustees and a justice of the peace, Carlyle was entrusted with certain civic duties. He was responsible for completing Christ Church, building the courthouse, a public warehouse, a wharf, and the Presbyterian Meeting House, and extending Duke Street to Lumley Point. As a large landowner and a well-to-do member of the gentry, Carlyle was one of the first to import racehorses, which were bred at Torthorwald, one of his three plantations.

In March 1755, General Edward Braddock, commander-in-chief of His Majesty's forces in North America, arrived in

Alexandria with 1,600 troops on their way to drive the French out of the British territory west of the Alleghenies. Braddock, headquartered at Carlyle's house, met with five colonial governors on April 14, 1755 to discuss the colonies' financing of the expedition. The governors' refusal to ask their colonial assemblies to pay for the campaign was the first in a series of actions that led eventually to the Revolutionary War.

Carlyle wrote to his brother George on August 15, 1775: "... their was the Grandest Congress held at my home ever known on this Continent, Gov. Shirley, of New England, Morris of pensilvania, Delaney of New York, Sharp of Maryland, Dinwiddie of Virginia, General Braddock Comador Keeple & Many other Gentlemen were there several days & concerted the plan for this presint campain, in which was determined Braddock troups was to attack Fort Duquesne, in which he unhappily failed. . . ."

Carlyle was appointed commissary for the Virginia militia, in charge of providing all food, clothing, and ammunition for the troops fighting the French and Indian War and the Revolutionary War. Carlyle also looked after George William Fairfax's estates while the latter was in England and kept an eye on Mount Vernon while George Washington was off fighting wars.

In addition to his association with William Hicks, Carlyle formed a partnership with John Dalton, a fellow Scotsman, around 1752. The firm of Carlyle and Dalton lasted until Dalton's death twenty-five years later. Through the years, there were other business ventures, involving real estate, shipping, farming, an iron foundry, a grist mill, and a store.

As Carlyle's business expanded, his standing in the community grew, as well. In 1747, he married Sarah (Sally) Fairfax, the daughter of Colonel William Fairfax and a cousin of the powerful Lord Fairfax. Sarah's sister Ann was the wife of Lawrence Washington, half-brother of George Washington. John and Sarah had seven children, only two of whom survived infancy. After Sarah's death in 1761, Carlyle married Sybil West, the daughter of Alexandrian Hugh West. They had three sons, two of whom died young, and Sybil died in childbirth in 1769.

THE BUILDING

John Carlyle began building the house in 1751, a few years after his marriage to Sally Fairfax. In 1752, when the house was nearly finished, the walls were weakened during a storm and had to be completely rebuilt. The Carlyles moved into the house the day their first son was born, August 1, 1753.

Most Alexandria houses at that time were one- or two-story structures built of wood or brick. Carlyle's, however, was a country house in town, built of stone and modeled after the English and Scottish manor houses he had known in his youth. While most town houses were built close to the street, Carlyle's house was sited quite far from the road, with two dependencies, an office and a kitchen, placed at the front and side property lines. The land sloped down to the river behind the house, where a warehouse and gardens were located. (In the 1770s, Alexandrians began "banking out," or filling in, the land at the river's edge, creating what are now Lee Street and Union Street.)

The design for the house probably came from one of the

architectural design books found in most eighteenth-century gentlemen's libraries, such as Adam's *Vitruvius Scoticus*, James Gibbs's *Book of Architecture*, or William Salman's *Palladio Londenensis*. With a stone façade, a single projecting pavilion, and stone quoins at each corner, the exterior is similar to many eighteenth-century houses in northern England and Scotland.

Carlyle House

Carlyle left his property to his son when he died in 1780. One year later, after his son's death, the estate was divided between his two grandsons. Three-year-old Carlyle Fairfax Whiting inherited Torthorwald, one of the country estates, which was on the site of the present Fairlington. The town house and other property passed to John Carlyle Herbert, whose father was the president of the Bank of Alexandria, and the Herbert family lived in the Carlyle house for many years. John Herbert sold part of the property to the bank, which constructed a brick building on the northeast corner of the property, at the corner of Fairfax and Cameron Streets.

In 1827, the house was sold to pay the debts of John's uncle, Thomas Herbert. In 1848, James Green, a well-to-do Alexandria furniture manufacturer whose factory stood two blocks away on Prince Street, converted the bank building into the Mansion House hotel. He modernized the old house and moved in with his family. In 1855, Green connected the house to the hotel and built a four-story hotel addition that completely blocked the view of John Carlyle's house from Fairfax Street.

During the Civil War, when Northern troops occupied Alexandria, the hotel was converted into a Union army hospital but reopened as a hotel in August 1865. The hotel building—then called the Braddock House—became run down after Green's death in 1880. The property was converted into apartments and changed hands several times. During World War I, the wing that connected the house to the hotel was torn down, making the house freestanding again. Although the house was still blocked by the apartments on Fairfax Street, it was refurbished and opened to the public as a museum.

In 1941—two hundred years after John Carlyle settled in Virginia—Lloyd L. Schaeffer purchased the house and continued to maintain it as a museum until the 1960s, when its existence was threatened by urban renewal. In 1969, the Northern Virginia Regional Park Authority decided to make the Carlyle House the focal point of a new urban park. Most of the hotel was demolished in 1973. The restored Carlyle House opened in 1976 as a major event of Virginia's Bicentennial celebration.

TOURING THE MUSEUM

One room on the ground floor, five rooms on the first floor and four on the second floor are open to the public. The house is decorated with period furnishings, according to the inventory taken in 1780 after John Carlyle's death. The only objects owned by Carlyle himself are a snuffbox in the master bedroom and portraits of John's father and brother.

GROUND FLOOR

In the brick-floored reception area, exhibits depict the early history of Alexandria and the restoration of the Carlyle house. One of the most interesting features is a copy of the plan of Alexandria, drawn by seventeen-year-old George Washington after the town's lots were auctioned in 1749.

A display in the adjacent servants' hall shows items, such as bread crumbs, fuller's earth, lemons, and castile soap, that were used to remove stains in the colonial era. Wrought iron kettles and pots in the large open fireplace are a reminder of the eighteenth-century mode of cooking.

DINING ROOM

FIRST FLOOR

A closet for storing silver and other valuable items, next to the fireplace, is an unusual feature of the dining room. You can see how sugar was prepared in the eighteenth century. It was shaped into a cone, wrapped in paper and tied with string. Sugar nippers were used to cut small chunks, which were then stored in a bowl or tea caddy.

The floral prints on the walls were a popular decorative note during the 1700s. They were originally seed catalogs, promoting flowers that bloomed during particular months.

Notice the doors and window seats of pine, which have been painted to look like mahogany.

JOHN CARLYLE'S BEDROOM

A green four-poster bed with blue-and-white hangings dominates this white-walled room. The printed fabric of the valance and hangings features a pineapple motif, symbolizing hospitality. Four green beds such as this one were listed in John Carlyle's 1780 inventory.

A portrait of Rachel Murray Carlyle, John Carlyle's mother, hangs over the mantel. Nearby are a small, eighteenth-century drop-leaf table, a clothes press, and a Chippendale mahogany corner chair.

John Carlyle's silver-and-cowrie shell snuffbox, with his family crest embossed on the lid, is in the bookcase. It may have been purchased when Carlyle visited England in May 1751. The bookcase would have been filled with books from Carlyle's 220-volume library, which included a complete set of the works of Voltaire.

Four-poster bed in John Carlyle's bedroom

ENTRANCE HALL

This wide center hall, which was used for dinners and dancing, is typical of a Georgian-style house. The bright green Windsor chairs and settee are similar to those John Carlyle probably ordered from Philadelphia. Painted floor cloths, such as the two seen here with a design of large, marbleized squares, were often used instead of carpets during the eighteenth century. The wide floorboards are the original ones, laid when the house was built in 1753.

LARGE PARLOR

The pale blue woodwork in this room is especially noteworthy. Notice the swan's neck pediment with carved pineapple and rosettes over the doors and the chair rail with a Greek key motif.

The Carlyle family used this room for entertaining, and the table is sometimes set for dessert, with tarts, jellies, sweetmeats, cookies, and apples.

A copy of a Hesselius portrait of John Carlyle hangs over the mantel, and a companion portrait of John's brother, George, is between the windows. Twenty framed views of

View of the large parlor

London and vicinity—similar to those in Carlyle's collection—grace one of the walls. A game table nearby holds checkers and a backgammon set.

SMALL PARLOR

The Prussian blue used for the woodwork in this room was the most expensive paint color in the colonial era. This room has been set up as an office—although Carlyle's office was actually in a small building on Fairfax Street—to demonstrate how goods were traded during the eighteenth century. The value of coins was determined by their weight, as indicated by the scales on the desk. The leather letter box holds invoices for the goods that arrived packed in barrels and crates, such as the one on display that is marked with John Carlyle's initials.

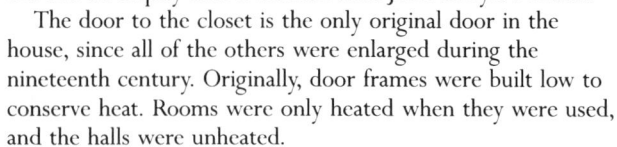

View of the small parlor

The door to the closet is the only original door in the house, since all of the others were enlarged during the nineteenth century. Originally, door frames were built low to conserve heat. Rooms were only heated when they were used, and the halls were unheated.

SECOND FLOOR

STAIR LANDING

Notice the Palladian window that provided both light and ventilation, as well as a view of the gardens below.

In the mid-nineteenth century, James Green installed a circular staircase with a balcony at the second floor level.

UPSTAIRS HALL

During the summer, this hall was probably used as an informal parlor or family sitting room. Now it is often used for rotating exhibits concerning the customs and crafts of the eighteenth century.

Halls on either side of this wide central hall, which lead to the bedrooms, are an unusual architectural feature in an eighteenth-century home, providing both privacy and ventilation.

CARLYLE DAUGHTERS' BEDROOM
Sarah and Anne, the only children of John and Sarah Carlyle who survived infancy, are believed to have shared this room. The sheet music seen here reminds visitors that both girls took music lessons at Mount Vernon with their friend Martha Parke Custis, Martha Washington's daughter.

Since this—the largest bedroom on the second floor—would have had the best view of the river, General Braddock was probably housed here in 1755. The chintz hangings on the four-poster bed blend with the cream-colored walls and light gold woodwork.

CARLYLE SON'S BEDROOM
Although rather sparsely furnished now, this bedroom originally belonged to George William Carlyle.

George William, John Carlyle's only surviving son, inherited the house when his father died in 1780. A member of Colonel Henry "Light Horse Harry" Lee's regiment, he lost his life in a Revolutionary War battle in South Carolina.

ARCHITECTURAL ROOM
This room shows the skeleton of the house, with the walls stripped to reveal the brick and sandstone used in the house's construction. The sandstone came from the Aquia Creek quarry once owned by George Washington and later used to build the Capitol. Sand and seashells were mixed together to form mortar.

Notice the dovetailed joists and the original bearing beam of the floor.

The stone hearth is original. Through the years, alterations were made in the dimensions of the fireplace with the change in heating technology.

The original lathing and plaster can be seen in the ceiling. In restoring the house, the front was capped with limestone, since the original sandstone is no longer available. James Green added stucco to the façade in the 1850s. It was removed and the side and rear façades were restuccoed during the restoration.

GADSBY'S TAVERN MUSEUM

134 North Royal Street
Alexandria, Virginia 22314
703/838-4242

METRO	King Street. Transfer to bus to Old Town.
HOURS	10 A.M. to 5 P.M. Tuesday through Saturday; 1 to 5 P.M. Sunday.
TOURS	Throughout the day, at fifteen minutes before and fifteen minutes after the hour. Last tour each day at 4:15 P.M.
ADMISSION	$3, adults; $1, children aged 11 to 17; free, children under 11 accompanied by paying adult.
HANDICAPPED FACILITIES	Access to the first floor only.
AUTHOR'S CHOICE	Tap Room, first floor Assembly Room, second floor Ballroom, second floor

In this historic Georgian building, George Washington and his friends dined, drank, and discussed important events of the day. The adjoining building, which was once a famous hotel, houses a restaurant on the first floor that re-creates the food, drinks, and ambiance of the colonial era.

Gadsby's Tavern Museum

HISTORY

The smaller brick building was constructed approximately 1770, probably by John Carlyle, whose home was on the other side of the Market Square. Carlyle was the executor of the estate of the original landowners, Charles and Anne Mason.

In the 1770s, the Hawkins family operated a tavern here, with Mrs. Mary Hawkins assuming responsibility when her husband died. John Wise bought the building in 1782. Six years later, Wise moved to larger quarters at the corner of Cameron and Fairfax Streets and began renting the building to a series of tenants.

In 1792, Wise built the adjoining Federal-style brick house, now known as 138 North Royal Street. Outbuildings—a kitchen, stable, coach house, wash house, and necessary—were located in the courtyard behind the building.

At various times in the 1790s, the 1770 building was used as a boarding house, a coffee house, and a private men's club. The 1792 building next door served as the City Hotel and Tavern, with John Gadsby as proprietor from 1796 to 1808. Under Gadsby's supervision, it became one of the finest and most expensive establishments in the nation.

Gadsby moved to Baltimore, Maryland, in 1808 to operate a tavern and then settled in Washington in the 1820s. He was the proprietor of various hotels, including the National Hotel at Sixth Street and Pennsylvania Avenue, until his death in 1844. During the 1830s and 1840s, Gadsby lived in Decatur House on Lafayette Square.

Both buildings, which were sold by Wise in 1815, were always inns, rather than private homes. The City Hotel retained its name and function until approximately 1878. After that time, both buildings housed a variety of commercial establishments.

American Legion Post 24 saved the buildings from demolition in 1929. They were restored by the city in honor of the 1976 Bicentennial celebration. The museum is now owned and operated by the City of Alexandria.

TOURING THE MUSEUM

Many taverns flourished in Alexandria during the late eighteenth and early nineteenth centuries. Gadsby's, a stagecoach stop strategically located near the Market Square, was one of the most popular.

Notices posted on tavern bulletin boards provided information about events in the town and the arrival and departure of ships anchored in the Potomac River. Eighteenth-century taverns were similar to men's clubs and patrons often spent several hours there, eating, exchanging information, visiting with friends, or spending the night.

George Washington was perhaps the most famous patron. He owned a small town house one and one-half blocks away, on Cameron Street. Since that house did not have a kitchen, Washington frequently dined here when Mary Hawkins operated the tavern and, later, during Gadsby's tenure.

On November 5, 1798, less than a year before his death, Washington stood on the steps of Gadsby's Tavern as the Alexandria Independent Infantry Blues, a company of volunteer soldiers, passed in review. It was his final but unofficial military review.

The museum interprets the period from approximately 1770 to 1810, when Gadsby's Tavern was the social, political, and business center of Alexandria.

TAP ROOM   FIRST FLOOR

A typical eighteenth-century tap room has been re-created, with blue-and-white Canton china in the corner cupboard and a sugar loaf and sugar nipper on the sideboard. Many foods and beverages that were commonly available in Alexandria during the period are displayed on the tables.

Canvas-back duck was a popular dish, as was Sally Lunn bread. This turban-shaped loaf is a specialty of the Gadsby's Tavern restaurant next door.

SMALL DINING ROOM
This room across the hall could be rented for private dinners or meetings. It was also available for games of chess, checkers, cards, or loo. Gambling, although illegal, was fairly common in eighteenth-century America.

Notice that the doors to the tap room and the small dining room are painted green—a color that may have been used to indicate public rooms.

SECOND FLOOR

ASSEMBLY ROOM
Candles glowed when this handsome room was used for dances, political meetings, and entertainments that included a traveling ventriloquist and a man with a learned pig. From time to time, it was also used by merchants and traveling doctors and dentists.

Note the random width pine flooring, parts of which may be original.

THIRD FLOOR

BEDROOMS
Tavern keepers were required to provide sleeping accommodations in order to operate an "ordinary" in colonial Virginia. Three bedrooms nestled under the eaves of the roof satisfied this requirement for Mary Hawkins's customers.

During busy times, three or four travelers might share each bed; trundle beds and pallets on the floor accommodated additional guests. As you can see, these white-washed rooms were simply furnished with just the bare necessities—rope-strung beds and chamber pots. There were no fireplaces above the second floor. In some colonial inns, linens were not always changed regularly. Because of these inconveniences, women travelers generally stayed with family or friends, rather than in taverns.

A bedroom in the 1770 building

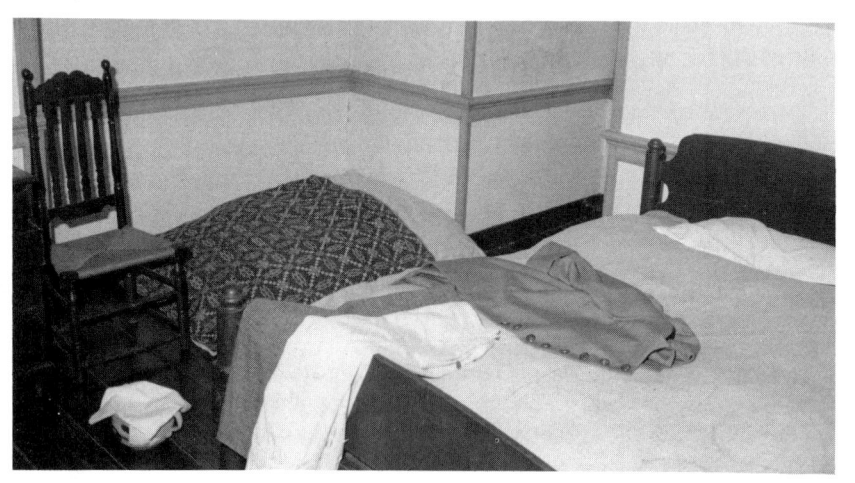

1792 BUILDING
Reached today from the landing above the Assembly Room, this City Hotel building contained fourteen guest rooms. Three private bedrooms are open to the public.

Eighteenth-century travelers reported that Gadsby's accommodations, at $1.50 per day, were elegant but expensive.

The first bedroom contains a portrait of John Gadsby by his grandson John Gadsby Chapman, who painted the mural of Pocahontas in the United States Capitol building.

The second bedroom is simply furnished with a field bed, table, chair, and looking glass.

Private accommodations became more common by the end of the eighteenth century, enabling women to stay in hotels. The four-poster, chintz-draped bed and traveling desk in the third bedroom would have been suitable for women guests.

BALLROOM

George Washington celebrated his last two birthdays in this spacious, high-ceilinged room. The tradition continues today, as Alexandrians commemorate the first president's birthday with a ball here every February.

The mirror frame and cast-iron coal grate were included in the inventory of John Gadsby's possessions. The original woodwork from this ballroom is now in the Metropolitan Museum of Art in New York City. The woolen draperies are faithful reproductions of period window hangings.

Re-creation of an eighteenth-century ball at Gadsby's Tavern

CAMERON STREET ICE WELL

Chunks of ice cut from the frozen Potomac River were stored in subterranean ice wells. Instead of locating this remarkably preserved well near the outbuildings in back of the hotel, builder John Wise placed it on Cameron Street near the corner of North Royal Street. A brick tunnel connects the well to the hotel basement.

Ice was used to chill wine and punch as early as 1790. It was also used to make the ice cream that Dolley Madison first served at the White House in 1809. In June 1805, John Gadsby apparently had more ice than he needed because he advertised it for sale at eight cents a pound.

The well is visible through a glass cutaway section a few steps down from the sidewalk.

ROBERT E. LEE BOYHOOD HOME

607 Oronoco Street
Alexandria, Virginia 22314
703/548-8454

METRO	Braddock Road.
HOURS	10 A.M. to 4 P.M. Monday through Saturday; 1 P.M. to 4 P.M. Sunday. Open by appointment only December 15 to February 1, except for Robert E. Lee birthday celebration.
TOURS	Walk-in tours whenever the house is open. Group tours by appointment.
ADMISSION	$3, adults; $1, students aged 11 to 17; free, children under 10; group rates.
SPECIAL EVENTS	Celebrations of Robert E. Lee's birthday in January, Fitzhugh-Custis wedding in July, and Marquis de Lafayette's visit in October. Candlelight Christmas tours.
AUTHOR'S CHOICE	Parlor, first floor Portraits of Robert E. Lee, stairway Mrs. Lee's bedroom, second floor

Robert E. Lee

Although best known for its connection to the family of Robert E. Lee, this handsome Federal house also has historic associations with George Washington and the Marquis de Lafayette.

HISTORY

The house was built in 1795 by John Potts of Pottstown, Pennsylvania. Potts, a friend and business associate of George Washington, was one of the founders of the Potomac Canal Transportation System, which aimed to increase trade with settlers in the West.

William Fitzhugh bought the house in 1799 and lived here until his death in 1809. Since his son, William Henry, was under age, the house was placed in trust and was rented by the Lee family, who had been living at 611 Cameron Street, Alexandria, in 1812. Robert E. Lee lived here between the ages of five and eighteen, when he left for the U.S. Military Academy at West Point.

Lee was born at the family plantation in Stratford, Westmoreland County, Virginia, January 19, 1807. His mother, Ann Hill Carter Lee, was a descendant of Robert "King" Carter, one of the wealthiest landowners in Virginia. His father, Colonel (later General) Henry "Light Horse Harry" Lee, was a dashing cavalry officer who served with George Washington during the Revolutionary War. Colonel Lee was also a member of the Virginia House of Delegates and the Continental Congress, and was the governor of Virginia from 1792 to 1795. Colonel Lee's epitaph for George Washington, "First in war, first in peace, and first in the hearts of his countrymen," is still remembered today.

When Robert was only five years old, his father was injured

while trying to protect a friend from rioters in Baltimore. Several months later, Colonel Lee went to Barbados in an effort to regain his health. Unfortunately, he became seriously ill during the return voyage in 1818 and died on Cumberland Island off the coast of Georgia. Mrs. Lee continued to live in this house until 1825. Seventeen different families occupied the house until 1967, when it became a museum.

A number of historic events have taken place here. George Washington was a frequent visitor when the house was occupied by its original owner, John Potts, and the second owner, William Fitzhugh. Washington sometimes dined here after attending services at nearby Christ Church.

Other historic events include the Marquis de Lafayette's visit to the widowed Mrs. Lee during his triumphal tour of America in October 1824, and the wedding of Mary Lee Fitzhugh and George Washington Parke Custis, Martha Washington's grandson, in 1804.

THE BUILDING

Structurally, this handsome red brick Federal house is the same as when it was built, except for the addition of plumbing, heat, and electricity. Many original details remain, including the Adam-style ceiling molding, and the lock on the front door, which was installed upside down.

Note the symmetry of the design, the fanlight over the entrance door, and the date "1795" on an upper corner of the building.

Four rooms on the first floor and three rooms upstairs are open to the public. All are furnished with period pieces.

FIRST FLOOR

ENTRANCE FOYER
Portraits of Robert E. Lee and his wife hang on either side of the front door. They are copies by Gregory Stapko of William E. West's 1838 paintings. The Lee and Carter family coats of arms can also be seen here.

DRAWING ROOM
The room is furnished with Hepplewhite chairs and a green satin camelback sofa. A portrait of Lucy Carter Fitzhugh, Mrs. Robert E. Lee's great-grandmother, is over the mantel.

Known as the Lafayette Parlor, it was here that the widowed Mrs. Henry "Light Horse Harry" Lee entertained the Marquis de Lafayette, who had served with her husband during the Revolutionary War. The "Welcome Lafayette" banner on display was sold to raise money for Lafayette's visit.

This is the room in which Mary Lee Fitzhugh married George Washington Parke Custis, the owner of Arlington House. Their daughter, Mary Ann Randolph Custis, became Robert E. Lee's wife in 1831. The piano, harp, and music stand recall the musical ability of Robert E. Lee's mother, who was a talented pianist and singer.

Mary Ann Custis Lee, the wife of Robert E. Lee

DINING ROOM
On November 17, 1799, less than a month before his death, George Washington noted in his diary that he dined here with William Fitzhugh after attending services at Christ Church.

A portrait of Colonel Henry "Light Horse Harry" Lee, Robert E. Lee's father, hangs over the mantel. Colonel Lee trained and equipped his own cavalry unit during the Revolutionary War.

Other paintings include portraits of William and Anne Randolph Fitzhugh and Robert E. Lee. The Directoire console table is one of four pier tables in the house.

MORNING ROOM

The objects in this room, which is three steps down from the dining room, reflect many of the interests of eighteenth- and nineteenth-century families, including a well-thumbed Latin and Greek version of Homer's *Iliad*.

A chess set and mother-of-pearl counters for the game of loo are on a table. Also on display is a "perspective glass," an ingenious device that projects pictures on a wall. An engraving of twenty-seven-year-old Martha Washington hangs over the sofa. It is based on John Wollaston's 1751 portrait of her.

The blue-and-white Canton china in the cupboards on either side of the fireplace may have come to Alexandria during the height of the China trade.

WINTER KITCHEN

This brick-floored kitchen retains its original fireplace, crane for holding kettles, and servants' bells. Note the iron oven installed in the wall by John Potts, who was an ironmonger in Pennsylvania. In the 1920s, the owner of the house went to Stratton in London, the company that had manufactured the oven, to try to find a missing part. In addition to locating the missing item, Stratton found the original bill of sale and the name of the clipper ship that brought the oven to America in 1795.

The high value placed on sugar in the colonial era is illustrated here. Paper-wrapped cones of sugar were stored in locked sugar chests, together with coffee, tea, and spices. Pieces of sugar were cut with a nipper, pulverized with a wooden mortar and pestle, and sifted in a horsehair sifter before being used.

A copy of the document restoring Robert E. Lee's citizenship hangs near the fireplace. Lee lost his citizenship during the Civil War and never regained it because the oath of allegiance he wrote when the war ended went astray. A century later, in 1975, his citizenship was restored posthumously by President Gerald Ford.

STAIRWAY

Five portraits of Robert E. Lee line the stairway to the second floor, showing Lee at various stages in his military life. They reveal the progression from an eighteen-year-old cadet at the U.S. Military Academy, to a second lieutenant, an officer in the Mexican War, superintendant of the U.S. Military Academy, and, finally, commander-in-chief of the Army of the Confederacy. The pastel portraits are copies by David Sylvett, based on paintings and photographs. Lee, who resigned his U.S. Army commission after thirty-two years of service, is the only American who was ever offered the command of two opposing armies.

From the stair landing, you can see a towering magnolia tree that may have been planted by Robert E. Lee's mother around 1812. Originally, the terraced gardens extended a full block to Pendleton Street.

SECOND FLOOR

CHILD'S BEDROOM

Furnished as a nursery, this room on the second floor landing may have been occupied by five-year-old Robert when the Lee family moved here in 1812. Furnishings include a dolls' house, a china infant feeder, and a child's wooden walker.

Robert's father died when he was eleven years old. Until he left for West Point seven years later, he was considered the man of the family, responsible for caring for his mother and sisters. An older brother was a lawyer; another brother was a naval officer, and an ailing older sister lived periodically in Philadelphia with a relative who was a doctor. Mrs. Lee, who suffered from arthritis, reportedly said that Robert was both a son and a daughter to her and she did not know what she would do without him.

MRS. LEE'S BEDROOM

Mrs. Lee's room is a short flight of stairs up from the nursery. Notice the original Adam mantel and the fine proportions of the room, with its thirteen-foot ceiling.

The Sheraton four-poster bed boasts its original black-and-gold paint, with a Greek key design around the top railing. A painting of Shirley, the Carter ancestral home, stands on the desk. Nearby are a miniature Sheraton cane-seat chair and a small four-poster bed with crewel hangings that were probably samples of eighteenth-century products. The Oriental sewing box with ivory fittings, ca. 1820, was a gift to the museum from a former docent.

HALLWAY

Original documents signed by historic figures are mounted on the walls. The signatures include those of George Washington, the Marquis de Lafayette, Robert "King" Carter, "Light Horse Harry" Lee, and Robert E. Lee.

FAMILY BEDROOM

This room, which probably served as a guest room as well as a family bedroom, may have been occupied by George Washington on one of his frequent trips to Alexandria from Mount Vernon. Eighteenth-century plantation owners sometimes stayed overnight in taverns, sleeping three or four to a bed, but most preferred to stay with friends whenever possible. Women and children who traveled always stayed with friends or relatives—never in taverns.

Notice the fire screen, which opens to form a desk. It is similar to one carried by the Marquis de Lafayette on his travels throughout the country. Since ladies' makeup had a wax base in the nineteenth century, a screen was frequently placed in front of the fire to keep their makeup from running.

Also note the "Beau Brummel," a man's dressing table and shaving stand that was often used in traveling.

Clothing and coverlets were stored in the cabinets on either side of the fireplace. The leather letter case was made in Alexandria during the nineteenth century.

LEE-FENDALL HOUSE

614 Oronoco Street
Alexandria, Virginia 22314
703/548-1789

METRO	Braddock Road.
HOURS	10 A.M. to 4 P.M. Tuesday through Saturday; Noon to 4 P.M. Sunday. Closed occasionally when the house is rented for private functions.
TOURS	Walk-in tours whenever the house is open. Last tour 3:45 P.M. Group tours by appointment.
ADMISSION	$3, adults; $1, students 11 to 17; group rates.
MEMBERSHIP	Lee-Fendall House Associates from $25.
AUTHOR'S CHOICE	Lee family portraits Dining room, first floor Nursery, second floor Dolls' houses, third floor

For more than one hundred years, members of the Lee family occupied the spacious, white frame house at the corner of North Washington and Oronoco Streets. Since the house originally owned by Edmund Jennings Lee is on the other side of North Washington Street and the boyhood home of Robert E. Lee is diagonally across Oronoco Street, this intersection is traditionally known as "Lee Corner."

Labor leader John L. Lewis lived here for thirty-two years.

Today, the furnishings and the focus are on family life in Alexandria from 1850 to 1890.

HISTORY

In 1785, Philip Richard Fendall built this house for his second wife on a half-acre of land obtained the previous year from his cousin, Lieutenant Colonel Henry "Light Horse Harry" Lee. Fendall, an attorney, was the first president of the Bank of Alexandria and a director of the Potomac Canal Company.

Fendall was called "the magnetic Mr. Fendall" because he

had three wives, all of whom were Lees. His first wife was Sarah Lettice Lee, a cousin from Maryland. When she died, Fendall wed Elizabeth Steptoe Lee, who was the widow of Philip Ludwell Lee of Stratford and the mother of Matilda, "Light Horse" Harry Lee's first wife. Continuing the Lee dynastic tradition, Fendall's third wife was another cousin, Harry Lee's sister Mary.

Thirty-seven members of the Lee family lived here on and off for 118 years, from 1785 to 1903. The house was modernized in the 1850s, with the addition of central heating, gas lighting, and running water. During the Civil War, the building was requisitioned to serve as a hospital for Union soldiers.

The family of Robert Downham, a well-known Alexandria entrepreneur, occupied the house until John L. Lewis, president of the United Mine Workers Union, purchased it in 1937. Among other improvements, Lewis added an elevator to the third floor. When Lewis died in 1969, the house was purchased by the Virginia Trust for Historic Preservation, which administers it as a nonprofit educational corporation and museum. Edmund Jennings Lee's law library is housed in the museum director's office.

THE BUILDING
Visitors enter through the side gate on North Washington Street, which leads to a sun porch that was added in the 1850s. Lee family memorabilia can be seen in three rooms on the first floor and three rooms on the second floor. One room on the third floor and the garden are also open to the public.

ENTRANCE HALL   FIRST FLOOR
The two marble-topped mahogany pier tables and mirrors are Lee family heirlooms. A silver tray holds calling cards, a reminder of the days when etiquette required formal visits according to strict protocol. During the Victorian era, a call had to be returned within five days.

FORMAL PARLOR
This room was used only when the family had guests. Otherwise, there was no heat, and dust covers were placed over the furniture. Philip Fendall entertained George Washington and other colonial patriots here.

The damask-covered sofas and the piano date from the 1840s or 1850s, and the ceiling molding was installed in the eighteenth century.

SOUTH PARLOR
This family parlor reveals some of the changes the house has undergone during its two-hundred-year history. In the 1850s renovation, marble mantels were installed, windows were enlarged to a then-stylish size, and the porch adjacent to the parlor was added. The porch also served as a greenhouse.

The slant-front desk is a Lee family heirloom with an interesting history. It had been in this house before being moved to Bedford, a plantation in the Shenandoah Valley. During the Civil War, Union troops burned Bedford, but the family managed to save the desk. Scorch marks from the fire are still visible on one of its drawers.

Portraits of "Light Horse" Harry Lee and Richard Henry

Lee, who signed the Declaration of Independence, hang on the west wall. A portrait of Richard Henry Lee's brother Arthur hangs over the fireplace. Arthur Lee was a statesman and diplomat who secretly obtained the first French promise of military aid for the colonies during the Revolutionary War. As one of three American commissioners sent to Paris in December 1776, he signed the Treaty of Alliance between France and the United States in February 1778.

DINING ROOM

It became customary during the Victorian period to designate one room as the dining room. Previously, meals had been served in whichever room was the warmest during the winter or the coolest in the summer. Eating habits also changed during the Industrial Revolution. Eighteenth-century families usually had their main meal at 3 P.M. Victorians, however, dined early in the evening.

In this room across the hall from the family parlor, the table is set for dessert. There is an apple at every place, in keeping with the Victorian emphasis on healthy foods. Some of the special serving dishes and utensils that evolved in the mid-nineteenth century can be seen, including a cheese dish and cheese scoop, a sardine dish and fork, and a banana bowl.

A copy of Peale's portrait of twenty-eight-year-old "Light Horse" Harry Lee hangs on the wall. In the spring of 1789, Harry Lee was dining here with his in-laws, the Fendalls, when the mayor of Alexandria visited and asked him to write the farewell address from the citizens of Alexandria to George Washington, who was soon to assume the presidency of the United States. A framed copy of the speech, in which Lee called Washington "the best of men and our most beloved fellow citizen," is here. You can also see the account of Lee's funeral oration for Washington that appeared in the January 15, 1800, issue of the New York *Spectator*. It contains the well-known phrase, "first in war, first in peace, and first in the hearts of his countrymen."

STAIRWAY

Lee portraits line the stairway hall leading to the second floor. Pictured here are Richard Lee, who came to Jamestown, Virginia, from Shropshire, England, in 1636 and his wife, Ann Constable, a ward of Sir Francis Wiatt, the governor of Virginia. Their portraits were painted in London in 1662, probably by Sir Peter Lely. The first member of his family to come to America, Richard Lee was a fur trader, merchant, and large landowner who also served as secretary of the Virginia Governor's Council.

Also pictured are Thomas Lee, who built Stratford Hall, the Lees' American ancestral home; his wife Hannah Ludwell Lee; Edmund Jennings Lee, and his wife Sarah Lee.

On the stair landing is Harry Lee's certificate of membership in the Society of the Cincinnati, signed by George Washington, president of the society.

SECOND FLOOR

SOUTH BEDROOM

This room retains the original fireplace mantel and random width pine floor boards that were installed when the house was built in 1785.

The rosewood furniture—bed, dresser, wardrobe, and

washstand—were exhibited at the Philadelphia Centennial Exposition in 1876. The red velvet tete-a-tete is unusual because of its open back.

The names of Mary Lee, her cousin Myra Lee Civalier, and the Civaliers' dog, Hal, have been etched in the windowpane, with the date 1895. Myra Lee Civalier was a well-known Alexandria actress who also held dance and exercise classes in the entrance hall of this house.

A somber portrait of Charlotte Henderson hangs over the mantel. The daughter of a Marine Corps commandant, she was the niece of Louis Cazenove who remodeled the house during the 1850s.

Notice the lock of Henry Clay's hair, "cut by a lady of Port Gibson April 1846." Clay was a close friend of Philip Fendall, Jr.

NORTH BEDROOM

This room is furnished as it might have been for a teenage girl, such as Maude Downham, who once lived here. She was the daughter of Robert Downham.

Most of the furniture was manufactured by James Green, a noted Alexandria furniture maker. Among the noteworthy items are a small desk that formerly belonged to the Downham family. Louis Cazenove's traveling trunk is here, and a ceramic footwarmer stands on the hearth, waiting to be filled with hot water.

NURSERY

Cribs replaced cradles during the Victorian period and attitudes toward children changed. They were allowed to crawl on the floor, to play and get soiled—unlike in the colonial era.

In the nursery, you can see a Sears and Roebuck "Indestructible Minerva" doll with a metal head and a stuffed body. Other objects on display—some of which may have been salesmen's samples—include dolls, a toy crib, a hobby horse, a miniature cupboard with doll dishes, a doll carriage, and the marbles and blocks that delighted Victorian children.

DOLLS' HOUSES   THIRD FLOOR

A collection of dolls' houses from the nineteenth and early twentieth centuries showcases early American art and architecture.

The collection includes a miniature general store and antique shop made from fish crates, found in Fredericksburg, Virginia; a copy of a two-hundred-year-old house in Milton, Massachusetts; a Victorian town house; a greenhouse; an early American kitchen, and an example of "tramp art." The latter was made by drifters, using cigar boxes, fruit, and vegetable crates, and was sold or traded for food between 1870 and 1940.

Originally, several small buildings stood where the garden is   **GARDEN**
now. Philip Fendall conducted his law practice in one building. A two-story structure housed slaves and, later, servants. In addition, a dove cote, a rabbit warren, a well, and stables were once located in the garden.

The well, which was Alexandria's largest when it was dug, became contaminated in 1850 and was converted into a privy. Local archaeologists are currently excavating it.

The brick-paved paths lined with boxwood, roses, azaleas, and seasonal plantings provide a quiet haven for visitors.

THE LYCEUM

201 South Washington Street
Alexandria, Virginia 22314
703/838-4994

METRO	King Street. Transfer to bus for Old Town.
HOURS	10 A.M. to 5 P.M. daily. Closed Thanksgiving, Christmas Day, and New Year's Day.
TOURS	Group tours by appointment.
ADMISSION	Free.
HANDICAPPED FACILITIES	Ramp and handicapped entrance at rear of building. Elevette to second floor for those needing assistance.
MUSEUM SHOP	Historical books, prints, gifts, eighteenth-century reproductions.
SPECIAL EVENTS	Fall and spring lecture series; concerts, films, and special historical programs. Annual Scottish Preview the Saturday after Thanksgiving.
MEMBERSHIP	The Lyceum Company from $20.
AUTHOR'S CHOICE	Alexandria exhibits, first floor

For approximately twenty years before the Civil War, the Lyceum was the cultural heart of Alexandria. Converted into a private home after the war and eventually remodeled into offices, it has now been restored to serve as Alexandria's history museum. The Lyceum collects, preserves, exhibits, and interprets the history and culture of the City of Alexandria and the surrounding Northern Virginia area.

HISTORY
Benjamin Hallowell, a nineteenth-century Quaker schoolmaster who was Robert E. Lee's tutor, founded a community organization, the Lyceum Company, to present literary and scientific lectures. The organization was so popular that it soon outgrew its rented quarters.

Under Hallowell's leadership, the Lyceum Company, together with the Alexandria Library Company, constructed this handsome Greek Revival building in 1839. The contract

The Lyceum

called for "a fine building, a little back from the street . . . surrounded by an iron railing, and a beautiful yard of flowers and ornamental shrubbery."

The library and historical collection occupied the first floor. John Quincy Adams was among those who spoke in the second floor lecture hall, which was decorated with marble busts of Seneca and Cicero.

The Lyceum flourished in the years before the Civil War. It was redecorated and remodeled in 1858. When the war began three years later, however, the building was converted into a barracks for the Alexandria Artillery and Loudoun Guards. During the Union army occupation of Alexandria, the building was requisitioned for use as an army hospital.

Tastes changed after the war, and the Lyceum Company apparently became inactive. People sought entertainment, rather than enlightenment. The building gradually became rundown. John Bathurst Daingerfield bought the property at an auction and remodeled it into a private home for his daughter, Mary, and her husband, Captain Philip Beverly Hooe. Daingerfield willed the building to his grandson, John Daingerfield Hooe, when Mary died.

In 1900, Dr. and Mrs. Hugh McGuire purchased the house. It remained in their family until 1938, when it was sold and remodeled for commercial use. From 1940 until the 1960s, the offices of the Alexandria Chamber of Commerce, insurance agents, realtors, architects, and others were located here.

Saved from demolition in 1970 by local preservationists, the building was restored in 1974 and converted into Alexandria's Bicentennial Center in 1976. In 1985, the Lyceum became Alexandria's history museum. Owned and operated by the City of Alexandria, it is once again a cultural and intellectual center, devoted to preserving the heritage of the past.

TOURING THE MUSEUM

Changing exhibitions that focus on various facets of Alexandria's history are presented on the first floor. The lecture hall on the second floor is devoted to museum programs, meetings, concerts, and special events.

The permanent collection, spanning three centuries of Alexandria's history, features prints, documents, photographs, paintings, ceramics, silver, and furniture. Highlights from the collection are on display in "Colonial to Contemporary: The Collections of The Lyceum." Among the objects on view are the Joynt collection of Alexandria-made silver and locally produced nineteenth-century stoneware.

You can also see a desk, wardrobe, and sideboard manufactured in Alexandria by the Green and Brothers Furniture Company. James Green was a prominent Alexandria furniture manufacturer. In the 1860s, his firm employed more than six hundred workers who made furniture that was shipped throughout the South and West.

The Lyceum's museum shop is one of the few places in the country where you can find a "busy-body," a copy of an eighteenth-century security device. When this three-way mirror is attached to the outside of an upper-story window frame, you can see visitors at the front door without being seen.

MOUNT VERNON

Mount Vernon, Virginia 22121
703/780-2000

TO REACH	Follow George Washington Parkway south, about eight miles beyond Alexandria.
HOURS	March through October: 9 A.M. to 5 P.M. daily; November through February: 9 A.M. to 4 P.M. daily.
ADMISSION	$6, adults; $5.50, senior citizens over 62; $3, children aged 6 to 11. No admission charge on Washington's birthday holiday, the third Monday in February.
HANDICAPPED FACILITIES	Ramp at entrance. First floor and grounds accessible to the disabled.
FOOD SERVICE	Snack Bar open 9:30 A.M. to 5:30 P.M. daily, until 4:30 P.M. November to February. Mount Vernon Inn open for lunch 11 A.M. to 3:30 P.M. Monday through Saturday, until 4 P.M. Sunday; and dinner 5 P.M. to 9 P.M. (No dinner service Sunday.) Dinner reservations recommended. Call 703/780-0011.
MUSEUM SHOP	Books, postcards, and wide selection of gift items. Herbs and plants for sale in the museum shop during the winter and at the main entrance gate during the summer.
MEMBERSHIP	Friends of Historic Mount Vernon memberships from $50.
AUTHOR'S CHOICE	Large dining room, first floor Study, first floor Kitchen

Mount Vernon provides a glimpse into the private life of George Washington—farmer and southern gentleman—that balances his public image as a soldier and statesman. It also sheds light on plantation life in the eighteenth century.

For more than forty-five years, despite long absences fighting wars and running the government, his heart was at Mount Vernon. He was concerned with enlarging and furnishing the mansion, landscaping the grounds, and operating the plantation.

HISTORY

John Washington, George Washington's great-grandfather, emigrated from England to Westmoreland County, Virginia, in 1659. He obtained land along the upper Potomac River, known as Little Hunting Creek Plantation, in 1674. Augustine Washington, George's father, acquired the land in 1726. Nine years later, the family, which included three-year-old George, moved to Little Hunting Creek Plantation from their home on Popes Creek in Westmoreland County. They lived there approximately five years before moving to Ferry Farm near Fredericksburg, on the Rappahannock River.

George's brother Lawrence inherited the plantation in 1740 and renamed it in honor of British Admiral Edward Vernon, his naval commander in the Caribbean. After their father died in 1743, Lawrence invited George to stay with him and his wife at Mount Vernon. In 1754, two years after Lawrence's death, George began to lease the estate from his sister-in-law, and acquired the property upon her death in 1761.

From 1752 to 1759, Washington was away from home for long periods of time, serving as aide to General Braddock and as commander of the Virginia militia. His younger brother John Augustine—and, later, a cousin, Lund Washington—managed the plantation in his absence. In January 1759, George married Martha Dandridge Custis, a wealthy widow with two young children, John Parke and Martha Parke Custis.

As commander-in-chief of the Continental Army, Washington was away from home from 1775 to 1783. Martha joined him every winter during his northern campaigns. He returned to Mount Vernon only twice during the Revolutionary War, stopping there briefly on his way to and from Yorktown in 1781. After the war, Washington looked forward to retirement on his plantation, but his plans were thwarted when he was elected president in 1789. During his eight-year term, he returned home only fifteen times, for visits that ranged from a few days to several months. Despite his absences, Washington supervised his plantation closely, receiving weekly reports from his manager and sending detailed instructions for work to be done.

The end of Washington's second presidential term in March 1797 meant that he was able—finally—to enjoy a quiet life at Mount Vernon. He died two-and-a-half years later, in December 1799, and Martha died in 1802.

During his forty-five years as master of Mount Vernon, Washington increased the size of his holdings from 2,126 acres to nearly eight thousand acres with five farms. The estate was divided after his death, with the house and four thousand acres willed to his nephew, Bushrod Washington, the son of John Augustine. The remaining property was bequeathed to Martha Washington's granddaughter Nelly Custis and her husband, Lawrence Lewis, and to two grandnephews.

In 1829, Bushrod Washington, an associate justice of the U.S. Supreme Court, left the mansion to his nephew John Augustine Washington, who died three years later. John Augustine's widow deeded the property to her son, John Augustine Washington, Jr., in 1850. Washington found it difficult to keep up Mount Vernon and tried unsuccessfully to sell it to the State of Virginia and the federal government.

In 1853, Ann Pamela Cunningham of South Carolina organized the Mount Vernon Ladies' Association (the first patriotic women's organization in the country), and launched a campaign to save and restore the estate. (Her mother had seen Mount Vernon from the deck of a Potomac River steamboat, and was shocked by its rundown condition.)

Cunningham, a semi-invalid reared in a sheltered Victorian environment, wrote letters to newspapers appealing to the women of the United States to save the historic property. In those days, a woman's name appeared in print only twice in her lifetime—when she was married and when she died. At first, the Cunningham letters were signed simply "A Southern Matron." Later, however, she defied convention and used her own name. Among those who rallied to the cause was Edward Everett of Massachusetts, a statesman and orator, who contributed over $69,000 in lecture and writing fees—nearly one-third of the amount needed—to purchase Mount Vernon.

In 1858, the association paid $200,000 for the property and began a search for furnishings that had been at Mount Vernon or objects associated with the Washingtons. The association, a private, nonprofit organization, is still responsible for the operation and maintenance of the mansion and grounds.

THE BUILDINGS

The central part of the house, a simple one-and-a-half-story structure, was probably built by Augustine Washington, George's father, in 1735. In 1757, George Washington enlarged it to a two-and-a-half-story house. He had the pine façade bevelled and "rusticated," a process involving the use of varnish, paint, and sand to create the appearance of stone.

Washington continued to add to the house for the next twenty-eight years, using designs culled from the fashionable architectural books found in every eighteenth-century gentleman's library.

The south wing was added in 1774, and, in 1776, the north wing, containing the large dining room, was built. The covered walks leading to the outbuildings on either side of the house were constructed between 1778 and 1780.

A southern plantation was a self-contained village, with virtually everything needed by the master, his family, and the servants produced on the premises. In 1786, approximately ninety people lived at Mount Vernon, and more than a hundred and fifty people lived on Washington's four other farms. One year, the shoemaker made 217 pairs of shoes and mended 199 pairs. At least ten women were kept busy spinning wool, flax, and cotton into cloth, which was then made into clothing.

The house is surrounded by a number of small buildings that served various functions. Clustered around the courtyard are the kitchen, butler's house, gardener's house (also used, at various times, by the shoemaker and the tailor), storehouse, and office, where visitors sometimes stayed. Service lanes on either side of the mansion led to the smokehouse, washhouse, coachhouse, stables, spinning house, icehouse, greenhouse, and slaves' quarters.

Mount Vernon

THE MANSION

Fourteen rooms are open to the public on two floors. In 1980, after removing as many as twenty layers of paint from the walls, researchers discovered the original paint colors. Visitors accustomed to the soft gray-blues and gray-greens of

Williamsburg, Virginia, may be surprised by Mount Vernon's brilliant palette. The bright pigments—which faded eventually—were a sign of wealth and high fashion.

Southern hospitality may have originated with plantation society. No stranger ever went hungry and no friend ever lacked a bed. Martha and George Washington seldom dined alone. They had dinner guests or dined out every day for twenty years. After Martha's son, John Parke Custis, died in 1781, the Washingtons raised his two youngest children, George Washington Parke Custis and Nelly Custis.

The bright green color may be the first thing you notice upon entering the dining room, which was used for large receptions as well as formal dinners. Agricultural motifs are worked into the design of the plaster ceiling and the mantelpiece, as a symbol of Washington's life as a farmer. The elaborate Italian marble mantel was a gift from Samuel Vaughan, an admirer and friend in England. When it arrived in 1785, Washington protested that it was "too elegant and costly" for his "republican style of living."

Notice that chairs are lined up in front of the windows. Servants would probably have brought in a trestle table and placed the chairs around it when preparing the room for guests.

In ordering furnishings for the mansion, Washington frequently stressed that they should be "good and fashionable in their several kinds." He paid close attention to their price, durability, and style. In 1761, for example, he objected to the seventeen-guinea price of a mahogany wine chest and bottles that had been ordered. Writing to his English agent, he said, "Surely, here must be as great a mistake, or as great an Imposition as ever was offered by a Tradesman."

Washington frequently entertained guests on the piazza, with its panoramic view of the Potomac River. While the piazza was being built, he sent detailed instructions about the English flagstones he wanted to have installed there.

The passage, or center hall, was often used as a parlor in warm weather, with doors open at either end for ventilation. The paneled walls have been grained to resemble mahogany. The key to the Bastille, a gift to Washington from General Lafayette, is displayed on the wall between the downstairs bedroom and the dining room. The key has remained there ever since Washington hung it in 1790, except for a two-week period in July 1989 when it was loaned to the French government to commemorate the two hundredth anniversary of Bastille Day.

The music room, or "Little Parlor," contains Nelly Custis's harpsichord, which was made in London in 1793. The portraits and the marine prints are all either original or duplicates of those owned by the Washingtons.

The next room, known as the West Parlor, is much more formal, with paneled walls, a decorated ceiling in the style of Robert Adam, and the Washington coat of arms carved into the pediment over the mantel. The blue walls are reminiscent of the brilliant aquamarine of a Winslow Homer watercolor. The walls of the bedroom across the hall, which was often used by guests, are painted a similar shade of blue.

The wood paneling in the family dining room is painted a bright vertigris green. The table is set for the sweetmeats course, served after dessert.

On the second floor, you can see six bedrooms, including the room occupied by General Lafayette, with matching chintz bedhangings, draperies, and upholstery; Nelly Custis's bedroom, containing the mahogany crib used by her first child, and the bedroom occupied by the Washingtons, where the former president died. A flight of stairs leads from that room to Washington's first floor study.

Here, more than in any other room in the house, you can sense the spirit of Washington. One wall is dominated by a ceiling-high bookcase. A copy of a marble bust of Washington, carved from life by French sculptor Jean-Antoine Houdon in 1785, can be seen. (The original is in Mount Vernon's museum.) Other furnishings include a terrestrial globe, ordered from England in 1790; a handsome Hepplewhite secretary-bookcase made by John Aitken in Philadelphia around 1797, and a leather-covered revolving desk chair made in New York around 1790. It was in this secluded room that Washington sent letters to his friends in the new government and his agents in England, reviewed his farm accounts, wrote in his diary, and supervised the operations of his five farms.

THE GROUNDS

Some of the trees that line the bowling green in front of the mansion were planted by Washington. He was deeply involved in every aspect of Mount Vernon's operations, from the agricultural to the purely decorative.

After visiting the house, stroll around the grounds and see the various outbuildings, which provide an insight into the economy of an eighteenth-century Virginia plantation. A museum contains Washington family memorabilia, including the clay bust of Washington modeled by Houdon, books, and porcelain. Notice Washington's sunglasses—tortoiseshell frames with a hinged visor containing tinted lenses. In the adjacent museum annex, a model of Mount Vernon indicates its various stages of construction, and exhibits show items uncovered during archaeological research.

George and Martha Washington are buried in the family tomb, beyond the stables at the end of the south service lane. In his will, Washington stipulated that a new brick tomb be built "at the foot of what is commonly called the Vineyard Inclosure" and that other relatives be reinterred there from the old family vault.

After Washington's death, Congress requested permission to rebury him beneath a marble monument in the new Capitol. Although Mrs. Washington agreed and a crypt was provided, the plan was never carried out. In 1831, the bodies of George and Martha Washington were removed from the old family vault to another vault inside this brick enclosure. In 1837, the Washingtons' bodies were transferred from the vault to two marble sarcophagi that were placed inside the enclosure.

Bushrod Washington, John Augustine Washington, Nelly Custis Lewis, and one of her daughters are among the family members buried here.

POPE-LEIGHEY HOUSE

Woodlawn Plantation
Mount Vernon, Virginia 22121
703/780-3264

TO REACH	Follow George Washington Parkway south, about eleven miles below Alexandria.
METRO	Huntington (six-and-one-half miles).
BUS	Fort Belvoir.
HOURS	9:30 A.M. to 4:30 P.M. daily except Thanksgiving and Christmas Day, March through December. Weekends only, January and February.
TOURS	On the hour and half-hour.
ADMISSION	$4, adults; $3., students and senior citizens. Combination ticket for Woodlawn and Pope-Leighey House: $8, adults; $6, students and senior citizens.
HANDICAPPED FACILITIES	Partially accessible to the disabled.
MUSEUM SHOP	Postcards and books relating to Frank Lloyd Wright and architecture.
SPECIAL EVENTS	Annual celebration of Frank Lloyd Wright's birthday.
MEMBERSHIP	National Trust for Historic Preservation from $15, and Friends of the Pope-Leighey House from $25.
AUTHOR'S CHOICE	The architecture The living-dining area

Located on the grounds of Woodlawn Plantation, this is the only Frank Lloyd Wright-designed house in Virginia. And, just as Woodlawn typifies the grace and symmetry of an eighteenth-century Georgian mansion, the Pope-Leighey House represents an innovative, twentieth-century American approach to architecture.

HISTORY

In the summer of 1939, Loren Pope, a fifty-dollar-a-week editor at the *Washington Evening Star*, wrote to architect Frank Lloyd Wright, "There are certain things a man wants during life, and, of life. Material things and things of the spirit. The writer has one fervent wish that includes both. It is for a house created by you. Will you create a house for us? Will you?"

Wright replied, "Dear Loren Pope: Of course I am ready to give you a house."

Pope, who had read Wright's *Autobiography*, was impressed by the architect's work. But lending institutions did not share his enthusiasm for Wright's revolutionary ideas. Finally, the *Evening Star* gave him a $5,700 construction loan, which was repayable at twelve dollars a week. Pope was also responsible for the room, board, and a small weekly fee for Gordon

Chadwick, then an apprentice at Wright's Taliesin West in Arizona, who supervised the job.

Construction began in 1940 in a wooded area of Falls Church, Virginia. As sometimes happens, costs escalated—occasionally as much as thirty percent—between the time a price was estimated and materials were purchased. The Popes moved into the house in the spring of 1941. The final cost of the building was seven thousand dollars, including furnishings. Mr. and Mrs. Pope and their son lived here for six years before moving to a farm in Loudoun County, Virginia. Pope later recalled that "The day we left, I sat on the fireplace hob and wept. Our five-year-old son came up to me and said, " 'Daddy, I don't want to leave this house.' "

Despite the dire predictions of those who were skeptical about the design originally, the Popes found many potential buyers. Mr. and Mrs. Robert Leighey purchased it in 1946 for seventeen thousand, five hundred dollars.

In the early 1960s, plans for Interstate 66 called for the highway to run through the property. In order to save it, the widowed Marjorie Leighey donated the house and its contents to the National Trust for Historic Preservation. She stipulated that the Trust would rebuild the house on another site and give her lifetime occupancy rights. She also helped to finance the move to Woodlawn. While the house was being dismantled in 1964, Mrs. Leighey went to Japan to teach for five years. She returned in 1969 and lived here until her death in 1983.

THE HOUSE

Wright developed a type of modestly priced house he called "Usonian," a term derived from Samuel Butler's name for the United States in his book, *Erewhon*. Usonian houses were designed for specific clients and specific sites, and were never mass produced. They were also designed to be expandable if a family needed more room.

The Pope-Leighey House

As a Midwestern architect, the low, open spaces of the plains were reflected in Wright's Prairie style homes. He called his architecture "organic," explaining that it is "Architecture that develops from within outward in harmony with the condition of its being, as distinguished from one that is applied from without."

Wright had a clearly defined architectural philosophy. A house should harmonize with its environment, and each element—including the windows and the furniture—was integral to the whole design. He built in much of the furniture, and designed such accessories as china, lamps, and table linens, believing that they, too, should harmonize.

The Pope-Leighey house is small in size but big in ideas. Wright invented and named the carport, believing that garages were unnecessary, especially in low cost homes. The cantilevered carport breaks up the boxy look and gives the appearance of length. The use of natural materials—cypress wood, brick, and glass—eliminated the need for periodic painting. Recessed lighting was in keeping with the simplicity of the house, and was less expensive and easier to maintain than hanging fixtures. A flat roof, radiant heating in the concrete floors, and the use of piano hinges on the folding doors to the kitchen were Wright innovations.

In just twelve hundred square feet of floor space, Wright managed to include a living and dining room, two bedrooms, a study, a kitchen, and a bathroom, all on one level. There is neither an attic nor a basement. Despite its small size, the uncluttered look of built-in furniture and the broad expanse of windows create a sense of spaciousness.

Wright's innovative building techniques aroused skepticism at the time. Engineers and contractors predicted that the flat roof would not bear the weight of a snowfall; that the concrete floors would be cold, despite the heating pipes underneath them, and that the cypress walls were not strong enough to last. The walls were built as units and then joined at the corners, under the supervision of Howard C. Rickert, a master carpenter. They were constructed by screwing cypress siding onto both sides of a core of plywood which had been covered with building paper. When assembled, no further finishing, painting or plastering, either inside or outside, was required. Electrical wiring and heat passed through the floors and ceilings.

From the tile-floored foyer, it is just a few steps to the compact, brick-walled kitchen, with its space-saving, folding doors. A small study, now used as a gift shop and office, adjoins the kitchen.

The L-shaped living-dining room, with an eleven-and-a-half-foot-high ceiling, is the heart of the house. Its open design typifies Wright's belief that doors and walls were not needed, except for privacy in bedrooms and bathrooms. Bookshelves line the walls, and the fireplace—which Wright associated with comfort, protection, and a sense of family—is a central feature.

Wright designed a multi-section table unit. Three sections form a dining table, and other parts serve as tables in the living room. A few pieces of Wright-designed china from the Imperial Hotel in Tokyo, which he designed between 1916 and 1922, are on the dining table. The cushioned plywood chairs are also Wright designs. Although movable, all of the chairs, tables, and bed frames were designed to appear built-in.

A hallway, two bedrooms, and a bathroom lead from the foyer. Clerestory windows around the perimeter of the walls, embellished with a geometric design created by the architect, provide light and ventilation. The house, built before homes were air-conditioned, was designed so that a natural flow of air could circulate throughout the house.

It is interesting to consider how controversial the Pope-Leighey house seemed to be when it was first built. After living here for six years, Loren Pope submitted an article to *House Beautiful*, entitled "The Love Affair of a Man and His House." When it was finally published in August, 1948, an editorial note said, "We held it for more than a year before we decided to be brave enough to publish it. We say 'brave' because it will make a lot of our readers very angry. But since it is true that a house is so much more than mere shelter, we think people ought to know about it."

In his article, Pope wrote, "Buildings are close to our lives and influence them, consciously or subconsciously. Mr. Wright's buildings are a tangible expression of his philosophy. He thinks of America as synonymous with freedom. And to him, freedom has many ingredients; among them truth, courage, frankness, and space to live in, uncramped. All these things are a part of the house and proclaim themselves, eloquently but quietly . . . It is like living with a great and quiet soul. Some of its peace and calm carry over to you . . . It is the only kind of house fit for man to live in. It is a lift for his soul as well as shelter for his body. It is an implicit sermon on truth, beauty, and simplicity. It does not intrude, but is always there for comfort."

In a speech at the Pope-Leighey house nearly fifty years after it was built, Loren Pope talked about his former home. He said, "Keats said beauty is truth and truth beauty. Wright's buildings let materials be their own ornament. Form followed function, which helped make them organic, like a tree, a cactus, or a man. The outdoors and the indoors flowed into each other as one living space. To me, they exemplified Keats's statement."

WOODLAWN PLANTATION

**9000 Richmond Highway
Mount Vernon, Virginia 22121
703/780-4000**

TO REACH	Follow George Washington Parkway south, about eleven miles below Alexandria.
METRO	Huntington (six-and-one-half miles).
BUS	Fort Belvoir.
HOURS	9:30 A.M. to 4:30 P.M. daily except Thanksgiving, Christmas, and New Year's Day.
TOURS	Guided tours on the hour and half-hour. Last tour at 3:30 P.M. Written translations in French, Spanish, and German. Special "signing tours" for hearing-impaired by special arrangement.
ADMISSION	$5, adults; $3.50, students and senior citizens. Combination ticket for Woodlawn and Pope-Leighey House: $8, adults; $6, students and senior citizens. $2, admission to grounds only. Ages 5 and under, free.
HANDICAPPED FACILITIES	First floor accessible to the disabled.
MUSEUM SHOP	Books, postcards, tee shirts, gifts, toys, handmade items, china, glass, and cards.
SPECIAL EVENTS	Concerts, lectures, seminars; needlework exhibit in March; craft fair and 19th Century Rose Week in May; children's needlework workshops in August; national quilt show in October, and "A Woodlawn Christmas" in December.
MEMBERSHIP	National Trust for Historic Preservation from $15 and Friends of Woodlawn from $25.
AUTHOR'S CHOICE	The portico
The music room
The gardens

When you drive up the long, tree-shaded road leading to Woodlawn Plantation, the twentieth century—especially the traffic on Route 1—seems far away. Located three miles south of Mount Vernon, this nineteenth-century oasis was built by members of George Washington's family.

HISTORY

In February 1799, George Washington gave two thousand acres of Dogue Run Farm, part of his Mount Vernon property, as a wedding gift to his foster daughter, Eleanor Parke "Nelly" Custis, and her husband, Major Lawrence Lewis, who was Washington's nephew. The Lewises lived at Mount Vernon during the planning and construction of their home. Washington died in December 1799, before construction began.

The Lewises and their two children moved into the unfinished mansion in 1802, after the death of Martha

Washington. Nelly Lewis had many talents. She spoke four languages, painted, sang, played the harp and pianoforte, and enjoyed doing needlework. An 1817 account of a visit to Woodlawn noted that ". . . in addition to her brilliant acquirements she is a pattern of every domestic virtue and an excellent housekeeper and this I am surprised to hear is the characteristic of the Virginia ladies generally."

Lewis, the son of Washington's sister, Betty, was raised at Kenmore in Fredericksburg, Virginia. He had read some law before serving in the Army, and was chief executor of George Washington's estate.

After the death of Lawrence Lewis in 1839, Nelly went to live with her son, Lorenzo, at his plantation, Audley, in Berryville, Virginia. Woodlawn was sold in 1846 to Jacob and Paul Troth and Chalkley and Lucas Gillingham, Quakers from Philadelphia. They cut down and sold many of the trees for cordwood and ships' timbers, and divided the land into small farms. The mansion was used as a school and a Friends Meeting Place until the Quaker Meeting House was built nearby.

From the early 1850s until the turn of the century, the house served, at various times, as a Baptist Sabbath School and as the focal point of a land development project and tourist center.

In 1901, it was purchased by Paul Kester, a New York playwright. Kester, his brother Vaughn, their mother, and sixty cats occupied the house for four years, and made various architectural changes. In 1905, Elizabeth M. Sharpe, of Pennsylvania, purchased Woodlawn for $25,000. She lived there until her death in 1925, resisting offers from many buyers, including President and Mrs. Woodrow Wilson. With the aid of architects Edward Donn, Jr., and Waddy Wood, she rebuilt some of Kester's additions to conform to the original design, and added formal gardens.

Senator and Mrs. Oscar W. Underwood of Alabama, the last private owners, continued to modernize and restore the house and gardens. The Underwood family occupied the house until Mrs. Underwood's death in 1948, except for a two-year rental by Secretary of War Harry W. Woodring during the 1930s.

In 1948, Woodlawn was purchased by a group of public-spirited citizens who donated it to the National Trust for Historic Preservation. Many of the furnishings that Nelly Custis brought from Mount Vernon can be seen in the ten rooms that are open to the public.

THE BUILDING

The house was designed by Dr. William Thornton, the first architect of the U.S. Capitol. Thornton also designed the Octagon and Tudor Place, and may have been the architect of Dumbarton House and Dumbarton Oaks.

Construction began in 1800 and continued until 1805. The house, of Flemish bond brick, is a late Georgian style, with two wings connected by hyphens to the main house. Most of the exterior shutters and windowpanes are original. Symmetry was an important feature of Georgian architecture, so rooms frequently had two doors—one of which might be a false door or used to conceal a closet—to achieve a sense of balance.

In Paul Kester's 1901 restoration of the then-rundown property, the hyphens and wings were raised to their present height. Sharpe later rebuilt some of Kester's additions to

Woodlawn Plantation

conform with the original design. She also added formal gardens.

ENTRANCE HALL

FIRST FLOOR

You enter a large hall, which was originally the north hyphen and servants' hall connecting the mansion and plantation office. In the 1901 restoration, this area was used as a ballroom. A similar room on the south side of the house, originally a wash house and pantry, connected the dining room and kitchen.

Displays trace the history of Woodlawn and its occupants.

PORTICO

From the graceful portico you can see the trees of Mount Vernon in the distance. Two hundred years ago, the trees were not so tall and Nelly Custis Lewis reportedly enjoyed standing here, spyglass in hand, looking at her former home.

FAMILY PARLOR

In this cozy room, with its tea table and chairs placed before the fireplace, the family met for daily prayers, and entertained close friends. The portrait over the mantel, showing Nelly Lewis about the time of her marriage, is a copy of a Gilbert Stuart painting in the National Gallery of Art. The vases on the mantel, decorated with an American eagle, shield, and the initials "G.V." (sic) were reportedly a gift from Lafayette to George Washington. The two silhouettes on the mantel were done by Charles Willson Peale.

The footstool with a lion worked in needlepoint is an example of Nelly Lewis's artistry with a needle. The firescreen nearby protected ladies' faces from the heat of the fire and kept their wax-based makeup intact. Notice a small painting of George Washington and a portrait of the Lewises' only surviving son, Lorenzo. And don't miss the earliest known picture of Woodlawn—a faded lithograph by John Robert Murray of Lawrence Lewis and his family showing the house to Lafayette during his triumphal visit to America in 1824.

MASTER BEDROOM

In southern plantation houses, the master bedroom was frequently on the first floor, away from children and guests but close to the center of plantation life. "The Apotheosis of George Washington," a brown-and-white toile de Jouy fabric, covers the wing chair, and is also used for draperies, bed curtains and a dust ruffle on the Lewises' crown-canopied, four-poster mahogany bed. The fabric is a copy of one that was originally used in the house, which Nelly Lewis described as "a toile with Washington Crowned by Fame."

The needlepoint footstool with its dog design is similar to the lion footstool in the parlor. Nelly Lewis made both of them for her grandchildren. She was working on the unfinished needlework on the frame here at the time of her death.

CENTER HALL

A wide center hall such as this, a popular feature in southern homes, was frequently used for entertaining. Opening the doors at either end provided cross ventilation.

The portrait of George Washington hanging above the French Empire sofa was painted by Rembrandt Peale. The small portraits of George and Martha Washington are studies by Edward Savage for later paintings. Nelly Lewis commissioned Hiram Powers to sculpt the marble bust of Washington near the entrance to the portico. After she left Woodlawn, she reportedly placed it in the garden at Audley as a reminder of her family and former home.

MUSIC ROOM

Notice the plaster crown molding and the Italian marble mantel which were installed when the house was built. The embroidered firescreen and the harp stool are examples of Nelly Lewis's needlework. Portraits of Nelly and Lawrence Lewis painted by John Beale Bordly about 1832 grace the walls of this room, which often echoed to the strains of Lawrence's violin and Nelly's harp, pianoforte, and mandolin.

The wall color is Turner's Patent Yellow, named for English artist Joseph M.W. Turner, whose oil paintings and watercolors prefigured the Impressionists in their interplay of light and color.

DINING ROOM

The Hepplewhite drop-leaf table is set for dessert with lavender Spode bone china. Notice the unusual three-part fruit chiller or ice cream server. The cane-seat, curly maple chairs

The dining room

are original pieces, made between 1800 and 1840. A knife box that belonged to George Washington stands on the sideboard. Nearby is a copy of one of Edward Savage's best-known paintings, showing George and Martha Washington looking at a map of the District of Columbia with Martha's grandchildren, George Washington Parke Custis and Nelly Custis, and Billy Lee, Washington's favorite manservant.

A portrait of Elizabeth Bordley Gibson of Philadelphia, Nelly Lewis's childhood friend, hangs above the Italian marble mantel. Elizabeth and Nelly exchanged about two thousand letters, beginning with their boarding school days. The letters have been an invaluable source of information about Woodlawn and its earliest inhabitants.

UNDERWOOD ROOM
Named in honor of the last private owner of Woodlawn, Senator Oscar W. Underwood, this was originally a laundry room. Nelly's Needlers, a group of volunteers responsible for fundraising projects at Woodlawn, made the needlepoint seats for the Chippendale chairs.

STAIRCASE
As you go up the wide, curving stairway, notice the seascape painted on a panel underneath the window near the top of the stairs. It was painted by George Washington Parke Custis, Nelly's brother, as a wedding gift to the Lewises.

BOY'S ROOM — SECOND FLOOR
The Lewises had eight children—four girls and four boys. Only one son, Lorenzo, survived infancy. This room with its blue walls, original pine floors, eagle-decorated Federal bed, and stuffed birds and animals reflects Lorenzo's hobbies of taxidermy and ornithology. About thirty stuffed birds remain at Woodlawn from Lorenzo's once-large collection. The picture, *A Spaniard on a Jackass*, was worked in needlepoint by Nelly Lewis.

Notice the tin bathtub on the floor, an example of nineteenth-century hygiene. Hot water was brought to the bedrooms from the kitchen, and indoor plumbing was unknown.

WHITE BEDROOM
Used as a ladies' guest bedroom, the four-poster, king-size bed, known as a Butler patent bed, was large enough to accommodate two or three guests. Nelly Lewis created the *Young Cavalier* needlepoint picture at age seventy-two; it was her last work.

LINEN ROOM
Since there is no fireplace, this little room adjacent to the balcony was not used during the winter. It served as a school room, as well as a linen storage room.

LAFAYETTE ROOM
Lafayette stayed in this men's guest bedroom during his 1824 visit. He traveled with the marble-topped folding French desk you see here. The four-poster Sheraton canopy bed, also made in France, was a high-style piece.

GIRLS ROOM
This room is furnished as it might have been in 1815, when the Lewises' three daughters were aged 16, 10, and 2. A rocking horse, doll carriage, child-size chairs, dolls, and an English dolls' house would have delighted the girls for hours. Their samplers and drawings are on the walls.

GARDENS
Brick paths lead through gardens fragrant with boxwood, crape myrtle, and seasonal plantings. A long axial walk, shaded by a double row of locust trees planted in floral borders, is the central feature of the gardens. The brick walk ends at a gazebo, which was frequently included in late eighteenth- and early nineteenth-century gardens.

The original flower garden—now occupied by Fort Belvoir housing—is marked by a gate at the far end of the lawn. An ancient apple tree is an indication that an orchard may have been here, too.

The nineteenth-century gardens were restored in 1960 by the Garden Club of Virginia. Because the rose was important to the Lewis family, more than three dozen beds of roses, bordered in boxwood, were included in the garden plan. Most of the varieties, including the moss, cabbage, tea, China, damask, and Bourbon roses, were known before 1850, and may have been grown by the Lewises.

In addition to the formal gardens, there are several nature trails, designed by the National Audubon Society.

ART GALLERIES

DOWNTOWN

David Adamson Gallery
406 Seventh Street, N.W. (20004)
202/628-0257
10 A.M. to 4:30 P.M. Tuesday through Saturday.
Contemporary paintings and prints by local to international artists. Also publisher of limited edition lithographs.

Fendrick Gallery
Relocating downtown Spring 1992. Call 301/652-5909 for information.
9:30 A.M. to 5:30 P.M. Monday through Saturday.
Contemporary American paintings, drawings, prints, sculpture, and furniture as art.

Mahler Gallery
406 Seventh Street, N.W. (20004)
202/393-5180
10:30 A.M. to 5:30 P.M. Tuesday through Friday; Noon to 5:30 P.M. Saturday.
New works by Washington area artists.

Mickelson Gallery
709 G Street, N.W. (20001)
202/628-1734
9:30 A.M. to 5 P.M. Monday through Friday, 9:30 A.M. to 3 P.M. Saturday.
Prints and paintings by contemporary American and international artists, with an emphasis on traditional realism. Framing and restoration.

Watergate Gallery, Ltd.
Watergate Mall
2552 Virginia Avenue, N.W. (20037)
10 A.M. to 6 P.M. Monday through Saturday.
Works by area artists.

Washington Project for the Arts
400 Seventh Street, N.W. (20004)
202/347-4813
Gallery open 10 A.M. to 5 P.M. Monday through Friday, until 7 P.M. Thursday, 11 A.M. to 5 P.M. Saturday.
Bookworks, artists' bookstore, open 10 A.M. to 6 P.M. Monday through Friday, until 7 P.M. Thursday, 11 A.M. to 5 P.M. Saturday.
A multidisciplinary, contemporary arts center that encourages young and emerging talent, and promotes new and experimental works in the performing, visual, and literary arts.

Zenith Gallery
413 Seventh Street, N.W. (20004)
202/783-2963
10 A.M. to 6 P.M. Monday through Friday, 11 A.M. to 6 P.M. Saturday.
Contemporary paintings, prints, neon art, sculpture, woven tapestries, fiber wall hangings, stained glass, ceramics, wearable art, jewelry, crafts, and furniture.

DUPONT CIRCLE

Addison/Ripley Gallery, Ltd.
9 Hillyer Court, N.W. (20008)
202/328-2332
11 A.M. to 5 P.M. Tuesday through Saturday, and by appointment.
Contemporary art in all media, concentrating on—but not limited to—local artists.

Affrica
2010 1/2 R Street, N.W. (20008)
202/745-7272
Noon to 6 P.M. Wednesday through Saturday, and by appointment.
Traditional arts of Africa, including museum quality masks, figures, pottery, furniture, textiles, and beadwork.

Anton Gallery
2108 R Street, N.W. (20008)
202/328-0828
Noon to 5 P.M. Tuesday through Saturday, and by appointment. Occasionally open on Sunday.
Contemporary American paintings, sculpture, drawings, and prints.

Art, Science and Technology Institute
Museum of the Third Dimension
2018 R Street, N.W. (20008)
202/667-6322
Fine art holograms, including one of the largest holograms in the world. Display of opto-electronics recording equipment.

Baumgartner Galleries, Inc.
2016 R Street, N.W. (20009)
202/232-6320
11 A.M. to 6 P.M. Tuesday through Friday, Noon to 5 P.M. Saturday.
Contemporary art.

Brody's Gallery
1706 Twenty-first Street, N.W. (20009)
202/462-4747
11 A.M. to 5:30 P.M. Tuesday through Saturday, and by appointment.
Contemporary fine art: paintings, prints, works on paper, sculpture, and photography.

Carega Foxley Leach Gallery
1732 Connecticut Avenue, N.W. (20008)
202/462-8462
By appointment.
Contemporary regional paintings and sculpture.

de Andino Fine Arts
1609 Connecticut Avenue, N.W. (20008)
202/462-4772
11 A.M. to 5 P.M. Tuesday through Saturday.
Modern and contemporary art.

Foundry Gallery
9 Hillyer Court, N.W. (20008)
202/387-0203
11 A.M. to 5 P.M. Tuesday through Saturday.
Contemporary and experimental paintings, constructions, and works on paper.

Geoffrey Diner Gallery
1730 Twenty-first Street, N.W. (20008)
202/483-5005
Noon to 6 P.M. Tuesday through Saturday.
Twentieth-century decorative arts, including turn-of-the-century American paintings, arts and crafts, furniture and accessories.

Jane Haslem Gallery
2025 Hillyer Place, N.W. (20008)
202/232-4644
11 A.M. to 5 P.M. Tuesday through Saturday, and by appointment.
American paintings, prints, and works on paper from 1900 to the present. Specialty American print "innovators" since World War II. Original political cartoons and comic strips.

Gallery K
2010 R Street, N.W. (20009)
202/234-0339
11 A.M. to 6 P.M. Tuesday through Saturday.
Contemporary paintings and sculpture by young American and European artists.

Gallery 10
1519 Connecticut Avenue, N.W. (20036)
202/232-3326
11 A.M. to 5 P.M. Tuesday through Saturday.
A member artists' gallery featuring contemporary art and new talent.

Henri Gallery
1500 Twenty-first Street, N.W. (20036)
202/659-9313
11 A.M. to 6 P.M. Tuesday through Saturday; 2 to 6 P.M. Sunday.
Contemporary paintings, drawings, some photographs, constructions, and sculpture.

Jones Troyer Fitzpatrick Gallery
1614 Twentieth Street, N.W. (20009)
202/328-7189
11 A.M. to 5 P.M. Wednesday through Saturday.
Contemporary art, with a special emphasis on photography and works on paper.

Kathleen Ewing Gallery
1609 Connecticut Avenue, N.W.
Suite 200 (20009)
202/328-0955
11 A.M. to 6 P.M. Wednesday through Saturday.
Emphasis on contemporary photography and works on paper by Washington area artists. More than thirty artists represented.

Kimberly Gallery
1621 Twenty-first Street, N.W. (20009)
202/234-1988
11 A.M. to 6 P.M. Tuesday through Saturday.
Contemporary Latin-American art.

Marsha Mateyka Gallery
2012 R Street, N.W. (20009)
202/328-0088
11 A.M. to 5 P.M. Wednesday through Saturday, and by appointment.
Contemporary painting, sculpture, and works on paper by American and European artists.

Nancy Drysdale Gallery
2103 O Street, N.W. (20037)
202/466-4550
11 A.M. to 5 P.M. Tuesday through Saturday.
Paintings, sculpture, photographs, and commissioned site-specific projects for architectural settings. Nationally known contemporary artists.

Osuna Galleries, Inc.
1919 Q Street, N.W. (20009)
202/296-1963
10 A.M. to 5 P.M. Tuesday through Saturday.
Contemporary American paintings, seventeenth-, eighteenth-, and nineteenth-century European works of art, and contemporary and colonial Latin American paintings.

Pensler Galleries
2029 Q Street, N.W. (20009)
202/328-9190
10 A.M. to 5 P.M. Tuesday through Saturday.
Nineteenth- and twentieth-century American paintings and drawings.

Robert Brown Contemporary Art
2030 R Street, N.W. (20007)
202/483-4383
Noon to 6 P.M. Tuesday through Saturday.
Contemporary European paintings, graphics, and drawings. Also works by local and nationally known American artists.

St. Luke's Gallery
1715 Q Street, N.W. (20009)
202/328-2424
10 A.M. to 6 P.M. Tuesday through Saturday.
European Old Master paintings, prints, and drawings.

Studio Gallery
2108 R Street, N.W. (20009)
202/232-8734
11 A.M. to 5 P.M. Tuesday through Saturday.
A cooperative gallery exhibiting paintings, sculptures, and prints by its member artists.

Tartt Gallery
2017 Que Street, N.W. (20009)
202/332-5652
11 A.M. to 5 P.M. Tuesday through Saturday.
Vintage and twentieth-century photography, painting, sculpture, and decorative arts by nationally known and local artists.

Touchstone Gallery
2009 R Street, N.W. (20037)
202/223-6683
11 A.M. to 5 P.M. Tuesday through Saturday, Noon to 5 P.M. Sunday.
Contemporary paintings, sculpture, photography, prints, and ceramics.

Trocadero Far Eastern Art
1501 Connecticut Avenue, N.W. (20036)
202/234-5656
10:30 A.M. to 6 P.M. Tuesday through Saturday.
Far Eastern art with an emphasis on Buddhist sculpture and Chinese porcelains. Large selection of stone sculpture from the second through the twelfth centuries. Fine Chinese furniture and early Chinese bronzes.

Veerhoff Galleries
1604 Seventeenth Street, N.W. (20009)
202/387-2322
9:30 A.M. to 6 P.M. Tuesday through Saturday.
Realistic oil paintings by contemporary Washington area artists. Antique and turn-of-the-century prints and graphics. Contemporary posters and prints. Framing and restoration.

Venable, Neslage Galleries
1803 Connecticut Avenue, N.W. (20009)
202/462-1800
10 A.M. to 6 P.M. Tuesday through Saturday.
Original contemporary American and European paintings, prints, and sculpture. Frederick McDuff paintings featured. Established 1892.

Washington Center for Photography
9 Hillyer Court, N.W. (20008)
202/234-5517
Noon to 5 P.M. Thursday, Friday, and Saturday. 1 P.M. to 5 P.M. Sunday.
Members' exhibitions. Also, juried shows featuring members and others, including nationally known photographers.

Washington Printmakers' Gallery
2106 R Street, N.W. (20008)
202/332-7757
11 A.M. to 5 P.M. Tuesday through Saturday.
A cooperative, featuring original hand-pulled prints by more than two dozen Washington artists, including many nationally and internationally known.

MIDTOWN

Arts Club of Washington
2017 Eye Street, N.W. (20006)
202/331-7282
10 A.M. to 5 P.M. Tuesday through Friday; 10 A.M. to 2 P.M. Saturday; 1 P.M. to 5 P.M. Sunday.
Exhibitions in all media, featuring local, nationally known, and international artists.

Franz Bader Gallery
1500 K Street, N.W. (20036)
202/393-6111
10 A.M. to 5 P.M. Tuesday through Saturday.
Contemporary paintings, prints, and sculpture, with an emphasis on Washington area artists.

Colonnade Gallery
Marvin Center, Third Floor
George Washington University
800 Twenty-first Street, N.W. (20052)
202/994-8400
9 A.M. to 10 P.M. daily.
Exhibitions by students and other artists in various media.

The Dimock Gallery
George Washington University
Lisner Auditorium, Lower Level
730 Twenty-first Street, N.W. (20052)
202/676-7091
10 A.M. to 5 P.M. Tuesday through Friday, Noon to 5 P.M. Saturday. Also open for selected performances in Lisner Auditorium.
Eight to ten special exhibitions annually, including many faculty and student related. University collection comprises nearly 3,500 paintings, sculpture, graphic arts, Washingtoniana, and pre-Columbian art.

Federal Reserve Board Art Gallery
C Street between 20th and 21st Streets, N.W. (20551)
202/452-3686
11:30 A.M. to 2 P.M. Tuesday through Friday, and by appointment.
Located in a 1937 building, exhibitions feature a wide range of nineteenth- and twentieth-century subjects.

Jewelerswerk Galerie
2000 Pennsylvania Avenue, N.W. (20551)
202/293-0249
10 A.M. to 7 P.M. Monday through Friday; 10 A.M. to 6 P.M. Saturday.
Specializing in European and American contemporary jewelry.

GEORGETOWN

Adams, Davidson Galleries
3233 P Street, N.W. (20007)
202/965-3800
10 A.M. to 5 P.M. Tuesday through Friday, Noon to 6 P.M. Saturday.
Nineteenth-century American paintings, watercolors, drawings, and sculpture. Special interest in Hudson River School, Luminism, and American Impressionism.

Alif Gallery
1204 Thirty-first Street, N.W. (20007)
202/337-9670
Contemporary Arab art.

Alla Rogers Gallery
1054 Thirty-first Street, N.W. (20007)
(Piazza in Canal Square)
202/333-8595
11:30 A.M. to 6 P.M. Tuesday through Saturday.
Washington artists, as well as those from Central and Eastern Europe. Art from the USSR, including icons, paintings, sculpture, graphics, glass, and ceramics.

American Hand
2906 M Street, N.W. (20007)
202/965-3273
11 A.M. to 6 P.M. Monday through Saturday, 1 P.M. to 5 P.M. Sunday.
Contemporary American ceramics and international designs for the home and tabletop.

Atlantic Gallery
The Foundry Building
1055 Thomas Jefferson Street, N.W. (20007)
202/337-2299
10 A.M. to 6 P.M. Monday through Saturday; 1 P.M. to 5 P.M. Sunday.
Traditional art, featuring marine prints and paintings, and Washington views.

Cherub Gallery
2918 M Street, N.W. (20009)
202/337-2224
11 A.M. to 6 P.M. Monday through Saturday
Art Deco and Art Nouveau etchings, drawings, prints, and glass.

Circle Gallery
1413 Wisconsin Avenue, N.W. (20007)
202/338-6455
11 A.M. to 4 P.M. Tuesday through Saturday.
A nonprofit gallery providing exposure to mature but little-known regional artists in all media, both abstract and naturalistic.

Deco Gallery
3302 M Street, N.W. (20007)
202/333-6060
11 A.M. to 9 P.M. Monday through Saturday; 11 A.M. to 6 P.M. Sunday.
Sculpture in bronze, acrylic, and crystal luminière. Also contemporary paintings.

Dunham Gallery
3075 Canal Towpath, N.W. (20007)
202/337-7860
11 A.M. to 3 P.M. Thursday; 10 A.M. to 7 P.M. Friday; Noon to 4 P.M. Saturday; 1 P.M. to 5 P.M. Sunday.
Nineteenth- and twentieth-century American and European paintings.

Galerie Jacque
1054 31st Street, N.W. (20007)
202/342-0494
11:30 A.M. to 6:30 P.M. Tuesday through Friday; 12:30 P.M. to 6:30 P.M. Saturday and Sunday.
European and American Barbizon style paintings.

Galerie Lareuse
2820 Pennsylvania Avenue, N.W. (20007)
202/333-5704
Etchings, lithographs, drawings, and paintings by twentieth-century masters.

Georgetown Gallery of Art
3235 P Street, N.W. (20007)
202/333-6308
11 A.M. to 5 P.M. Tuesday through Saturday, and by appointment.
Specializing in the sculpture and graphics of Henry Moore.

Gregory Gallery
3112 M Street, N.W. (20007)
202/625-1677
Noon to 7 P.M. Tuesday through Friday; Noon to 4 P.M. Saturday and Sunday.
Contemporary Russian art.

Guarisco Gallery
2828 Pennsylvania Avenue, N.W. (20007)
202/333-8533
10 A.M. to 5:30 P.M. Monday through Friday, Noon to 5 P.M. Saturday.
Fine nineteenth-century European, British, and American oil paintings and watercolors.

Maurine Littleton Gallery
1667 Wisconsin Avenue, N.W. (20007)
202/333-9307
Noon to 6 P.M. Tuesday through Saturday.
International studio glass and contemporary ceramics. Prints, paintings, and drawings also shown if executed by a glass or ceramic artist represented by the gallery.

Merrill Chase Galleries
3300 M Street, N.W. (20007)
202/333-7701
11 A.M. to 8 P.M. Monday through Friday; 11 A.M. to 7 P.M. Saturday; 11 A.M. to 6 P.M. Sunday.
Works of art by nineteenth- and twentieth-century masters, as well as contemporary artists.

Old Print Gallery
1220 31st Street, N.W. (20007)
202/965-1818
10 A.M. to 5:45 P.M. Monday through Saturday.
Antique prints, including city views, historical scenes, natural history, and Western Americana. Original sixteenth- to nineteenth-century maps.

P & C Art Inc.
2400 Wisconsin Avenue, N.W. (20007)
202/965-2485
3301 M Street, N.W. (20007)
202/965-4630
10 A.M. to 7 P.M. Tuesday through Saturday; 12:30 P.M. to 6 P.M. Sunday.
Also
212 King Street
Alexandria, Virginia 22314
703/549-2525

10 A.M. to 7 P.M. Monday through Wednesday; 10 A.M. to 9 P.M. Thursday through Saturday; Noon to 6 P.M. Sunday.
Also
825 E. Rockville Pike
Rockville, Maryland 20852
301/251-0360
10 A.M. to 7 P.M. Monday through Saturday; 12:30 P.M. to 5 P.M. Sunday. Original graphics, sculpture, and art posters. Established 1976.

Shogun Gallery
1083 Wisconsin Avenue, N.W. (20007)
202/965-5454
11 A.M. to 6 P.M. daily.
Original eighteenth-, nineteenth-, and twentieth-century Japanese prints. Also framing and appraisals.

Spectrum Gallery
1132 Twenty-ninth Street, N.W. (20007)
202/333-0954
10 A.M. to 5 P.M. Tuesday through Saturday, 2 to 5 P.M. Sunday.
A cooperative gallery representing all disciplines—painting, printmaking, sculpture, ceramics, and jewelry.

Susan Conway Carroll Gallery
1058 Thomas Jefferson Street, N.W. (20007)
202/333-4082
11 A.M. to 5 P.M. Tuesday through Saturday.
Contemporary art, also nineteenth- and twentieth-century works.

Taggart and Jorgensen Gallery
3241 P Street, N.W. (20007)
202/298-7676
11 A.M. to 5 P.M. Monday through Saturday.
Nineteenth- and early twentieth-century American paintings emphasizing American Impressionism.

Washington Studio School Gallery
3232 P Street, N.W. (20007)
202/333-2663
11 A.M. to 4 P.M. Tuesday through Saturday.
A non-profit gallery featuring group and solo shows by emerging and established artists.

UPPER NORTHWEST

A Salon, Ltd./ Willow Street Gallery
6925 Willow Street, N.W. (20012)
202/882-0740
Noon to 5 P.M. Thursday through Sunday.
An artist-run organization dedicated to promoting and encouraging the work of Washington-area artists through exhibitions and other programs.

Art Barn Gallery
2401 Tilden Street, N.W. (20008)
202/244-2482
10 A.M. to 5 P.M. Wednesday through Saturday, Noon to 5 P.M. Sunday.
Works of art in all media by area artists. Saturday adult and children's art classes.

Brazilian-American Cultural Institute
4103 Connecticut Avenue, N.W. (20008)
202/362-8334
10 A.M. to 8 P.M. Monday through Thursday; 10 A.M. to 5 P.M. Friday.
Exhibitions of Brazilian art from September through June. Also permanent collection of Brazilian plastic art.

Arthur and Marjorie Dadian Gallery
Wesley Theological Seminary
Center for Arts and Religion
4500 Massachusetts Avenue, N.W. (20016)
202/885-8745
1 P.M. to 6:30 P.M. Tuesday through Friday; 1 P.M. to 4 P.M. Saturday.
Three or four exhibitions each year, highlighting the intrinsic power of art to reflect the human experience and to serve as visual theological proclamations.

Farrell Collection
2633 Connecticut Avenue, N.W. (20016)
202/483-8334
10 A.M. to 9 P.M. Monday through Saturday; Noon to 6:30 P.M. Sunday.
Works by nationally known artists in ceramics, glass, wood, and jewelry.

Jackie Chalkley
3301 New Mexico Avenue, N.W. (20016)
202/686-8882
10 A.M. to 5:30 P.M. Monday through Saturday.
Also
Willard Hotel, Suite 130 (20005)
202/638-3060
10 A.M. to 6 P.M. Monday through Saturday.
American crafts, limited edition handmade and designer clothing, and special art jewelry.

Meridian House International
1630 Crescent Place, N.W. (20009)
202/667-6800
1 to 4 P.M. Monday through Friday. Call for Sunday hours.
A nonprofit institution dedicated to international understanding through exchanges of people, ideas, and the arts. Sponsors exhibitions featuring artists from every area of the world.

Sherley Koteen Associates
2604 Tilden Place, N.W. (20008)
202/363-2233
By appointment.
Contemporary American art, highlighting works in clay, glass, fiber, wood, and mixed media by ranking artists from all parts of the United States.

Watkins Art Gallery
The American University
4400 Massachusetts Avenue, N.W. (20016)
202/885-1670
10 A.M. to 5 P.M. Monday through Friday, 1 P.M. to 5 P.M. Saturday.
Regularly scheduled exhibitions of works by American University faculty and students; selections from the permanent collection of American art; special exhibitions of regional artists and other subjects.

MARYLAND

Sandra Berler
7002 Connecticut Avenue
Chevy Chase, Maryland 20015
301/656-8144
By appointment.
Fine photographic prints.

Bethesda Art Gallery
P.O. Box 722
Glen Echo, Maryland 20812
301/320-6048
American fine prints from the first half of the twentieth century, with emphasis on the twenties, thirties, and forties. Periodic exhibitions at the Woman's Club of Bethesda. Call for information.

Capricorn Galleries
4849 Rugby Avenue
Bethesda, Maryland 20814
301/657-3477
10 A.M. to 5 P.M. and 7 P.M. to 9 P.M. Tuesday through Friday, 10 A.M. to 5 P.M. Saturday, 1 to 5 P.M. Sunday.
Contemporary American realism; emerging national artists.

The Glass Gallery
4720 Hampden Lane
Bethesda, Maryland 20814
301/657-3478
11 A.M. to 5 P.M. Tuesday through Saturday.
Contemporary art glass, including sculptural, decorative, and functional pieces by studio artists.

Goldman Fine Arts Gallery
Jewish Community Center
6125 Montrose Road
Rockville, Maryland 20852
301/881-0100
Noon to 4 P.M. Monday through Thursday and 7:30 P.M. to 9:30 P.M. Monday and Thursday, 2 to 5 P.M. Sunday.
Contemporary and historical objects and works of art dedicated to an expression of the Jewish experience.

Images International
4600 East-West Highway
Bethesda, Maryland 20815
301/654-2321
11 A.M. to 4 P.M. Monday; 10 A.M. to 6 P.M. Tuesday through Saturday; Noon to 4 P.M. Sunday.
European and American paintings and works on paper.

Montpelier Cultural Arts Center
12826 Laurel-Bowie Road
Laurel, Maryland 20708
301/953-1993
10 A.M. to 5 P.M. daily, except holidays.

Art exhibitions, classes, workshops, concerts, and poetry readings in Prince Georges County's first community arts center on the grounds of an eighteenth-century Georgian mansion.

Schweitzer Japanese Prints
6313 Lenox Road
Bethesda, Maryland 20816
301/229-6574
By appointment.
Nineteenth-, twentieth-century, and contemporary Japanese prints and woodblock books.

Strathmore Hall Arts Center
10701 Rockville Pike
Rockville, Maryland 20852
301/530-0540
10 A.M. to 4 P.M. Monday through Friday, 10 A.M. to 3 P.M. Saturday.
Multidisciplinary arts center with year-round exhibitions of local, regional, and national artists' works, indoor and outdoor concerts, and Montgomery County Authors Collection of books—all located in a turn-of-the-century mansion.

Takoma Park Gallery
7000 Carroll Avenue
Takoma Park, Maryland 20912
301/270-1950
10:30 A.M. to 4 P.M. Saturday and Sunday, and by appointment.
Specializing in Honduran primitive and contemporary art.

University of Maryland Art Gallery
2202 Art-Sociology Building
College Park, Maryland 20742
301/454-2763
10 A.M. to 4 P.M. Monday through Friday, until 9 P.M. Wednesday; 1 to 5 P.M. Saturday and Sunday.
Six exhibitions each academic year, including two Master of Fine Arts thesis exhibitions, ranging from historical to contemporary art in all media. Also permanent collection of 700 objects, including WPA mural studies, contemporary prints, and African tribal sculpture.

VIRGINIA

Andreas Galleries, Inc.
8545 Leesburg Pike
Vienna, Virginia 22182
703/448-2222
9 A.M. to 6 P.M. Monday through Friday, Noon to 4 P.M. Saturday.
Contemporary European and American paintings and sculpture.

Arlington Arts Center
3550 Wilson Boulevard
Arlington, Virginia 22201
703/524-1494
11 A.M. to 5 P.M. Tuesday through Sunday.
Juried and curated shows of emerging artists from Virginia, Maryland, and the District of Columbia. Also educational programs in Arlington's only permanent visual arts center.

Athenaeum
Northern Virginia Fine Arts Association
201 Prince Street
Alexandria, Virginia 22314
703/548-0035
11 A.M. to 4 P.M. Wednesday through Saturday; 1 P.M. to 4 P.M. Sunday.
Exhibitions of works by regional artists.

Auburn Fine Arts Gallery
110 S. Columbus Street
Alexandria, Virginia 22314
703/548-1932
11 A.M. to 5 P.M. Tuesday, Thursday, and Saturday; 11 A.M. to 8 P.M. Friday; Noon to 5 P.M. Sunday, and by appointment.
Traditional oil paintings by European and American artists.

Buffalo Gallery
127 South Fairfax Street
Alexandria, Virginia 22314
703/548-3338
11 A.M. to 5 P.M. Tuesday through Saturday; 1 to 5 P.M. Sunday, and by appointment.
Art of the American west; limited edition prints and posters; contemporary Southwest pottery; Plains Indian beadwork, and Native American basketry, circa 1900-15.

Ellipse Art Center
4350 N. Fairfax Drive
Arlington, Virginia 22203
703/516-4466
11 A.M. to 6 P.M. Tuesday, Wednesday, and Saturday; 11 A.M. to 7 P.M. Thursday; 11 A.M. to 8 P.M. Friday.

Six shows each year featuring contemporary, traditional, and historical visual and performing arts showcasing regional, national, and international artists.

Emerson Gallery/McLean Project for the Arts
1234 Ingleside Avenue
McLean, Virginia 22101
703/790-0123
11 A.M. to 4 P.M. Tuesday through Saturday.
A nonprofit gallery featuring the works of contemporary Washington area artists.

Factory Photoworks Gallery
105 N. Union Street, #344
Alexandria, Virginia 22314
703/683-2205
10 A.M. to 5 P.M. daily, closed Wednesday.
A cooperative gallery of twelve photographers working with a variety of subject matters and media.

Gallery 4
115 South Columbus Street
Alexandria, Virginia 22314
703/548-4600
10 A.M. to 5 P.M. Tuesday through Saturday
Contemporary paintings, watercolors, drawings, and prints.

Gallerie Julian
506 King Street
Alexandria, Virginia 22314
703/548-6203
Also
1055 Thomas Jefferson Street, N.W. (20007)
202/333-5162
10 A.M. to 6 P.M. Monday through Wednesday; 10 A.M. to 10 P.M. Thursday through Saturday; Noon to 6 P.M. Sunday.
Original art and limited edition graphics by contemporary American and European artists

Greater Reston Art Center
One Fountain Square
11911 Freedom Drive, Suite 110
Reston, Virginia 22090
703/471-9242
11 A.M. to 5 P.M. Tuesday through Saturday; Noon to 5 P.M. Sunday.
Works by contemporary artists, primarily of the Eastern seaboard.

Hamilton Gallery
1311 King Street
Alexandria, Virginia 22314
703/836-1010
10 A.M. to 5 P.M. Monday through Saturday.
Modern graphics, oils, watercolors, and wildlife prints. Custom framing.

Liros Gallery, Inc.
320 King Street
Alexandria, Virginia 22314
703/549-7881
9 A.M. to 5:30 P.M. Monday through Friday, 10 A.M. to 4 P.M. Saturday.
Fine works of art of the eighteenth and nineteenth centuries. Oils, watercolors, old prints, and Russian icons.

Studio Antiques and Fine Art
628 N. Washington Street
Alexandria, Virginia 22314
703/548-5188
10 A.M. to 5 P.M. Monday through Saturday; Noon to 5 P.M. Sunday.
European and American paintings from the eighteenth to the early twentieth century, shown in conjunction with period furniture and accessories.

Torpedo Factory Art Center
105 North Union Street
Alexandria, Virginia 22314
703/838-4565
10 A.M. to 5 P.M. daily, except Thanksgiving, Christmas, and New Year's Day.
Over 165 professional artists, working in all media, and five cooperative exhibition galleries, located in a former munitions plant.

SPECIAL PLACES FOR PRIVATE FUNCTIONS

Sponsorship by a member and/or a large fee to the organization is often required. Certain restrictions concerning smoking or the serving of alcoholic beverages may also apply.

American News Women's Club
1607 Twenty-second Street, N.W. (20008)
202/332-6770

Army and Navy Club
901 Seventeenth Street, N.W. (20006)
202/628-8400

Arts Club of Washington
2017 Eye Street, N.W. (20006)
202/331-7282

Art Museum of the Americas
201 Eighteenth Street, N.W. (20006)
202/458-6022

The Athenaeum
201 Prince Street
Alexandria, Virginia 22314
703/548-0035

Clara Barton House
5801 Oxford Road
Glen Echo, Maryland 20812
301/492-6245

Belle Grove
Box 137
Middletown, Virginia 22645
703/869-2028

Capitol Hill Club
300 First Street, S.E. (20003)
202/484-4590

Carlyle House
121 North Fairfax Street
Alexandria, Virginia 22314
703/549-2997

Cleveland Park Club
3433 Thirty-third Place, N.W. (20008)
202/363-0756

Congressional Club
2001 New Hampshire Avenue, N.W. (20036)
202/332-1268; 202/332-1155

Corcoran Gallery of Art
Seventeenth Street and New York Avenue, N.W. (20006)
202/638-3211
Corporate use only.

Cosmos Club
2121 Massachusetts Avenue, N.W. (20008)
202/387-7783

Decatur House
748 Jackson Place, N.W. (20006)
202/842-0920

Dumbarton House
2715 Que Street, N.W. (20007)
202/337-2288

Folger Shakespeare Library
201 East Capitol Street, N.E. (20003)
202/544-4600

Gadsby's Tavern
138 North Royal Street
Alexandria, Virginia 22314
703/548-1288

Gunston Hall
Lorton, Virginia 22079
703/550-9220

Historical Society of Washington, D.C.
Heurich Mansion
1307 New Hampshire Avenue, N.W. (20036)
202/785-2068

International Club of Washington
1800 K Street, N.W. (20006)
202/862-1400

Thomas Law House
461 N Street, S.W. (20024)
202/829-8640

Robert E. Lee Boyhood Home
607 Oronoco Street
Alexandria, Virginia 22314
703/548-8454

Lee-Fendall House
614 Oronoco Street
Alexandria, Virginia 22314
703/548-1789

The Lyceum
201 South Washington Street
Alexandria, Virginia 22314
703/838-4994

Meridian House International
1630 Crescent Place, N.W. (20009)
202/667-6800
Corporate and nonprofit use only.

Montpelier Mansion
9401 Montpelier Drive
Laurel, Maryland 20707
301/953-1376

Morven Park
Route 3
Box 50
Leesburg, Virginia 22075
703/777-2414
Weddings and corporate use only

National Building Museum
Office of Special Events
401 F Street, N.W. (20001)
202/272-3555

National Museum of Women in the Arts
1250 New York Avenue, N.W. (20005)
202/783-5000

National Press Club
529 Fourteenth Street, N.W. (20045)
202/662-7500

Oatlands
Route 2
Box 352
Leesburg, Virginia 22075
703/777-3174

The Octagon
1799 New York Avenue, N.W. (20006)
202/638-3105
Corporate use only.

Oxon Hill Manor
6901 Oxon Hill Road
Oxon Hill, Maryland 20745
301/839-7782

The Phillips Collection
1600 Twenty-first Street, N.W. (20009)
202/387-2151

Pisces Club
3040 M Street, N.W. (20007)
202/333-4530

Rockville Civic Center Mansion
603 Edmonston Drive
Rockville, Maryland 20851
301/309-3001

Sewall-Belmont House
144 Constitution Avenue, N.E. (20002)
202/546-3989

Lillian and Albert Small Jewish Museum
Jewish Historical Society
701 Third Street, N.W. (20001)
202/789-0900

Strathmore Hall Art Center
10701 Rockville Pike
Rockville, Maryland 20852
301/530-0540

Textile Museum
2320 S Street, N.W. (20008)
202/667-0441

Tudor Place
1605 Thirty-second Street, N.W. (20007)
202/965-2262

University Club
1135 Sixteenth Street, N.W. (20036)
202/862-8800

Washington Club
15 Dupont Circle, N.W. (20036)
202/483-9200

Washington Dolls' House and Toy Museum
5236 Forty-fourth Street, N.W. (20015)
202/244-0024

Newton White Mansion
2708 Enterprise Road
Mitchellville, Maryland 20716
301/249-2004

Woodrow Wilson House
2340 S Street, N.W. (20008)
202/673-4034

Woman's National Democratic Club
1526 New Hampshire Avenue, N.W. (20036)
202/232-7363

Woodend Mansion
Audubon Naturalist Society
8940 Jones Mill Road
Chevy Chase, Maryland 20815
301/652-8107; 301/652-9188

Woodlawn Plantation
9000 Richmond Highway
Alexandria, Virginia 22121
703/780-4000

CHECKLIST OF SPECIAL COLLECTIONS

AFRO-AMERICAN
Bethune Museum-Archives
National Museum of African Art
National Museum of American Art
National Museum of American History
National Portrait Gallery

AMERICAN INDIAN
Hillwood
Interior Department Museum
National Museum of American Art
National Museum of Natural History
National Portrait Gallery

ARCHITECTURE
National Building Museum
The Octagon
Pope-Leighey House

ART—Ancient
Dumbarton Oaks
National Gallery of Art
National Geographic Society
National Museum of Natural History
Textile Museum

ART
17th and 18th Centuries
Corcoran Gallery of Art
Diplomatic Reception Rooms
National Gallery of Art
National Museum of American Art
National Portrait Gallery
White House
Woodlawn Plantation

ART
19th and 20th Centuries
Arlington House
Barney Studio House
Corcoran Gallery of Art
Decatur House
Diplomatic Reception Rooms
Dumbarton House
Ford's Theatre
Hirshhorn Museum and Sculpture Garden
National Gallery of Art
National Museum of American Art
National Museum of Women in the Arts
National Portrait Gallery
Phillips Collection
Sewall-Belmont House
Tudor Place
Woodlawn Plantation

ART—Asian
Freer Gallery of Art
National Museum of Natural History
National Gallery of Art
Arthur M. Sackler Gallery

ART—Folk
Art Museum of the Americas
Capital Children's Museum
National Gallery of Art
National Museum of American Art

ART—Hispanic
Fondo del Sol

ART—Latin-American
Art Museum of the Americas
Organization of American States

CERAMICS AND PORCELAIN
(See also, Decorative Arts)
Arts and Industries Building
Freer Gallery of Art
Hillwood
National Gallery of Art
National Museum of American History
Renwick Gallery
Arthur M. Sackler Gallery

CHILDREN
Capital Children's Museum
Holocaust Memorial Museum
Interior Department Museum
Marine Corps Museum
National Air and Space Museum
National Capital Trolley Museum
National Geographic Society
National Museum of American History
National Museum of Natural History
Navy Museum
Old Stone House
Washington Dolls' House and Toy Museum

CIVIL WAR
Arlington House
Clara Barton House
Ford's Theatre
Robert E. Lee Boyhood Home
Lee-Fendall House
Marine Corps Museum
National Museum of American Art
National Portrait Gallery
Navy Museum
Petersen House
Tudor Place

DECORATIVE ARTS (Furniture, Silver, Porcelain, Glass, Objets d'Art)
Anderson House
Arlington House
Arts and Industries Building
Carlyle House
Corcoran Gallery of Art
DAR Museum
Decatur House
Diplomatic Reception Rooms
Dumbarton House
Dumbarton Oaks
Freer Gallery of Art
Hillwood
Historical Society of Washington, D.C.
Mount Vernon
National Gallery of Art
National Museum of American History
The Octagon
Old Executive Office Building
Pope-Leighey House
Renwick Gallery
Arthur M. Sackler Gallery
Sewall-Belmont House
Tudor Place
White House
Woodlawn Plantation

DOCUMENTS
Folger Shakespeare Library
Historical Society of Washington, D.C.
Holocaust Memorial Museum
Library of Congress
Marine Corps Museum
National Archives

GARDENS
Carlyle House
Dumbarton Oaks
Enid A. Haupt Garden
Robert E. Lee Boyhood Home
Lee-Fendall House
Hillwood
Mount Vernon
Old Stone House
Tudor Place
Woodlawn Plantation

GLASS (See also, Decorative Arts)
National Gallery of Art
National Museum of American History
Renwick Gallery

HISTORIC HOUSES
Anderson House
Arlington House
Barney Studio House
Clara Barton House
Bethune Museum-Archives
Carlyle House
Decatur House
Dumbarton House
Dumbarton Oaks
Gadsby's Tavern Museum
Hillwood
Historical Society of Washington, D.C.
Robert E. Lee Boyhood Home
Lee-Fendall House
Mount Vernon
The Octagon
Old Stone House
Petersen House
Pope-Leighey House
Sewall-Belmont House
Tudor Place
White House
Woodrow Wilson House
Woodlawn Plantation

JEWELRY
Dumbarton Oaks
Hillwood
National Gallery of Art
National Museum of Natural History
Renwick Gallery

JUDAICA
B'nai B'rith Klutznick Museum
Holocaust Memorial Museum
Jewish Historical Society
National Museum of American History

LIBRARIES
Folger Shakespeare Library
Library of Congress

MILITARY
Anderson House
Marine Corps Museum
National Museum of American History
Navy Museum

PHOTOGRAPHY
Corcoran Gallery of Art
Historical Society of Washington, D.C.
Jewish Historical Society
Library of Congress
National Archives
National Gallery of Art
National Geographic Society
National Museum of American Art

PORTRAITS
Corcoran Gallery of Art
Diplomatic Reception Rooms
National Gallery of Art
National Museum of American Art
National Museum of Women in the Arts
National Portrait Gallery
Tudor Place
White House
Woodlawn Plantation

PRINTS AND DRAWINGS
Corcoran Gallery of Art
Folger Shakespeare Library
Hirshhorn Museum and Sculpture Garden
Library of Congress
National Gallery of Art
National Museum of American Art
National Museum of American History
National Museum of Women in the Arts
National Portrait Gallery
Phillips Collection

RELIGIOUS ART
Corcoran Gallery of Art
Fondo del Sol
Hillwood
Jewish Historical Society
National Gallery of Art

RUSSIAN ART
Hillwood

SCIENCE
Marine Corps Museum
National Air and Space Museum
National Geographic Society
National Museum of American History
National Museum of Natural History
Navy Museum

SCULPTURE
Corcoran Gallery of Art
Hirshhorn Museum and Sculpture Garden
National Air and Space Museum
National Gallery of Art
National Museum of African Art
National Museum of American Art
National Portrait Gallery

TEXTILES
Dumbarton Oaks
National Museum of African Art
Textile Museum

TRANSPORTATION
Marine Corps Museum
National Air and Space Museum
National Capital Trolley Museum
National Museum of American History
Navy Museum

VICTORIANA
Arts and Industries Building
Historical Society of Washington, D.C.
Lee-Fendall House
National Building Museum
National Museum of American History
Old Executive Office Building
Renwick Gallery
Washington Dolls' House and Toy Museum

WASHINGTONIANA
Historical Society of Washington, D.C.
Jewish Historical Society
Smithsonian Institution Building

SELECTED BIBLIOGRAPHY

Anderson, Isabel, ed. *Larz Anderson: Letters and Journals of a Diplomat.* New York: Fleming H. Revell Company, 1960.

Anthony, Irvin. *Decatur.* New York and London: Charles Scribner's Sons, 1931.

Applewhite, E. J. *Washington Itself.* New York: Alfred A. Knopf, 1983.

Beale, Marie. *Decatur House and Its Inhabitants.* Washington: National Trust for Historic Preservation, 1954.

Behrman, S.N. *Duveen.* New York: Vintage Books, a division of Random House, 1952.

Berry, Heidi L. "The Wright Time," *The Washington Post,* 7 July 1988.

Bonsal, Stephen. *Edward Fitzgerald Beale, a Pioneer in the Path of Empire 1822–1903.* New York and London: G.P. Putnam's Sons, 1912.

Caemmerer, H. Paul. *Historic Washington.* Washington: Columbia Historical Society, 1948.

Cameron, Julia. "Women's Art Museum? A Gentle Dream Finally Begins To Take Shape," *Chicago Tribune,* 16 February 1986.

Carmichael, Leonard and Long, J. C. *James Smithson and the Smithsonian Story.* New York: G.P. Putnam's Sons, 1965.

Christmas, Anne. "Recollections of Wilson," *Washington Evening Star,* 18 December 1970.

Conroy, Sarah Booth. "Doing Justice to an Old Capitol Chamber," *Washington Post,* 8 May 1975.

Conroy, Sarah Booth. "At the Renwick, They're Knocking 'Art' Off Its Pedestal," *Washington Post,* 23 January 1972.

Conroy, Sarah Booth. "Washington's Granddaughter Slept Here," *Washington Post,* 5 June 1988.

Dowell, Susan Stiles. "Washington Legacy: Tudor Place Recalls the Roots of Our Greatness," *Southern Accents,* March 1991.

Duveen, James Henry. *The Rise of the House of Duveen.* New York: Alfred A. Knopf, 1957.

Fede, Helen Maggs. *Washington Furniture at Mount Vernon.* Mount Vernon: Mount Vernon Ladies' Association of the Union, 1966.

Finley, David Edward. *A Standard of Excellence: Andrew W. Mellon Founds the National Gallery of Art at Washington.* Washington: Smithsonian Institution Press, 1973.

The First Ladies Hall. Washington: Smithsonian Institution Press, 1985.

Fitzgerald, Dr. Oscar P. *History in the Washington Navy Yard.* Washington: 1986. Unpublished paper.

Folsom, Merrill. *Great American Mansions and Their Stories.* New York: Hastings House, 1984.

Forgey, Benjamin. "Birth of the Women's Museum—The Building: Retrofitting a Classic." *Washington Post,* 5 April 1987.

Fowler, Robert H. *The Assassination of Abraham Lincoln.* Washington: Eastern Acorn Press, 1984.

Freeman, Douglas Southall. *Robert E. Lee,* 4 vols. New York: Charles Scribner's Sons, 1934–35.

Freyer, Bryna. *Royal Benin Art in the Collection of the National Museum of African Art.* Washington and London: Smithsonian Institutution Press, 1987.

Fromme, Babbette Brandt. *Curators' Choice: An Introduction to the Art Museums of the U.S.,* southern edition. New York: Crown Publishers, Inc., 1981.

Alexandria, Va.: Gadsby's Tavern Museum, n.d. "Tavern Outbuildings," "Finances in Alexandria," "The Ice Well," "Dormer Bedrooms—1770 Tavern Building," "The Ballroom Window Hangings."

Getlein, Frank and Lewis, Jo Ann. *The Washington, D.C., Art Review.* New York: Vanguard, 1980.

Hall, Delight. *Alice Pike Barney Memorial Collection.* Washington: Smithsonian Institution, 1965.

Hogarth, Paul. *Walking Tours of Old Washington and Alexandria.* McLean, Va.: EPM Publications, Inc., 1985.

Hunter, Marjorie. "This Is the Dream House That Wright Designed," *The New York Times,* 16 March 1985.

Jacobs, Flora Gill. *Dolls' Houses in America: Historic Preservation in Miniature.* New York: Charles Scribner's Sons, 1974.

Jacobsen, Hugh Newell, ed. *A Guide to the Architecture of Washington, D.C.* New York: Frederick A. Praeger, 1965.

Janson, H.W. *History of Art.* New York: Harry N. Abrams, Inc., 1971.

Johnson, Gerald W. and Wall, Charles Cecil. *Mount Vernon: The Story of a Shrine.* New York: Random House, 1953.

Junior League of Washington. *The City of Washington: An Illustrated History.* New York: Alfred A. Knopf, 1985.

Kainen, Jacob. "Gallery: The Phillips Gallery," *Washington Post/Potomac*, 14 March 1971.

Katz, Herbert and Marjorie. *Museums, U.S.A., A History and Guide*. Garden City, N.Y.: Doubleday and Company, Inc., 1965.

Lee, Richard M. *Mr. Lincoln's City*. McLean, Va.: EPM Publications, Inc., 1981.

Robert E. Lee. Washington: Eastern Acorn Press, 1983.

The Living White House. Washington: White House Historical Association, 1966.

MacDougall, William. "Priceless Home Site Once Sold for Tobacco," *Washington Evening Star*, 11 October 1958.

McCue, George. *The Octagon*. Washington: American Institute of Architects Foundation, 1976.

Mayer, J.P. ed. Tocqueville, Alexis Charles Henri Maurice Clerel de. *Democracy in America*. Garden City, N.Y.: Doubleday and Company, Inc., 1969.

Montague, Ludwell Lee. *The Lees of Virginia*. Alexandria, Va.: The Society of the Lees of Virginia, 1967.

Munson, James D. *Col. John Carlyle, Gent., A True and Just Account of the Man and His House*. Alexandria, Va.: Northern Virginia Regional Park Authority, 1986.

Museums USA. Washington: National Endowment for the Arts, 1974.

Newman, Sasha M. *Arthur Dove and Duncan Phillips, Artist and Patron*. New York: George Braziller, 1981.

Newsletter, April 1991. Washington: The United States Holocaust Memorial Museum.

Newsletter, August 1991. Washington: The United States Holocaust Memorial Museum.

Official Guide to the Smithsonian. Washington: Smithsonian Institution Press, 1981.

The Old Executive Office Building: A Victorian Masterpiece. Washington: Executive Office of the President, 1984.

Park, Edwards and Carlhian, Jean Paul. *A New View From the Castle*. Washington and London: Smithsonian Institution Press, 1987.

The Phillips Collection in the Making: 1920–1930. Washington: Smithsonian Institution, 1979.

Phillips, Duncan. *A Collection in the Making*. New York: E. Weyhe, 1926.

Phillips, Duncan. *The Enchantment of Art*. Washington: Phillips Publications, 1927.

Phillips, Duncan. *The Leadership of Giorgione*. Washington: American Federation of Arts, 1937.

Phillips, Marjorie. *Duncan Phillips and His Collection*. New York: W. W. Norton and Company, revised edition 1982.

Pope, Loren. "The Love Affair of a Man and His House," *House Beautiful*, August, 1948.

Pope, Loren. "Five Decades Later." Talk at Pope-Leighey House, Spring, 1989.

Proctor, John Clagett. "In Hallowed Arlington," *Washington Evening Star*, 30 May 1948.

Rathbun, Richard. *The National Gallery of Art: Department of Fine Arts of the National Museum*. Washington: Government Printing Office, 1916.

Richard, Paul. "Birth of the Women's Museum—The Art: Genteel to a Fault." *Washington Post*, 5 April 1987.

"The Opulent New-Old Renwick," *Smithsonian*, November 1972.

Saarinen, Aline B. *The Proud Possessors*. New York: Random House, 1958.

Seligman, Germain. *Merchants of Art: 1880–1960, Eighty Years of Professional Collecting*. New York: Appleton-Century-Crofts, Inc., 1961.

Sherman, Lila. *Art Museums of America: A Guide to Collections in the United States and Canada*. New York: William Morrow and Company, Inc., 1980.

The Smithsonian Experience: Science - History - The Arts . . . The Treasures of the Nation. Washington: Smithsonian Institution, 1977.

Spaeth, Eloise. *American Art Museums, an Introduction to Looking*. New York: McGraw-Hill Book Company, 1969.

Tayloe, Benjamin Ogle. *Our Neighbors on Lafayette Square*. Washington: Junior League of Washington, 1982.

Taylor, John Russell and Brooke, Brian. *The Art Dealers*. New York: Charles Scribner's Sons, 1969.

Templeman, Eleanor Lee. *Virginia Homes of the Lees*. Arlington, Va.: Eleanor Lee Templeman, 1985.

Towe, Emily. "Our Changing Capitol," *Washington Star/Sunday*, 2 November 1958.

Tyman, Kathleen. "Four Centuries of Artistic Expression To Be Housed in Women's Museum." *Washington Times*, 22 February 1983.

Voges, Nettie Allen. *Old Alexandria: Where America's past is present*. McLean, Va.: EPM Publications, Inc., 1975.

Walker, John. *Self-Portrait with Donors*. Boston: Little, Brown and Company, 1969.

We, the People: The Story of the United States Capitol. Washington: The United States Capitol Historical Society, 1963.

Welcome to Woodlawn. Woodlawn Foundation, n.d.

White, Jean. "36 Million Items Are Stacked in the World's Biggest Library," *Washington Post and Times-Herald*, 14 March 1958.

Whitehill, Walter Muir. *Dumbarton Oaks: The History of a Georgetown House and Garden, 1800–1966*. Cambridge,

Massachusetts: Harvard University Press, 1967.

The White House: An Historic Guide. Washington: White House Historical Association, 1982.

Widder, Robert B. *A Pictorial Treasury of the Smithsonian Institution*. Philadelphia and New York: Chilton Books, a division of Chilton Company, 1966.

PHOTO CREDITS

Smithsonian Institution, 11, 12, 14, 75; Freer Gallery of Art, Smithsonian Institution, 16, 17, 19 (Acc. no. 30.54), 20; Hirshhorn Museum and Sculpture Garden, Smithsonian Institution, 24, 25; National Air and Space Museum, Smithsonian Institution, 31, 33; National Gallery of Art, 38, 41, 42, 46; Washington Convention and Visitors Association, 45, 187, 286; National Museum of African Art, Smithsonian Institution, 47, 49, 50; National Museum of American History, Smithsonian Institution, 51, 53, 54, 59; National Museum of Natural History, Smithsonian Institution, 61, 62, 66; Arthur M. Sackler Gallery, Smithsonian Institution, 69, 72, 73; Architect of the Capitol, 79, 87, 88, 89; Library of Congress, Lincoln Inauguration, 85, 96, 97; Folger Shakespeare Library, 90, 92, 93; Navy Museum, 103, 104; Sewall-Belmont House, 108, 109; National Building Museum, F. Harlan Hambright, 111, 118, 119; National Archives, 113; National Park Service, 114, 115, 139, 234, 235, 252, 261, 262, 263; National Museum of American Art, Smithsonian Institution, 123, 124, 125, 126; National Museum of Women in the Arts, 128, 129, 131; National Portrait Gallery, Smithsonian Institution, 133, 134, 135, 137; Jewish Historical Society of Greater Washington, 140; William Edmund Barrett, 143, 205, 223; Art Museum of the Americas, 145, 146, 147; Bethune Museum-Archives, 148; B'nai B'rith Klutznick Museum, 149, 150; Corcoran Gallery of Art, 152, 155; Daughters of the American Revolution, 157; Decatur House, 158; U.S. Department of State, 164; Richard Cheek, desk, 164, 165; U.S. Department of the Interior, 166; National Geographic Society, 168; American Institute of Architects, 170, 171, 173; White House, 174, 176, 178; Renwick Gallery, National Museum of American Art, Smithsonian Institution, 181, 182, 184, 185; White House Collection, 190, 191; Textile Museum, 195, 216, 217; Society of the Cincinnati, 197; Barney Studio House, National Museum of American Art, Smithsonian Institution, 199, 202; Fondo del Sol Visual Art and Media Center, 203; Phillips Collection, 209, 212, 213; Textile Museum, 217; Woodrow Wilson House, 220, 221; National Society of the Colonial Dames of America, 224; Dumbarton Oaks Research Library and Collection, 228, 231, 233; Tudor Place Foundation, 237, 238; Sarah Hood, painting, 237; Hillwood, 240, 241, 242, 244; Washington Dolls' House and Toy Museum, 248, 249; Mount Vernon Ladies' Association, 251; William J. McCaw and Associates, 257; Stabler-Leadbeater Apothecary Shop, 258; Northern Virginia Regional Park Authority, 266, 267, 268; Gadsby's Tavern Museum, 270, 272, 273; Robert E. Lee Boyhood Home, 274, 275; Lyceum, 282; National Trust for Historic Preservation, 290; Woodlawn Plantation, Marler, 295; Frederick E. Paton, 296.

Drawings, U.S. Holocaust Memorial Museum, 26; Smithsonian Institution, 76; National Trust for Historic Preservation, 159, 219; Society of the Cincinnati, 196; Textile Museum, 214; Lee-Fendall House, 278.

INDEX

Abbey, Edwin Austin, *The Trial of Queen Katherine*, 183
Abbot, Charles, 74
Adam, Robert, 235; Adam style, 246
Adams, John, 171, 190; portraits of, 42, 192; prayer, 193
Adams, John Quincy, 87, 159; portrait of, 191
Adas Israel Synagogue, 140–41
Air and Space Museum, National, 13, 29–34
Alexandria: map, 9; Historic buildings, Carlyle House, 264–69; Gadsby's Tavern Museum, 270–73; Robert E. Lee Boyhood Home, 274–77; Lee-Fendall House, 278–81; Lyceum, 282–83; Stabler-Leadbeater Apothecary Shop, 258–59
Allston, Washington, 154
American History, National Museum of, 51–59
American Institute of Architects, Octagon House, 170–73
American News Women's Club, 308
American Red Cross, 252–55. *See also* Clara Barton
American Revolution. *See* Revolutionary War
Amherst College: Folger Shakespeare Library, 92
Anderson, Isabel: portrait, 198
Anderson, Larz, 196–98
Anderson House, 196–98
Andrews, E. F., *Martha Washington*, 190
Anthony, Susan B., 109
Apothecary shop: Stabler-Leadbeater Apothecary Shop, 258–59
Architects: Architects Collaborative, 172; John Blatteau, 165; Charles Bulfinch, 84; Gordon Bunshaft, 23; Jean Paul Carlhian, 48, 69, 75; Adolph Cluss, 14; Gordon Chadwick, 289–90; Paul P. Cret, 92, 144, 180; Edward Donn, Jr., 294; William Parker Elliot, 121; Ernest Flagg, 154; James I. Freed, 27; George Hadfield, 262; Stephen Hallett, 82, 83; James Hoban, 175, 184; Hornblower and Marshall, 210; Thomas Jeckyll, 19–20; Philip Johnson, 127, 231; Edward Vason Jones, 163, 165; Albert Kelsey, 144, 180; Keyes, Condon Florance, 130; Fiske Kimball, 225; Frederick Rhinelander King, 229; Benjamin Henry Latrobe, 83, 88, 102, 187; Little and Brown, 198; McKim, Mead, and White, 52, 188, 210; Sarah O'Neil Manion, 247; Montgomery C. Meigs, 85, 117–19; John Granville Meyers, 206; Robert Mills, 121, 127, 175, 224; Alfred B. Mullett, 175; Notter, Finegold, and Alexander, 27; Gyo Obata, 30; Horace W. Peaslee, 225; Pei, Cobb, Freed, and Partners, 27; I. M. Pei and Associates, 37, 44–45, 154; Paul J. Pelz, 95; Charles A. Platt, 18; John Russell Pope, 37, 39, 113, 176, 215; James Renwick, Jr., 12, 74, 76, 153, 181–83; Shepley, Bulfinch, Richardson and Abbott, 48; John L. Smithmeyer, 95; Edward Durrell Stone, 167; Dr. William Thornton, 82, 83, 170–71, 294; Alexander Trowbridge, 92; Richard von Ezdorf, 176, 178, 179; Thomas U. Walter, 84, 85; Thomas T. Waterman, 160; Waddy B. Wood, 130, 176, 201, 215, 218, 294; Frank Lloyd Wright, 154, 289–92; Wyeth and King, 210; Junzo Yoshimura, 69
Architecture: National Building Museum, 111, 117–19; Octagon, 143, 174. *See also* Architects, above
Archives: Arthur M. Sackler Gallery, 68; Bethune Museum-Archives, 148; B'nai B'rith, Philip Lax Gallery of B'nai B'rith History and Archives, 151; Daughters of the American Revolution (DAR) Museum, 157; Lillian and Albert Small Jewish Museum, 141; National Archives, 112–13; National Museum of African Art, 47; U.S. Holocaust Memorial Museum, 28
Argand, Aimé: oil lamps, 160–61, 190
Arlington House, 3, 260–63
Army and Navy Club, 308
Art galleries, 1, 299–307
Art Museum of the Americas, 2, 144–47, 308
Art museums: Art Museum of the Americas, 2, 144–47; Corcoran Gallery of Art, 2, 152–55; Dumbarton Oaks, 2, 228–33; Fondo del Sol, 203–4; Freer Gallery of Art, 16–21; Hirshhorn Museum and Sculpture Garden, 22–25; National Gallery of Art, 2, 35–46; National Museum of African Art, 47–50; National Museum of American Art, 120–27; National Museum of Women in the Arts, 128–31; National Portrait Gallery, 132–37; Phillips Collection, 2, 208–13; Renwick Gallery, 181–85; Arthur M. Sackler Gallery, 68–73
Arthur, Chester A., 188
Arts and Industries Building, Smithsonian, 11, 14–15, 52, 74
Arts Club of Washington, 308
Athenaeum, 308
Avery, Milton, 23, 211

Bacon, Francis, 24
Bader, Gretta, 119
Balling, Ole Peter Hansen: portraits by, 133
Balthus (Balthasar Klossowski de Rola), 24
Barlow, Joel, 204
Barney, Alice Pike, 3, 199–202
Barney, Laura, 199, 200, 201
Barney, Natalie, 199, 200
Barney Studio House, 199–202
U.S.S. Barry (destroyer), 104
Bartlett, Paul, 238
Barton, Clara, 85, 122; portrait, 252; house, 252–55, 308
Barye, Antoine-Louis: bronzes, 153
Bateman, Hester, 131
Baziotes, William, 123
Beale, Edward Fitzgerald, 159–60
Beale, Marie (Mrs. Truxtun), 160, 161
Beale, Truxtun, 160
Beall, Col. Ninian, 224, 228–29, 236

Beaux, Cecilia, *Ethel Page*, 131; *Isabel Anderson*, 198; *Caroline Peter*, 239
Bell, Alexander Graham, 136, 229
Bellangé, Pierre-Antoine, 191; armchair, 191
Belle Grove, 308
Belmont, Alva (Mrs. Oliver H.P.), 109
Benton, Thomas Hart, *Achelous and Hercules*, 123
Berenson, Bernard, 211
Berkowitz, Leon, 123
Bernhardt, Sarah, 200
Bethune, Mary McLeod, 148
Beverley, Jane Peter, 239
Bierstadt, Albert, 122; *Among the Sierra Nevada Mountains, California*, 125; *Mount Corcoran*, 155; *The Rocky Mountains*, 193
Bingham, George Caleb, *Lighter Relieving a Steamboat Aground*, 191
Blatteau, John, 165
Bliss, Mildred and Robert Woods, 228, 231; collections, 229–32
B'nai B'rith Klutznick Museum, 149–51
Boehm, Joseph Edgar, *James McNeill Whistler*, 135
Bonheur, Rosa, *Sheep by the Sea*, 131
Bonnard, Pierre, 2, 212; *The Palm, Circus Rider, The Open Window, Woman With Dog, The Riviera, Early Spring*, 213
Booth, John Wilkes, 2, 114–16
Bordly, John Beale, *Nelly Lewis, Lawrence Lewis*, 296
Botero, Fernando, 145
Both, Jan, *Landscape With Cows and Sheep*, 184
Botticelli, Sandro, *Adoration of the Magi*, 36; *Giuliano de Medici, Portrait of a Youth*, 39
Boucher, François, 244
Bourdelle, Pierre, 210
Bracquemond, Felix: tile mural, 15
Braddock, General Edward, 264–65, 269
Brady, Mathew, 112, 134, 152, 183, 238
Brancusi, Constantin, *Sleeping Muse*, 22
Braque, Georges, 212
Brizzi, Ary, 146
Bronzino, Agnolo, *A Young Woman and Her Little Boy*, 39
Brooks, Romaine, 123; *Una, Lady Troubridge*, 123
Brown, Everald, *Totem*, 145
Brown, J. Carter, 39, 40
Bruce, Ailsa Mellon, 37, 41
Brumidi, Constantino, 86–87; Capitol dome, 86
Buberl, Caspar: frieze, 118
Buchanan, James, 188
Bulfinch, Charles, 55, 84
Bunshaft, Gordon, 23
Buoninsegna, Duccio di, *Nativity With the Prophets Isaiah and Ezekiel*, 38
Burke, Admiral Arleigh, 103
Bush, George, 177–78
Byrd, Richard E., 169

Calder, Alexander, *Fish*, 24; *Two Disks*, 44; Untitled mobile, 45; *The Gwenfritz*, 52
Calhoun, John, 89
Capital Children's Museum, 80–81
Capitol, 82–89; Congressional Chambers visitors' pass, 88

Capitol Hill: map, 5
Capitol Hill Club, 308
Caribbeana Arts Festival, 204
Carlhian, Jean Paul, 48, 69–70, 75
Carlyle, John, 264–66
Carlyle House, 264–69, 308
Caro, Anthony, *National Gallery Ledge Piece*, 45
Carolus Duran, Charles Émile Augustus, 108
Carreño, Mario, *Caribbean Enchantment*, 145
Carroll, Charles, 224
Carroll, Daniel, 108
Carter, President Jimmy and Rosalyn, 188
Carter, Robert "King", 274, 277
Cassatt, Mary, *Child in a Straw Hat*, 41; *The Caress*, 126; *Study of Reine*, 131; portrait of, 135
Castagno, Andrea del, *Portrait of a Man*, 38
"Castle," Smithsonian Institution, 12–13
Catlin, George, 124–25, 198; *Ju-ah-kis-gaw, Woman With Her Child in a Cradle*, 124
Centennial Exposition, 1876, 14–15, 29, 52
Cervantez, Pedro, *Los Privados*, 127
Cézanne, Paul, *Boy in a Red Waistcoat*, 37; *The Artist's Father, Still Life With Apples and Peaches, Houses in Provence, Still Life With Peppermint Bottle*, 41, 212, *Self-Portrait, Mont Sainte Victoire, Provençal Landscape Near Les Lauves*, 213
Chadwick, Gordon, 289–90
Chand, Nek, sculpture garden, 81
Chandor, Douglas, *Winston Churchill*, 137; Marjorie Merriweather Post, 240
Chapman, John G., 272
Chardin, Jean-Baptiste Siméon, *A Bowl of Plums*, 211, 212
Chase, William Merritt, *Shinnecock Hills*, 126
Checklist of collections, 311–13
Children, of interest to, 311; Capital Children's Museum, 80–81; Interior Department Museum, 166; National Air and Space Museum, 29–34; National Capital Trolley Museum, 256–57; National Geographic Society, 167–69; National Museum of American History, 51–59; National Museum of Natural History, 60–67; Discovery Room, 64; Insect Zoo, 67; National Society of Children of the American Revolution Museum, 157; Old Stone House, 234–35; Washington Dolls' House and Toy Museum, 248–49
Christy, Howard Chandler, *General Douglas MacArthur*, 137
Church, Frederic Edwin, 122; *Niagara Falls*, 154–55
Cincinnati, Society of the, 196–98
Clara Barton House, 252–55
Clark, William A. collection, 153
Clay, Henry, 89, 109, 159, 171, 281
Cleveland, Grover, 117, 192
Cleveland Park Club, 308
Cluss, Adolph, 14
Cole, Thomas, 122; *The Voyage of Life*, 42; *Subsiding of the Waters of the Deluge*, 125
Collections checklist, 311–13
Colonial Dames of America, National Society of the: Dumbarton House, 224–27
Concerts: Anderson House, 196; Capitol, 82; Clara Barton House, 252; Corcoran

Gallery of Art, 152; Dumbarton Oaks, 228; Folger Shakespeare Library, 90; Hirshhorn Museum and Sculpture Garden, 22; Library of Congress, 94, 97; Lyceum, 282; National Air and Space Museum, 29; National Building Museum, 117; National Gallery of Art, 35; National Museum of American Art, 120; National Museum of Women in the Arts, 128; Phillips Collection, 208; Renwick Gallery, 181
Conger, Clement E., 162
Congressional Club, 308
Constable, John, *A View of Salisbury Cathedral From Lower Marsh Close*, 42
Constitution and Bill of Rights, 112, 113
Container Corporation of America Collection, 123
Cook, Howard Norton, 123
Cooper-Hewitt Museum, New York, 13
Copley, John Singleton, *The Copley Family*, *Watson and the Shark*, 42; *Self-Portrait*, *Andrew Oliver*, 135; *Mrs. John Montresor*, *Alice Hooper*, 163
Corcoran, William Wilson, 85, 152–53, 160, 175, 181–82; portraits of, 152, 183
Corcoran Gallery of Art, 152–55, 308
Corcoran School of Art, 152–53, 182
Cornè, Michele Felice, *The Landing of the Pilgrims*, 163
Cosmos Club, 308
Crawford, Thomas, 85; *Freedom*, 79, 154
Credi, Lorenzo di, *Self-Portrait*, 38
Cret, Paul P., 92, 144, 180
Crockwell, Douglass, *Paper Workers*, 127
Cropsey, Jasper Francis, *Autumn on the Hudson River*, 43
Cunningham, Ann Pamela, 285
Custis, Eleanor Parke (Nelly), 260, 263, 274, 285, 287, 288, 293, 294, 295, 296, 297
Custis, Eliza Parke (Mrs. Thomas Law), 3, 227
Custis, George Washington Parke, 238, 260–61, 275, 287, 297; paintings by, 263, 297
Custis, John IV, 238
Custis, John Parke, 260, 285, 287
Custis, Martha Parke, 285
Custis, Mary Ann Randolph (Mrs. Robert E. Lee), 238, 261, 262–63

Dale, Chester, Collection, 36, 41
Dahlgren, John, 103
Daingerfield, John Bathurst, 283
Dalton, John, 265
Daughters of the American Revolution (DAR) Museum, 156–57
Daumier, Honoré, 24; *The Deputies*, 44; *Three Lawyers*, 212
David, Jacques-Louis, *Napoleon in His Study*, 41
Davidson, Jo, *Gertrude Stein*, 137
Davis, Gene, 123, 209
Davis, Jefferson, 84, 85, 159–60
Decatur, Stephen, 104, 158–59
Decatur House, 3, 158–61, 308
Declaration of Independence, 96, 112–13, 121
Degas, Edgar, 24; sculptures, 44; *Mary Cassatt*, 135; *Dancers at the Bar*, 212
de Kooning, Elaine Fried, *Bacchus #3*, 131

de Kooning, Willem, 24
Delaunay, Sonia Terk, *Study for Portugal*, 130
de Tocqueville, Alexis, 89
de Weldon, Felix: *Iwo Jima*, 101
Dewing, Maria Oakey, *Garden In May*, 126
Dewing, Thomas Wilmer, 17, 122; *The Spinet*, *Summer*, *Lady in White*, 126
Diebenkorn, Richard, 37
Dine, Jim, 123
Dinosaurs, National Museum of Natural History, 60, 62
Discovery Room, National Museum of Natural History, 64
Donn, Edward, Jr., 294
Douglass House, Frederick, 47
Dove, Arthur G., 211, 212
Downham, Robert, 179
Drewes, Werner, 123
Dumbarton House, 3, 223, 224–27, 308
Dumbarton Oaks, 2, 228–33
Dupont Circle, 204; area map, 7
Dupont-Kalorama Museums Consortium, 204; Museum Walk, 204
Durand, Asher Brown, *Georgianna Frances Adams*, *Mary Louisa Adams*, 126
Durand-Ruel, Joseph, 211
Dürer, Albrecht, 154
Duveen, Joseph (Lord Duveen of Millbank), 36

Eakins, Thomas, 24; Battle of Trenton bas-reliefs, 25; *The Biglin Brothers Racing*, 43; *The Pathetic Song*, 155; *Miss Amelia Van Buren*, 213; *William Rush's Model*, 125
Edouart, Auguste, silhouettes, 134–35
Eisenhower, Dwight D., 85–86, 109, 122, 133, 174
El Greco, 39, 211; *The Repentant Peter*, 212; *The Visitation*, 232
Elliot, William Parker, 121
Elliott, Charles Loring, *William Wilson Corcoran*, 152
Emmett, Rowland: *S.S. Pussiewillow II*, 34
Eskimos: National Museum of Natural History, 64
Eugénie, Empress, jewelry, 66; portrait of, 244
Ezekiel, Moses Jacob, 182

Fabergé, Carl, 242, 245; Imperial Easter egg, 242
Fairfax, Sarah (Sally), 265
Farrand, Beatrix, 233
Faulkner, Barry, *Declaration of Independence*, *Constitution*, 113
Fendall, Philip Richard, 278–79
Fern, Alan, 135
Ferris, Keith, *Fortresses Under Fire*, 34
Figari, Pedro, 145, *The Market Place*, 146
Fillmore, Millard, 84
First Ladies Hall, 51, 55
Fitzhugh, Lucy Carter, 275
Fitzhugh, Mary Lee, 275
Fitzhugh, William, 274
Flagg, Ernest, 154
Flagg, James Montgomery, 133
Folger, Henry Clay, 91–92
Folger Shakespeare Library, 2, 90–93, 308

Fondo del Sol Visual Art and Media Center, 203–4
Fontana, Lavinia, 129; *Portrait of a Noblewoman*, 131
Ford's Theatre, 2, 114–16
Foucault pendulum: National Museum of American History, 54
Fragonard, Jean-Honoré, 41; *A Young Girl Reading*, 41
Frank, Robert, 37
Frankenthaler, Helen, 37, 123; *Ponti*, 130; *Spiritualist*, 131
Franklin, Benjamin, bust of, 135; portraits, 165, 190–91; printing press, 121
Freed, James I., 27
Freer, Charles Lang, 2–3, 16–18, 25, 68; portrait, 16
Freer Gallery of Art, 16–21, 68
French, Daniel Chester, 95; *History*, 96; *Narcissa, Abraham Lincoln*, 126; Dupont Circle fountain, 204
Frost, Patricia and Phillip Collection, 123
Fukushima, Tikashi, 147; *Green*, 147

Gadsby, John, 159, 271
Gadsby's Tavern, 270–73, 308
Gainsborough, Thomas *Mrs. Richard Brinsley Sheridan*, 41–42
Gallatin, Albert, 108
Garber, Paul E., Preservation, Restoration and Storage Facility, 34
Garbisch, Edgar William and Bernice Chrysler Collection, 36
Gardens, 312; Dumbarton Oaks, 233; Enid A. Haupt Garden, 74–75; Hillwood, 241; Lee-Fendall House, 281; Old Stone House, 235; Organization of American States, Aztec Garden, 147, 180; Tudor Place, 239; White House Jacqueline Kennedy Garden, 189; Woodlawn Plantation, 298
Gauguin, Paul, *Self-Portrait*, 41; *Eve*, 44
Georgetown: map, 7
Gérard, Marguerite, *The Beloved Child*, 246
Giacometti, Alberto, 24
Giant Bible of Mainz, 96
Gibbons, Grinling, 198
Gibson, Elizabeth Bordley: portrait of, 297
Gillingham, Chalkley and Lucas, 294
Giorgione, 211, 212
Giotto, 154
Goh Annex, 210
Goh, Yasuhiro, 210
Gorlia, Émile, 48
Gottlieb, Adolph, 123
Goya, Francisco José de, 212
Grant, Ulysses S., 140, 182
Graves, Nancy, 131
Gray, Gen. Alfred M., 101
Green, James, 266, 281, 283
Greenberg, Harold and Sylvia Sculpture Garden, 151
Greenough, Horatio, statue of George Washington, 55
Gregory, John, bas-reliefs, 92
Greuze, Jean Baptiste, *Benjamin Franklin*, 165
Guillen, Asilia, 147
Gunston Hall, 308

Gutenberg Bible, 96

Haas, Richard, 48
Hadfield, George, 262
Hallett, Stephen, 82, 83
Hallowell, Benjamin, 282
Hals, Frans, 36
Hampton, James, *The Throne of the Third Heaven of the Nation's Millennium General Assembly*, 81, 123–24
Hanks, Nancy, 129
Harmsworth, Sir Leicester Collection, 123
Harnett, William M., *My Gems*, 43
Harrison, Mrs. Benjamin: china, 189
Hartley, Marsden, 211
Harvard Unviersity: Dumbarton Oaks, 228, 229
Hassam, Childe, 122; *The South Ledges, Appledore*, 126
Haupt Garden, Enid A., 48, 74–75
Hawkins, Mrs. Mary, 270
Healy, George Peter Alexander, 132, 135, *Mrs. Albert J. Myer, Mrs. Thomas B. Bryan*, 184; *John Tyler*, 192; *Rutherford B. Hayes*, 193
Heda, Willem Claesz, *Banquet Piece With Mince Pie*, 40
Hemphill, Herbert Waide, Jr., Collection of American Folk Art, 123
Henderson, Archibald, 99
Hendler, Mr. and Mrs. L. Manuel Collection, 123
Henry, Joseph, 29; statue of, 12
Herbert, John Carlyle, 266
Herbert, Thomas, 266
Hermitage Museum, 36, 39
Heurich, Christian, 205–6; house, 205–7
Hicks, Edward: *Peaceable Kingdom*, 43
Hicks, William, 264, 265
Hillwood, 240–47
Hirshhorn, Joseph J., 3, 22–23; collection, 23–24, 48, 50
Hirshhorn Museum and Sculpture Garden, 22–25
Historic houses, 312; Arlington House, 3, 260–63; Barney Studio House, 199–202; Bethune Museum-Archives, 148; Carlyle House, 264–69; Clara Barton House, 252–55; Decatur House, 158–61; Dumbarton House, 224–27; Dumbarton Oaks, 228–33; Ford's Theatre, 2, 114–16; Gadsby's Tavern Museum, 270–73; Hillwood, 240–47; Historical Society of Washington, D.C., 205–7; Lee-Fendall House, 278–81; Robert E. Lee Boyhood Home, 274–77; Mount Vernon, 284–88; Octagon, 3, 143, 170–73; Old Stone House, 234–35; Petersen House, 138–39; Pope-Leighey House, 289–92; Sewall-Belmont House, 108–9; Stabler-Leadbeater Apothecary Shop, 258–59; Tudor Place, 236–39; White House, 186–93; Woodlawn Plantation, 293–98; Woodrow Wilson House, 218–221
Historical Society of Washington, D.C., 205–07, 308
Hoban, James, 175, 186, 191
Hofmann, Hans, *Fermented Soil*, 127
Holladay, Wilhelmina ("Billie"), 128–29, 130

Holocaust, U.S. Memorial Council, 26
Holocaust, U.S. Memorial Museum, 1, 26–28
Holocaust, U.S. Research Institute, 28
Homer, Winslow, 44, 123, 287; *Breezing Up*, 43
Hope diamond, 65–66
Hoover, Herbert, 113
Hopper, Edward, *Sunday*, 213; *Ryder's House*, 127
Hornblower and Marshall, 210
Hôtel d'Orsay, Grand Salon, 155
Houdon, Jean-Antoine, *George Washington*, 134, 288
Houston, Sam, 89
Hubbell, Julian, 253–55
Humphrey, Hubert H., 177

Inaugural balls: Old Patent Office, 122; Old Pension Building, 117
Ingres, Jean Auguste Dominique, 154
Inman, Henry, *Angelica Singleton Van Buren*, 193
Inness, George, 122
Insect Zoo: National Museum of Natural History, 67
Interior Department Museum, 166
International Club of Washington, 308

Jacobs, Flora Gill, collection, 248–49
Jackson, Andrew, 121, 159, 171, 190, 193
Jackson, Martha Memorial Collection, 123
Janssen, Geraert, *William Shakespeare*, 93
Japanese Americans: Museum of American History, 58
Jay, John, 104–5, 164; portrait of, 164
Jean-Gilles, Joseph, 147
Jeckyll, Thomas, 19–20
Jefferson, Thomas, 82–83, 88, 95, 108, 121, 171, 186, 187, 188, 190; statue of, 165
Jewish Historical Institute, 27–28
Jewish Historical Society of Greater Washington, 140–41
Johansen, John C., *Signing of the Treaty of Versailles*, 136
John, Augustus, *Tallulah Bankhead*, 133
Johns, Jasper, 37
Johnson, Eastman, 123; *The Girl I Left Behind Me*, 125
Johnson, Lyndon B., 23, 174, 177, 188
Johnson, Philip, 127, 229, 231
Johnson, S. C., Collection, 123
Johnson, William H., 123, 125
Jones, Edward Vason, 163
Jones, John Paul, 104–5
Kainen, Jacob, 123, 209
Kalorama area, Washington, D.C., 204
Kauffmann, Angelica, 129; *Dr. John Morgan*, 135
Kantor, Morris, 123
Kelly, Ellsworth, 37
Kelsey, Albert, 144, 180
Kennedy, John F., Center for the Performing Arts, 13
Kester, Paul, 294
Key, Francis Scott, 52–53; desk, 238
Keyes Condon Florance, 130
King, Charles Bird: *Young Omahaw, War Eagle, Little Missouri, and Pawnees*, 124

King, Frederick Rhinelander, 229
King, Martin Luther, Jr., 137
Klee, Paul, 209, 212, 213
Kline, Franz, 123; *Merce C.*, 127
Knaths, Karl, 212
Kokoschka, Oskar, 212
Kollwitz, Kathe: *The Farewell, Rest In His Hands*, 130
Kress, Samuel H. Collection, 36

Lafayette, Marquis de, 83, 84, 166, 171, 236, 237, 262, 275, 277, 295, 297
Lam, Wilfredo, 145–46; *Lisamona*, 146
Lamb, Venice and Alastair Collection, 48
Lane, Fitz Hugh, *Lumber Schooners at Evening on Penobscot Bay*, 43
Langley, Samuel P., 29. 74
Lannuier, Charles Honoré, 192, 246
Latrobe, Benjamin Henry, 83–84, 88, 159, 187
Laurencin, Marie, *Portrait of a Girl in a Hat*, 131
Law House, 308
Leadbeater, Edward Stabler, 259
Lee Family of Virginia: Arlington House, 260–63; Lee-Fendall House, 178–81; Robert E. Lee Boyhood Home, 274–77
Lee, Ann Hill Carter, 274
Lee, Arthur, 280
Lee, Edmund Jennings, 278
Lee, Elizabeth Steptoe, 279
Lee, George Washington Custis, 261, 262
Lee, Henry "Light Horse Harry", 274–75. 278. 279–80
Lee, Mary, 279
Lee, Robert E., 236, 238–39, 260–62. 282; boyhood home, 274–77, 309
Lee, Mrs. Robert E. (Mary Ann Randolph Custis), 238, 261, 262–63
Lee-Fendall House, 278–81, 309
Lehmbruck, Wilhelm, *Seated Youth*, 44
Léger, Fernand, *Nude on a Red Background*, 24
Leighey, Mr. and Mrs. Robert, 290
Lely, Sir Peter, 280
L'Enfant, Pierre Charles, 44, 82, 121, 186, 198; membership badge designed by, 196; grave site, 262
Leonardo da Vinci, 36; *Ginevra de'Benci*, 38
Lerner, Abram, 23, 24
Leutze Park, 98
Lewis, John L., 278, 279
Lewis, Maj. Lawrence, 293, 294, 295; portrait of, 296
Lewis, Mrs. Lawrence (Eleanor Parke "Nelly" Custis), 260, 263, 274, 285, 287, 288, 293, 294, 295, 296, 297
Lewis, Lorenzo, 294, 295, 297
Lewis, Victor, *Walking With Her Blue Umbrella*, 147
Leyland, Frederick R., 19–20
Liautaud, Georges, *Crucifixion*, 147
Libraries: Daughters of the American Revolution (DAR), 157; Executive Office of the President, 177; Folger Shakespeare Library, 90–93; Freer Gallery of Art, 16; Historical Society of Washington, D.C., 207; Library of Congress, 94; National Museum of African Art, 47; National

Museum of Women in the Arts, 128; U.S. Holocaust Memorial Museum, 28. *See also* Archives
Library of Congress, 83, 94–97
Lichtenstein, Roy, 37; *Look Mickey*, 46
Lillian and Albert Small Jewish Museum, 140–41, 309
Lincoln, Abraham, 29, 85, 122; assassination, 114–15, 138; china, 189; Gettysburg Address, 96; Petersen House, 138–39; portrait, 193; statues, 86, 96; Lincoln Museum, 2, 115–16
Lindbergh, Charles, *Spirit of St. Louis*, 30
Lippi, Filippino, *Portrait of a Youth*, 38
Lippold, Richard, *Ad Astra*, 30
Little and Brown, 198
Louis, Morris, 123, 209; *Beta Kappa*, 46
Lowendal, Constance de, *John Paul Jones*, 135
Lozowick, Louis, 123
Lyceum, 282–83, 309

Mabe, Manabu, *Agony*, 147
Madison, Dolley, 3, 171, 187, 192
Madison, James, 15, 95, 171; portrait, 42; statue of, 97; Treaty of Ghent, 108, 171
Makovski, Konstantin, *The Boyar Wedding*, 244
Maldonado, Estuardo, *Pictography*, 146
Mall: map, 5
Manet, Édouard, *Gare Saint-Lazare*, 41; *The Old Musician*, 41; *Ballet Espagnol*, 212
Manion, Sarah O'Neil, 247
Manship, Paul, 123
Maps: Capitol Hill, 5; Downtown, 6; Dupont Circle area, 7; Georgetown, 7; Kalorama area, 7; Mall, 5; Midtown, 6; Old Town Alexandria, 9; Upper Northwest, 8; Washington metropolitan area, 8
Marie Antoinette, Queen, chairs, 244–45; desk, 44; jewelry, 66
Marie Louise, Empress, jewelry, 66
Marin, John, 211, 212
Marine Corps Historical Center, 98
Marine Corps Museum, 98–101
Marsh, Reginald, *George Tilyou's Steeplechase*, 127
Martin, David, *Benjamin Franklin*, 165, 190–91
Mason, Charles and Anne, 270
Matisse, Henri, 24, 25; *Backs*, 25; cutouts, 46; *Studio, Quai St. Michel*, 213
Matta, Roberto, 145
Mauter, Conrad, 246
Mazarin, Cardinal, *Triumph of Christ* tapestry, 43
McCall, Robert, *The Space Mural, A Cosmic View*, 32
McKim, Mead, and White, 52, 188, 210
McLaren, Sidney, *Creative Imagination*, 147
Meigs, Montgomery C., 85, 117–19
Mellon, Andrew W., 3, 36–37, 136; collection, 41
Mellon, Paul, 37, 41
Mercier, Charlotte, 129
Meridian House International, 309
Merion, Maria Sibylla, *Dissertation in Insect Generations and Metamorphosis in Surinam*, 130
Meserve, Frederick Hill, collection, 134
Metropolitan Washington area: map, 8
Meyers, John Granville, 206

Michelangelo Buonarroti, 154
Mills, Robert, 121, 127, 175, 224
Minton tile, 15, 84, 177, 179
Miró, Joan, 24
Mitchell, Joan: *Dirty Snow*, 131
Mondrian, Piet, *Diamond Painting, Red, Yellow and Blue*, 46
Monet, Claude, *Saint-Adresse*, 37; *Waterloo Bridge, London*, 41
Monroe, James, 83, 171, 187, 191–92, 193; portrait, 42
Montpelier Mansion, 309
Moon rocks, 66
Moore, Arthur Cotton Associates, 210
Moore, Henry, *Two Piece Reclining Figure: Points*, 25; *Knife Edge Mirror Two Piece*, 45
Moran, Thomas, 122; *The Chasm of the Colorado*, *The Grand Canyon of the Yellowstone*, 124–25
Morse, Samuel F. B., *The Old House of Representatives*, 84, 154; *Self-Portrait*, 135; *James Monroe*, 192; telegraph, 15, 89
Morisot, Berthe, 129; *The Cage*, 131
Morven Park, 309
Moses, Anna Mary Robertson ("Grandma"), 157
Mott, Lucretia, 109
Mount Vernon, 3, 237, 239, 251, 284–88, 293, 294, 295
Mount Vernon Ladies' Association, 285
Mowbray, Henry Siddons, 198
Mullett, Alfred B., 175–76
Myers, George Hewitt, 3; 214–15; collections, 215–16

Nakian, Reuben, *Harry Hopkins*, 137
National Air and Space Museum, 29–34
National Archives, 112–13
National Building Museum, 117–19, 309
National Capital Trolley Museum, 256–57
National Gallery of Art, 35–46
National Geographic Society, 167–69
National Learning Center, 80–81
National Museum of African Art, 47–50
National Museum of American Art, 120–27
National Museum of American History, 51–59
National Museum of Natural History, 60–67
National Museum of Women in the Arts, 128–31, 309
National Portrait Gallery, 132–37
National Press Club, 309
National Society of Children of the American Revolution Museum, 157
National Trust for Historic Preservation, 160, 219, 290, 294
National Women's Party headquarters, 108–09
Natural History, National Museum of, 60–67
Naval Historical Center, 103
Navy Museum, 102–07
Newton White Mansion, 309
Noguchi, Isamu: *Grey Sun*, 127
Noland, Kenneth, 12, 123, 209; *Another Time*, 46
Notter, Finegold, and Alexander, 27

Oatlands, 309
Obata, Gyo, 30

Octagon, 3, 143, 160, 170–73, 187, 309
Ohtake, Tomi, *Number 9*, 147
O'Keeffe, Georgia, 24; *Alligator Pears in a Basket*, 130, 131
Old Executive Office Building, 113, 174–79
Old Patent Office Building (National Museum of American Art and National Portrait Gallery), 120–27, 132–37
Old Stone House, 234–35
Oldroyd, Osborn H. Collection, 115, 116, 139
Organization of American States, 144, 180
Oriental rugs: Textile Museum, 214–17
Otero, Alejandro, *Delta Solar*, 30
Oxon Hill Manor, 309

Pacheco, Maria Luisa, *Composition*, 146
Paderewski, Jan, 233
Paley, Albert, entrance gates, 181
Pan American Union. *See* Organization of American States.
Panini, Giovanni Paolo, *Interior of the Pantheon*, 39
Paul, Alice, 109; portrait, 108
Peacock Room (James McNeill Whistler), 19–21
Peale, Charles Willson, 2, 42, 122, 295; *Mrs. James Smith and Grandson*, 126; *The Stoddert Children*, 226
Peale, Rembrandt, 2, 42, *Edward Shippen Burd of Philadelphia*, 126; *Thomas Jefferson*, 192; *Rubens Peale*, 135; *Rubens Peale With a Geranium*, 42; *George Washington*, 134, 164, 296; *Martha Washington*, 134, 164
Peale, Rubens, 2, 42, portraits of, 42, 135
Peary, Robert E., 169
Peeters, Clara, 128; *Still Life of Fish and Cat*, 131
Pei, Cobb, Freed, and Partners, 27
Pei, I. M., 37, 44–45, 154
Pelz, Paul J., 95
Perlman, Herman and Sara Collection, 150
Perry, Charles O., *Continuum*, 30
Perry, Lilla Cabot, *Lady in Evening Dress*, 131; *Lady With a Bowl of Violets*, 130
Perry, Commodore Matthew: Navy Museum, 107
Peter, Dr. Armistead, 239
Peter, Armistead III, 236, 238, 239; *Caroline Peter*, self-portrait, 238
Peter, America, 237, 239 ,
Peter, Britannia, 237, 238, 239
Peter, Caroline: 239; portraits of, 238, 239
Peter, Laurence: portrait of, 237
Peter, Martha Parke Custis, 236, 237, 238, 239, 285; portrait of, 238
Peter, Robert, 236, 238
Peter, Thomas, 236, 237, 239; portrait of, 238
Petersen House, 138–39
Peto, John Frederick, *The Old Violin*, 43
Phidias, 154
Phillips, Duncan, 2, 3, 209–13; portrait, 209
Phillips, Marjorie, 209–10, 211–12; portrait, 209; *Night Baseball*, 213
Phillips Collection, 208–13, 309
Photography, Corcoran Gallery of Art, 152; Historical Society of Washington, D.C., 207; Library of Congress, 94, 97; National Archives, 112–13; National Museum of American Art, 122; National Portrait Gallery, 134
Picasso, Pablo, 24, 44, 46; *Woman With Baby Carriage*, 24; *The Frugal Repast*, 37; *Family of Saltimbanques*, 46
Pisces Club, 309
Platt, Charles A., 18
Poleo, Hector, *Andean Family*, 148
Polesello, Rogelio, *Orange On Magenta*, 146
Pollock, Jackson, *November 7, 1951, Lavender Mist*, 24; *Going West*, 127
Pope, John Russell, 37, 39, 113, 176, 215
Pope-Leighey House, 289–92
Pope, Loren, 289–92
Post, Charles W. collections, 247; portrait of, 243
Post, Marjorie Merriweather: Hillwood, 240–47; jewelry, 66
Potts, John, 274, 276
Powers, Hiram, 125–26; *Eve Tempted*, 125; *The Greek Slave*, 125, 155, 184; *Martin Van Buren*, 193; *George Washington*, 296
Prendergast, Maurice, 212
Presidents: National Museum of American History, Ceremonial Court, 54, First Ladies Hall, 55; papers, Library of Congress, 96; National Portrait Gallery, Hall of Presidents and Rotunda, 133–34; Mount Vernon, 284–88; White House, 186–93; Woodrow Wilson House, 218–21; working at Old Executive Office Building, 174. *See also* individual names

Quantico, Air-Ground Museum, 99
Quilts: Daughters of the American Revolution (DAR) Museum, 157; exhibit, Decatur House, 158

Ramsay, Allan, *Portrait of a Lady*, 226
Raphael, 154; *Alba Madonna*, *Saint George and the Dragon*, 36, 39
Ratner, Philip, 151
Rauschenberg, Robert, 46, 123; *Reservoir*, 127
Ray, Man, 123
Reagan, Ronald, 134
Ream, Vinnie, and Abraham Lincoln, 86
Reis, Dr. Henry, 48
Rembrandt van Ryn, 36, 40, 85, 154; *Self-Portrait*, *The Mill*, 40
Remington, Frederic, *Fired On*, 124
Renoir, Pierre Auguste, *A Girl With a Watering Can*, 41; *The Luncheon of the Boating Party*, 211–12
Renouf, Émile, *The Helping Hand*, 183
Renwick, James, Jr., 12, 74, 181–82; gate, 76
Renwick Gallery, 121, 175, 181–85
Reynolds, Sir Joshua, 154
Ribera, Jusepe di, *The Martyrdom of Saint Bartholomew*, 37
Richardt, Ferdinand, *Independence Hall in Philadelphia*, 191
Rickey, George, *Three Red Lines*, 25
Riesener, Jean-Henri, commode, 242; desk, 44
Righetti, Francesco, *Mercury*, 41
Riley, Bridget, *Cerise, Olive, Turquoise Disks*, 131
Rimmer, William, *The Falling Gladiator*, 125

Ripley, S. Dillon, 47, 68
Ripley Center, S. Dillon, 48, 74
Rivers, Larry, *The Athlete's Dream*, 127
Riviera, José de, *Infinity*, 52
Robbins, Warren, collection, 47
Roby, Sara Foundation Collection, 123
Rock of Dumbarton, 224, 228, 236
Rockville Civic Center Mansion, 309
Rodin, Auguste, 24, 25; *The Burghers of Calais*, 25; *Walking Man, Hand With Female Figure*, 44
Roentgen, David, 245
Roesen, Severin, *Still Life With Fruit*, 126 *Still Life With Flowers*, 165
Roosevelt, Franklin D., 105, 174
Roosevelt, Theodore, 18, 63, 174, 181, 188, 189, 190, 193, 200; portrait of, 190
Roszak, Theodore, *Construction in White*, 127
Rothko, Mark, 46, 212
Rothko, Mark Foundation, 46
Rouault, Georges, 212
Rubens, Peter Paul, 154; *Daniel in the Lions' Den*, 40
Ruysch, Rachel, *Flowers in a Vase*, 131
Ryder, Albert Pinkham, 122, 125, 212; *Siegfried and the Rhine Maidens*, 43 *With Sloping Mast and Dipping Prow, Flying Dutchman, Jonah*, 125

Sackler, Arthur M., 68–69; collections, 70–74
Sackler, Arthur M. Gallery, 3, 48, 68–74
Saenredam, Pieter Jansz, *Cathedral of Saint John at 's-Hertogenbosch*, 40
St. Denis, Ruth, 200
Saint-Gaudens, Augustus, 96
Saint-Mémin, Charles de, *Dr. William Thornton, Col. John Tayloe*, 172
Salisbury, Frank O. 91
Sanchez, José Luis, *Queen Isabella*, 180
Sargent, John Singer, 24, 122; *Elizabeth Winthrop Chanler*, 125; *Theodore Roosevelt*, 190; *Betty Wertheimer*, 125; *Mrs. Henry White*, 154; *The Mosquito Net*, 191
Sarnoff, Lolo, *Gateway to Eden*, 131
Savage, Edward, *Congress Voting Independence*, 135; *George Washington, Martha Washington*, 297; *The Washington Family*, 172–73, 297
Schaeffer, Lloyd L., 266
Scheffer, Ary, *General Lafayette*, 88
Sené, C., 245
Schussele, Christian, *Men of Progress*, 136
Seurat, Georges, *The Lighthouse at Honfleur*, 41
Sewall-Belmont House, 108–09, 309
Sewall, Robert, 108
Shahn, Ben, 137
Shakespeare, William: Folger Shakespeare Library, 90–93
Sharpe, Elizabeth M., 294, 295
Shepley, Bulfinch, Richardson and Abbott, 48
Sirani, Elisabetta: *Virgin and Child*, 129
Sloan, John, *The Wake of the Ferry II*, 213
Sloane, Eric, *Earth Flight Environment*, 32
Small, Lillian and Albert Jewish Museum, 140–41, 309
Smith, David, *Sentinel* series, 46
Smithmeyer, John L., 95
Smithson, James, 13; tomb, 12

Smithsonian Institution, 2, 12–13, 52, 121; Arts and Industries Building, 11, 14–15, 52; Castle, 12–13, 74; Freer Gallery of Art, 16–21; Hirshhorn Museum and Sculpture Garden, 22–25; National Air and Space Museum, 29–34; National Gallery of Art, 13, 35–46; National Museum of African Art, 47–50; National Museum of American Art, 120–27; National Museum of American History, 51–59; National Museum of Natural History, 52, 60–67; National Portrait Gallery, 132–37; Paul E. Garber Preservation, Restoration and Storage Facility, 34; Renwick Gallery, 121, 175, 181–85; Arthur M. Sackler Gallery, 3, 48, 68–74; previsit information package, 12
Society of the Cincinnati: Anderson House, 196–98
Soto, Jesus Rafael, *Hurtado Scripture*, 146
Sousa, John Philip, 98
Spartali, Christine, portrait by James McNeill Whistler, 21
Stabler, Edward, 258
Stabler-Leadbeater Apothecary Shop, 258–59
Stanley, Henry Morton, 199
Stanley, John Mix, 124
Stanton, Elizabeth Cady, 109
Stapko, Gregory, 275
Star-Spangled Banner, 13, 52–53
State Department, Diplomatic Reception Rooms, 162–65
Still, Clyfford, 123
Stone, Edward Durrell, 167
Stone, William Oliver, *William Wilson Corcoran*, 183
Strathmore Hall Art Center, 309
Stuart, Gilbert, 42, 134; 198; *John Adams*, 42; *John Quincy Adams*, 191; *Mrs. Adams*, 191; *Thomas Jefferson*, 42; *Dolley Madison*, 192–92; *James Madison*, 42; *James Monroe*, 42; *William Thornton, Mrs. Thornton*, 173; *George Washington*, 42, 134, 190; *Martha Washington*, 134
Sully, Thomas, *Lady With a Harp: Eliza Ridgely*, 42; *Andrew Jackson*, 154; *Thomas Jefferson*, 165; *James Monroe*, 164; silhouette of, 135
Sully, Robert, *James Sully*, 226
Supreme Court, old Chamber, 83. 88–89
Suvero, Mark di, *Isis*, 25
Sylvett, David, 276
Syme, John, *John James Audubon*, 193
Szyzlo, Fernando de, *Cajamarca*, 146

Tack, Augustus Vincent, 209, 211, 212
Taft, William Howard, 174, 179, 180, 229
Tamayo, Rufino, 145–46; *Man Contemplating the Moon*, 146
Tanguy, Yves, *The Look of Amber*, 46
Tanner, Henry Ossawa, 125
Tayloe, Benjamin Ogle, 171
Tayloe, Col. John III, 170–71, 187
Taylor, David W., 103
Textile Museum, 2, 195, 214–17, 309
Thayer, Abbott Handerson, 17; *The Stevenson Memorial*, 125; *Flower Studies*, 126
Thomas, Alma, *Iris, Tulips, Jonquils and Crocuses, Orion*, 131

Thomas Law House, 308
Thornton, Dr. William, 82, 83, 170–71, 225, 229, 236, 237, 294; *Thomas Jefferson*, 164; portrait of, 172
Thornton, Mrs. William, 238
Tingey, Captain Thomas, 103
Tingey House, 103
Titian (Tiziano Vecelli) *Venus With a Mirror*, 36, 39
Torres-Garcia, Joaquin, *Constructivism*, 146
Toyota, Yutaka, *In the Time Before Nothing*, 147
Treaty of Ghent, 108, 173
Treaty of Paris, 164
Trolley Museum, National Capital, 256–57
Troth, Jacob and Paul, 294
Truitt, Ann: *Summer Day*, 131
Truman, Harry, 177; White House renovation, 188, 193
Trumbull, John, 86, 198; *John Adams*, 192; *George Washington*, 237
Tryon, Dwight William, 17
Tudor Place, 236–39, 309
Tudor Place Foundation, 236
Twachtman, John, 122, *Round Hill Road*, 126

Ulrey, A. Mueller, *Mrs. Woodrow Wilson*, 220
Underwood, Sen. Oscar W., 294, 297
University Club, 309

Valadon, Suzanne: *Nude Doing Her Hair*, *Bouquet of Flowers in an Empire Vase*, 131
Van Buren, Martin, 159. 188, 191
Van der Weyden, Rogier, *Saint George and the Dragon*, 40
Vanderlyn, John, *George Washington*, 88
Van Dyck, Sir Anthony, 36; *Marchesa Elena Grimaldi*, *Queen Henrietta Maria With Her Dwarf*, 40
Van Eyck, Jan, *Annunciation*, 36, 39–40
Van Gogh, Vincent, *Roses*, 37; *Flower Beds in Holland*, 41; *The Road Menders*, 212
Varden, John, collection, 120–21
Vedder Elihu, 95
Velasquez, José Antonio, *San Antonio de Oriente*, 147
Velazquez, Diego Rodriguez de Silva, 154
Vermeer, Jan, *Woman Holding a Balance*, 40
Verrocchio, Andrea del, bust of Giuliano de Medici, 39
Vever, Henri, collection, 70
Vidal, Miguel Angel, *Equilibrium*, 146
Virginia Trust for Historic Preservation, 279
von Ezdorf, Richard, 176, 178, 179
Vonnoh, Robert, 220; *Ellen Axson Wilson and Her Daughters*, 221
Vos, Hubert, *Alice Barney*, 202

Wakabayashi, Kazuo, *Blue and Black*, 147
Walker, Edward and Mary Collection, 152
Walker, John, 3
Walter, Thomas U., 84, 85, 118
Washington, city of, 2, 102, 120–21, 132, 186–87; burning of the Capitol, 83, 95, 238; burning of the Navy Yard, 103; burning of the White House, 187
Washington Club, 309
Washington Dolls' House and Toy Museum, 248–49, 309
Washington family, 226, 284–85
Washington, George, 3, 121, 166, 226, 227, 258, 270, 271, 277, 288, 293, 294, 297; busts of, 288, 296; his letter to Touro Synagogue, 150; Mount Vernon, 284–88; portraits of, 42, 88, 89, 134, 163, 172–73, 190, 237, 295, 296; Society of the Cincinnati, 196–98; china, 189; furniture, 238, 239; statue, 55; uniform, 58
Washington, Lawrence, 284–85
Washington, Martha, 224, 226–27, 236. 237, 260–61, 284–88, 293–94; portraits of, 164, 172–73, 190, 297
Washington Gallery of Modern Art, 153
Washington Metropolitan Area: map, 8
Washington Navy Yard, 98, 102–03
Waterman, Thomas T., 160
Webster, Daniel, 84, 89, 171
Weir, J. Alden, 123
West, Benjamin, 122; *Helen Brought to Paris*, *Self-Portrait*, *Mary Hopkinson*, 126
West, Sybil, 265
Whistler, James McNeill, 2, 44, and Alice Pike Barney, 200, 201, and Charles Lang Freer, 2, 17–18; bust of, 135; in Freer Gallery of Art, 17–21; *Wapping on Thames*, 43; *Valparaiso Harbor*, *Head of a Young Woman*, 126
White House, 186–93; First Ladies Hall, National Museum of American History, 55
White, Newton Mansion, 309
White, Stanford, 17
Whiting, Carlyle Fairfax, 266
Whitman, Walt, 85, 122, 247
Widener, Joseph E. collection, 36, 41
Williams, Capt. William G., 237
Wilson, Edith Bolling, 218–21, 294
Wilson, Ellen Axson, 220; portrait of, 221
Wilson, Woodrow, 218–21, 294
Wintherhalter, Franz, *Empress Eugénie*, 244
Wise, John, 270–73; portrait of, 272
Wollaston, John, *Mrs. Lucy Parry*, 126
Woman's National Democratic Club, 310
Wood, Waddy B., 130, 176, 201, 215, 218, 294
Woodend Mansion, 310
Woodlawn Plantation, 289, 293–98, 310
Woodrow Wilson House, 218–21, 310
Woodrow Wilson International Center for Scholars, 12, 13
Wright, Frank Lloyd, 154, 289–92; architectural philosophy, 290–91; Imperial Hotel china, 291
Wright, Orville and Wilbur, 1903 Flyer, 30
Wyeth, Andrew, *Dodges Ridge*, 127
Wyeth and King, 210

Yoshimura, Junzo, 69

Another Ross Guide . . .

NEW YORK CITY MUSEUMS
A ROSS GUIDE

Ideal for gifts or reference, it includes

- 60 museums, historic houses, and other special places open to the public in the New York metropolitan area
- 122 art galleries
- 37 museums and historic houses available for private functions
- a checklist of special collections
- nearly 150 illustrations
- 7 maps

This carefully researched guide is *the only book of its kind* featuring in-depth descriptions of New York's very special attractions. Following the same handy format as WASHINGTON, D.C. MUSEUMS: A ROSS GUIDE, the book includes biographies and historical backgrounds, comprehensive reports on museum collections, anecdotes, and information on hours, admission fees, museum shops, restaurants, libraries, handicapped facilities, and public transportation.

ORDER FORM

To: AMERICANA PRESS
P.O. Box 71004
Chevy Chase, MD 20813
301/718-9808

Please send me _____ copies of NEW YORK CITY MUSEUMS: A ROSS GUIDE and/or _____ copies of WASHINGTON, D.C. MUSEUMS: A ROSS GUIDE by Betty Ross at $14.95 each, plus postage and handling. (In Maryland, add $.75 sales tax for each book.)

Postage and Handling: $2.50 for the first book and $.50 for each additional book.

Enclosed is $ _____

Name _____

Address _____

_____ Zip _____